Fifty Years in Time and Space

A Short History of *Doctor Who*

Frank Danes

Frank Danes

Fifty Years in Time and Space

A Short History of *Doctor Who*

Unauthorised

Published in 2013 by St Mark's Press
20 Close Road
Pavenham, Bedfordshire MK43 7PP
www.stmarkspress.com

No Tharil shall outlive the day of the feast.

ISBN: 978 1 907062 18 6

Printed and bound in the United Kingdom by Henry Ling Limited, at the Dorset
Press, Dorchester, DT1 1HD

For Emma, Tom, Zoë and Matthew

and my parents

Charles and Marion

Contents

Introduction

This book is a brief guide to the British Broadcasting Corporation's series *Doctor Who,* fifty years old on 23rd November 2013. It is one of the longest running television series in the world and, after *Coronation Street,* is the second longest running in the United Kingdom (if we discount the fifteen years or so it was out of regular production). *Doctor Who* fans bask in pleasure when they remember that their series is older than *Star Trek,* erroneously seen by many as the world's most famous science fiction show. *Star Trek*'s pilot episode was made in 1964 but the series was not broadcast until 1966. *Doctor Who* began three years earlier, on Saturday 23rd November 1963. This was the day after President Kennedy's assassination shocked the world and dominated both the public consciousness and the airwaves. The BBC's new adventure series attracted little attention on its first day and the first episode, "An Unearthly Child", was repeated before the second on Saturday 30th November 1963. The original series ran from 1963-1989, with an eighteen month pause in transmission from 1985-6; a TV movie followed in 1996 as an unsuccessful attempt to revive the show, which finally returned as a ratings success and the BBC's flagship drama in 2005. It has been in production ever since.

Eleven actors to date have played the Doctor on television: seven in the original run, one in the TV movie and three in the revived series from 2005. There have been two cinema films, three professionally produced theatre plays and thousands of novelisations, novels and stories in comic strip and audio form. *Doctor Who* is not so much a television programme as a product.

This book aims to be a guide to fifty years of the series for those who like *Doctor Who* and want to learn more about it. It aims to be of interest to readers who enjoy the post 2005 revival and want to know more about the original series. I also hope it will be of interest to the die hard, knowledgeable fans who, perhaps lifelong fans like me, devour anything about *Doctor Who* that they can get their hands on. It is inevitably a personal reading of the series and is coloured by my own critical preferences: any book about the programme which doesn't demonstrate the author's own views would, I think, be very dull. I haven't religiously covered every single story – there are over 240 at time of writing (April 2013) – and I haven't provided a plot précis or production details of every one. Interested readers can find these in many of the programme guides that are available online or in book form. I hope readers will forgive me for jumping around and pursuing the bits I'm most interested in. Since these bits include all of *Doctor Who*, I hope most issues are touched on, in more or less detail.

I was born in 1965 – on a Saturday, in fact, and just in time to watch "Galaxy Four" episode two. Some of my earliest memories are of watching the programme: I remember my twin brother and I putting our hands over the screen when the Yeti appeared, prompting yells of "Get those twins away from the television!" from my elder brothers. I must have seen "Seeds of Death" (1968) and "The Evil of the Daleks" (1967), although I have no memory of them, as I thought the Silurians in "Doctor Who and the Silurians" (1970) were Ice Warriors and I was not only able to remember the Daleks when they reappeared in "Day of the Daleks" (1972) but was able to correct a nursery worker at my pre-school when she erroneously called the Marx toy Dalek, which graced our playgroup, "a robot". My brother and I went down the road to watch the programme in colour in the early seventies, at a time when a colour television cost something in the region of £2000 in today's money; we would return to tell our father, who watched the programme in black and white, what colour the monsters had been (usually green). I co-edited a fanzine in the 1980s, did some professional writing, got a degree in English and American Literature and became a secondary school English teacher. I've always been a *Doctor Who* fan even as I have become (in script editor Terrance Dicks' words) older, fatter, greyer, but not noticeably wiser.

1

The Genesis of *Doctor Who*

In 1963, the BBC was looking for a programme to fill the gap between the Saturday afternoon sports magazine *Grandstand* and the highly popular *Juke Box Jury*. Then, as now, it wanted to beef up its Saturday evening schedule against stiff opposition from ITV, the British independent television network.

This was one of several stars which came into alignment to bring *Doctor Who* to British television screens on 23rd November, 1963. Another was the appointment of Sydney Newman as Head of Drama at the BBC. A feisty Canadian, Newman had held a similar position at ABC television, one of the ITV franchises. There, he had created *The Avengers* – in its Ian Hendry, pre-fantasy guise – and *Armchair Theatre*. The BBC regarded the success of Newman's shows with admiring eyes and persuaded him to come and work for the corporation. Newman praised what worked well at the BBC and ruffled feathers in shaking up the organisation where necessary. He completely overhauled the BBC script unit, whose in-house writers wrote the drama output for television, and established the model for a production team which would be adopted by the new *Doctor Who* series: a producer would oversee all aspects of production and a story editor (later, a script editor) would commission and edit the scripts from BBC staffers and freelance writers.

In 1962, the BBC had commissioned the wonderfully named Donald Bull and Alice Frick to report on the viability of making programmes in the science fiction genre. The BBC had had much success in the genre and wanted to explore its possibilities further: Nigel Kneale's three *Quatermass* series in the 1950s had been tours de force, iconic science fiction serials which had emptied the pubs of viewers rushing home to catch the latest instalment. (Kneale had a certain degree of disdain for *Doctor Who* itself, thinking the premise was a terrible idea and the sort of thing which one should think of only to reject at once. He also noted that the programme shamelessly pillaged his plots on occasions: for example, there are marked similarities between *Quatermass and the Pit* (1958/9) and "The Daemons" (1971), both serials hinging on the manipulation of humankind's development by alien intervention.) Bull and Frick reported in late 1962 and suggested adapting some literary science fiction by such writers as John Wyndham. They advised against some types of science fiction adventure as too fanciful and difficult to realise.

Sydney Newman and Donald Wilson, the Head of the Script Department, considered the need for a new family Saturday evening drama in the light of Frick and Bull's report, and a follow-up report by Frick and John Braybon. Newman came up with the basic premise for the series. It was to be about a traveller who was able to move about in space and backwards, forwards and sideways in time. Eschewing the usual criteria for a hero, Newman decreed that the hero, or anti-hero as he quickly became, was to be a crotchety old man, at least 350 years old. He was to travel with human companions who were to be points of identification for the audience: a heroic male, a young woman and a teenager. The hero shouldn't have a name but a title: Doctor. One story about the show's development at this point has it that Hugh David, one BBC writer who did some initial work on the series, was discussing the programme with another writer in a restaurant. He wrote "Doctor..." on a piece of paper and, wondering what his name should be, added: "who?" It was thus quickly established that a central dramatic drive of the new series should be the mystery around the Doctor's character: who was he and where did he come from? The question was endlessly deferred as the Doctor and his companions found themselves faced with the far more urgent question of surviving from week to week, and was only finally answered in Patrick Troughton's last story, "The War Games" (1969).

Having established the basics, Newman handed the show over to other writers to develop. These included Donald Wilson and Mervyn Pinfield, who became the show's associate or executive producer: the crew on the first season story "The Sensorites" (1964) nicknamed the bald, bewhiskered aliens "Mervyns" because they said they looked like him. David Whitaker was appointed as *Doctor Who*'s first story editor and Newman brought a former colleague over from ABC Television to act as producer. This was the twenty eight year old Verity Lambert, whose appointment raised eyebrows and some hackles at the male-dominated BBC.

Once the series had been commissioned in early 1963, its details were quickly fleshed out. Some early ideas for the Doctor were that he was to be virtually senile, bewildered by his surroundings and completely unable to comprehend his space machine. His eyes were to blaze with anger and suspicion if he suspected his human companions of interference. Some of these elements survived into the finished programme, or at least the pilot: here, the Doctor addresses Ian contemptuously as "Schoolmaster" and is scornful of Ian and Barbara's incomprehension when they enter the TARDIS. The Doctor's selfishness and lack of heroism in "The Daleks" (1963-4) is also a remnant of the initial character treatment, although he was starting to move in the direction of heroism as early as the middle of that serial.

Several ideas were discussed for the Doctor's space machine. An invisible sphere was suggested but then discarded because it was difficult to realise and, anyway, couldn't have been seen on screen. Someone suggested that a craft that sophisticated would have to be disguised if the primitive natives of planet Earth weren't to investigate it. This idea quickly developed into the notion that it could disguise itself wherever it goes, although the notion of building a new prop for every serial was quickly squashed on cost grounds. Why not have its disguise mechanism broken in the first story? Then viewers could have the fun of seeing an everyday object in fantastic settings. Perhaps influenced by C. S. Lewis's wardrobe as a gateway into another world (from *The Lion, the Witch and the Wardrobe* (1950)), the space machine's exterior would be a similar large box: a police box, then as familiar on British streets as, say, post boxes are today.

The series was commissioned for an initial run of thirteen 25 minute episodes. David Whitaker started to commission scripts. The Australian BBC staff writer Anthony Coburn was to write the first serial and the characters started to take shape. It was made clear that "Doctor Who" was the name of the programme and not the name of the character: the "Who" suffix was a question about the character's origins and some of the early documentation adds a question mark to the series' name: *Doctor Who?* Had they stuck with the question mark (which strangely became a feature of the costumes for Doctors four to seven, long after the Doctor's origins as a Time Lord had been established), they might have pre-empted the confusion about the Doctor's name which has dogged the programme ever since. William Hartnell's credit on the end titles was always given as "Dr Who", with the abbreviated form of "Doctor" implying that the next word was his name; the character was called "Dr Who" in scripts and stage directions but not in dialogue. The Doctor's granddaughter's name does indeed seem to be "Susan", but the first story's script indicates that she borrowed her surname, Foreman, from the gates of the scrapyard where the TARDIS first landed. Ian addresses the Doctor as "Doctor Foreman" in episode two: "Eh? Doctor who? What is he talking about?" Hartnell soliloquises. This was the first auto-referential use of the programme's name in dialogue; later in the second episode, when Barbara refers to him as "Doctor

Foreman", Ian corrects her: "That's not his name. Who is he? Doctor who?" The character was colloquially called "Doctor Who" but fans and the production team knew he was just "The Doctor". This point was lost on the makers of the two Peter Cushing Dalek films (*Dr Who and the Daleks* in 1965 and *Daleks: Invasion Earth 2150 A.D.*, 1966) where the character, now a human scientist who has invented the TARDIS, introduces himself as "Dr Who" and is addressed as such by other characters. Similarly, the ghastly 1960s TV comic strip, which began in 1964, usually called him "Dr Who". Perhaps this usage bled into the television programme's continuity, which went a bit pear shaped in "The War Machines" (1966): new script editor Gerry Davis failed to edit lines where the megalomaniac computer WOTAN demands: "Dr Who is required. Bring him here."

Aside from this howler, the production teams thereafter used "Who" as a joke. The Doctor adopts the alias "Doktor von Wer" in "The Highlanders" (1966-7); Jon Pertwee's sprightly Edwardian roadster Bessie, introduced in 1970, has the number plate "Who 1" (changed to "Who 7" at Sylvester McCoy's suggestion for its appearance in the 1989 story "Battlefield") and there are many quips of the "What Doctor? Doctor who?" variety along the way. Passing himself off as his android double, the Doctor warns the android Warrant Officer Benton to beware of the real article in 1976's "The Android Invasion": "We don't know who's who." In a bid to please the fans (it did), John Nathan-Turner changed the actor's credit from "Dr Who" or "Doctor Who" to "The Doctor" for Peter Davison's run in 1981, and this has been the case ever since (although Christopher Eccleston was credited as "Doctor Who" in the programme's titles, presumably to match the new series with the colloquial naming of the character as the series was re-launched: no point in confusing people). Steven Moffat returned to the question in Matt Smith's second series (2011): "Silence Will Fall" when the ultimate question is asked, which Dorium reveals is, "Doctor who?" In the 2012 series, Moffat played around with the Doctor's title and name again as Matt Smith whirls around the TARDIS console, asking himself (or calling himself?) "Doctor Who?"

Waris Hussein was contracted to direct the first story. 2005 showrunner Russell T Davies has approvingly noted the radicalism of the original story's production team: produced by a young woman and directed by a young, Asian and gay man. Verity Lambert considered actors to play the Doctor. Hugh David, a writer and actor who had done some initial work on the series, was considered but ruled himself out: he didn't want to return to acting in a long running series. Lambert thought of Cyril Cusack and Michael Hordern but her final choice was William Hartnell. Hartnell was in his fifties and had had a distinguished film career, turning in outstanding performances as the gangster Dallow in *Brighton Rock* (1947) and *The Yangtse Incident* (1957), of which a critic had written that Hartnell, even when silent and filmed from the back, acted everyone else off screen. Hartnell had become somewhat stuck in a rut playing tough sergeants and army types in films like *Carry on Sergeant* (1958) and television series like *The Army Game* (ITV, 1957-1961); he had dismissed the latter as "rubbish". Verity Lambert had been struck by Hartnell's performance as the talent scout in the film *This Sporting Life* (1963). Here, the character's air of slight incompetence and pathos touched her and seemed exactly right for the Doctor: at least, as the early treatment notes had conceived him.

Lambert and Hussein invited Hartnell to lunch. Accounts of what happened at their first meeting differ. Hussein has said that Hartnell was bemused, asking, "I don't know quite what you people want from me. What do you want from me?" Lambert said that she handed Hartnell the script for the first episode "and he just loved it". The Doctor was cast and BBC publicity noted that "this [was] Mr Hartnell's first role for the BBC".

The companions were also cast. William Russell, an experienced television actor who had found fame in *The Adventures of Sir Lancelot* (ITV, 1956-7), was to be Ian Chesterton; Jacqueline Hill was to play Barbara Wright; Carole Ann Ford was to play Susan. As the Doctor had been partly conceived as an elderly anti-hero, the role of dashing young hero was to be taken by Ian: he could handle the rough and tumble of their adventures which the Doctor's age and temperament precluded. In 1974, producer Barry Letts made a similar decision in casting Ian Marter as the dynamic young naval lieutenant Harry Sullivan before casting the fourth Doctor, reasoning that if an older actor were cast (Graham Crowden was under consideration), Harry could handle the rough stuff.

The companions of 1963 were worlds away from the capable Amy or Rose of the revived series. Ian Chesterton is a square jawed, decent Englishman who speaks with a received pronunciation (or BBC) accent. He is a science teacher at Susan's school; Barbara is a history teacher, the companions thus representing the two aspects of the new series: science (fiction) and history. Using teachers as identification points was old fashioned even in 1963; even by the end of Hartnell's run, the companions became a modern mini-skirted secretary, Polly, and the cockney sailor Ben Jackson. Ian is obviously heroic, taking charge of the travellers' attempts to escape "The Cave of Skulls" (1963) in the first story and trying to organise the Thals into a fighting force against the Daleks in the second. (When I showed an episode of "The Daleks" to a year seven class in 2006, most of them, accustomed to the heroic David Tennant and Christopher Eccleston, assumed that Ian was the Doctor.) Barbara is highly intelligent and resourceful and not just the screaming stereotype which later companions were said to become. She often defies the Doctor. In the first story, the Doctor wants to abandon an injured caveman to his death so that they can escape to the TARDIS: Barbara insists on helping him ("They must be out of their minds!" the Doctor exclaims, incredulously); in the second, Barbara insists on their moral duty to help the Thals when the Doctor implies it is none of their business. By the time of "The Aztecs" (1964), Barbara embraces the persona of the goddess Yetaxa in a bid to stop the Aztecs' practice of human sacrifice, defying the Doctor who tells her it is wrong and futile ("You can't rewrite history. Not one line.")

Susan was conceived by Sydney Newman as a point of audience identification for younger, or teenage, viewers. It was Anthony Coburn who scripted her as the Doctor's granddaughter, perhaps inspired by Little Nell's relationship with her grandfather in Dickens's novel *The Old Curiosity Shop* and certainly motivated by a need to sidestep any prurient questions about why a young girl should be travelling with a much older man. She is nominally fifteen and a student at Ian and Barbara's Coal Hill School. The school itself is another sign of the series' radicalism: it is a comprehensive and is thus closer to many of the viewers' own school experience than the private or boarding schools of such other popular, contemporary icons as *Whacko!* or the *St Trinian's* film series. Carole Ann Ford said that character was sold to her as being an *Avengers* type lady, but there were to be no signs of Cathy Gale's leather suits or high kicking action and Ford left the series after a year. She gives a wonderful and convincing performance as a brave and intelligent young woman. Indeed, the first two seasons are notable for the outstanding performances of their principals, who never send the series up and always play it straight: something essential if the "preposterous" (to use a contemporary viewer's word) situations are to be sold to the viewers. Verity Lambert criticised some later (presumably the McCoy) eras of the show for not taking themselves seriously and thereby ruining the illusion.

Doctor Who was never conceived as a children's programme, although it has been often identified as such. Writing in *The Daily Sketch* in the early 1970s, Gerald Garrett described it as "the children's own programme which adults adore"; actor Frazer Hines created gasps of dismay at a 1980 convention when he said he thought it was a children's programme. There is nowhere in the early documentation which mentions it is intended for children and its scheduling suggests it was intended to keep hold of the family audience from *Grandstand* and hold it over for *Juke Box Jury*. It never patronised children, which accounts for its popularity with them. Perhaps it is the place that science fiction holds in the British psyche which partly accounts for *Doctor Who*'s identification as a children's programme: many are sniffy about science fiction and think it not respectable as a genre or "childish", thus it must be for children. These are not cultural assumptions in America, where science fiction is taken somewhat more seriously and no-one dismissively assumed that *Star Trek* (1966-69), for example, was a children's programme.

Nevertheless, many within the BBC assumed the programme was for children even at its conception: the Children's Department was miffed that the show was to be made by the Drama Department, thus affording it arguably greater kudos, and not by the Children's Department. It responded by eyeing the programme with suspicion. One of the earliest criticisms of the programme's violence was by the BBC Children's Department, which objected strongly to Susan threatening Ian with a pair of scissors and using them to slash at her bed, presumably as an Ian substitute, in "The Brink of Disaster" (the third story, 1964).

Verity Lambert was horrified to learn that the new, technically complex series was not to be allocated studio space at the gleaming Television Centre but in the ancient studios at Lime Grove, where lights were worked by sliders on the walls and the cameras were so ancient that zooms could only be accomplished by physically trundling them towards the actors. Were the forces of suspicion at the BBC, dubious about and jealous of the favour *Doctor Who* enjoyed with Sydney Wilson, flexing their muscles? Lambert protested, but got nowhere. *Doctor Who* was to be made at Lime Grove on a tiny budget. The designers discovered that a full scale police box prop wouldn't fit into the lifts at Lime Grove. The prop had to be scaled down: the larger props used in the 2005 revival are much closer to the original police box height. Considering the restrictions, the standard of the finished programmes was miraculous: the journey across Asia to Cathay (in "Marco Polo", 1964) was achieved in a tiny studio and so impressed some Walt Disney executives that they wanted to adapt that serial into a film (nothing came of it).

Peter Brachacki was assigned to design the first episode and was responsible for the look of the TARDIS interior, a design as identifiable and iconic as the Daleks or K9 to the series' imagery. The original set introduced the roundelled walls which have featured in every subsequent redesign to the present day. Brachacki reasoned that, if the TARDIS was to have only one operator, all the controls would need to be readily accessible: hence the hexagonal control console which, again, has been a staple of TARDIS interior designs. In "Journey's End" (2010), the Doctor and his companions joyously and cheesily pilot the TARDIS together with one at each side of the console. The Doctor explains that six Time Lords would have originally piloted a TARDIS, something at odds with the original design conception and news to fans who had watched the original stories. Brachacki also included two huge roundelled doors which usually opened immediately onto the exterior, visible from the control room. Stepping outside the TARDIS, the police box doors usually shut in unison with the roundelled interior doors: a magical and extraordinary image for the original viewers. The TARDIS interior of the film *Dr Who and the Daleks* (1965) was, by contrast, a dull affair, a tangled mess of wires which abandoned the hexagonal console and the roundelled walls. The huge roundelled doors were replaced by the white interior doors of the police box, a design poached for the new TARDIS interiors from "Rose" (2005) onwards.

Although the TARDIS's control room was a wonder of design for the original viewers, Waris Hussein was recorded as saying that the designer had apparently thrown some flats together in five minutes and pushed off. Hussein was very angry about it but there was no time to redesign the set. The cameras rolled on "An Unearthly Child" in September 1963, mere months after the programme had been conceived.

The first version of "An Unearthly Child" is usually described as a pilot, but, as William Russell has said, "That was no pilot – that was an attempt to get it right first time!" This unscreened episode features a much more aggressive and alien Doctor and a much stranger Susan. Susan tells her teachers that she was born in the forty ninth century (in the second, broadcast recording, this becomes, "I was born in another time, another world") and there are two fluffed attempts at entering the TARDIS when the interior doors fail to shut properly. Perhaps some of the problems stemmed from the difficulties of recording such a technically demanding and new type of programme on only two cameras at Lime Grove. Sydney Newman saw the finished episode, took Hussein and Lambert out to dinner and told them he should sack the pair of them. Instead, he told them to re-record the episode and make it better.

Re-shooting episode one, "An Unearthly Child", gave Verity Lambert and story editor David Whitaker a chance to iron out the difficulties of the first attempt. The Doctor's costume was tweaked and his abrasiveness softened in the first step towards making him a more heroic character (a process fully accomplished by the end of the first season); he patronises Ian and Barbara but is no longer contemptuous and scornful. Susan was similarly softened and became much more like a human teenager than the pilot's extraordinarily alien girl. The new episode was shot on four cameras, not two, and the entrance into the TARDIS went smoothly. The *Radio Times*, the BBC's listing magazine, unobtrusively publicised the new series and listed it each week as "An Adventure in Space and Time". The first episode was broadcast on Saturday 23rd November, 1963 at 5.15 p.m..

2

Into the Time Vortex: seasons one to three

Sydney Newman had stipulated that *Doctor Who* stories should go forwards, backwards and sideways in time. Forwards and backwards was fine, but what did "sideways" mean? It seemed to indicate unfamiliar dimensions and was not realised until "Planet of Giants" (1964), when the TARDIS crew arrive back on contemporary Earth but are only one inch high.

The basic idea for "Planet of Giants" was in the series' pre-production documents. It was the first story by academic Louis Marks, who later wrote the well-received serials "Day of the Daleks" (1972), "Planet of Evil" (1975) and "The Masque of Mandragora" (1976). Sadly, "Planet of Giants" is thin stuff: the TARDIS crew are too small to interact with the humans and the villain's plot – to market a deadly insecticide – is small beer anyway. Newman ordered that the serial should be cut down from four episodes to three and episodes three and four were edited together. There was a gap of four years between "Giants" and the next "sideways" in time adventure, by which point memories of Newman's conceptual ideas had somewhat faded: this was "The Mind Robber" (1968), a Troughton tale which takes place in the fantasy void of the Land of Fiction.

If interpreting the "sideways" in time instruction was challenging, it was easy to satisfy the forwards and backwards remit. Newman indicated that future – or science fiction – stories should alternate with historical stories set in Earth's past. These fulfilled the edict of Lord Reith, the BBC's first Director General, that the corporation should inform as well as entertain and, unlike its commercial rivals, give the public not what they wanted but something better. As Robert Holmes (script editor 1974-1977) noted, part of the original brief for *Doctor Who* was to teach children history: fortunately, as he went on to observe, the entertainment principle quickly dominated. The First Doctor thus encounters such historical figures as Marco Polo, Kublai Khan, the Emperor Nero, Robespierre, Napoleon, Richard the Lionheart and Wyatt Earp. More liberties were taken with historical stories when Dennis Spooner took over from David Whitaker as story editor: Spooner had a somewhat cavalier attitude towards historical fact and increased the humour. Noting that viewers apparently preferred the science fiction stories, the production team phased out the historicals after "The Highlanders" (1966), the story which introduced Jamie

McCrimmon (Fraser Hines) as a companion. The next straight historical story was Terence Dudley's "Black Orchid" in 1982, set in the 1920s and featuring Peter Davison's Fifth Doctor: Christopher Bidmead, who favoured hard science fiction, noted that he had rejected Dudley's script when he had been script editor of the previous season and opined that "Black Orchid" should never have been made.

Dennis Spooner's light-hearted approach to history culminated in "The Time Meddler" (1965). The story is noteworthy on several levels. An historical setting and plot – Viking invaders (with names like "Sven") raid a Saxon village – are enlivened by science fiction elements: the Time Meddler himself, who wants to help Harold to win the Battle of Hastings by supplying him with atomic bazookas. This jolly idea is worlds away from the serious tone of "Marco Polo" only a year earlier and typical of Spooner's quirky sense of humour. Writing alternative episodes of "The Daleks' Masterplan" (1965-6) with Terry Nation, Spooner ensured that he left the Doctor and his companions in as impossible a situation as possible at the end of his episodes before handing over to Terry Nation. Nation replied in kind and both authors scratched their heads over the problem the other had set.

The Meddling Monk is another member of the Doctor's race, the first (after Susan) to be encountered in the series. In a cliffhanger which must have been totally unexpected to the original viewers, companions Vicky and Steven enter a tomb and find themselves inside another TARDIS. The Monk himself is delightfully played by actor Peter Butterworth, who had seen distinguished war service as a serial escaper from German prisoner of war camps. He returned as the Monk in "The Daleks' Masterplan" (1965-6).

"The Time Meddler" was the first of the "pseudo historicals", stories set in Earth's past but enlivened by a science fiction element. This imaginative fusion resulted in some of the series' best loved stories (such as "The Talons of Weng-Chiang" in 1977). Meetings between the Doctor and famous historical figures were, however, phased out by the end of Hartnell's run. Writing "The Time Warrior" in 1974, Robert Holmes agreed to set the story in medieval times on the specific condition that he didn't have to include any real figures from the period. Re-launching the show in 2005, Russell T Davies re-launched the pseudo-historical and had the Doctor meet famous historical people. Reflecting the script writers' background in English literature, there was an emphasis on meeting writers: Christopher Eccleston's Doctor meets Charles Dickens, David Tennant's Doctor meets William Shakespeare and Agatha Christie. Other characters were those who children might know from their history lessons: the Tenth Doctor encounters Queen Victoria and Queen Elizabeth I; Matt Smith's Doctor knows Winston Churchill well and has met him off screen before the events of "Victory of the Daleks" (2010). Others were less well known: Madame de Pompadour is "The Girl in the Fireplace" (2006) and Queen Nefertiti travels with the Eleventh Doctor in "Dinosaurs on a Spaceship" (2012). Davies' and Moffat's resurrection of the pseudo-historicals is one of many examples of their looking to the Hartnell era for inspiration: from 2005, the Time Lords have gone and the Ninth, Tenth and Eleventh Doctors wander in time and space without them in the background – as had the first and second Doctors until "The War Games" (1969). Matt Smith's Doctor reboots the Universe and even the Daleks forget who the Doctor is in the 2012 season, thus recreating the original scenario of other characters having no idea who he is and giving Moffat a chance to air the "Doctor who?" jokes again.

Doctor Who stories had individual episode titles until the penultimate serial of season three, "The Savages" (1966), when they were given an overall title and episode numbers. The titling of individual episodes was in keeping with the programme's original premise that this was a *continuing* "adventure in space and time": one story led directly into the next and viewers had no idea when one story was to end and another to begin. Thus original viewers of "The Daleks" would have suspected that the story was to end at the conclusion of its fourth instalment: the Doctor and his companions have escaped with the Thals from the Dalek ambush, say farewell to the latter and wish them luck, and prepare to leave in the TARDIS. Only then does the Doctor realise that the Daleks have taken the ship's fluid link and they cannot leave: they must return to the city to retrieve it. Only then do the viewers realise that the story is not over after all. This continuous story telling left no room for speculative gaps between stories, in which the Doctor might have other adventures to help fans plug the gaps created by continuity mistakes, as is the case from at least the 1970 series onwards.

The practice of naming individual stories was also presumably abandoned because it became too tedious to think of a new title every week. Some are simply variations on each other, as in the third story's two episodes, "The Edge of Destruction"/"The Brink of Disaster" (1964). Russell T Davies again looked to the original episodes for inspiration in the 2005 revival: individual episodes, even of two or three part stories, were to have individual episode titles (with the solitary exception – in eight years from 2005 to 2012 – of "The End of Time" parts one and two: the 2009/2010 Christmas and New Year specials).

The first serial combines science fiction and history. Episode one introduces us to the Doctor (his first words: "What are you doing here?") and to the TARDIS. Susan explains, "I made up the name from the initial letters: Time and Relative Dimension in Space." This explanation was fine for the ephemeral medium of television, when programmes would be shown once or at the most twice and then forgotten, and Anthony Coburn could hardly have been aware that he was sparking one of the show's first continuity controversies. Was Susan a solar engineer who had worked on the Time Lords' first time and space machines and had named them? Did she win a Gallifreyan competition and the prize was to name the time ships? Was the fourth word "dimension" or "dimensions"? Susan says "dimension"; so do Paul McGann in the TV movie (1996) and Christopher Eccleston in "Rose" (2005: he was apparently ad-libbing; the script said "dimensions"); other Doctors say "dimensions". Perhaps Susan's claim that she "named" the TARDIS is evidence of the original conception that the Doctor built it (as Patrick Troughton once said, although the Tenth Doctor tells Rose, "They were grown, not built" and Jack Harkness tries to grow one on his desk in *Torchwood*): this was a hint picked up by the makers of the 1965 film *Dr Who and the Daleks* (1965) in which Dr Who (sic), played by Peter Cushing, proudly informs Roy Castle's Ian that the TARDIS is "my greatest invention". "The War Games" in 1969 firmly establishes that TARDISes were built by the Time Lords and the Doctor stole one because he was bored, which contradicts what Susan said six years previously: but this was in the days before home video, DVDs and cable television repeats and perhaps no-one could really remember. Terrence Dicks once said that *Doctor Who* script editors' attitude to the programme's continuity was the same as the definition of history in the book *1066 and All That* (1930): "what you can remember".

Episode two establishes that the TARDIS's chameleon circuit (called such in the novelisations) has broken: the Doctor tuts, "It's still a police box. Why hasn't it changed? Dear dear dear. How very disturbing." Barbara works out that the TARDIS should "[disguise] itself wherever it goes" and Susan confirms that's right. Why then does it adopt the form of a London police box when it lands in a 1963 junkyard? As Ian says in "An Unearthly Child", "What on earth's it doing here? These things are usually on the street." Shouldn't the TARDIS have become an old wardrobe or something (or would that be too close to *The Lion, the Witch and the Wardrobe*?) to blend in with the other junk? Or was the chameleon circuit already starting to malfunction? It chose a contemporary London artefact, but one from the wrong place. Presumably Anthony Coburn had forgotten that the police box form was supposed to blend in with its surroundings (it didn't) and the circuit didn't break until the end of episode one. Those as wants to can already have continuity fun with the first few minutes of *Doctor Who*.

The second, third and fourth parts of the first story are set on prehistoric Earth. A stone age tribe has lost the secret of fire: the ice age is coming and without fire, they will die. The cave men didn't speak in the original script but do in the finished version. Coburn gives them a pleasingly poetic speech style to contrast with the time travellers': recalling cooked meat, Horg says, "I remember how the meat and fire joined together." Eloquent cavemen were not to everyone's taste and a contemporary critic scratched his head over the well-chiselled 1960s looks of a stone age tribe that speaks perfect English. He would have perhaps preferred the production team to pull out a few teeth and restore the original script's grunts for verisimilitude, but he did hit on a perennial problem in science fiction television: all the aliens speak contemporary English. This was recognised as a dramatic necessity and makers of the original series quietly ignored it: *Star Trek*'s team issued all Star Fleet personnel with a universal translator as a get-out clause. In "The Masque of Mandragora" (1976), the hypnotised Sarah asks the Doctor how she is able to understand Renaissance Italian. This witty, auto-referential reference to a question the series had always quietly avoided immediately alerts the Doctor to the fact that she has been turned against him: only a hypnotised companion would ever question the conventions of the show. "It's a Time Lord gift I let you share," he later explains. Perhaps this telepathic gift isn't always effective, as the Doctor can only speak "a little" Tibetan to K'anpo Rinpoche in "Planet of the Spiders" (1974), or perhaps Hinchcliffe and Holmes had forgotten what Letts and Dicks had established two years earlier, which seems much more likely. Realising that twenty first century audiences were much more likely to scoff at the convention, and anxious to avoid any ridicule that had dogged the original series in its final years, Russell T Davies addressed the issue in the revived series' second story, "The End of the World", in 2005. Conversing with her first aliens in the far future, Rose asks the Doctor why they all speak English. "You hear English," the Doctor explains. He goes on to say that the TARDIS translates for her. This isn't quite what the Doctor said in "The Masque of Mandragora" but Davies makes it clear that the Doctor is an essential part of the telepathic circuit in David Tennant's first story "The Christmas Invasion" (2005). The humans are only able to hear the

Sycorax's speech as gibberish until the Doctor awakens from his regeneration trauma coma (an awakening brought about by smelling Jackie's nice hot cup of tea in a pleasingly British moment). When Rose hears the Sycorax leader speaking English, she knows that the Doctor and the TARDIS are translating for her and the Time Lord has recovered. Continuity for Terrance Dicks and for Russell T Davies was "what you can remember". However, Dicks was working in an age where stories were shown once – or twice at the most; Davies was a fan with a fan's access to home video, VHS and DVD and could, when he pleased, make references to past stories which pleased the fans but were unnoticed by the general viewer and didn't interfere with the story telling.

If language was one problem for the Tribe of Gum, as they were called in the script but not on screen, costuming was another. Derek Newark, who played Za, recalled that he was asked if he was a hairy man at his audition.

"Pardon?"

"Are you a hairy man?" Newark paused and then asked if they wanted him to strip off. It was then explained that, if he was to play a primitive human being, excessive body hair might be an advantage. Carole Ann Ford recalled that the animal skins they were given to wear were full of insects.

The attention of the world was focussed on the assassination of President John F. Kennedy on 23rd November 1963 rather than on the new science fiction serial which debuted quietly that Saturday evening. Those who watched it said it made a stir. Sixth Doctor Colin Baker was a law student at the time; coming home to his digs, he caught the opening minutes as he came up the stairs and said he was still standing in the same place, transfixed, twenty five minutes later. Another viewer said he had been similarly transfixed as a child, there being nothing like *Doctor Who* on British television in 1963. The BBC repeated "An Unearthly Child" before the second episode, "The Cave of Skulls", on Saturday 30th November and six million people watched the first story. This wasn't bad but nor was it an unbounded critical success. Verity Lambert was preparing to wind up the series after the third serial "The Edge of Destruction" (1964), thus completing the BBC's initial order of thirteen episodes. Some elements in the BBC, such as the Children's Department, might have been happy to see the new series go. Some had been shocked by the violence of the first story: Ian observes that all the skulls in "The Cave of Skulls" have been split open and Kal is mauled by an (unseen) sabre toothed tiger. My mother turned the television off at this point, concerned at the effect on my brothers aged three, five and seven. It soon went on again and, somewhat to her amusement, most of my family was glued to the programme for the next fifty years. Concerns and complaints about the series' violence were an immediate feature of reaction to *Doctor Who* and dogged the series throughout its run. John Nathan-Turner (producer 1980-89) said that, in his prayers at night, he asked that anti-sex and violence campaigner Mrs Mary Whitehouse had watched the programme and disliked it, as her protests always put another two million on the viewing figures. Certainly, *Doctor Who*'s depiction of violence and peril helped to contribute to the ambivalent position it held in the BBC and led some in the corporation to dislike it heartily: if it was a children's programme, why was it made by the Drama Department? And if it was for children, why was it so horrific?

In creating the series, Sydney Newman had specified that the science fiction stories were not to contain "Bug Eyed Monsters" or BEMs. Perhaps he intended them to be thoughtful, imaginative explorations of existing science along the lines of some of John Wyndham's stories. Anthony Coburn's second script for the series, "The Masters of Luxor", was such a tale and concentrated on human characters rather than monsters. It was never made. David Whitaker had commissioned a story from Terry Nation, who was best known as a comic writer for Tony Hancock but who had contributed a script to the BBC's anthology science fiction series *Out of the Unknown*, which Whitaker had seen and liked. Nation turned in a seven part tale introducing some strange creatures called Daleks.

It is said that Lambert and Whitaker didn't much like it but had no other script ready to go into production. "The Daleks" (aka "The Mutants") it had to be for story two.

In 1963, the designer assigned to each serial was responsible for virtually all the designs, bar costume. Staff designer Raymond Cusick was not only responsible for the very effective petrified jungle sets in the second story, but also for the Daleks' city and the Daleks themselves. When the four travellers enter the city in "The Dead Planet" (1963), episode one of the story, it is clear that it is not built for human beings: floors, walls and corridors are made of metal and the doors are far too small for even average sized people to enter with comfort. This was the series' first alien environment and it was wonderfully effective. Cusick also designed the Daleks from a somewhat sketchy description in Nation's script. Nation had been inspired by watching the Georgian State dancers, who wore long dresses and appeared to glide across the floor: he wanted the Daleks to move like that. The script stipulated they were to be hideous machine-like creatures without human features; the eye was on a flexible shaft, arms with mechanical grips carried strange weapons. One BBC staffer blithely suggested spraying cardboard tubes silver and bedecking an actor with them. Cusick produced two designs, determined to break up the human form entirely. He sketched an actor sitting in a chair and drew the basic shape around him. When Barbara asks Ian if he thinks there might be someone inside them, this might be an auto-referential joke about the actor inside the prop: such was the strangeness of the movement that many viewers assumed the Daleks must be radio controlled, complete machine creations, as Barbara herself at first thought. Cusick explained that he demonstrated the movement to someone by pushing along a salt or pepper cellar, although, contrary to legend, a condiments set had not inspired the actual design.

Four Daleks were made. The job was contracted out to the firm Shawcraft as BBC departments were over-stretched with other shows. Shawcraft was responsible for many of the creations of the show's early years, including the Slyther and the Mechanoids. In an attempt to make the Daleks easier to build, Raymond Cusick had broken the base down into a series of studded panels. He had originally wanted a smooth, sloped cone. Once the Daleks were finished, Shawcraft asked him why he hadn't specified a smooth look for the base, as it would have been so much easier for them to construct.

The Daleks arrived at the rehearsal room and William Russell said the cast all laughed at them, thinking them ludicrous. Hartnell was unhappy about being cut by one of the Dalek's shoulder bands if it slid past him, and sellotape was applied to some of the supposedly sharp edges. One of the crew noted that this made not a blind bit of difference, but it was important to keep the show's star happy. The Dalek operators rehearsed in the bases without the top half. Once camera rehearsals began, director Christopher Barry found it impossible to tell which Dalek was which and which actor was inside each one (apparently a perennial confusion with Dalek stories, as some of the studio footage from "Death to the Daleks" (1974) reveals). He opted to tape numbers onto the domes and then was able to issue clear directions: "Dalek one – go left; Dalek two, circle right" and so on. The reels of sellotape used to stick on the numbers were jammed into the Daleks' shoulder collars. Numbers and reels are clearly visible in BBC publicity shots for the serial and some illustrators for early books and comic strips about the Daleks assumed that the numbers were part of the designs and that the sellotape reel was a speaker for the Dalek voice. Both features were erroneously retained in some drawings, notably in *The Dalek Book* (1964). Perhaps Mike Tucker and his team remembered the numbered Daleks when they came to revamp the beasts for the revived series' episode *Dalek* (2005) as all bronze Dalek domes carry an identification symbol under the eye stick.

Nation's script immediately chimed with the popular imagination and viewing figures for "The Daleks" rose from six million for "An Unearthly Child" to nine million for this second story. They peaked at ten million for the third story "The Edge of Destruction", perhaps as a result of word of mouth recommendations that this new show was worth watching. Certainly, the Daleks ensured *Doctor Who*'s success and the BBC commissioned another batch of thirty or so episodes: enough to take the show through to the end of its first season.

The radioactive, ashen forest in "The Dead Planet" resonated with contemporary terrors about nuclear war. It was broadcast only a year after the Cuban missile crisis, the point at which humanity had come closest to a nuclear holocaust, a war in which "the fruits of victory would turn to ash in our mouths" as an American diplomat had told the United Nations. The flesh and blood part of the Daleks was a hideous mutation created by years of radiation after the neutronic war with the Thals "many centuries ago". Susan is terrified at having to encounter the Thals as the Daleks assure her they must be "disgustingly mutated". In fact, the mutation cycle has gone full circle and they are tall, attractive and mostly blond humanoids. Presumably the Thals mutated more quickly because they stayed out in the open: the embittered Daleks, by contrast, retreated into their city, built themselves travel and survival machines and, in a horrifying twist to viewers who feared radiation sickness, became dependent on the radiation that would kill the Thals. Nuclear holocaust appeared to haunt Nation as a theme and he returned to it in his 1970s series *Survivors* and in the first series of *Blake's Seven* (1978).

The Second World War had ended only eighteen years before the Daleks' first appearance and it is very quickly apparent that they are Nazis in armoured pepperpots. They use Susan to get them the Thals' anti-radiation drug and then refuse to let the time travellers have any — "Let them die", one Dalek grates – thus, like the Nazis, treating people as means and not as ends. The Daleks are interested in leaving their city and colonising the rest of the planet: they need *lebensraum* and cannot see why they should share their world with a supposedly inferior species. When the drug is demonstrated to be poison for them, they determine to explode another neutron bomb to increase the radiation levels on which they have become dependent: they will then be able to colonise the rest of the planet. By happy coincidence, the bomb will also kill all the Thals. The Doctor protests that the plan is "sheer murder" and a Dalek corrects him: "No. Extermination." The word is a clear reference to the Nazis' so-called "final solution" and it is a neat piece of irony that the supposed inferior species in fact resembles the Nazi Aryan ideal – an apt comment on the absurdity of racism. If viewers hadn't got the point yet, the story's second director, Richard Martin, makes it clear by ending the scene quoted above with the Daleks lining up, raising their sucker sticks in salute and chanting their war cries in unison. Daleks also gave Nazi salutes in their second story, "The Dalek Invasion of Earth" (1964). Referencing the appeasers of Hitler in the 1930s, and perhaps glancing at conscientious objectors in the war itself, Ian attempts to convince the pacifist Thals to fight the Daleks. They refuse until he proposes to exchange one of their females for the TARDIS's missing component: perhaps the Daleks would like to experiment on her. One of the Thals knocks Ian down, thus proving his point – made many times by the series – that sometimes evil must be fought if it is to be defeated.

Episode one of the story, "The Dead Planet", ends with Barbara, separated from her friends, exploring the city on her own. She comes to a door at the end of a corridor – a dead end. Turning round, she sees something which terrifies her and screams. The end credits roll. The something is obviously a Dalek: what the viewers see is the alien point of view as it trundles towards her, its sucker stick clear on the right of the shot. (This shot was virtually repeated in "Dalek" (2005): Rose is trapped by the closed bulkhead and we see her from the Dalek's point of view as it advances.) We don't see a whole Dalek because Shawcraft hadn't finished them, but contemporary accounts say viewers were excited and astonished. Nation has said that his phone didn't stop ringing on the night "The Dead Planet" was shown, with people demanding, "What the hell was it?" They had to wait till next week to find out and the viewing figures inexorably rose.

Sydney Newman was furious when he saw some of the early episodes of "The Daleks" and summoned Verity Lambert for a dressing down. Lambert recalled that he hated the Daleks, thinking them the worst kind of science fiction cliché, and he raged at her: "Jesus, bug eyed monsters" – the very thing he had stipulated must not appear in the show. Lambert defended herself: "They are not! They are survivors of an atomic war." Newman was not convinced and said "Uh huh." It says much for Newman's good grace and strength of character when he saw the viewing figures and apologised to Verity Lambert. She recalled that he said, you guys obviously understand *Doctor Who* much better than I do, so go ahead and do your own thing. Here was a creator willing to pass on his baby to someone else who could do it better: something of a contrast to *Star Trek* creator Gene Roddenberry, who continued to offer suggestions and storylines to his successors long after he had moved on as executive producer of the franchise. Newman congratulated Verity Lambert on the second Dalek story and said he had loved it.

Britain apparently went Dalek crazy in 1964. Quick to cash in on the Daleks' success, Britain's manufacturers rushed out "robot action" battery operated Daleks, Dalek slippers, Dalek wallpaper and turned the water pistol into "Dr Who's Anti-Dalek Fluid Neutraliser". The BBC meanwhile gave two of its Daleks props away to a Dr Barnardo's children's home and said, at first, that it had no plans to bring the creatures back. In the face of endless enquiries and petitioning from the press and from children, and belatedly awakening to a cash cow when they eventually saw one, the BBC confirmed that the Daleks would return at some point. Raymond Cusick had been largely responsible for the Daleks' success with his superb, iconic design but it was Terry Nation who co-owned the copyright with the BBC and coined in the royalties, earning enough to buy himself an agreeable country house where he installed four of the beasts. As a BBC staff designer who received a salary in place of royalties, Cusick made not a penny. Eventually, the BBC recognised that he had played some part in the Daleks' success and gave him a one-off payment of a few hundred pounds, which Cusick considered derisory. Later in the 1960s, the children's BBC magazine programme *Blue Peter* showed viewers how to make their own model Dalek and one of the presenters remarked that whoever had designed the originals deserved a *Blue Peter* badge. These were given out as rewards for success, endeavour or for appearing on the show: 1980s companion Ace wore one on her bomber jacket. Cusick wrote in, said he had designed them, and duly received his badge.

The production team were keen to capitalise on the success of the Daleks and one monster after another was created, at least partly, in the hope that it would emulate the merchandising success of Terry Nation's creations. Hopes were pinned on the Voord, the Zarbi and the Chumblies but nothing much came of them, although the Zarbi and their Vortis companions the Menoptra did merit a badge each – now hotly sought by collectors and a snip at £85 a piece on eBay. The Mechanoids, spherical robots introduced in "The Chase" (1965), were virtually redesigned Daleks. Small toys were made of them and they featured in the Dalek strip in the comic *TV21*, but they never reappeared in the series and the toys quickly vanished from toyshops.

British cinema, ever keen to capitalise on small screen successes, approached the BBC with a view to making a film of the first Dalek serial. This approach was fronted by Milton Subotsky and Max J. Rosenberg, producers of horror films which rivalled the output of Hammer studios. They created a company called Aaru productions to make the first *Who* feature film.

It was common practice in the 1950s and 1960s to turn television programmes into cinema films. Television was ephemera and programmes were usually only shown once and then never seen again. Films, however, could be seen as many times as an audience member could stump up the admission fee. Moreover, films could reach a wider, more international audience than the original programme: Hammer films had remade the first two 1950s *Quatermass* serials as films, replacing Nigel Kneale's troubled professor with a confident American played by Brian Donlevy as a precondition for stateside sales, much to Kneale's chagrin. Furthermore, feature films could be made in colour at a time when television was emphatically small screen and black and white. Acknowledging the equal appeal of the Doctor and the Daleks to the public, the movie poster for the film announced the title as *Dr Who and the* (in a small font) with the word *DALEKS* shouted in giant capitals along the width of the poster's bottom. The illustration replicated this wording by showing the new TARDIS crew cowering in apparent awe as giant, colourful Daleks sweep past them. The poster also made a simple and direct appeal to those who had enjoyed the black and white serial, proclaiming, "NOW ON THE BIG SCREEN – IN COLOUR!"

There appear to have been some thoughts about using the television cast, but they were busy making the series proper. The film was duly recast. Subotsky has explained that they had to use an internationally recognised star if the film was sold abroad and Peter Cushing was cast as Dr Who (sic). The script stuck closely to Nation's original but crammed seven episodes into 79 minutes: terribly short by today's standards but the right length for Saturday morning at the children's pictures. The film, unlike the series, is specifically aimed at children. The Doctor is much more of an amiable old buffer than Hartnell's edgy and unpredictable original; Susan (often "Susie") becomes a twelve year old granddaughter, Barbara another granddaughter and the gallant Ian Chesterton a bumbling oaf played by Roy Castle. The film is exciting and colourful and the story sweeps along, although the heavy eye make up of the Thals excited some comments: presumably the fascist Daleks thought this was another sign of their decadence. The extras for these perfect physical specimens were Covent Garden porters, who apparently were not happy at being asked to shave off their body hair to reveal their rippling torsos. In the original serial, a Thal is killed when he tries to cross a bottomless cavern in a cave under the Dalek city. In the film version, he falls onto a convenient ledge. The film, made quickly with a main eye on profit, effectively capitalised on Dalekmania and a sequel was commissioned. This was 1966's *Daleks: Invasion Earth 2150 A.D.*. Peter Cushing's Doctor introduced viewers to the idea that another actor could play the part, which perhaps eased the production team's fears when they had to consider whether to replace the ailing William Hartnell or end the series. I watched *Dr Who and the Daleks* for the first time in 1973, when it premiered on BBC 1 as part of the "High Adventure" early evening film series. I remember looking through the *Radio Times* and being surprised and aggrieved to find that the Doctor was not being played by Jon Pertwee; although I had watched other Doctors, I could barely remember them and had been mystified by finding some old bloke with long hair pretending to be the Doctor in an old annual. The film is cheap, cheerful and fun; writing in 1977, the *Radio Times* film critic Philip Jenkinson wrote, "*Star Wars* it ain't, but they must have spent a few quid on the cardboard and papier mâché."

David Whitaker adapted "The Daleks" (1963-4) for the first (and best) *Doctor Who* novelisation. This included the third version of the introduction of the TARDIS crew, including "An Unearthly Child" and the human inventor Dr Who of the film. *Doctor Who in an Exciting Adventure with the Daleks* (1964) is told in the first person by Ian Chesterton, now an ex-schoolmaster who has tried, and failed, to get a job as a rocket scientist. Returning from his job interview, he stops his car at last in a thick fog and encounters Barbara, who has been involved in a road accident. The driver of the other vehicle, a military truck, is dead and Barbara's passenger, Susan English (not Foreman), has disappeared. Barbara has been giving Susan some private coaching at her flat and has insisted on driving her home in the fog, ignoring Susan's protests. Ian is alarmed to hear someone strike a match so near to a car accident: this is the Doctor, who has come to investigate. Ian observes that the match never seems to burn down. "Just a little invention of mine," the old man observes. Ian is surprised to find a police box in the middle of Barnes Common and the adventure at that point more or less follows the script of "The Daleks" although, as it is written from Ian's point of view, much is left out. Whitaker's writing is excellent and the prose is worthy of John Wyndham. *Doctor Who* aficionados in the early sixties thus had three versions of "The Daleks" to choose from: the original television serial (which, admittedly, they could only access in memory), the Aaru film and the novel.

(Strictly speaking, the title of Whitaker's novel is *Doctor Who*. The "in an exciting adventure with the Daleks" bit is an explanatory strapline, not part of the title. However, both the original novel *and* the Paul McGann TV movie were called *Doctor Who* only: vanilla and not elaborated. This is unhelpful, when *Doctor Who* is also the title of the series proper. Thus the strapline has become confused with the book's title, which is, was, and remains, plain *Doctor Who*. It is clearly essential to be correct on this vital point.)

If the film could afford a much larger budget than the television series, the television series was running out of money by the end of the second story. David Whitaker wrote a two episode filler "The Edge of Destruction" / "The Brink of Disaster", set entirely on board the TARDIS and featuring only the regular cast. This is as tense and strange as it is slow: the TARDIS is apparently infiltrated by a strange force which causes the travellers to lose touch with their surroundings. Ian and Barbara think they are once again teaching at Coal Hill School and Susan threatens Ian with a pair of scissors. The Children's Department protested. Fantasy violence with Daleks was one thing, but real violence with objects which children could find around the home was quite another. The first season continued with a journey across thirteenth century Europe in "Marco Polo" (1964), notable for effective shooting of an epic journey in a tiny studio and for Polo's voice-over narrating their voyage and stating his irritation with the Doctor. The science fiction/historical/science fiction pattern continued. After reaching Cathay, they crew hunted for the six Keys of Marinus in an eponymous adventure. Again scripted by Terry Nation, this was sub-standard peril-of-the-week fare and very much in the vein of 1930s and 1940s cinema adventure serials like *Flash Gordon*. It was again designed by Raymond Cusick, who had to create a different environment for each episode on a tiny budget. On the DVD release of the story, he was asked, "Are you proud of your work on 'The Keys of Marinus'?" Cusick replied musingly, "Am I proud of my work on 'The Keys of Marinus'?" He paused. "No," he said.

John Lucarotti, who had written the acclaimed "Marco Polo", turned in another intelligent and thoughtful script with the next story, "The Aztecs". Barbara is mistaken by the Aztecs for the reincarnation of the goddess Yetaxa, a role she embraces in an attempt to make the Aztecs abandon their barbaric practice of human sacrifice. The Doctor protests and argues, "You can't change history. Not one line." This is one of the first attempts in the series to grapple with the complications and ambiguities of time travel. The Doctor argues that history is fixed, has happened and cannot be changed. Barbara ignores him, even to the extent of half seeming to believe in her new persona. "Not Barbara," she corrects the Doctor. "Yetaxa." Her *idées de grandeur* meet their come-uppance: the sacrifice she saves is most indignant at being denied his moment of glory and the Aztecs continue in their bloodthirsty ways. History absorbs her attempt to change it and she becomes part of established events. This was an idea the series returned to in "Day of the Daleks" (1972), in which a band of guerrillas from the future arrive back on Earth during the Doctor's twentieth century exile, determined to assassinate Sir Reginald Styles. Styles, they argue, was responsible for the world war which led to the Dalek invasion: having led the peace delegates to his country house for final negotiations, he exploded a bomb which killed the lot of them and plunged the world into war. All but one of the guerrillas, Shura, return with the Doctor to the Dalek ruled Earth of the future and the Doctor realises the truth: Shura, left alone and determined to finish the mission, detonated the bomb which kills Styles and the delegates. "You're trapped in a temporal paradox," the Doctor sternly announces. "Styles didn't cause that explosion and start the wars. You did it yourselves." The guerrillas, like Barbara, attempt to change history but become part of its inexorable pattern and flow.

The original production team realised that time travel paradoxes were something to be handled very carefully and the 1960s stories tend to avoid them. If the Doctor cannot change history – presumably defined as events before 1964, when "The Aztecs" was made – why, they asked, is he able to change events in the future or on different planets? As a time traveller, he lives outside time: past and future are alike to him, so, if he can't change historical events, surely he shouldn't be able to change future ones either? In "Day of the Daleks", Jo asks the Doctor why, if the guerrillas can't kill Styles on their first attempt (he's out of the country), don't they just reset their time machines to the previous evening and have another go? "That's the Blinovitch Limitation Effect," the Doctor explains. He is about to define this but he and Jo are called away by the guerrillas before he gets a chance. Script editor Terrance Dicks cheerfully explained that this was because the Blinovitch Limitation Effect didn't bear close scrutiny and was inserted to plug a plot hole which the viewers might have worked out for themselves.

The question asked – and avoided – by the original production team was eventually answered under Russell T Davies's period as showrunner of the revived series. In James Moran's 2008 story "The Fires of Pompeii", Donna insists that they must save the Pompeiians before Vesuvius erupts and is upset when the Doctor refuses. He explains that there are fixed points in time which cannot be changed: one is Pompeii's destruction by Vesuvius. Other points in time are fluid and can be changed. Viewers thus had to wait forty four years before the First Doctor's objections to Barbara changing history were properly explained, which is part of the fun of sticking with *Doctor Who*, particularly with our contemporary production teams' keenness to extrapolate good ideas from the original series to create good stories.

"The Aztecs" is the first story to feature romance for the Doctor. Hartnell, unlike the Tenth Doctor, was no inveterate snogger, but he shares a cup of chocolate with an elderly Aztec lady, Cameca. As every Key Stage Two pupil knows from their history project in year four, the Aztecs were one of the first people to discover the blessings of chocolate (although they don't learn it was considered an aphrodisiac), and Cameca explains that the sharing of the drink signals their engagement. Ian, much amused, congratulates the Doctor on the news. The Doctor seems unfussed about his impending nuptials, perhaps suggesting that Time Lords and human beings are genetically and genitally compatible, something assumed by Rose and Martha in the revival. Even Susan muses on the type of man she would like to marry, determined to choose for herself, and anticipating her romance and marriage with David Campbell, one of the freedom fighters in series two's "The Dalek Invasion of Earth" (1964).

3

Regeneration

Season one concluded with the familiar pattern of alternating science fiction and historical stories. "The Sensorites" (1964) is a slightly dated affair and the humans' rocket ship seems to have come out of a 1940s film serial; its twenty eighth century crew wear buttoned shirts and jackets with rocket logos. The starship Enterprise it ain't. The Sensorites themselves are effective designs. They joined the Zarbi and Menoptra, equally impressive creations from season two's "The Web Planet" (1965), in the first *Doctor Who* annual, largely written by story editor David Whitaker. The publishers also wanted to include the Daleks but Terry Nation was using them in their own series of annuals, independent of the Doctor.

Jacqueline Hill (Barbara) is absent from much "The Sensorites" as she was on holiday. It was common practice in the 1960s to write out characters when the actor needed a break or was unwell: this was an absolute necessity when the series ran for forty-odd weeks of the year and one episode was made a week. The production team cheerfully accommodated William Hartnell's request for a week off from an episode of "The Dalek Invasion of Earth" (1964) – he was unwell – and speedily rewrote the script to incapacitate the Doctor, who spends most of the episode unconscious, with his back to the camera, and played by an extra. In "The Celestial Toymaker" (1966), the Doctor is rendered invisible and only his pre-recorded voice is heard: Hartnell was on holiday.

The season concluded with Dennis Spooner's first story for the series, "The Reign of Terror". Set in the French revolution, it sees Barbara and Susan carted off to the guillotine and is inflected more towards humour – Spooner's preference – than some of the earlier historicals. Cast and crew completed the next story, "Planet of Giants", which was held over to start season two, and then departed on holiday. Spooner took over from Whitaker as story editor from the third story, "The Rescue" (1965).

Season two's second story is remarkable for establishing the template for the next forty eight years, and certainly for Pertwee's first three seasons, which he spends in exile as UNIT's scientific adviser on contemporary Earth. "The Dalek Invasion of Earth" (1964) is the first alien invasion story. Nominally set two hundred years in the future in

2164, the level of human technology and fashion is very much of the 1960s, as noted by a *Radio Times* reviewer of the Peter Cushing film version, which followed suit: "Fashion pundits please note – in 2150, we'll all be wearing sixties casuals." The story draws heavily on the Daleks' origins as symbols of the Nazis in depicting an England smashed by heavy bombardment. Some humans cower in cellars and plot resistance while others are carted off to a concentration camp in Bedfordshire. In short, this is England as it would have been if a Nazi invasion had been successful. Terry Nation draws heavily on the heroism of resistance fighters in occupied Europe: the poorly armed resistance attacks the vastly superior Dalek force aboard their spaceship and are repulsed with heavy losses; the crippled scientist Dortmun (an image Nation would return to in the similarly wheelchair bound Davros) launches a suicide attack against a squad of Daleks, determined to take a few with him so that Barbara and resistance fighter Jenny can escape. Verbal and visual imagery is from the Second World War, still very much in living memory, and is sometimes disturbing. The humans in the Daleks' camp are called "slave workers" and are on starvation rations; the Dalek in charge of the concentration camp is referred to as the "kommandant"; humans trade jewellery for food with a black marketeer who slips in and out of the camp unnoticed; an old woman and her daughter mend clothes for the slave workers and betray Barbara and Jenny to the Daleks for the sake of a few tins of food and oranges; the Daleks raise their sucker arms in Nazi salutes; the punishment for not working hard enough is extermination; and so on. The Robomen are unthinking servants of the Daleks, human beings turned into machines who pitilessly enforce discipline with whips and truncheons in a clear reference to the SS and the Gestapo. In one sequence, the Doctor, Susan and Tyler (another resistance member) evade the Daleks in the London sewers but have themselves to evade alligators which escaped from the zoo when the city was first bombed. This sequence was perhaps inspired by actual events: knowing that bombing was coming in 1940, zoo keepers shot the more dangerous animals in Regent's Park zoo for fear that they would escape if it was bombed. The alligator that actually appears on screen appears to be a sweet little baby one and is about eight inches long, but the idea was dramatically good.

The Robomen are a concept that doesn't perhaps stand the test of time and, like elements of "The Keys of Marinus" (1964), appears to have come straight from *Buck Rogers* type pulp film serials of the 1940s. In creating them, Nation was responding to one of the problems of the

Daleks which has dogged all of their appearances in the original series. Designed for only one story, the Daleks work beautifully in the television studio: in "The Daleks" (1963-4), they can't even leave the smooth floors of their city. Once they are taken out on location, problems begin. Designer Spencer Chapman disrupts the Daleks' smooth lines by plonking them on a larger base unit which can accommodate larger wheels - their original smaller bases are clearly visible – and gives them radio discs on their backs. This is handy for the Doctor, who defeats them by interfering with the signals that allow them to move and to communicate with each other. These new Daleks are bigger than their original counterparts but now clearly contain an actor, when the originals were designed to conceal that they were operated by one.

Daleks in London can't climb stairs, so need someone to do it for them. Hence the need for the more mobile Robomen. The Daleks' lack of mobility led to endless jokes, exemplified in a Birkett cartoon of 1978: confronted with a flight of stairs, the leader of a group of Daleks says, "Well, this certainly buggers up our plans to conquer the universe." The cartoon was printed on the cover of scripts for "Destiny of the Daleks" (1979) issued to actors and crew and perhaps prompted Tom Baker's taunting of a Dalek as he escapes up a rope: "If you're supposed to be the superior race of the universe, why don't you try climbing after us?" Fans suspected the auto-referential line to be inserted by new script editor Douglas Adams, who was ever alive to the series' absurdities, and they disapproved of it as drawing attention to the Daleks' dramatic limitations and thus spoiling the suspension of disbelief. It is hard to see Nation writing the line and he disliked the production team's handling of his original script for "Destiny of the Daleks". Even back in the 1960s, production crews scratched their heads over the Daleks' technical limitations. Hover Daleks were suggested for "The Chase" (1965) but they were not technically possible.

Birkett's card is still widely available today but was redundant even before the end of the original series. The Colin Baker story "Revelation of the Daleks" (1985) has an understated moment where a Dalek hovers (a shot realised using a commercially available model Dalek produced by Sevans Models) but this was soon forgotten by viewers. The end of episode one of Sylvester McCoy's "Remembrance of the Daleks" (1988) has the Doctor run up some cellar stairs to escape an Imperial Dalek. It then follows him. This was considered enough of a dramatic surprise – confounding those cynical viewers who shouted, "Run up the stairs!" to the Doctor – that it merited an episode ending on its own. The sequence was reprised in the revived series episode "Dalek" (2005) when Rose and Adam evade the Dalek by running up a flight of stairs. "Great big alien death machine," smarms Adam, "defeated by a flight of stairs." "Elevate," grates the Dalek, and follows him. Fans cheered across the U.K.

In "Day of the Daleks", the Robomen are replaced by the ape-like Ogrons as more mobile servants, although they might have been a feature of Louis Marks's original scripts for that story, which didn't feature the Daleks. Nevertheless, the human guerrillas are opposed by the Daleks' gorillas. Production teams in the later 1970s also felt that the Daleks' dialogue was terribly slow and dull and slowed down the story telling: hence the perceived need to bring back Davros in "Destiny of the Daleks" (1979) and every subsequent Dalek story in the original series. Davros, with his more human speech patterns, could handle the dialogue better than the Daleks, although an irritating effect of his continuous inclusion was that the Daleks themselves took a back seat in 1980s Dalek stories.

The Dalek operators themselves in "The Dalek Invasion of Earth" lamented the Daleks' limitations in different terms. Once inside their props, other actors tended to forget about them, and Dalek actors were left without refreshments when their fellows went to have their tea breaks. Comfort breaks were a similar problem. On location, the operators solved it by trundling their Daleks over drains at the side of the road, where they could blissfully relieve themselves in peace. One actor recalled setting the trend and a line of Daleks formed behind him, all queuing for the loo.

Sydney Newman may have loved "The Dalek Invasion of Earth" but sadly it has not really stood the test of time. The DVD draws attention to floor managers saying "Cue!" before a line of slave workers leaves the Dalek spaceship; Daleks zoom down its ramp, apparently – judging from a bang – to crash into something off-screen. The Dalek voices were produced by actors speaking into a ring modulator (an effect originally created for a robot voice in a pre-*Who* radio play), but the crew never remembered to write down the modulator's settings. Thus Dalek voices throughout the original series differ from story to story in their pitch and level of distortion: something that Nicholas Briggs, an actor and fan who has provided the Dalek voices since 2005, would never dream of doing. The Dalek voices in their invasion serial are particularly piping and barely distorted: they sound like a bad imitation of a Dalek voice by someone in a pub or playground. Furthermore,

David Graham's Dalek voices are pre-recorded and played in live on set: they frequently overlap Peter Hawkins' live voices, and the result is chaos. (These actors are best known for providing, respectively, the voices of Parker in *Thunderbirds* and Captain Pugwash in the eponymous cartoon.) Some effects make fans wince. Ian and the Doctor watch the arrival of the Dalek saucer in episode one: on the DVD, viewers can choose between a *TV21* / revived series flying saucer thundering over the London streets, or opt for the original, a silver pie dish suspended from wires which is every bit as good as those in Ed Wood's film *Plan 9 From Outer Space* (1959).

Before the advent of home video, fans' folk memories of this story were partly based on plot summaries and impressive photos published in such vehicles as the *Doctor Who Tenth Anniversary Special* (BBC, 1973). Some of course had actually seen and remembered its first broadcast. However, much of the affection for and excitement generated by mention of this serial arguably arises from its transmutation into the cinema film, *Daleks: Invasion Earth 2150 A.D.* (1966). This was Peter Cushing's second outing as the Doctor and was regularly shown on BBC television in the 1970s. Its imagery was repeated in some of the scenes of the Dalek invasion of Cardiff in *The Stolen Earth* (2008) and the cover art for the 1976 novelisation *Doctor Who and the Dalek Invasion of Earth* (1977) by Terrance Dicks. Here, the Roboman and Dalek on the cover were based on the film's versions, with illustrator Christos Achilleos adding a gas mask, goggles and a machine gun to the Roboman for added dehumanising horror (the Robomen in the television production apparently wear adapted lamp shades or waste paper baskets and speak like *Monty Python*'s Gumbies). The flying saucers raking London with fire are also from the movie version.

This second *Doctor Who* film was an attempt to cash in on Dalekmania and to build on the box office success of the first film, *Dr Who and the Daleks*, released a year earlier. Such was the success of the Daleks that the Doctor doesn't even feature in the film's title and cinema trailers concentrated on the Daleks themselves, only mentioning in passing that "Dr Who" is played by Peter Cushing. It is a much better, less childish and more exciting outing than the first film. Producers Subotsky and Vegoda had apparently listened to audience feedback from children who had seen *Dr Who and the Daleks* and were apparently disappointed that the Daleks only exterminated one person. There are effective extermination scenes a-plenty in the second film. Stuntman Eddie Powell, who doubled for Christopher Lee in the contemporaneous *Dracula* films for Hammer, and would go on to work as the eponymous *Alien* in Ridley Scott's 1979 film, runs to escape from the Dalek saucer over wrecked shop roofs and is brought down by Dalek firepower. Powell actually caught and injured his foot in the shop awning as he went down – something visible if you freeze frame the DVD. He is surrounded by Daleks, who exterminate him. There is a mass extermination of Philip Madoc, who plays the sneering black marketeer Brockley, later in the film. The Daleks' guns in both films were realised by shooting carbon dioxide fire extinguishers through their hollow exterminators. This was arguably a much more effective visual effect than the television equivalent: for all the 1960s Dalek stories, the extermination effect is achieved by turning the picture negative (an image which survived through the 1970s and 1980s to the present day, when Dalek extermination rays reveal an x-ray of the people they are blasting: an extrapolation of a negative). One problem with the film Daleks' firepower is that, although it is now clear which Dalek is firing, their range is limited by the range of the fire extinguisher (about eight feet). An American film critic erroneously assumed that the Daleks fired nerve gas. This is quite wrong.

The film benefited from a greater adherence to the original television version than *Dr Who and the Daleks*. Original story editor David Whitaker rewrote much of the dialogue and the tone is grittier and more serious, although the Nazi imagery was considerably toned down from the television original. The Daleks themselves sport the new vertical solar panels introduced into the 1965 television serial, "The Chase" as an explanation for the Daleks' new power source outside their city. The budget was bigger than the first film – and many times larger than the television series' – allowing for impressive visuals of the Daleks' saucer and massed Daleks on location. The acting is of a higher quality: accomplished actor Ray Brooks plays David, whose television romance with Susan is cut as the film's Susan is much younger than Carole Ann Ford's; Bernard Cribbins (who was to play companion Wilfred Mott against David Tennant's Doctor from 2007-2010) replaces Roy Castle as comic relief Tom Campbell and Barbara is inexplicably replaced by Louise (Jill Curzon), the Doctor's niece. Andrew Kier, who was to play the screen Quatermass in Nigel Kneale's approved Hammer film of *Quatermass and the Pit* (1967), provides Scottish gravitas as resistance fighter Wyler, who befriends Susan. Peter Cushing was ill for some of the shoot and the schedule had to be rearranged around his absence; some have argued that his illness affects his performance and that he is not quite the sprightly Doctor of *Dr Who and the Daleks*.

Better though the second film was, it was released when interest in the Daleks was waning and it barely broke even at the box office. Subotsky and Rosenberg had the rights to make a third film, but this was shelved. In a 1980s interview, Subotsky said that this was to have been called *Dr Who's Greatest Adventure* and would have featured two Doctors (Patrick Troughton was playing the part on television when the third film would have been released). Subotsky went on to make *At The Earth's Core* (1976), featuring Doug McClure and a burrowing machine akin to the Mole from *Thunderbirds*. Peter Cushing plays scientist Dr Abner Perry and gives a performance that is virtually identical to his Doctor, thus suggesting that he could have continued as the screen Doctor with great success. Who might have played the other Doctor in *Dr Who's Greatest Adventure* remains a mystery, and how a human Dr Who might have regenerated is anyone's guess.

Aimed at children and intended to make money, the two 1960s Dalek films are fondly remembered parts of *Who* history. They also started a repeated series of attempts to bring the Doctor to the big screen; rumours of films have been rumbling since the 1970s and pre-production has started on actual films. In 2012, Steven Moffat quelled excitement over reports that a film was actually in pre-production by stating emphatically that any new film would have to include the television cast and would have to tie in with present programme continuity. As the television cast are heavily involved in making the ongoing series – as were William Hartnell, Carole Ann Ford, Jacqueline Hill and William Russell when the two Dalek films were made – it seems highly unlikely that a film will materialise for the time being.

Susan leaves the TARDIS at the end of "The Dalek Invasion of Earth" to marry freedom fighter David Campbell. Carole Ann Ford, who played her, had become unhappy with what she saw as the lack of development of Susan's character. David Whitaker, now working under new story editor Dennis Spooner, wrote a two part story originally entitled "Dr Who and Tanni", to introduce Susan's replacement. This became "The Rescue" (1964), Tanni was renamed Vicki and Maureen O'Brien was contracted to play her. The actress was at the beginning of her career and unprepared for the high public profile the role brought her. She recalled people recognising her on the London Underground and nudging each other and for many years was uncomfortable with her association with the series, unwilling to give interviews and sometimes vehemently wishing that fanzine editors would leave her alone. She became more reconciled to her place in the series' history as it neared its thirty fifth anniversary.

"The Rescue" is one of the series' neglected gems; beautifully written by David Whitaker and well acted by a small cast, it centres on a crashed spaceship in the far future. Vicki is one of the survivors and so is Bennett, crippled by the crash. Vicky lives in terror of the alien Koquillion, who stalks around the ship, intimidating its occupants. The Doctor discovers that Koquillion is Bennett in disguise; Bennett had originally murdered the crew, including Vicki's father, but is himself killed by the aliens native to the planet. Now completely alone, Vicki gratefully accepts the Doctor's invitation to accompany him on his travels. "In that old box?" she asks. "We can go anywhere and everywhere in that old box," the Doctor chuckles. Ian and Barbara are keen that the Doctor should invite Vicki aboard, partly because they like her very much themselves, and partly because they believe she can help to fill the gap that Susan has left. "The Rescue"'s themes of grief, loss and the healing power of compassion are touching and we are immediately drawn to Vicki, beautifully played by Maureen O'Brien. The actress prepared carefully for the shoot by "becoming" her character according to the Method school of acting, much, she recalls, to the amusement of the three established regulars.

Vicki is, to all intents and purposes, Susan with another name. She is human, granted, rather than a member of the Doctor's own race, but comes from the far future and is bewildered by Ian and Barbara's lack of technical knowledge: she has no idea what an aspirin is and is surprised on hearing the Beatles in "The Chase" (1965): "I'd no idea they played classical music." Like Susan, she is young, inexperienced and needs protecting; like Susan, the Doctor enjoys a grandfatherly relationship with her and takes her under his wing. Hartnell's Doctor often puts his arm around her protectively, especially when danger threatens, as at the end of one of the episodes "The Web Planet" (1965) when the Animus immobilises the Doctor and Vicki with a sticky spray of web. Like Susan, she leaves the TARDIS to be married off (often the fate of female companions of the first four Doctors): unlike Susan, she knows that her choice of husband will entail her own death, for her name is changed to Cressida, her husband is Troilus and the Trojan War is coming to its end ("The Myth Makers", 1965).

Vicki's similarity to Susan was a blessing to the story editors. Some script writers hadn't grasped that Susan was leaving and they could easily replace her name with Vicki's without causing any material damage to the story. Peter Purves was later to complain that the original script for "Galaxy Four" (1965) had been written for Ian and Barbara and he had been given Barbara's lines. The actor was singularly fed up at having to be afraid of the Drahvins, the race of female villains, whom he described as "singularly un-Amazonian". Confusion over companions was a consequence of hurried writing, itself attributable to the production of so many episodes a year. The issue grew to a head in Patrick Troughton's time, when unsuitable scripts were rushed into production because there was no replacement available, and was one of the reasons that the number of episodes was cut from about forty a year to twenty five or so in 1970, when the series moved into colour and Jon Pertwee became the Doctor.

Companions come and go with a somewhat bewildering rapidity in Hartnell's time. Discovering that the Daleks' time machine can return them to Earth – albeit in 1965 rather than 1963 – Ian and Barbara opt to leave the Doctor at the end of "The Chase" (1965). Ian offers too little money for his bus fare and the incredulous conductor asks, "Where have you been, the moon?" "No, but you're close," Ian quips. The teachers are replaced by Steven Taylor (Peter Purves), an astronaut imprisoned by the Mechanoids in "The Chase". Peter Purves, best known in the 1970s as one of the regular presenters on the BBC children's magazine show *Blue Peter*, originally appeared in episode two of "The Chase" as hillbilly tourist Morton Dill, who encounters the Daleks at the top of the Empire State Building. Purves's performance impressed the production team who offered him a regular role as Steven: Purves, who was newly married and needed the money, accepted with relief. Vicki is replaced first by Trojan handmaid Katarina, who was swiftly dispatched out of a spaceship's airlock when new story editor Donald Tosh realised her limitations: coming from that period of history, she wouldn't understand a lock, let alone a spaceship. Her replacement is space security agent Sara Kingdom, played by Jean Marsh, who had once been married to Jon Pertwee. Sara only featured in one story, the twelve episode epic "The Daleks' Master Plan" (1965-6), in which she shoots her brother Brett Vyon, believing him to be a traitor. Vyon was played by Nicholas Courtney, who went on to play the British commander of the United Nations Intelligence Taskforce, Brigadier Alistair Gordon Lethbridge-Stewart, one of the show's best loved characters (and longest lived: Courtney created the role in "The Web of Fear" in 1968 and was still playing him in *The Sarah Jane Adventures* forty years later). Sara, like Katarina, is killed off, aged to death by the Daleks' time destructor in another sequence that had sensitive souls bristling with concern at the effect of such horror on their children. They were the last companions to die until "Earthshock" in 1982, fondly remembered to this day for the death of Adric.

Yet another companion joins the TARDIS at the end of "The Massacre", Dodo Chaplet (Jackie Lane), who only lasted five stories. The production team allowed Jackie Lane to use a Cockney accent in filming for her first full story, "The Ark" (1966), but higher powers let it be known that principal characters should speak BBC English: thus Dodo alternates between received pronunciation and Cockney in alternate film or studio sequences. The Doctor's fondness for Dodo in "The Ark" is not especially believable, considering that they had only just met, and one suspects some hasty scriptwriting for a generic companion figure. Dodo slips away from the series in "The War Machines" (1966), where she isn't even granted a farewell scene. Yet another set of replacements are Londoners from the swinging sixties, seen by script editor Gerry Davis as necessary to bring the show up to date. These are the middle class Polly, notable for her long legs and miniskirts, and the cockney sparrow Able Seaman Ben Jackson.

This bewildering parade of companions through apparently revolving TARDIS doors can be partly accounted for by changes in the production team and partly by actors' desires to move on from unrewarding roles. Verity Lambert left, to be replaced as John Wiles and then Innes Lloyd as producer; Dennis Spooner moved on, to be replaced by Donald Tosh and then Gerry Davis as script editor. Each production team had different ideas about who would be suitable as a companion, and each didn't always think much of the previous team's choices. William Hartnell was especially unhappy about the departure of his first three companions. He got on well with Ian's replacement Steven (Peter Purves) and instructed Purves in the art of acting for television, suggesting that he made hand gestures near his face so that they could be picked up in close up: this perhaps explains the First Doctor's habit of gripping his lapels. Steven Taylor at least stayed for some eighteen months and provided some continuity while female companions came and went, although Peter Purves himself wasn't entirely happy in the role. Interviewed in the late 1970s, he said he didn't think he was always very good and there was a tendency to overact when surrounded by peril and monsters. He also got tired of uttering "such earth-shattering lines as, 'What's happening Doctor?' and 'Doctor, look out!' and the inevitable, 'Where are we, Doctor?' " Not being a fan of the Daleks, he said he wished he'd never signed on the dotted line when he learnt they were to feature in twelve consecutive episodes (actually eleven, as they are absent from the Christmas Day episode, "The Feast of Stephen" (1965)). In the same interview, Purves explained that he stayed on because he needed a regular income; he also liked Bill Hartnell and they got on well together. Hartnell was upset when Purves said he wanted to move on and couldn't understand why the younger actor would turn his back on regular money in an ongoing part when he had a young family to feed. Indeed, Purves went from *Doctor Who* to unemployment and a job delivering cars while he looked for other acting jobs.

Terrence Dicks has argued that an actor can play the Doctor for five or so years without reaching the limits of the part, but the role of the companion is much more limited: two years is about as much as anyone can stand. Dicks said that this was in the nature of the companion's role, especially female companions, who are there to look pretty, ask questions, scream, get captured and have the Doctor rescue them. This is a not unfair summary of the companion's function in the black and white stories, until the advent of women's liberation, as feminism was sometimes known in the 1970s, led to the creation of more capable companions like Dr Liz Shaw and Sarah Jane Smith. The Patrick Troughton story "The Moonbase" (1967), contains the following exchange:

Polly: You found something?

Doctor: Oh Polly, I only wish I had. Why not make some coffee to keep them all happy while I think of something?

Polly: All right.

Polly sympathetically squeezes the Doctor on the shoulder as she accepts that her role, like the good 1960s secretary she is, is to make the coffee while the clever men think of solutions. In the 1983 special "The Five Doctors", Janet Fielding (playing Tegan) objected to a scene in which the First Doctor (now played by Richard Hurndall) tells her to make tea for the recovering Fifth Doctor (Peter Davison). A rewrite was hurriedly inserted to placate both Tegan and Janet Fielding as the Fifth Doctor asks Tegan to humour the First Doctor; he was much more old fashioned when he was younger.

If such was the role of the female companion, it wasn't surprising that actresses didn't always want to play them for long. Some didn't want to get involved at all. Offered a recurring role as the Doctor's companion in the series, Pauline Collins, who played Samantha in "The Faceless Ones" (1967) turned Innes Lloyd down. She returned to play Queen Victoria in the 2006 story "Tooth and Claw".

Although Dicks' description of the companion's function is slightly tongue in cheek, and Barbara and Susan were much more resourceful than it suggests, it is true that the relationship between the Doctor and the women was formed by the sexual politics of the time. Christopher Eccleston dismissively remarked upon the "paternalistic know-all and underwritten female companion" of the original series (his Doctor's relationship with Rose being *so* much more modern). *Doctor Who* has arguably struggled throughout its history to escape its roots in sixties gender politics, but as long as there was an older Doctor and younger female companions, there was something paternalistic and arguably sexist about the relationship, even as late as 1987-9 with the seventh Doctor and the much younger Ace. As a younger and physically attractive Doctor, Peter Davison was told not to put his arm around Tegan, Nyssa or Peri, to negate any charges of hanky panky in the TARDIS. He was, however, allowed to put his arm around the male Adric or Turlough. Apparently viewers, alive to a heterosexual subtext, wouldn't see a homosexual one. Tegan and Nyssa were even given their own shared bedroom in the TARDIS, a clearly feminine space with no signs of intrusion from the Doctor. Russell T Davies changed the dynamic of the companion and Doctor altogether by bringing sexuality and romance to the fore: both Rose and Martha are in love with the Doctor in the revived series. Thus Davies liberated the series from 1960s gender politics and irritated some fans (who preferred adventure to "soap opera" romance), and some gay fans, who had felt at home with the Doctor's inclusive asexuality.

William Hartnell was unhappy about the endless changes in the show's third season. He was also unwell, suffering from undiagnosed arteriosclerosis which made it hard for him to remember his lines. He could be crotchety and difficult on set. Gerry Davis said that he cared very, very deeply about the programme; perhaps Hartnell's irascibility was partly caused by his frustration at not being able to play the part as well as he would have liked. He would dry up and forget his lines or utter malapropisms: in "The Daleks", he mentions that the Thals have left "gloves" outside the TARDIS and quickly corrects the word to "drugs". Such mistakes survive in the finished episodes. In its early days, *Doctor Who* episodes were recorded in sequence with cameras moving from one set to another and scenes played in order, in real time, as though the actors were in a play. There might be one or, at the most two, recording breaks in an episode – for example, for a costume change, special effect or to move into the TARDIS set in "An Unearthly Child" – but that was all. These recording conditions determined that there should be several companions in the TARDIS: if there were more than, say, two principals, there were more possibilities for the cameras to pick up their ongoing stories on several different sets. The Doctor could have only one companion when the conditions of recording changed with the advent of colour. Videotape in the early 1960s was incredibly expensive and editing it almost unheard of; once programmes had been recorded, film copies were made of them for overseas sales (and occasional repeats) and the videotape itself was recorded over for another programme. It thus wasn't possible to retake fluffed lines and fluffed scenes unless something went badly wrong, and Hartnell's moments of drying and malapropisms become more apparent on screen as his time as the Doctor went on and, sadly, his illness worsened. Verity Lambert was furious when a preoccupied Hartnell completely forgot his lines and necessitated a very expensive retake on an early episode. The twenty eight year old producer berated him for his "inexcusable" lack of professionalism and Hartnell, to his credit, accepted the rebuke and apologised. In a late Hartnell story, "The War Machines" (1966), the actor gives an excellent performance in the filmed sequences, presumably because film cameras made retakes and short takes possible; he is sometimes quite incoherent in its videotaped studio scenes.

Innes Lloyd, the new producer, realised that the punishing schedule of the show was taking its toll on Hartnell. The decision was made to continue with the series for a fourth season but to change the leading actor. Vere Lorrimer, who worked on "The Celestial Toymaker" (1966), recalled that one possibility was to have the Doctor change his form as a result of the Toymaker's interference. The Toymaker had rendered him invisible: could he look like a different person when he returned? In the end, the production team reasoned that the Doctor, because he was an alien, should have the power to change his form as part of his life cycle. At the end of "The Tenth Planet" (1966), Hartnell announces that his old body is getting a bit thin and collapses on the floor of the TARDIS. Before the astonished gaze of Ben and Polly, his face is suffused with a blazing light, which subsides to reveal the features of the second Doctor, Patrick Troughton.

4

The New Doctor

"I've been renewed," the new Doctor explained. "Part of me, part of the TARDIS. Without it I couldn't survive." Today's viewers are more than used to the Doctor changing his form. Speculation about who is to be the new Doctor is part of the fun of watching the new series, but it came as an utter surprise to viewers in 1966. Hartnell changed into Patrick Troughton without a fanfare. The transformation wasn't even at the end of the season. There had been some short articles in the newspapers explaining that Hartnell was leaving, but nothing like the media circus that now accompanies a change of Doctor, and most viewers were completely unprepared. This wasn't called a regeneration: the word "regeneration" wasn't used until "Planet of the Spiders" in 1974, to prepare viewers for Jon Pertwee's transformation into Tom Baker. Some of the thinking in 1966 was that this was a rejuvenation: Patrick Troughton's Doctor was William Hartnell's Doctor when younger. "Dr Who is a modern phoenix," proclaimed that year's *Dr Who Annual* of the new Doctor. As the mythical phoenix could rise from its ashes to be reborn at the moment of its death, so the Doctor could rise again. There was also the intriguing indication that the TARDIS was a necessary part of the transformation process, suggesting that it was more than just a vehicle – it was a life support machine. Might this account for the number of regenerations that have taken place inside the TARDIS? Hartnell/Troughton, Davison/Colin Baker, Colin Baker/McCoy, Eccleston/Tennant, Tennant/Smith … perhaps the Doctor prefers to change there, knowing that his machine will aid his passing. In the fifth Doctor's debut story "Castrovalva" (1982), writer Christopher Bidmead gave the TARDIS a "zero room", a zone of tranquillity and healing in which the Time Lord could recover from his regeneration trauma.

Patrick Troughton was a distinguished and highly experienced character actor on stage, radio, film and television. He had been shortlisted for Johnny Ringo in "The Gunfighters" (1966), a role which had eventually gone to Laurence Payne, who later returned to give wonderful support performances as the doomed Morix in "The Leisure Hive" (1980) and the corrupted scientist Dastari in "The Two Doctors" (1985). Troughton was initially reluctant to accept the role of the Doctor. He had apparently watched the show with his children and loved William Hartnell's performance, but also believed that *Doctor Who* had been "done to death and wouldn't last". This is an ironic comment from our point of view in the series' fiftieth anniversary year but it reflected the falling viewing figures and the feelings of many in the BBC that the show, like its leading man, was getting tired. Troughton was asked several times if he would like the part and kept turning it down until, apparently, the BBC offered him a fee that, with a large family, he couldn't refuse. Troughton was a chameleon of an actor and able to play practically anything; he may have felt constrained by committing to a lead role in such a long running series and he both missed the challenge of other roles and feared typecasting. Barry Letts (producer 1970-1974) observed that he shouldn't have been worried, as he walked out of *Doctor Who* into the Duke of Norfolk in the BBC's prestige drama series *The Six Wives of Henry VIII* (1970), starring Keith Michell. Troughton, like Hartnell, found the demands of producing forty episodes a year exhausting and often longed to return to the freedom of being a "jobbing" actor. He was tempted to resign when Deborah Watling left as Victoria in 1967. His weariness showed when he was filming "The War Games". Troughton asked a visual effects man to demonstrate how big an explosion, which the Doctor was supposed to be next to, would be. The visual effects man assured him it would be fine, but Troughton insisted, and the explosion was tested: it was so big that it would have easily caught him in its blast. "Now you know why I wanted you to test it," he explained to the explosives expert. These sort of incidents wore Troughton down and he thought, very firmly, after three years that enough was enough. When he and Peter Davison were shooting "The Five Doctors" in 1983, Davison confessed that he was unsure how long he should continue as the Doctor. He had done two complete years and was itching to return to other roles and other shows, which he had longingly observed being rehearsed next to *Doctor Who* in the BBC's rehearsal facilities. Troughton advised him to do three years, the same number he had done.

For years after leaving the show, Troughton said that he was "wearied" by reminders of his association with it. It didn't annoy him, he said, it just wearied him. He was reluctant, as he had been when he was the Doctor, to give interviews about playing the part. In the early 1980s, he turned down an invitation to appear at a *Doctor Who* Appreciation Society convention, arguing that telling people how the programme was made would spoil the illusion; he wrote that he wished the society well and he was sorry to disappoint people, but that was how he felt. Troughton similarly needed some persuasion to overcome his doubts about appearing in the 1973 tenth anniversary story, "The Three

Doctors", eventually agreeing to do it because he had left the programme three years ago, was no longer solely associated with it, and it would be his first appearance in colour. Pertwee and others recalled that there were some clashes between the Doctors on the set, but that's another story. It was in fact Jon Pertwee who persuaded Troughton to accept some invitations to conventions because they were great fun. Pertwee recalled how they had chased each other up the aisles of an American convention hall having a water pistol fight, to the delight of the fans. Having had a change of heart, Troughton enjoyed reprising the role (for the second time) so much in the twentieth anniversary special, "The Five Doctors" (1983), that he asked producer John Nathan Turner if he could do another one. He did return in the much less well regarded 1985 story "The Two Doctors", this time with Frazer Hines as Jamie. Troughton had allegedly wanted to appear with Zoe and Jamie, his last two companions, in "The Three Doctors" twelve years earlier, so having Jamie in 1985 belatedly fulfilled half his wish. Janet Fielding, who played companion Tegan, asked Troughton if he still wanted to do stage work: "Oh darling, I don't want to do all that shouting in the evenings," he replied. Happy to be associated with *Doctor Who* in the 1980s, and getting lots of fun from it, Troughton tragically died from a heart attack while attending a convention in Georgia in 1987.

Troughton's slight ambivalence towards the programme as its star in 1966-1969 can be partly explained as the sense of frustration which a first class actor can feel when tied down to a particular part. Fans, who assume the leading actor loves the programme as much as they do, sometimes find this hard to understand. Troughton certainly enjoyed many aspects of the show. Barry Letts, who directed him in "The Enemy of the World" (1967-8), recalled that he was always enthusiastic and always had inventive, good ideas. One sequence in David Whitaker's script said that the Doctor should paddle in the sea: Troughton thought this was a bit dull, and suggested he should wear a 1920s bathing costume and go for a swim, which was duly filmed. In some stories, Troughton had opportunities to show his chameleon-like qualities as an actor by having the Doctor disguise himself as, variously, a washer woman and a British official in the First World War; in "The Enemy of the World", he relished playing Salamander, the Doctor's double, as a Mexican-accented world dictator. Troughton got on well with his co-stars and particularly with Frazer Hines as Jamie, with whom he remained friends for life. Wendy Padbury, Hines and Deborah Watling, who played the second Doctor's companions, all speak warmly about Troughton and fondly of their memories of working with him. He was something of a practical joker, too. In "The Abominable Snowmen" (1967), Victoria (Deborah Watling) is hypnotised and the Doctor makes a loud noise to try and break her trance. She doesn't even flinch. In rehearsal, Frazer Hines and Troughton picked up a heavy chest that was part of the set dressing, lifted it high and let it smash to the ground: Watling, nicknamed "leather lungs" by the crew for her powerful screaming, never came down off the ceiling. In "Fury from the Deep" (1967), Watling's last story, the TARDIS crew come across mounds of foam on the beach, left behind by the intelligent seaweed monster that menaces the humans. The foam was produced in industrial quantities by a new foam machine, which the story used to the full. Frazer Hines said that, by this point, he and Patrick Troughton had been working together for so long that they only had to look at each other to see what the other was thinking. He and Troughton ran up behind Deborah Watling, grabbed her, picked her up, and dunked her in the foam.

Patrick Troughton is one of the finest Doctors and arguably the only Doctor in the original series who always turns in a consistently excellent performance. When he was cast as the eleventh Doctor, Matt Smith watched some DVDs of his predecessors to bring him up to speed on the programme, and said that he was most impressed by Troughton's classic story "The Tomb of the Cybermen" (1967). Smith's wonderful performance as the Doctor could be said to be influenced by Troughton's. One of the original producers of the show argued that Patrick Troughton was the first "real" Doctor: Hartnell had created the part and had made it his own, but his was not a template that could be followed. Troughton had perhaps the hardest job in forging a new identity for the Doctor which viewers could accept. He was gentle, clever, kind, funny and eccentric but was also capable of showing steel and was unswerving in his moral outrage and disgust at evil and exploitation. In one novelisation, Terrance Dicks writes that the Doctor plays the fool to give himself time to think, and this is very apposite for Troughton's Doctor. People wouldn't always take him seriously and would under-estimate him: then he would surprise or defeat them. In "The Moonbase" (1967), the Doctor potters about and gets under everybody's feet. The very people who shout at him that he's an idiot and should get out of the way are surprised when they discover he has been quietly gathering evidence of the Cybermen's infiltration of the base, which he uses eventually in their defeat. In "The Tomb of the Cybermen", the Doctor asks Victoria, who has been torn away from

Victorian England, if she is happy with them and if she still grieves for her father. He gently explains that he can remember his own family when he wants to, and encourages her to think that their lives are different from everybody else's: nobody else in the Universe can travel in time and space. From showing such compassion and thoughtfulness in one scene, he immediately pretends to agree with megalomaniac Eric Klieg's aims in reviving the Cybermen: they will give him total power, even over the thoughts of others. Klieg is pleased that the Doctor accepts his brilliance: the Doctor replies, "Well, now I know you're mad. I was just trying to make sure." The Second Doctor is always brave, as when he confronts the armed and dangerous Klieg, or demands to know the Cybercontroller's plans when the others shrink away in terror. The Third Doctor can't believe his ears when he hears his predecessor lambast the mad, renegade Time Lord Omega about being plucked away while he was minding his own business by a "horrible great jelly". "What are you trying to do?" Pertwee hisses. "Testing the limits of his self control. They're not very good, are they?" Troughton replies. The Pertwee Doctor relaxes: "No. No, they're not." The Doctors' methods are different, but their aim – to assess the threat that Omega poses – is the same, and the Second Doctor rightly earns his successor's respect.

Patrick Troughton is one of my favourite Doctors. It took him some time to arrive at the performance which is now so admired. When he was cast, he admits that he wasn't sure how to play it at all. He had a make-up and costume test in which he blacked up as a pirate. Sydney Newman, the show's creator who was still involved in some of the show's major creative decisions, said that Troughton should play the Doctor as "a cosmic hobo" (American slang for a tramp). The image stuck. Troughton wore a version of William Hartnell's costume, but with much less elegance. The trousers were baggier, he dispensed with the waistcoat, and favoured a rumpled shirt and a ragged bow tie (the bow tie was resurrected by Matt Smith as particularly "Doctor-ish", again suggesting Troughton's influence on his portrayal). Clothes in his first and third incarnation were rather important to him: now, it seemed as though he couldn't care less. Newman's choice of a "cosmic hobo" for the second Doctor was an apt, small piece of genius which exactly fitted the magpie wanderer in time and space, and is still influential in today's Doctor.

It is true that some of the early Troughton stories have an uncertain tone, with Troughton, and the writers, not entirely sure how the part should be played. There is a lot of dressing up and disguise and Troughton doesn't always seem at ease with Ben and Polly, the companions he had inherited from William Hartnell; they were retained to help viewers accept that this new Doctor was still *the* Doctor, as Sarah Jane Smith was retained for the Pertwee / Baker transformation in 1974-5. Troughton seems much more at his ease when Jamie, his first companion, takes centre stage and when Ben and Polly are eased out for Victoria and, later, for Zoe. William Hartnell always had confidence in Troughton, however, describing him as "the *only* actor" who could play the new Doctor.

Having said all this, the Second Doctor is the hardest to write about because so few of his stories still exist in their entirety. The BBC not only recorded over original videotapes: they also junked episodes of television programmes which they considered no longer useful. It is mind bogglingly hard to imagine such a mindset today, but the BBC archives decided in the 1970s that it simply didn't have enough shelf space for all the programmes the corporation had produced, and that programmes which it couldn't fit on its shelves should be destroyed. Building more shelves didn't seem to occur to them. In the 1960s and 1970s, programmes were rarely repeated and the actors' union Equity demanded punishingly high repeat fees for old shows. The actors were understandably driven by worries that, if the BBC kept showing repeats, they would stop making new programmes and actors would be out of work. Current practice shows they needn't have worried, and actresses like Wendy Padbury have said what an agreeable surprise it is to have a cheque for a video release of a programme made thirty or so years ago: it isn't a lot, but it pays for the week's supermarket shop.

Furthermore, the BBC in the 1970s had a policy of not repeating programmes that didn't feature the current Doctor. This policy was only overturned in 1981 when producer John Nathan Turner promoted a series of repeats from the first four Doctors, under the umbrella title, "The Five Faces of Doctor Who", as a way of reminding people that there had been other Doctors before the seven year reign of Tom Baker, and with the aim of thus helping them to accept the new Fifth Doctor, Peter Davison. The BBC even applied this restriction on using any image of the Doctor other than the current one to the range of novelisations of the stories then released by Target books (which, in total, sold eight million copies and contributed considerably to children's literacy). In Tom Baker's time, Target was instructed only to use Baker's face on the cover; stories from different Doctors were not to include the lead actor's face.

But in the 1960s and 1970s, there was no cable or satellite television, no VHS or DVD and the only usefulness of old shows, as far as BBC

Enterprises (the BBC's commercial arm) was concerned was to sell them to overseas broadcasters. Once overseas stations no longer wanted them, the shows were junked. Thousands of programmes were literally burned. The Pertwee stories had been made in colour but BBC Enterprises had produced black and white film copies for export to countries which didn't have colour television. Some colour Pertwee episodes were exported to the United States, but when this market dried up, Enterprises took the extraordinary decision to destroy the colour originals and keep the black and white film copies.

Ian Levine, a fan and consultant on the show in the 1980s, went to BBC Enterprises to buy some old *Doctor Who* film prints. He discovered the first Dalek story on the desk, marked "for destruction". Incredulous, Levine asked what it was doing there. "No-one wants them," was the reply. "They're just old black and white films." Levine wanted them, and told the BBC Enterprises person that he wanted to buy "The Daleks" (1963) right there. It is thanks to him and others like him that we can still enjoy so many of the 1960s episodes.

Patrick Troughton's Doctor suffered particularly from BBC Enterprise's purges. While most of William Hartnell's stories were retained, Troughton's output was butchered. A few single episodes were retained as historical examples of the sort of thing television had produced in the 1960s, of interest to researchers: many were junked, including both, highly regarded, Troughton Dalek stories. A few complete stories were retained from Troughton's final years as the Doctor.

With the advent of VHS and satellite television in the 1980s, and a change of heart by Equity – who perhaps accepted that the maw of multi-channel television had to be fed with something, and why not repeats if they could negotiate acceptable fees for their members? – the BBC stopped junking old shows and turned its energy, ironically, to recovering those it had destroyed. "The Tomb of the Cybermen" was returned from Hong Kong television in 1992. New video technology made it possible to combine the colour picture from American domestic video recordings of *Doctor Who* – which were not of broadcast quality – with the black and white film prints retained by the BBC, and "The Daemons" was the first recoloured story to be released on VHS in 1993. Technology is now so advanced that colour can sometimes be restored from the black and white film alone, which is how a colour episode of "Planet of the Daleks" (1973) episode three, came to be released on DVD in 2009; apparently the black and white film had traces of the original colour, which could be enhanced by computer. (Here, my level of technological understanding peaks; I am Jo Grant to the restoration team's Doctor.)

In spite of occasional discovery of old episodes – "Galaxy Four": "Air Lock" (1965) and "The Underwater Menace" episode 2 (1967) were returned in 2011 – more than half of Troughton's output has been lost. It is thus very difficult to write about his time as the Doctor. Some argue that we can do so, as audio recordings of all his stories exist and have been commercially released with linking narration. There are also telesnaps of lost episodes: these are off-screen stills taken at the time of the original broadcast and retained by directors and others as a record of the programme before the days of domestic video recorders. We can reconstruct the experience of watching Troughton by listening to the audio, looking at the telesnaps and using our imaginations to fill in the gaps. However, this does not appeal to everyone, and perhaps not the casual, non-fan viewer of the show, as an agreeable activity. It doesn't replace the experience of watching the programme on the television, where it belongs, and it doesn't make for reliable judgements of those programmes which no longer exist in their entirety. This is particularly the case for those stories of which only one or two episodes remain. *Doctor Who* stories in the 1960s were told over four, six, seven or even ten weeks; the action unfolded slowly and single episodes from longer stories are unrepresentative of the experience of watching the whole. They can seem painfully slow: the Doctor, Jamie and Zoe barely feature in the surviving episode of "The Space Pirates" (1969) and seem to spend most of their time accepting their inability to escape from a pod drifting in space. The impression we have of Troughton's excellence as the Doctor is largely created by the complete, or very nearly complete, stories that do exist.

Although so few of Troughton's episodes remain, his era as the Doctor gave the programme some of its enduring tropes. One was an emphasis on monsters; another was the development of the story type known by fans as the "base under siege": humans in a base are attacked from monsters without and infiltrators within, who want to destroy, convert or do other unspeakable things to the poorly equipped human beings. Of course, the Hartnell era had given the programme monsters too – and without the appeal of the Daleks in the second story (what if the production team had opted for "The Masters of Luxor" instead?) the programme would probably never have survived beyond its initial thirteen weeks.

Both aspects – the monsters and the base under siege – came together in Hartnell's final story, "The Tenth Planet" (1966), which introduced the Cybermen. Several planets came into conjunction to create this highly regarded story. The first was new story editor Gerry Davis's decision to beef up the scientific content of the programme by hiring a scientific adviser (he was anticipating UNIT's decision to hire the Third Doctor in a similar capacity, perhaps). This was Dr Christopher (Kit) Pedlar, a surgeon and academic. Davis explained in an interview that, in his search for a scientific adviser, he invited several people into his office and asked them: if you wanted to take over the world using the newly finished Post Office Tower (now the BT Tower, privatised by the Conservative government in the 1980s), how would you go about it? Pedlar gave a considered and thoughtful reply. In the best traditions of intelligent science fiction, he extrapolated fiction from established scientific fact and theory. He speculated that a computer in the Post Office Tower could connect itself to all other computers in the world via telephone lines, and presciently anticipated the internet. Perhaps these computers could further exert control over human beings by sending a hypnotic signal over the same phone lines? Pedlar's ideas linked into the perennial fear expressed in science fiction and continually returned to in *Doctor Who*: that, instead of machines serving human beings, human beings would come to serve the machines or – even worse – become machines themselves. This fear saw its full expression in the Cybermen and, to a lesser extent, the Daleks. The latter were also symbols of dehumanisation, which human beings have always feared, but by fascism and Nazism more than mechanisation. Davis was impressed by Pedlar's ideas, hired him, and the conversation in the office became the basis for "The War Machines" (1966). Pedlar's lack of experience in writing for television necessitated another writer, Ian Stuart Black, translating his ideas into a workable script. In Troughton's period as the Doctor, Pedlar would co-write the scripts with Gerry Davis. Eventually they created *Doomwatch* (1969), a highly regarded science fiction series which warned of environmental dangers to the planet.

The friendship and collaboration between Pedlar and Davis led to their co-creation of the Cybermen, "cyber" here meaning mechanical rather than in the modern sense. These were half human, half machine. Pedlar had been involved in early research into heart replacement surgery and had become concerned about the possibilities of spare part surgery: human beings replacing parts of their bodies – perhaps perfectly good parts – with mechanical alternatives. What if they eventually replaced their irrational brains with computers, which were more efficient? What if the computers caused human beings to lose their empathy and emotions? What if they substituted such things with logic and – since it is logical that superior beings should rule the inferior – a desire for power?

The final planet in the conjunction was the more prosaic need to find a monster to replace the Daleks. Davis and producer Innes Lloyd could see the writing on the wall as far as the Daleks were concerned. They knew that Terry Nation had moved onto other projects with independent television (he eventually became script editor on the Tara King episodes of *The Avengers*); they also realised that the Daleks were money spinners and Nation would demand greater editorial control over their use. The culmination was Nation's decision to take the Daleks out of *Doctor Who* and launch them in their own series, designed for American television. There were, however, two Troughton Dalek stories, but both were written by David Whitaker; Nation apparently didn't like them but received a credit and a fee for the Daleks' use. The production team duly killed the Daleks off in a civil war in "The Evil of the Daleks" (1967). Watching their city in flames, the Doctor murmurs that this is "the final end…"

Terry Nation sketched out some ideas for his Dalek television series in *The Dalek Outer Space Book* (1966), one of the 1960s Dalek annuals which didn't feature the Doctor. He resurrected the character of Sara Kingdom from "The Daleks' Masterplan" (1965), gave her the strength of ten men and the Space Security Service as military back-up to fight the Daleks. A pilot script was written. The new series was to be filmed in colour when *Doctor Who* was still primarily shot on video in black and white. Studios were booked, pre-production began… and immediately ran into trouble. Nation turned to the BBC for financial help and for the loan of its Daleks. His company tried to place the new show on BBC 2, the only BBC channel to be broadcasting in colour. Its controller, David Attenborough, read the script, pronounced it "very exciting", a good adventure yarn in the *Doctor Who* tradition, and declined to show or invest in it as it was unsuitable for his channel. Nation eventually admitted defeat and his attempt to give the Daleks their own American series ran into the sands of Aridius. He did consider using the Daleks independently of the Doctor at the climax of series two of *Blake's Seven* when Blake and the evil Federation join forces to repel alien invaders. Why not the Daleks? Eventually, Nation opted for some rather dull shapeshifters who conveniently appeared most often as humanoids. The Daleks returned to *Doctor Who* after a gap of five years in "Day of the Daleks" (1972).

The Cybermen featured in no fewer than four Patrick Troughton stories, some better than others. "The Moonbase" (1967), their second outing, was essentially a retread of their first appearance in Hartnell's last story "The Tenth Planet" (1966): the Cybermen attempt to infiltrate an Arctic base/moonbase in order to convert the humans within into Cybermen. It didn't especially help that their appearance changed considerably for almost every story. The original Cybermen have been described as "rather absurd creatures" and looked as though they were the result of someone rooting around in the kitchen cupboards: they have silver bodies and chest units like reversed rucksacks, with a scaffolding-like head arrangement (not unlike the Robomen's) to hold up a massive torch. In fact, the design was an attempt to visualise Pedlar and Davis's intention that the Cybermen should be a parody of a human being. Human hands were visible – these were the only Cybermen whose actors didn't wear gloves – and the stocking masks over the actor's heads suggested the human features beneath. These Cybermen opened their mouths into a wide, static O shape to speak: the voices themselves were provided throughout the 1960s by actors elsewhere in the studio, and the combination of the static mouth and the weird, sing-song voice was both strange and disturbing. Pedlar's horror at humankind's dehumanisation as Cybermen was thus well realised. Recognising that her first attempt wasn't entirely successful, Sandra Reid redesigned the creatures for their next appearance, giving them a more robotic look that was basically followed in all subsequent designs to the present. The scaffolding helmet was reduced in size to become the familiar "jug handles" shape; the cloth face became metal and the mouth was now a pillar box slit. However, Reid retained the eeriness of the Cybermen's speech: a panel behind the mouth, operated by the actor, slid down when the Cyberman began speaking and slid up only when it had finished, an effect which terrified the young Sophie Aldred, who was to play the seventh Doctor's companion Ace in the late 1980s. This new design lasted all of two stories (although the Cybermen seen in "The Tomb of the Cybermen" had a few ribbons added), before they were changed yet again for "The Wheel in Space" (1968), which introduced Zoe as the Doctor's companion. This story's Cybermen were so delicate that the pipes on the costumes kept breaking: the Cybermen become increasingly static as the six parter progressed for fear that even more of the costume would fall to bits. There was yet another redesign for "The Invasion" (1968), which added the ear muffs to the jug handles and became the basis for the Cybermen design used in "Revenge of the Cybermen" (1975) and the radical redesign for the 1980s stories from "Earthshock" (1982) onwards.

Unlike the Daleks, the Cybermen's voices changed from story to story. The original sing-song chant was replaced by a buzzing voice created by the voice artistes putting a small buzzing disc – similar to those slipped into the mouth by Punch and Judy men to produce Mr Punch's voice – and articulating the lines in virtual silence: the microphones picked up the rest. Voices were provided chiefly by Roy Skelton – who provided Dalek voices until the series' demise in 1989 and also provided the voices of Bungle and Zippy in the children's series *Rainbow* – and Peter Hawkins, who also did Daleks and the eponymous hero of the cartoon *Captain Pugwash*. The Cybermen's 1960s voices, like so much of 1960s *Who*, were simple, strange and disturbing. When Russell T Davies brought the Cybermen back for the second season of the revived *Doctor Who* in 2006 (*Rise of the Cybermen / The Age of Steel*), the regenerated show looked, as it did in so many ways, back to the 1960s for inspiration. Davies insisted that the new Cybermen should have the Pierrot teardrop added for "The Wheel in Space" and "The Invasion" as a sign that they were sad at what had happened to them: indeed, the newly converted Cyberman Yvonne Hartman weeps a tear of oil at her conversion in "Doomsday" (2006). The new Cybermen voices provided by Nicholas Briggs (who, like Peter Hawkins and Roy Skelton, also did Daleks, though not Zippy or Captain Pugwash) recalled the Troughton era voices and an electric blue light (apparently Russell T Davies's favourite colour) snaps on when the Cyberman begins to speak and snaps off when he ceases, again recalling the effect in "The Moonbase" and "The Tomb of the Cybermen". Nicholas Briggs sent Davies an audio of about twenty slightly different Cybermen voices to choose from, all created – as was his Dalek voice – on his own ring modulator. Davies couldn't hear much difference between many of them and felt somewhat disorientated after listening to so many. By contrast, the actors who played Cybermen in "Revenge of the Cybermen" and the 1980s Cybermen stories provided their own voices, not always successfully. The Cyberleader in the former story, played by RSC actor Christopher Robbie, struts around with his hands on his hips and barks out his lines in a distinctly American accent; Graeme Harper, who directed "Rise of the Cybermen", said he thought the 1980s voices sounded like a bad Hollywood actor – a fair description of the plummy tones of David Banks, who played Cyberleaders in all of the 1980s stories.

Other monsters came and went as the production team, like their predecessors in the Hartnell era, wistfully tried to come up with a monster that would rival the Daleks in popularity. There were the

Quarks – "Deadly, robot servants of the cruel Dominators" – who looked rather unfortunately like walking fridges. They were played by child actors, which accounted for their diminutive height, and piped their threats in feminine voices. The production team presumably thought highly of them as they are among the aliens the Doctor shows the Time Lords in a "thought channel" at his trial ("The War Games" 1969) as examples of the evil in the Universe that must be fought. *TV Comic* thought highly of them too and used them frequently, and without their humanoid Dominator masters (a rather dull race of humanoid conquerers), as the enemy in their dreadful *Dr Who* (sic) strip, which bore even less relation to the television series than the Peter Cushing movies. The comic used the Quarks without the permission of their creators, Mervyn Haisman and Henry Lincoln, who were understandably displeased. *TV Comic's* editor had assumed that the rights to carry a *Doctor Who* comic strip entitled him to use the programme's other intellectual property, which was of course copyright to individual, self-employed writers. Haisman and Lincoln's displeasure at the purloining of the Quarks eventually led them to part company with the *Doctor Who* production office.

More successful and enduring than the Quarks were the Ice Warriors. Rather quaintly, and in the traditions of H. G. Wells (whose novel *The Time Machine* had had more than a glancing influence in the show's genesis), these were inhabitants of the planet Mars and made their eponymous appearance in a 1967 serial. Martians in science fiction were passé even in 1967; if H. G. Wells's contemporaries had thought that the markings on the surface of the red planet were canals constructed by the Martians, even children knew better in 1967 and were aware that Mars was a lifeless rock. Scriptwriter Brian Hayles took this into account in "The Ice Warriors". In their first appearance the Martians' spaceship landed on Earth many centuries ago, when there might conceivably have been life on Mars, and gets itself buried in a glacier. It is the Doctor's companion Jamie who names the Martians, Ice Warriors; the name apparently stuck with the humans and the production team, as they are invariably called Ice Warriors on screen in all their stories, perhaps to escape from the naivety of the name "Martians". The Ice Warriors are frozen in suspended animation and awoken by a process of ionisation in the twenty second century. This is an attempt by the humans to limit the impact of a new Ice Age – which occasionally replaced nuclear war in the 1960s and 1970s as the favourite feared apocalypse of popular imagination – by controlling the path of an advancing glacier: as it rolls forward, so it reveals the Ice Warriors' spaceship. The scientists' leader Clent has one of the ship's inhabitants, still trapped in a block of ice, brought back to the scientists' base for study (always a bad move in *Doctor Who*); the scientists speculate that he might be a Viking chieftain from examination of his mighty helmet. Of course, the creature thaws out and is revealed at the end of episode one to be still alive. Watching the episodes back to back, which was not possible when originally broadcast, it is obvious that the Ice Warrior's helmet and make up changes completely between episodes one and two.

Bernard Bresslaw, an actor best known for his appearances in the *Carry On* films, plays the Ice Warrior leader, Varga. He had just finished playing amorous berk Ken Biddle in *Carry On Doctor* before rehearsing "The Ice Warriors". Bresslaw was six feet seven inches tall, and is an impressive sight in his costume, towering menacingly over his captive, the Doctor's companion Victoria. He took the role seriously and considered the creature's design for inspiration for his performance: the reptilian Ice Warrior appears to have a soft skin, visible in its mouth and jaw parts, underneath an armoured exoskeleton (apparently inspired by a crocodile's back). Bresslaw used the creature's reptilian design to create its hissing, whispering voice, which recalled lizards and snakes for him. It was a simple and brilliantly effective decision and, like so much else in *Doctor Who*, immediately appealed to children who could copy both the voice and the Ice Warriors' lumbering gait. Here was something they could imitate in the playground while the Daleks were absent from the series. The Ice Warriors were frightening, strong and menacing, but fortunately so slow that the nimbler humans could run away from them: often a feature of *Who* monsters. Bresslaw also devised the Ice Warriors pulling their heads into their necks, tortoise like, again inspired by the design which recalled a tortoise in its contrast between hard shell and soft inner parts. Uniquely in the four Ice Warrior stories, Bresslaw's Varga also has a wheezy giggle, which he utters as he puts the Doctor to death by withdrawing air from the ship's airlock.

Innes Lloyd, the producer, managed to secure the services of the famous actor Peter Barkworth to play Clent. BBC executive colleagues were impressed: first Marius Goring (as corrupt scientist Maxtible in "The Evil of the Daleks" (1967)), now Peter Barkworth. "When are you going to get Laurence Olivier in *Doctor Who*, Innes?" he was asked. Eighteen years later, producer John Nathan-Turner heard rumours that Olivier was interested in appearing in the programme. He thought of offering him the part of the mutant in "Revelation of the Daleks" (1985); perhaps Lord Olivier, by now frail and elderly, didn't fancy a winter shoot near an icy pond in hideous make up and the part was taken by someone else. It seems a shame that Nathan-Turner didn't think of Olivier for Rassilon's cameo in "The Five Doctors" (1983).

The Ice Warriors returned in the following year's story "The Seeds of Death" (1969) heavily rewritten by script editor Terrance Dicks from Hayles's original script. Dicks apologised profusely to Hayles for the necessity of the rewrites and recalls that Hayles, after letting him explain at length, asked him if he was a Catholic? Dicks replied that he wasn't, and Hayles, who was, said his lengthy breast-beating had suggested a Catholic sensibility and he wasn't to worry as he, Hayles, didn't mind at all. "The Seeds of Death" was a money saving exercise: reusing the expensive Ice Warrior suits would save the team from having to design and build a new set of aliens, although there was enough money in the pot to create a new type of Ice Warrior. This was the Ice Lord, an aristocratic Martian in charge of the others, whose helmet only covered part of his face and lacked the plebeian warriors' jaw piece. He was played by Alan Bennion, who returned as Ice Lords for the two Jon Pertwee Ice Warrior tales.

After "The Ice Warriors", "The Seeds of Death" is something of a disappointment. Set on yet another moonbase, it recalls the events of "The Moonbase" a few years earlier, with the Ice Warriors replacing the Cybermen. It is yet another "base under siege" story and the Ice Warriors could really be swapped for any monster. Gerry Davis, who had introduced this sub-genre with "The Tenth Planet" in 1966, argued that one of its advantages was making the best use of the show's limited budget. Instead of building lots of small sets, most of the money went on one large, showcase set: the gravitron control room in "The Moonbase", the Ioniser control room in "The Ice Warriors", or the T-Mat control room in "The Seeds of Death". While these large sets are impressive for television science fiction in the 1960s – and similar in function and spectacle, although on a much smaller scale, to the massive villains' lairs of contemporary James Bond films – they did take up much of the available studio space. One consequence, Davis noted, was that they took up room which might have been available for the large TARDIS interior set: thus many of the 1960s stories stay out of the TARDIS's interior as much as possible or, when they do feature it, limit it to a couple of roundelled flats and the control console. Similarly, in the show's final season of its initial run in 1989, the TARDIS interior is only briefly shown in one story, "Battlefield". By this point, the set was so bashed about that it only comprised one flat and the console; low level lighting was employed to hide the flaws. The revived, post-2005 series avoided the problem entirely by having the TARDIS interior as a standing set (and saved money by featuring it all the time, especially in extra scenes shot for *Children in Need* and DVD specials). The new TARDIS set seen in "The Snowmen" (2012) was built in the series' new studio home in Roach Loch, Cardiff Bay, the BBC "Drama Village". It hadn't been possible to move Matt Smith's first TARDIS set from the previous studio at Upper Boat, so the opportunity was taken to redesign the set and return to the machine look of the 1970s serials, thus moving away from the idea that the TARDIS was organic and, in the Tenth Doctor's words, "grown, not built" ("The Satan Pit", 2006).

The other highly regarded Troughton monsters were the Yeti, who featured in "The Abominable Snowmen" (1967) and returned, slightly redesigned, in "The Web of Fear" the following year. Only two episodes survived the vandals' purge of the BBC archives but the stories can be enjoyed in the excellent Target novelisations and, less enjoyably for this writer, in the BBC audios of the TV soundtracks. (David Troughton reads the novelisation *Doctor Who and the Abominable Snowmen* on a BBC audio and download, and his realisation of his father's voice is a flawless delight.) The Yeti are robot servants of the disembodied Great Intelligence, an amorphous alien body which seeks physical manifestation first, in a Tibetan monastery in the 1930s and, second, in the London Underground in the 1960s. Both stories featured Jack Watling as Mr, later Professor, Travers, a professor of anthropology who leads an expedition to search for the Yeti in the 1930s and returns to battle their robot counterparts in contemporary London. Watling was the father of Deborah Watling, who played Victoria, and said it felt very strange to run down a Welsh mountain away from the Yeti, to be confronted by her dad at the bottom! "The Abominable Snowmen" featured one of the programme's first extensive shoots in Wales, where the actors froze and envied the Yeti in their lovely fur costumes. Local children, who had come along to watch the shoot, were far from being frightened of the Yeti: Troughton recalled that they thought they were lovely and kept patting their fur. He counted them as his favourite monster. One of the Yeti was played by extra John Levene, who also played Cybermen in the 1960s. He was eventually promoted to the role of Corporal Benton in "The Invasion" (1968), who became a regular UNIT character in the 1970s. Director Douglas Camfield praised his hard work, unfailing co-operation, and the fact that he, unlike other extras, didn't keep asking for a pay rise; hence he sanctioned his promotion out of the monster suit, into the human character.

The popularity of the Yeti ensured their quick return in "The Web of Fear" (1968). The Great Intelligence has now re-established its link with the Earth via a Yeti that is reactivated in a museum. This is achieved by the placing of its control unit, a small sphere, in the Yeti's chest: an image which terrified the young Paul McGann, who became the eighth Doctor, and who confused the Yeti control sphere with the image of Jesus revealing his sacred heart which he saw every Sunday in his Catholic church. The Yeti wreak havoc in the London Underground and cause the evacuation of the capital while the army tries to deal with this menace.

This scenario recalled the late Hartnell story "The War Machines" and set the template for Jon Pertwee's first three seasons, as well as providing story elements that are with us today. One of the regular army officers fighting the Yeti was a certain Colonel Lethbridge-Stewart, a talented soldier who is initially suspicious of the Doctor and even suspects him of being behind the menace. He was originally to be played by *Upstairs, Downstairs* actor David Langton, but Langton dropped out and Nicholas Courtney, who had been cast as Captain Knight, was promoted into the part. He was still playing Lethbridge-Stewart forty three years later.

Director Douglas Camfield sought London Underground's permission to shoot in the tube's tunnels, perhaps in the early hours of the morning when the trains weren't running. London Transport either refused, or demanded an outrageous fee (accounts vary), so the BBC built the tunnels themselves. These were so realistic that, after the story had been broadcast, the BBC received a letter from an angry London Transport threatening to sue them for filming in their tunnels after all.

It might be suggested that, if running up and down corridors is a standard *Doctor Who* technique to fill up the running time of flagging scripts, then fleeing down tube tunnels from the Yeti is an example of filling six episodes by running up and down extremely long corridors. Having said that, the Yeti in the Underground are one of the programme's enduring and iconic images, recalled by the general viewer of the original series in the same breath as the Daleks gliding over Westminster Bridge, the Sea Devils rising from the waters, and the giant maggots rearing out of the green slime. The former captain of the England cricket team Mike Gatting, a *Doctor Who* fan as a child and an adult, said that he had just got used to travelling on the tube on his own; his mother would give him the fare and tell him to sit close to the guards' compartment, for security. At this point, he watched "The Web of Fear" on television, and his new-found confidence deserted him.

"The Web of Fear" was well received by the press and the public. A third Yeti serial was planned, and Jack Watling's Professor Travers character was scheduled to appear in the next story of an alien invasion of the home counties, "The Invasion" (1968). Watling was unavailable, however, and a replacement professor was shoehorned into the script. At this point, the Yeti's creators, Mervyn Haisman and Henry Lincoln, fell out with the BBC over copyright issues. Although their next story "The Dominators", which introduced the Quarks, was filmed, they refused to give permission for their names to be used as writers, and the serial went out under the pseudonym of Norman Ashby. The Great Intelligence returned in the 2012 Christmas special "The Snowmen" in its first encounter with the Doctor and his third encounter with it.

The production team noted the success of "The Web of Fear". Plans were afoot to reshape *Doctor Who*. The team was feeling the strain of making so many serials every year and the small budget was heavily overstretched with the need to come up with different alien environments every three or four weeks. Script editor Terrance Dicks recalled that Derrick Sherwin, the new producer, kept commissioning stories and then rejecting them, even if they had been rewritten several times. Poor scripts, or scripts which were not ready, sometimes had to go into production. When director David Maloney was handed the script for a humorous serial about a prison in space, he protested, saying the script was terrible. Couldn't he make something else instead? The crafty Dicks had kept a script from new writer (and former policeman) Robert Holmes up his sleeve as a fall back. This was "The Krotons", originally submitted to the BBC as a science fiction play that had no connection with *Doctor Who*. Dicks, only too aware of, and exasperated by, the problems of finding workable scripts, had worked on "The Krotons" with Holmes as a possible stop-gap, rewriting it for *Doctor Who*. It was eventually broadcast over the new year of 1968-9. The intelligent science fiction script is sadly buried by grotesque over-acting and the ludicrous design of the Krotons themselves, which Dicks described as possibly the worst ever *Doctor Who* monster. Crystalline in origin, the Krotons look like supermarket cartons decorated with egg boxes topped off with a revolving lampshade. The only redeeming feature is their splendid voices, provided again by Roy Skelton, who based it on a South African sergeant major. The command that rings through the humanoids' learning hall at the episode one – "Stop! This is a warning. Leave the learning hall. All Gonds leave the learning hall now!" – is arresting, hilarious and eminently imitable. The South African accent was also an astute choice, linked as it then was with the oppression of apartheid and appropriate for a villainous alien race. The show returned to apartheid imagery in the Jon Pertwee story "The

Mutants" (1972).

The team thus felt oppressed by the need to find suitable scripts and the smallness of the budget. They were unhappy with the unconvincing realisation of alien worlds. If *Doctor Who* was to survive into the 1970s, they reasoned, it needed to be reshaped. The success of "The Web of Fear" led to the decision to ground the Doctor on Earth, where the home counties could double as the home counties rather than other planets, and money could be saved on alien sets. Derrick Sherwin had enjoyed Nicholas Courtney's performance as the Colonel: would he consider returning as a regular character? Courtney, wise like any actor to the advantages of regular work, agreed. Lethbridge-Stewart, now promoted to Brigadier, returned in "The Invasion" in 1968 as the head of the British section of the United Nations Intelligence Taskforce or UNIT, an international army dealing with the alien, "the odd, the unexplained". The army, with the Doctor, foil an attempted invasion of contemporary Earth by the Cybermen; Kevin Stoney, who had played galactic super villain Mavic Chen in "The Daleks' Master Plan" (1965-6), returned to give a splendid performance as treacherous industrialist Tobias Vaughn, who aids and betrays the Cybermen in a double-crossing attempt to rule the world himself.

The Doctor would have become UNIT's scientific adviser even if Troughton had continued in the role. As it was, he was ready to leave after three years. Terrance Dicks and Malcolm Hulke were tasked with writing a replacement script for a four part and a six part story which had, as was common at the time, fallen through. They very quickly came up with the epic adventure "The War Games" (1969), one of *Doctor Who's* best stories. At the time, however, viewing figures sagged dangerously around the three million mark for some of the middle episodes and serious consideration was given by the BBC to cancelling the series: after all, it had been on for six years, which was a good run for a television show, and the star wanted to leave. Wiser counsels prevailed and the show was renewed for another season. It would be made in colour, a new Doctor would be cast, and the number of episodes cut from around forty to about twenty five per year. All of this, it was hoped, with the new Earth-bound setting, would save money. It didn't.

Strangely enough, *Doctor Who* wasn't under the most severe threat of cancellation at the end of its sixth season, Patrick Troughton's last, but at the end of Jon Pertwee's successful first season, and the series' seventh, when the viewing figures had picked up healthily and Pertwee had been acclaimed in the role. Script editor Terrance Dicks and new producer Barry Letts were instructed by the BBC to come up with a Saturday evening replacement serial in 1970. One of their ideas was for a *Crocodile Dundee*-like serial featuring a bush Australian in modern London. This was a similar concept to the BBC's *Adam Adamant Lives!* (1966-1967) which Verity Lambert had produced on leaving *Doctor Who*, featuring a revived Victorian adventurer loose in contemporary, swinging London. It was intended to have been a rival fantasy show to ITV's *The Avengers*, but suffered from being made on video when *The Avengers* enjoyed the greater flexibility and enhanced look of film; it was also considered by many as frankly odd and was cancelled after only one season. Dicks and Letts also thought about remaking Nigel Kneale's *Quatermass* series of the 1950s and arranged a viewing in the BBC's internal cinemas. They considered the original productions to be ludicrously dated, a strange perspective from today's point of view, when Kneale's series are highly regarded and repeated exposure to early television on VHS and DVD has taught us to be tolerant of vintage production values. Perhaps, however, Dicks and Letts' viewing of the old *Quatermass* serials bore some fruit, as their plots were ruthlessly plundered in 1970s *Doctor Who*s, much to Nigel Kneale's irritation. The 1988 story "Remembrance of the Daleks" also makes a reference to Quatermass, this time as a character in the *Doctor Who* universe. Contemplating a Dalek infiltration of London in 1963 and bewildered about how to find an appropriate response, one character says to another: "I wish Bernard was here." "The British Rocket Group's got its own problems," she replies. Bernard is Quatermass's first name and the British Rocket Group is his creation.

Eventually, Dicks and Letts reported their inability to find a good concept to replace *Who* and the show was renewed for an eighth season. It went on from strength to strength as a mainstay of Saturday tea time viewing for the rest of the 1970s, and was not seriously threatened with cancellation until the arrival of Michael Grade at the BBC in the mid 1980s (see chapter eleven).

"The War Games" starts with the TARDIS landing in No Man's Land in the First World War. The Doctor, Jamie and Zoe are initially welcomed by friendly British soldiers, but the mysterious General Smythe hypnotises his officers into believing that they are deserters and German spies. The Doctor is apparently shot by firing squad at the end of episode one. Smythe is in fact a member of the War Lords, a race of aliens who have been abducting soldiers from different wars in Earth's history, transplanting them to an unnamed planet and leaving them to fight out their wars to the death. The War Lords' devilish plot is to bring together the survivors into one huge army and use it to conquer the galaxy. This potty scheme doesn't bear much scrutiny – won't the survivors be injured or exhausted? – so the story cracks along at a brisk pace to distract the viewer from the daft central premise. The TARDIS crew pass through one time zone to the next, encountering Roman soldiers and Confederates and Yankees from the American Civil War. Some of the soldiers have resisted the War Lords' conditioning and are able to pass through the time zones, recruiting similar veterans into a resistance to fight the War Lords.

In one excellent idea among so many, the War Lords are helped by the War Chief, played by Edward Brayshaw, who was to find fame as Mr Meaker in the BBC children's series *Rentaghost* (1976-1984), where he would sport a similarly alarming gringo moustache. The War Chief is a member of the Doctor's own race, who provides the War Lords with the space/time machines (apparently called SIDRATs, though not named as such on screen) required to ship the soldiers from Earth. Brought face to face with the Doctor, he proclaims: "You may have changed your appearance, but I know who you are." The Doctor is unmoved and unafraid: "Oh, do you?" The principle that members of the Doctor's race can recognise each other whatever their outward appearance is thus established: in "Terror of the Autons" (1971), the Master has no trouble recognising the Doctor, although he presumably has not previously encountered his third incarnation; in "The Deadly Assassin" (1976), Runciple the Fatuous recognises the Fourth Doctor and asks him if he's had a facelift.

Eventually, the War Lords are defeated by the resistance. Unable to send all the soldiers back to their own time on his own, the Doctor calls for help to his own people, the Time Lords. This is the first time they are named and the question implied by the programme's title – Doctor *Who?* – is answered after six years. The Doctor explains to Jamie that the Time Lords have immense powers: they have the secret of time and space travel, "we can live for ever, barring accidents", and that he ran away from them because he was bored. With all their great power, all the Time Lords ever do is observe; this wasn't enough for the Doctor, with a whole universe to explore, countless times, places and people to visit. He stole a TARDIS and fled.

It is suggested by the narrative of "The War Games" that the Time Lords were conceived in opposition to the War Lords; if the latter are the lords of war, the former are the lords of time. The Doctor has broken two of their laws: first, he stole a TARDIS (which was broken and in for repairs, which explains its unreliable steering and stuck chameleon circuit, and why the Doctor was able to get his hands on it in the first place); second, that he broke the most important law of the Time Lords by interfering in the affairs of other races. The Doctor is well aware that he risks sacrificing his freedom: by calling for the Time Lords' aid at the end of episode nine, he also gives away his own location in time and space and spends much of the rest of the story trying to escape from the Time Lords' grasp. In episode ten, the War Lord – an icy study of evil from the wonderful Philip Madoc – is tried by the Time Lords, who find his scheme diabolical, dematerialise him and place a force field around his planet so that it can no longer be a threat. They then turn their attention to the Doctor, who is put on trial.

In one of the series' best scenes, the Doctor mounts a defence of his actions and the programme's support of the just war theory: it is sometimes necessary to use violence to defeat evil. "True, I am guilty of interference, just as you are guilty of failing to use your great powers to help those in need." The Time Lords accept his defence and agree that there is evil in the universe that must be fought. The Doctor is hopeful: "You mean you're going to let me go?" Not entirely: the court's sentence is that the Doctor is to be sent to the planet Earth in the twentieth century, a world more vulnerable than the others, in exile, for as long as the Time Lords think fit. For that time, the secret of the TARDIS will be taken from him. The Doctor protests that he is known on Earth and it will be very embarrassing for him: the Time Lords reply that his appearance will change again as part of the sentence. When shown a succession of faces to choose from – thus establishing that Time Lords can have some choice in their appearance and partly excusing the dreadful regeneration scene in "Destiny of the Daleks" (1979) – the Doctor makes trouble and rejects the lot. Patrick Troughton's last moments as the Doctor have him spinning in a void, protesting, as the Time Lords choose his new body for him and send him into exile.

Although Pertwee was now cast, he does not feature in the regeneration scene in the final part of "The War Games". When we get our first glimpse of the Third Doctor in 1970, the TARDIS lands in a wood, the doors open, Pertwee stumbles out and promptly collapses. The series was now in colour, for those privileged viewers who could afford to rent or buy colour television (it is a sign of the Master's villainous extravagance that he insists on a *colour* television for his cell in 1972's *The Sea Devils*).

Meanwhile, there was the summer break to get through while science fiction audiences had to endure Saturday evenings without *Doctor Who*.

The BBC filled the gap in the schedule with a new science fiction series, imported from the United States. It was called *Star Trek*.

5

Exiled to Earth

The Doctor bitterly resented his exile to Earth: the new production team wasn't too happy about it either. In the end, it lasted for the seventh and eighth seasons. Terrance Dicks, continuing as script editor from the Troughton era, explained the show's new remit to his friend Malcolm Hulke. He had boarded with Hulke in the 1960s while learning his craft as a writer and the older Hulke had acted as something of a mentor. They wrote some scripts for *The Avengers* together and collaborated on "The War Games" in 1969. Hulke, who went on to write some of the best Pertwee scripts, considered Dicks's description of the new structure for *Doctor Who* and concluded: "Right, that basically leaves you with two plots: invasion from outer space or mad scientist." In fact, writers in the early seventies brilliantly undermined the series' self-imposed limitations. Hulke himself broke the mould in the second Pertwee story "Doctor Who and the Silurians" (1970), where the monsters were not alien invaders but had always been here, dormant and buried beneath the Earth. The Silurians were reptilian bipeds from the age of the dinosaurs, frozen for millions of years and awakened as a side effect of human technology (shades of Varga in "The Ice Warriors").

When the eighth season was confirmed after the BBC abandoned its flirtation with cancellation, new producer Barry Letts partially restored the Doctor's power of movement. The Time Lords periodically activated the TARDIS by remote control to send the Doctor to fix a problem for them, sometimes without telling him: they were thus revealed as a sneaky and devious lot who undermined their own official policy of non-interference in the affairs of other races. (We might compare *Star Trek*'s United Federation of Planets, which has a similar doctrine of non-interference unless its will needs to be stamped on an upstart civilisation: not a bad metaphor for 1960s US foreign policy.) The Doctor and Jo are sent to the planet Uxarieus in the twenty fifth century ("Colony in Space", 1971) to stop the Master getting his hands on the Doomsday Weapon, which would threaten the Time Lords' domination of the cosmos.

Jon Pertwee told the story of how he contacted his agent when he heard that Patrick Troughton was going to leave the programme. He wanted to put his own name forward; his agent wasn't sure this was the right career move, but phoned the BBC anyway and asked if they had considered his client, Jon Pertwee. There was silence from the other end. "Don't worry," Pertwee's agent said, "it's probably not a very good idea". "No, it's just that we're staggered," came the reply. "He's one of the two at the top of our list." The first choice was Ron Moody, fresh from his success as Fagin in the film of *Oliver!*, a treacly and sentimental adaptation of Dickens's great novel. One version of the story is that Moody was offered the part and turned it down. Much later in his career, he is said to have told Tom Baker he wished he'd accepted it.

Pertwee was well known as a comic actor who provided an amazing range of voices to the long-running BBC radio series *The Navy Lark*, inspired in part by his experience in the navy in the Second World War. He had featured in two *Carry On* films and in West Ends hits like *A Funny Thing Happened on the Way to the Forum*. Given his background in comedy, it seems possible that producer Peter Bryant was looking to replace Troughton with a like-for-like replacement performance inflected towards comedy. If this was the plan, Pertwee's reading of the part was quite different: he played the Doctor deadly straight after some comic business in his debut story (a result of post-regeneration trauma?), although he did disguise himself as a milkman and female cleaner – complete with funny voices – in "The Green Death" (1973). Like Tom Baker, Pertwee tapped into his own personality to play the Doctor: "I am Doctor Who and he is me," he told interviewers in the seventies.

Although Dicks and Letts were unenthusiastic about the Earth-bound setting, Pertwee embraced it enthusiastically, at least in public. "There's nothing more alarming than coming home to find a Yeti sitting on your loo in Tooting Bec" (a rather run down area of south London), he said in early interviews. This pointed to the contrast between the alien and the everyday that the 1970s stories exploited so successfully, following the template established in "The War Machines" (1966), "The Web of Fear" (1968) and "The Invasion" (1968). Chris Chibnall presumably remembered Pertwee's remark when he came to write the "red button" mini-episode "Pond Life" – featuring the home life of the Eleventh Doctor's companions Amy and Rory – to accompany the 2012 season. Opening his bathroom door early in the morning, Rory does a double-take when he sees an Ood sitting on the loo, blinking at him piteously.

The seventh season surrounded the Doctor with an ensemble cast of UNIT personnel who would carry the story with him. The Brigadier returned, initially with a different Captain for every story, including Paul

Darrow in "Doctor Who and the Silurians": Darrow would eventually find fame as the second, and then first, lead in *Blake's Seven*. Sergeants came and went too, although Corporal Benton, who had featured in a small way in "Invasion" (1968), reappeared in "The Ambassadors of Death" and "Inferno" (both 1970). The regulars settled down in the eighth season and Captain Mike Yates was introduced as a possible love interest for Jo Grant. Ian Marter auditioned for the part, was seriously considered and was eventually cast by Barry Letts three years later as the fourth Doctor's companion Harry Sullivan. Richard Franklin played Captain Yates and Sergeant Benton became the regular, resident sergeant.

Responding in a small way to the growth of feminism (or Women's Liberation as it was sometimes known back then), Pertwee's first companion was a very clever and capable scientist, Dr Liz Shaw. Sensibly clad in a suit for her first story, Liz was a far cry from some of the 1960s companions, whose primary purpose sometimes appeared to be to look pretty and glamorous. Brigadier Alistair Gordon Lethbridge-Stewart approaches Liz to be UNIT's scientific adviser when he is unable to locate the Doctor. She is immediately intrigued by the landing of two showers of meteorites in the same wood in Essex, knowing that the odds against such a thing are scientifically unacceptable. She takes little nonsense from the Brigadier and stands up to the Doctor as an equal, at least in the first story: she becomes more of an assistant for the rest of the season and the Brigadier later tells the Doctor she sees her role as "holding your test tubes and telling you how brilliant you are." Caroline John played the role beautifully as a scientist as near the Doctor's intellectual equal as it is possible to be. Presumably in an attempt to be as glamorous as the assistants of old, she affects mini-skirts and a huge hat in "The Ambassadors of Death". However, Barry Letts considered that her role in the series was limited: as she was clever, the Doctor had no need to explain things to her, and as she was capable of looking after herself, the opportunities for her to get captured and to need rescuing were limited. Not much of this could be said for the new companion Jo Grant, who joined the Doctor in "Terror of the Autons" (1971), the first story of season eight. Liz was unceremoniously written out in the gap between seasons: perhaps her lack of a proper farewell was explained by the production team's uncertainty about whether there actually would be an eighth season. In fact, Caroline John was expecting her first child when her final stories were shot and might have had to leave the series anyway, at least temporarily. Her husband, Geoffrey Beevers, played a UNIT corporal in "The Ambassadors of

Death", and appeared as the Master in "The Keeper of Traken" (1981).

Jo Grant was played by Katy Manning and was deliberately conceived as the antithesis of Liz. On her first meeting with the Doctor, she ruins the experiment he's working on, putting out his welding of the TARDIS's dematerialisation circuit with a fire extinguisher. The Doctor is horrified and tells the Brigadier that she's got to go. In fact, she stayed for three seasons. In a witty piece of scripting, Jo similarly ruins the experiment of Professor Clifford Jones when she encounters him in her last story, "The Green Death" (1973). He is trying to find a cure for the disease caused by the giant maggots and has prepared microscope slides of their slime; Jo knocks a jar of his nutritious fungus all over them and he is furious. As it was with the Doctor, Jo's ruining of a scientific experiment is clearly part of an unconscious courtship ritual. She eventually marries Professor Jones, describing him to the Doctor as "like a younger you." The Doctor bids her farewell and silently leaves her engagement party early; he climbs into Bessie and drives off into the sunset. In the novelisation of this story, Malcolm Hulke articulated what had been implied for the three years Jo had been part of the series: that in their time together, the Doctor had come to love her very much. Yet the love is not mentioned – it never needs to be – and is a far cry from Rose and Martha's noisy pining after the Doctor in the revived series. Similarly, his silent exit at the end of "The Green Death" is much more touching than the endless farewells of "Doomsday" (2006) and "The End of Time" part two (2010). Some fans found the companions' later love for the Doctor tiresome and considered it got in the way of telling the story. The implied love between the Doctor and Jo, and later the Doctor and Sarah, might be preferred as it never pushed the adventure to one side.

Jo is apparently about nineteen years old when we first encounter her. She tells the Doctor that she took General Science at A level (a contrast to the degrees taken by Liz); she later tells him "I didn't say I passed." The production team was delighted with Katy Manning's performance and she was a great favourite and friend of Pertwee's. Indeed, the whole cast apparently got on very well together and there was much fun and larking about on the set, sometimes to the irritation of the people who were trying to get the show in the can. The warmth between the regulars can perhaps be seen in the performances each gives in the UNIT stories. There seems to be little rivalry between the actors and they graciously give space for each other's performances: something that wasn't always so in a show that was so obviously a star vehicle as *Doctor Who*. We might again contrast *Star Trek*, where William Shatner –

Captain Kirk – allegedly insisted on hogging the close ups and the best lines, much to the alleged rage of his co-stars. Jo was a popular companion with children, who immediately identified with her gentleness and quietly expressed love for the Doctor. The relationship between them was that of a father and daughter, or perhaps an affectionate uncle and niece, and the Doctor, in the tall, handsome and protective form of Jon Pertwee, became a father figure for millions of children in a way that his two predecessors had, arguably, not managed. I remember talking in the playground at the end of my primary school years about Elisabeth Sladen's departure as Sarah in 1976: many of my friends had much preferred Jo to the sometimes spiky Sarah and several of them remembered how they had cried when she left in 1973. "I cheered when Sarah went," said one ingrate.

Popular as Jo was with children, her inclusion in the series did move its trajectory more firmly towards the younger audience. This is a problem for some fans, who are keen for the programme to be seen as a serious piece of science fiction: it wasn't a problem for the children watching at the time. I remember finding Liz a bit too serious: as a small child, watching her and Pertwee together was another example of watching the bewildering rituals and antics of grown-ups which were before me every day. Jo was a helping hand back into the series for younger children. She was no intellectual, so the Doctor could explain the story to her; although she was resourceful and bright, she also got captured and got into trouble, so the Doctor had to come and rescue her. She is easily hypnotised by the Master in "Terror of the Autons" (1971) and nearly succeeds in bombing the Doctor's lab; she leads a raid on the IMC spaceship in "Colony in Space" (1971) and is captured by their captain and cruel security chief.

After the seventh season, when they had been handed a template and cast largely tooled by the previous production team, Dicks and Letts thus reshaped the series into a more family-friendly and cosy mould in season eight. The futuristic Afrika-Korp-like UNIT uniforms were replaced by more regular army wear; the Brigadier was allowed to be funnier; the Doctor's black tail coats were replaced by soft velvet jackets in a variety of colours. Even the Doctor's hair was fluffier. So was the companion: if the 1970 series had responded positively to feminism, the 1971 series arguably took a step backwards. The pairing of Jo and the Doctor was the pairing Christopher Eccleston perhaps had in mind when he spoke disparagingly of "the paternalistic know-all and the underwritten female companion" of earlier years. Yet the viewing figures held up and even improved, *Doctor Who* continued to be a success, the show was renewed for season after season and all talk of cancellation was silenced for the rest of the decade. So much for political correctness.

In spite of a renewed slanting towards children in the eighth season, Jon Pertwee's time as the Doctor included some of the series' most intelligent and thoughtful scripts. In the best traditions of literary science fiction, the show was used as a vehicle to explore issues in the real world, as perhaps had not been the case since the introduction of the Cybermen and the Daleks in Hartnell's time. This renewed interest in real world issues was partly attributable to the pairing of Dicks with the new producer Barry Letts. Letts, a Buddhist, exemplified that faith's belief in the capacity of human beings to ruin themselves and the world through following the wrong path: this played well with Dicks's leaning, expressed in his work, towards liberal and left-of-centre politics. Two others joined the quartet of socially minded writers and had a considerable influence on the series' trajectory for the next five years. One of these was Robert Sloman, who wrote several scripts with Barry Letts; the other was Malcolm Hulke.

A recurring theme in Pertwee's era as the Doctor is the danger of uncontrolled, untested technology. In "Doctor Who and the Silurians" (1970), the cyclotron research establishment is created as an attempt to produce cheap, plentiful energy. Similarly, the Inferno project attempts to tap the power of the Earth's molten core to supply the planet's energy needs ("Inferno", 1970). Both projects appear to mirror contemporary British, and world, fascination with nuclear power; the "white heat of technology", in the words of British prime minister Harold Wilson (1964-1970, 1974-6) which, the public was told, would be so wonderful that the energy created would be limitless and, therefore, virtually free. Excited by its potential, not enough attention was paid to the by-products of nuclear power: nuclear waste that couldn't be disposed of, irradiation around the nuclear reprocessing plant at Sellafield and a higher than usual level of leukaemia in children who lived nearby, not to mention the horrors of Chernobyl and Fukushima that were to follow. In *Doctor Who*, the scientists behind the energy projects are not evil, but narrow minded and obsessed with their pet projects. Dr Lawrence resists all attempts to close down the cyclotron, eventually to the point of hysteria; Professor Stahlman arrogantly dismisses all the Doctor's objections to Project Inferno. In both stories, the by-products of using technology before it has been properly thought through and tested are, in fictional terms, as horrifying as the by-products of nuclear power. Lawrence's project awakens the

Silurians from their deep sleep; after murdering his older leader, the aggressive young Silurian flatly refuses to share the planet with upstart apes and initiates two projects to exterminate them. The first is a plague, originally used in his time to wipe out the apes which raided the Silurians' crops. It is hideously effective on human beings, but the Doctor and Liz find the cure. The second is to destroy the Van Allen Belt, which protects the Earth from the more harmful rays of the sun: without it, Liz explains, we would die of sunburn on a cloudy day. The awakening of the Silurians is an indirect effect of the use of technology and a warning that actions have consequences; it also highlights the impatience, even greed, of human beings who, hungry for solutions to real problems like the energy crisis, cling to pet schemes and close their ears to any objections that the technology is unreliable (shades of the controversy around releasing gas reserves by "fracking" at the time of writing – April 2013).

In "Inferno", the link between over-ambitious, untested technology and disaster is made even more apparent. Stahlman's project releases a slime that turns human beings into slavering, primitive monsters called Primords. Although unconvincingly realised on screen as hairy, fang toothed brutes who looked as though they had stepped out of an early movie of *Dr Jekyll and Mr Hyde* (aged four, I remember my brothers shouting "Hippy!" at them in 1970), the Primords are an effective metaphor for the greed and arrogance that motivates Stahlmann. Human beings who forgot their capacity to reason and follow their baser passions – here, of greed and arrogance – become animals. This is literally realised in the Primords of "Inferno" but is an idea that goes back as far as Shakespeare and the Elizabethans; it has a good pedigree long before science fiction or *Doctor Who*. If the Primords were not enough, the Doctor's tampering with the TARDIS's console transports him to a fascist, parallel Earth where Project Inferno does break through to the Earth's core: the resulting volcanic explosions destroy the planet. Returning to our Earth with this terrible warning, the Doctor discovers that all is not lost: Stahlman has become a Primord and the project is shut down. His experience leads the Doctor to muse that free will is not an illusion: it is Stahlman's choice whether he continues with the experiment of not; the Earth's destruction is not inevitable or pre-ordained but a result of human beings' choices. This is an environmental message that the Pertwee stories often repeat, and chimes with the emergence of the green movement in the Ecology Party (later the Green Party) and Friends of the Earth, both products of the early seventies.

The link between technology and its terrifying by-products is articulated most clearly in "The Green Death". This 1973 story is one of the series' most fondly remembered episodes, not least because it is "the one with the maggots" and provides some of the iconic imagery of *Doctor Who*: giant maggots sneaking up on people and attacking them. Written by Robert Sloman and an uncredited Barry Letts, "The Green Death" is one of the series' most uncompromising attacks on capitalism and greed. Global Chemicals has pioneered a chemical process that increases the energy yield of petroleum by more than 30%. Unfortunately, the by-product of the process is a filthy green slime which cannot be broken down by any chemical process. The company quietly flushes it down a disused coal mine and then denies all knowledge of it. The slime infects and eventually kills anyone who touches it – the green death – and causes a mutation of giant maggots which spread the infection. There is no cure.

Opposed to the irresponsibility of Global Chemicals is the Wholeweal Community led by Professor Cliff Jones, who eventually marries Jo Grant. Wholeweal protests against Global Chemicals ("More muck! More devastation! More death!") and seeks alternative, peaceful lifestyles. To prevent Wholeweal from becoming too twee and earnest, Sloman shows that it is not popular in the local community, who dub it "the Nuthatch". The villagers lost their jobs when the mine closed and are interested in the promise of jobs in Global Chemicals: Professor Jones is shouted down as a middle class do-gooder who doesn't understand their problems.

Nevertheless, while Global Chemicals seeks a solution to the fuel crisis that is devastating the British economy, Wholeweal seeks a solution to world starvation. Professor Jones is trying to exploit the possibilities of a high protein fungus which, of course, is discovered serendipitously to cure the green death itself: a maggot eats half of the fungus cake and dies. This is an obvious metaphor: the cure for the problems of rampant capitalism is environmentalism.

Much of the radicalism of Pertwee *Who* came from the writer Malcolm Hulke, who had, at one time, been a member of the Communist Party. Hulke's scripts are often attacks on capitalist greed. In "Colony in Space" (1971), the efforts of a group of colonists to found a farming community on a new planet are almost ruined by the rapacity of the Interplanetary Mining Corporation. IMC finds that the planet is rich in duralinium and is determined to strip-mine the colonists' home: it tries to scare them away by murdering two of their number and blaming it on savage native lizards, and then resorts to more open murder and intimidation. Again, there is an environmentalist theme. One of the terrors of the 1970s was over-population: in "Colony in Space", almost every square inch of Earth has been built on and human beings live cramped together in tiny, duralinium-based, apartments. Hence IMC's interest in Uxarieus: the planet's duralinium will provide over two million living units on Earth, and maximise the company's profits. The Doctor favours the colonists' alternative: human beings need space to live on and land to farm, rather than living like a lot of battery hens.

Having satirised ruthless multinationals and rapacious capitalism, Hulke also ties an environmental theme into the serial which he had previously used in "Doctor Who and the Silurians". The colonists' crops will not grow: even their cover crop withered and died. The planet's infertility is a by-product of the Doomsday Weapon built by its previous inhabitants: the Crab Nebula was created when the weapon was tested. Once the super race had designed and built the weapon as a pinnacle of its technological achievement, it went into decline and degenerated into various primitive species (shade of the Primords) who worship and fear the weapon. The Doomsday Weapon is maintained by a tiny, puppet like guardian (realised as a small puppet with a face like a cabbage) who needs its radiation to survive. The Master explains to the guardian that he intends to use the weapon to rule the cosmos; the guardian, horrified, agrees with the Doctor that such power must never be used. It commits suicide, the weapon is destroyed, the radiation disappears and the crops grow again. Some critics have criticised the scientific implausibility of the radiation immediately dispersing, but the narrative suggests that, once harmful technology is removed, nature and human beings will flourish. The happy ending also recalls science fiction's roots in Romantic literature: after the crisis, there is plenitude and growth.

We might at this point ask what possessed Hulke and the production team to call Pertwee's second story "Doctor Who and the Silurians", since it had been established for seven years that "Doctor Who" was not the character's name. After all, scripts had been called "Doctor Who and the ..." before, such as "Doctor Who and Tanni" (which became "The Rescue" (1964)), before the mistake had been picked up by eagle-eyed script editors. Similarly, the Doctor sometimes referred to himself as "Doctor Who" in scripts before they were edited. "Doctor Who and the Silurians" seems to have been a mistake that slipped through, or could be attributed to a new team that didn't fully grasp the series' vocabulary. After all, the story introduced the Doctor's

Edwardian roadster Bessie, which had the number plate Who 1, again implying that "Who" is the Doctor's name and causing earnest fans to turn cartwheels in their attempts to write the number plate into series continuity. It seems simplest to suggest that production teams make mistakes. Even Homer nods. One of the technical crew on the Radio Four *Doctor Who* play "The Paradise of Death" (1993), also by Barry Letts and starring Jon Pertwee, told me that the script continually referred to the Doctor's ship as "TARDIS" rather than "*the* TARDIS": it was only the presence of a fan in the recording studio which saved the mistake from being broadcast in the finished programme.

Before left-wingers could become too smug with the series' new political credentials, Hulke's final script for the series squarely targeted over-zealous environmentalists for its satire. In "Invasion of the Dinosaurs" (1974), London has been evacuated because of the appearance of terrifying prehistoric monsters. These provide the monster of the week that the Pertwee stories excelled at, but the real monsters are, as so often in the show, human beings themselves. The dinosaurs have been transported by a machine called the Timescoop, created and operated by Professor Whitaker (another dry performance from Peter Miles, who played Dr Lawrence in "Doctor Who and the Silurians" and thus cornered the market in fanatical scientists). Whitaker believes that human beings have ruined their planet with pollution, wickedness and war, and that the only solution is to roll back time to an earlier, greener state: a golden age, when human beings lived a simple agrarian existence and were in harmony with nature. Working with him are traitor Captain Mike Yates, who sabotages the Doctor's counter-moves at every turn, and Sir Charles Grover, a member of the Cabinet who wrote the acclaimed book *Last Chance for Man*. The Doctor applauds Grover's book and approves of the man, but Grover's environmentalism has led him to despair of solving the world's environmental problems: the only solution is to start again and avoid the mistakes which led human beings to despoil their planet. Grover's smiling conviction is horribly plausible (on the audio reading of the novel, Martin Jarvis makes him sound awfully like Peter Mandelson). Once the Doctor learns of the plan, he tells Mike that the Golden Age is an illusion and it never existed. Here, he is in good literary company: Shakespeare similarly harps back to the golden age in *As You Like It*, but the characters' attempts to capture it in the Forest of Arden are hardly successful and Arden is often shown in productions to be a bit grotty.

Sarah-Jane Smith is kidnapped by Grover and wakes up on a spaceship travelling away from Earth. On board are kindly environmentalists, who firmly believe that they are going to a new world not unlike Earth, peopled by kindly humanoids whom they will guide and help. Sarah realises the whole thing is a trick: the spaceship is a mock-up in a nuclear shelter under London; the planet they are travelling to is Earth in the past, when time has been rolled back and people in the present have ceased to exist. In response to Sarah's objections, Grover insists that this isn't murder as the people thus erased would never have existed. When she explains her findings to the idealists on the "spaceship", one of their leaders, Ruth, tells her that she mustn't say such things. Ruth then rapidly moves from wondering if Sarah will be happy with them to suggesting that she might have to be destroyed as a disruptive influence, for the good of the community, of course. Commenting on the story in the DVD extras, Terrance Dicks said that Hulke would have based Ruth on the sort of do-gooding leftie he would have known from his time in the Communist Party: Ruth, he said, is the sort of person who knows what's best for you and what you should think, and, if you disagree, will, most reluctantly, insist that you have to be sacrificed for the good of all. The idea is terrifying and all too true.

Eventually, the duped environmentalists insist that Operation Golden Age is evil and they will have no part in genocide. Whitaker and Grover activate the Timescoop and time starts going backwards. The Doctor, unaffected because he is a Time Lord, is able to reverse the process: time goes forward again but Whitaker and Grover, caught in the field of the Timescoop, have vanished. Where? "Back to their Golden Age," the Doctor says. "I hope they like it."

Excellent though the script is, there were huge production problems with "Invasion of the Dinosaurs". Producer Barry Letts was keen on dinosaurs in London because he believed they were now technically possible. He had been impressed by the Drashigs in "Carnival of Monsters" (1973) – and they are splendid, standing up well even for today's viewers – and wanted the BBC visual effects designers responsible for them to produce the dinosaurs for the new story. Unfortunately, the designers weren't available and the dinosaurs were farmed out to an external effects company who assured Letts that they could do the job convincingly. When the dinosaurs were delivered to the studio, Elisabeth Sladen said she could have cried. Letts was furious. The tyrannosaurus model was operated by a crank in its tail which allowed it to writhe and that was about it; all the dinosaurs shuffled along with rods in their legs and the larger tyrannosaurus head, used for close ups, doesn't match the smaller model. The dinosaurs were generally shot in the studio on video. Director Paddy Russell (one of *Who*'s few female directors) recalled that the only way Sarah could be seen in shot with a tyrannosaurus was to stand Elisabeth Sladen against a blue screen set, put the dinosaur model on another camera, and zoom out on Sarah until she was about the right size relative to the dinosaur. As the dinosaurs were on video, they don't match properly with the filmed exterior sequences and appear to be floating above the ground. There are, of course, no shadows. *Primaeval* it ain't. One or two shots are passable: there is a good glove puppet pterodactyl that smashes the window of the Doctor's jeep and attacks him; Sarah is locked in an aircraft hanger with a tyrannosaurus and, as a child, I remember being terrified as it woke up and tried to get at her, even as I realised that the effect wasn't that good.

The series was originally entitled "Timescoop" but was changed to "Invasion of the Dinosaurs" by the production team, ever on the look out for a catchy title. Hulke accepted the change but fell out with Dicks over a last minute decision to retitle episode one as simply "Invasion", to keep the inclusion of the dinosaurs as a surprise. The *Radio Times*, which Letts said was a law unto itself, revealed in the listings for episode one that the monsters were prehistoric, so the surprise was blown anyway. Hulke was angry because he feared that the dull retitling would have lost the story viewers and affected his reputation as a writer. Letts apologised and Hulke and Dicks made their peace, but Hulke said he had had enough of his work being interfered with and was glad that he was leaving television to concentrate exclusively on writing prose. One further consequence of the renaming of episode one was that the BBC wiped the colour print of it, believing it to be episode one of the Troughton Cybermen story "The Invasion" (1968). The story was not restored to full colour until its DVD release in 2012, when technical wizardry allowed episode one to be restored to at least some of its former glory.

Malcolm Hulke was among the first writers to be contracted by Target Books in 1974 to write new *Doctor Who* adaptations, called "novelisations" to indicate they were adaptations of scripts in novel form and, presumably, to distinguish them from original novels. Three *Doctor Who* novelisations had been published in the 1960s: *Doctor Who* [taglined] *In An Exciting Adventure with the Daleks* (1964; reissued by Target as the less-of-a-mouthful, *Doctor Who and the Daleks*); *Doctor Who and the Crusaders* (1964), both by David Whitaker, and *Doctor Who and the Zarbi* (1964) by Bill Strutton, an adaptation of his own scripts for "The Web Planet" (1964). These books were reissued with new covers by

Target in the 1970s and immediately sold so well that their editors asked the production team for more *Doctor Who* novels. Terrance Dicks, knowing that he was soon to move on from the series, offered to do some in spite of never having written a novel before. His first effort was the excellent *Doctor Who and the Auton Invasion*, based on Robert Holmes's script for "Spearhead from Space" (1970). Target had a habit of jazzing up the titles when it thought the original story title was too dull to catch the attention of children. Malcolm Hulke wrote six of the new novelisations: *Doctor Who and the Cave Monsters* (an adaptation of "Doctor Who and the Silurians", 1970); *Doctor Who and the Sea Devils* (originally entitled *Doctor Who and the Sea Monsters* to tie in with the first Silurian tale); *Doctor Who and the Doomsday Weapon* (from 1970's "Colony in Space" and a far better title than the original serial); *Doctor Who and the Space War* (adapted from the equally dully titled "Frontier in Space", 1973); *Doctor Who and the Green Death* and *Doctor Who and the Dinosaur Invasion*. Originally written for children, Hulke's novelisations are especially well regarded and stand up well as fine versions of the original stories. His prose is sometimes a little poor – he tends to repeat the same noun two or three times in three lines – but Hulke effectively takes advantage of the medium of the novel to expand intelligently on the original television scripts. On television, the Silurians were simply referred to as "Old Silurian" and "Young Silurian": in the novel, they have names and personalities. When he brought back the Silurians in 2010, Steven Moffat sent writer Chris Chibnall away to read *Doctor Who and the Cave Monsters* as source material for his scripts, and we can see Hulke's influence in the individualised Silurians of "The Hungry Earth" (2010): rather than being a race of indistinguishable, generic monsters like the Ice Warriors, these Silurians are individuals with their own conflicting agendas.

Hulke sometimes writes from the monster's point of view. In *Doctor Who and the Cave Monsters*, a Silurian that has wandered out on the moor tries to make sense of the humans, who all look alike to him: he refers to the moustached Brigadier as "fur under nose" to distinguish him from the other apes. In *Doctor Who and the Green Death*, episode five's cliff hanger is rendered from the maggot's point of view: as it edges up to the tasty treat of Jo's exposed thigh, it wriggles with happiness at the prospect of so much meat and blood just waiting to be sampled. (In the same novel, Jo also offers to go topless for Professor Jones to distract him from his experiments, but his mind is on his work: not a line that could be played in the television version.) The tyrannosaurus that menaces Sarah in the aircraft hanger (in *Doctor Who and the Dinosaur*

Invasion) remarks to itself upon her screaming and remembers that many of its meals make similar noises before it eats them. It moves its head towards her and finds it very puzzling when its nose bumps into something invisible: this is the glass of the office which is between it and Sarah.

In adapting Robert Sloman's scripts for "The Green Death", Hulke emphasises the story's anti-capitalism even more than the televised version. When told that Professor Jones has a Nobel Prize, Dr Stephens, the Head of (the renamed) Panorama Chemicals, is impressed; but, we are told, Dr Stephens was always impressed by success because he was a snob. Stephens gives the Brigadier a whisky made as a bi-product of Panorama's chemical process; he reminds the computer BOSS that their whisky is actually poisonous and BOSS chuckles because it will make money for Panorama Chemicals. Stephens remembers, as a small boy, listening to the radio to hear Adolf Hitler screaming, *"Ein Reich, ein Volk, ein Führer!"*: when BOSS's plans for world domination make him remember that broadcast, he turns against it.

Christianity also appears to be have been important to Hulke. His novels are laced with Christian references which are not found in the televised stories. In prison on Earth for his crimes against humanity, the Master says goodbye to Jo and asks that God will go with her. The prison governor, Trenchard, in the Master's thrall, tells him that he sometimes thinks the Master is the Devil. In *Doctor Who and the Doomsday Weapon*, Ashe, the colonists' leader, is fascinated by a book from antiquity he has brought with him from Earth which seems to be largely about somebody called God. In the book, there are four versions of a story about a man who sacrifices himself for others, which puzzles Ashe: why should anyone allow himself to die for others? Yet Ashe follows Christ's example when, at IMC's insistence, he is killed when he lifts off in the colonists' broken spaceship and it explodes. The other colonists have escaped from the ship under cover of darkness and Ashe's sacrifice is a ruse to save his friends and to convince IMC that the colonists have gone. In a particularly touching scene in the same novel, the Doctor teaches the colonists how to hold a funeral. Winton says they must dig "holes" for their dead, and the Doctor quietly corrects him to say "graves"; he encourages Winton to say good things about those who are lost, arguing that it's what the mourners expect, even though they don't know that they expect it. The Doctor is reconnecting human beings with the spirituality they have lost in their sterile, overcrowded, existence back on Earth. In *Doctor Who and the*

Green Death, Yates tells Stephens that he has no right to turn humanity into the company's slaves, arguing that God gave man the right of free will. Stephens concedes the point, but says that free will makes people unhappy. Under the rule of BOSS, people will sing happy songs and have an untroubled existence as contended slaves.

On television, *Doctor Who* had always wisely avoided established religion and had never offered an opinion on its truthfulness or otherwise. Some critics argue that, when religion does appear in the series, it's usually as a primitive cult and that therefore the series embraces atheism but the argument doesn't hold water: the existence of false religions does not negate the possibility that there is a true one. With their smaller circulation, the novelisations are perhaps the place for Christian reference, rather than a television series watched by millions which has a stronger potential to offend. We might contrast Hulke's light touch in the novels with Russell T Davies's occasional references to Christianity in the revived series. Christians were pleased when the Tenth Doctor tells Astrid that he "got the last room" in the Inn at Christ's nativity and was present at the first Christmas ("Voyage of the Damned" (2007)). They were less pleased when he indicates that the Resurrection never happened in the 2009 Easter special "Planet of the Dead", when the Doctor starts to say, "Although, what really happened was – " and is interrupted. Davies went further in the spin-off series *Torchwood*: in episode one, a character is brought back to life and splutters that there is nothing after death, thus denying the afterlife in the *Doctor Who* universe. These references could be seen as of a piece with Davies's other modernising agendas, which most Christians are comfortable with, in promoting gay characters and lifestyles, and casting regardless of the actor's colour. However, Davies, an atheist who told the BBC's Mark Lawson that Christianity is "just nonsense", unfortunately joins the contemporary Christianophobic zeitgeist. Richard Dawkins, anti-theist and husband of Lalla Ward, appeared in "The Stolen Earth" (2008) to explain that the planet has moved. As Dawkins' subject is biology rather than astronomy, there was no need for him to appear as an astronomical expert, although one might suggest he knows as much about astronomy as he does about theology. Russell T Davies enthused about Dawkins's cameo in the series: Dawkins repaid the favour by telling *Doctor Who* Magazine he didn't like *Doctor Who* and calling religious believers "faith heads", thus equating them with "crack heads" as addicted to a mind altering drug. Christianophobia insists that knocking Christianity is fair game and upsetting Christians doesn't matter. Under showrunner Steven Moffat, himself an atheist, such potentially offensive and controversial religious references have been notably and thankfully silenced.

Strangely, the Doctor himself was sometimes presented as a Christ substitute by Davies: millions of people all reverently murmur "Doctor!" at the same time in "Last of the Time Lords" (2008) and the Doctor is resurrected as a glowing super being who offers the Master forgiveness. The Master, like many of the viewers, is incredulous and wonders that he can be defeated by the power of prayer.

Having argued in favour of the liberal, pro-environmentalist and leftist leaning of the Pertwee *Doctor Who*, all were sometimes undermined or contradicted by various factors. Pertwee's Doctor claims he is a member of establishment clubs and is on good terms with senior civil servants; he is an expert on good food and wine and was once identified by the revived series writer Paul Cornell as a Tory. Verity Lambert, the show's original producer, considered the Doctor as a fundamentally anti-establishment character and was profoundly unhappy about this period of the series when he works for the military and, therefore, the establishment. Whereas American audiences are broadly supportive of, and comfortable with, the military – there were no complaints about the military set-up of the starship Enterprise and Star Fleet, for example – a large proportion of the British audience viewed the military with some suspicion. However, perhaps to counterbalance these views, the UNIT characters are treated with sensitivity and portrayed as human beings and individuals. The Brigadier is intelligent and reasonable, at least in his first season: he accepts it is his duty to follow his orders in supporting Dr Lawrence (in "Doctor Who and the Silurians") and Professor Stahlman (in "Inferno"), but opposes them when they become dangerously fanatical about their respective projects. Captain Mike Yates is shown to be an idealist who supports Operation Golden Age ("Invasion of the Dinosaurs", 1974) and turns his back on UNIT for what he sees as the good of humanity. The Brigadier allows him to leave UNIT quietly after extended sick leave rather than having him court-marshalled: a compassionate decision which acknowledges Mike's previous service. Mike then embroils himself in more trouble as he seeks peace of mind in a Buddhist meditation centre, only to discover it is being used to open a channel to malevolent alien forces ("Planet of the Spiders", 1974). These are soldiers who are flawed human beings, not the military blimps of popular prejudice. There is no contradiction between the sympathetic portrayal of the military and the show's occasional left-wing leanings: sensible socialists in Britain have always acknowledged the necessity of the nation's defence and prominent figures in the Labour Party served with distinction in the Second World War. Denis Healey, Secretary of State for Defence until 1970 and Chancellor of the Exchequer from 1974-9, commanded a beach regiment in the landings on the Italian coast in Anzio.

We might argue that Verity Lambert didn't perhaps watch the Pertwee series closely enough. The Doctor remains an anti-establishment figure and is as irritated by UNIT as he is resentful of the Time Lords. He chafes against his exile; working for UNIT, at least in Pertwee's first season, is something of a marriage of convenience. He makes it clear in "Spearhead from Space" (1970), his first story, that he will work for the Brigadier in return for a place to live, sleep and to try and get the TARDIS working again. Frequently, his obsession with doing so is his primary motivation in a story: in "Inferno" (1970), his main interest in Stahlman's project – to tap the Earth's core for its limitless source of free energy – is to use the energy thus released to power the TARDIS. In other stories, he is irritated by the Brigadier's problems as a distraction from his real work of resuming his travels in time and space. The Doctor often disagrees with the Brigadier's solutions and acidly remarks that "military intelligence" is "a contradiction in terms". He is horrified when Lethbridge-Stewart destroys the Silurians' base after the Doctor has sought a peaceful solution: the Doctor wants humans and Silurians to share the planet; the Brigadier thinks this is impossible and kills them. Again, the situation is complex and neither the Brigadier nor the Doctor is shown to be entirely right. The narrative suggests the Doctor is naïve to think that the Silurians would peacefully share the planet with the humans: they did, after all, release a disease that would exterminate humanity. After the Doctor has tried to negotiate, is the Brigadier right to exterminate them before they exterminate us? Or is the Brigadier's action a piece of racist genocide of ugly non-humans who probably deserve it? Barry Letts once offered an explanation of the Buddhist symbolism in "Planet of the Spiders" (1974), which he co-wrote with Robert Sloman, prefacing it with a reminder that we shouldn't take it too seriously. Perhaps we should remember this when we apply a serious analysis to an adventure serial, remembering that to do so is perhaps to contradict the show's tone and intention. However, the complex issues that are debated by the show again partly account for its popularity among children in its refusal to patronise its audience.

In spite of Nicholas Courtney's plaintive lament in a 1973 interview that "I don't want the Brig to look a twit", the Brigadier became more of a figure of fun as the Pertwee seasons progressed. This does not necessarily shore up Lambert's criticism of the Doctor working for the establishment by showing the establishment to be daft: rather, the production team took advantage of the dramatic possibilities of highlighting the humour in Courtney's splendid performance. For example, the Brigadier is shown to be ridiculously squeamish, wincing as the Doctor dissects a solid rubber doll – used to murder Mr Farrell – in "Terror of the Autons" (1971). He hurriedly cuts short the revelation of his love life by "Professor" Clegg in "Planet of the Spiders": Mr Clegg reveals his powers of extra-sensory perception by examining the Brigadier's watch, given to him by the sea ("Brighton, was it?") by "a young lady called... Doris... she said it was to express her gratitude for – " "All true, absolutely spot on," huffs the Brigadier, snatching the watch back. In "The Three Doctors" (1973), Courtney plays the part for laughs. Unable to transport the TARDIS and the Second Doctor to his rocky realm inside a black hole, the renegade Time Lord Omega transports the whole of UNIT HQ instead. Opening the door onto a barren landscape, the Brigadier opines that they have arrived in "Norfolk or somewhere like that"; he goes out to do a recce and muses, "I'm pretty certain that's Cromer."

6

I am the Master, and you will obey me

Assuming that it would ever be commissioned, Barry Letts and Terrance Dicks started to consider ideas for *Doctor Who*'s eighth season in 1970 and, in doing so, began to throw off the restraints imposed by the Troughton production team who had exiled the Doctor to Earth and hugely limited the range of stories that could be told. Letts was unhappy with the series' concentration, in its seventh season, on purely science fiction stories: he wanted to restore some of the freedom which came from inflecting the show more towards fantasy. This movement recalled the original guidelines to the series issued to writers in 1963: *Doctor Who* was to be neither straight science fiction nor historical drama nor fantasy, but writers were free to explore any genre which they felt best suited the story they wanted to tell. This flexibility is, of course, one reason why the programme has lasted so long: it has the most flexible format ever devised for any drama programme on television.

Dicks and Letts chatted in 1970 about the similarities between *Doctor Who* and Sherlock Holmes, with the straightforward, prosaically minded Brigadier playing Watson to the Doctor's Sherlock. (The links between the two heroes were highlighted again in 2010, when Mark Gatiss and Steven Moffat, writer and show runner of the revived series, came together to devise the highly successful, updated Conan Doyle series *Sherlock*.) If the Doctor was Sherlock, he needed a Moriarty. Terrance Dicks came back to the office next day and announced, "I've thought of a name for him and it's the Master." Barry Letts exclaimed, "That's brilliant!" Letts also said he knew exactly the right actor to play him: Roger Delgado, an actor with Spanish and sinister good looks who often played characters with mysteries and secrets to hide. The Master was named as such because, like "the Doctor", it was another academic title: this was never pointed out on screen, however, and completely escaped this viewer until Barry Letts pointed it out in an interview.

The Master is the antithesis of the Doctor and was superbly played by Roger Delgado. In the same way that none of the subsequent Doctors could make the part their own after the seven year domination of Tom Baker in the role (at least, in the original series), so it might be argued that none of the other subsequent Masters could come close to Delgado's suave original. Antony Ainley, who played the Master for eight years to Delgado's three, was hobbled by having make-up and a goatee beard that recalled Delgado's original and unfortunately invited unfavourable comparisons. Like the Doctor, the Master is a Time Lord who has escaped from Gallifrey in a stolen TARDIS; like the Doctor, he is brilliant, resourceful, charming and charismatic. Like the Doctor, he is a powerful hypnotist: while the Doctor uses his hypnotism to heal (for example, by releasing Victoria from the control of the Great Intelligence in "The Abominable Snowmen" (1967)), the Master uses it to dominate: his catchphrase, in his Delgado incarnation, is, "I am the Master: you will obey me." Unlike the Doctor, he has no wish to explore the Universe: his only goal is power and he wants to dominate it instead. The Doctor is dedicated to good and champions the weak against the strong: the Master is dedicated to evil and takes delight in crushing the weak beneath his heel. The Master is vicious, ruthless and sadistic, using his talents for his own amusement and gratification in his search for power. In casting Delgado, Barry Letts hit upon an actor who could be a match on screen for the dynamic Pertwee. Like Pertwee, Delgado is middle aged, good looking and has a beautiful speaking voice; like Pertwee, he is charming – he always scrupulously addresses Jo as "Miss Grant" or even, "My dear Miss Grant" – and likeable. He demands the best: the Master's TARDIS is a gleaming mark two, much to the Doctor's annoyance as he is unable to use its dematerialisation circuit, which he steals, in his own mark one; while the Doctor drives the sprightly Bessie, the Master has a chauffeur driven limousine in "The Mind of Evil" (1971) and, for that story only, is shown to smoke large cigars. Re-crafting the Master for the twenty first century, Russell T Davies's approach recalled the original Pertwee-Delgado dynamic: the Master (as played by John Simm) is apparently the same age as the Doctor, similarly good looking and similarly funny. There is a wonderful scene in "The Sound of Drums" (2008) when the American President can barely contain his rage when the Master, in response to his request that he be quiet, mimes zipping his lips and nods solemnly at everything the President says.

When season eight was given the green light, Letts and Dicks embarked on their plan to give the series "a good first night": a strong opening episode that would hook a large audience which would, it was hoped, stay with the show for the rest of the season. In 1971, this was the first appearance of the Master; in 1972, it was the reappearance of the Daleks for the first time in five years ("Day of the Daleks"); in 1973, it was "The Three Doctors" for the programme's tenth anniversary later that year; in season eleven, it was a new companion in Sarah Jane Smith and a new monster in the Sontaran, Lynx, and for season twelve, for which Letts produced only the first story, it was the arrival of the new

Doctor, Tom Baker. All bar the last of these debuts were heralded by some splendid *Radio Times* covers. Perhaps, in part, to entice more children to watch, the *Radio Times* contracted comics artist Frank Bellamy to draw some arresting, comic strip style covers. Their style immediately recalled the popular and well-drawn *Doctor Who* comic strip then running in *Countdown / TV Action*. The Master was thus introduced before his first episode was broadcast with a Bellamy drawn Pertwee saying, "That jackanapes! All he does is cause trouble", Jo Grant saying, "I shall obey!" and the Master himself, jaw thrust forward aggressively, saying, "I am usually referred to as **the Master!**" Aged six, I remember being particularly thrilled by Frank Bellamy's cover for the first *Radio Times* of 1972, whose headline announced "The Daleks are Back!": the Doctor, grim faced, is set against a red planetary background streaked with jagged lightning and menaced by two Daleks chanting, "You are the Doctor…You are the enemy of the Daleks…You will be exterminated…"

The Master makes his first appearance in "Terror of the Autons" (1971). This story is a virtual re-tread of the previous year's "Spearhead from Space", as "The Sea Devils" (1972) would be a virtual re-write of 1970's "Doctor Who and the Silurians", with the addition of the Master to the plots of the Nestenes and Sea Devils respectively. While assisting the Nestenes and Autons with their second invasion attempt, the Master has a lot of fun trying to kill the Doctor in various ingenious and nasty ways. He leaves a grenade as a calling card, hypnotises Jo into delivering a bomb to the Doctor's lab, and takes advantage of the Nestene's ability to animate any kind of plastic by having the Doctor's phone cord come to life and nearly strangle him. The Nestenes become as irritated as unemotional life forms can be by the Master's feud with the Doctor and warn him that he will be eliminated if the feud continues to interfere with their great plan.

The Master and the Doctor eventually meet in episode three and reveal a mutual liking and respect for each other. The Master says that the Doctor is his intellectual equal – "Almost" – and that he will kill him "but not without considerable regret". Later stories reveal that the Master and the Doctor were once friends on Gallifrey and went to the Time Lord Academy together. Jon Pertwee even went so far as to say that Nick Courtney had suggested the Master and the Doctor were brothers, and that this idea had been enthusiastically picked up by the production team until Roger Delgado's untimely death prevented its use. When this was put to him in an interview in the late 1970s, Courtney was amazed and had no memory of the suggestion at all. The idea fizzled on for years until Russell T Davies eventually scotched it in "The Sound of Drums" (2007): Martha asks the Tenth Doctor if he and the Master are brothers; the Doctor rolls his eyes and says that she has been watching too many soap operas. Nevertheless, the mutual respect and affection between the two Time Lords – although they despise each other's values absolutely – is apparent throughout Pertwee's tenure as the Doctor. "Terror of the Autons" was originally to have ended with the Doctor saying he would continue to fight the Master "until I destroy him or he destroys me". This was thought too downbeat and, to reflect the chemistry between the actors and the characters, was changed. The Doctor says he thinks the Master will turn up again. Jo expresses surprise that he doesn't seem too worried about the prospect; the Doctor smiles and replies, "I'm not. As a matter of fact, I'm rather looking forward to it."

Lest the Master be too attractive a character, Robert Holmes' script for "Terror of the Autons" shows him also to be a spiteful sadist. In episode one, he unnecessarily and viciously throws a scientist to his death from the steps of a radio telescope, simply because he is in the Master's way. Later, he delights in the humiliation of Professor Phillips, whom he has hypnotised and disguised as a clown in Rossini's circus. He devises a plastic armchair that swallows and suffocates whoever sits in it. The story also shows the Master's favoured method of murder: a matter concentration gun that shrinks his victims to the size of dolls. The Doctor discovers one of the radio telescope's scientists propped up in his own lunch box, in a very effective image by overlaying the actor into the lunch box with blue screen. Later stories – such as "The Deadly Assassin" (1977) and "Logopolis" (1981) – would instead opt for prop dolls or Action Men dressed in miniature costumes, to risible effect.

The Master appears as the major villain in every story of the 1971 season. Sometimes his appearance is delayed – his entrance as the Administrator in "Colony in Space" comes half way through the story – but there is an inevitability about it which becomes wearisome for some viewers. Letts and Dicks admitted it was a mistake to use him in every story. In "The Daemons", he memorably appears as the new vicar, the Reverend Mr Magister (Latin for "Master"): a good persona which the script doesn't fully exploit. After failing to persuade the Daemon Azal to pass on his planet-destroying powers to himself, the Master is finally captured by UNIT. This sequence was shot in a Wiltshire village. There is a story that director Christopher Barry asked the village children to boo the Master as he was taken into custody but, in a sign of how much they liked the character, they cheered him instead.

The Master appears occasionally for the next two seasons, in "The Sea Devils" (1972), "The Time Monster" (1972) and "Frontier in Space" (1973). One effect of the occasional use of his character was to dry up the offers of work Roger Delgado received after his first season. Casting directors hadn't woken up to the fact that he wasn't in every *Doctor Who* story and he was sometimes out of work. Delgado spoke about this to Barry Letts and said he thought he must leave as the Master; Letts was sympathetic and asked if he wanted to be written out quietly or to go out in a big bang. "Oh, let it be a big bang!" Delgado said enthusiastically. He had loved playing the Master and described the part as the man viewers loved to hate.

Some early story ideas were drawn up with the Master helping the Doctor against a threat that menaced them both, and there were some suggestions that the Master was pencilled in for the role that eventually became Lupton's in "Planet of the Spiders" (1974), Pertwee's swan song. Tragically, Roger Delgado was killed in a car accident while filming in Turkey. The news shook the tight-knit cast and was instrumental in persuading Katy Manning, and then Jon Pertwee, to leave. The Master's final appearance in his Delgado incarnation is in "Frontier in Space" (1973). Here, the Master joins up with the Daleks in an attempt to start a war between the rival empires of the Draconians and the humans; after their mutual destruction, the Daleks will mop up the survivors and dominate the galaxy. No doubt the Master intended to ditch them at some point along the way. He is last seen surrounded by Ogrons, desperately scrabbling for his gun to get a shot in at the departing Doctor.

As a character, the Master didn't reappear for three and a half years. Robert Holmes, who wrote "Terror of the Autons", reintroduced him as a crippled, skeletal form who frames the Doctor for the assassination of the Time Lord president in "The Deadly Assassin" (1976). Although the Master looks quite different, and is played with wonderful, vicious menace by Peter Pratt, his dialogue could have been written with Delgado in mind. He taunts the Doctor by explaining why it had to be him the Master chose to frame for the assassination: "Who else but you? So despicably good, so insufferably compassionate!" Producer Philip Hinchcliffe had stressed that the Master should be between regenerations so that a new actor could be eased into the part if a future production team wanted to bring back the character. At the end of "The Deadly Assassin", the Master's face is superimposed on his departing TARDIS (now in the form of a grandfather clock) and appears to be regenerating. This image was forgotten when he reappeared in "The Keeper of Traken" (1981), now played by Geoffrey Beevers but still maintaining his skeletal form. Beevers apparently used the same mask as Pratt but with the bulging eyes removed, as producer John Nathan-Turner insisted that an actor's eyes were hugely important to his performance. In fact, Beevers appears to be wearing make-up rather than the mask as the Master's skull teeth appear to be painted on his lips; his appearance is altogether less effective than the horror movie image of Peter Pratt in "The Deadly Assassin". At the end of his twelfth regeneration, the Master attempts to steal the Doctor's body, but instead opts for that of Tremas (Anthony Ainley), the father of new companion Nyssa. In a show-stopping climax to the final episode of "The Keeper of Traken" (1981), the Master's ravaged face merges with Tremas's and the new Master is born. With his goatee beard and swept back, black hair, he looks very like Roger Delgado, and fans throughout the land exhaled in ecstasy.

Anthony Ainley played the Master for the rest of the original series' run and provided some continuity in the face of rapidly changing Doctors. He appeared opposite Tom Baker, Peter Davison, Colin Baker, and Sylvester McCoy in the original show's final episode, "Survival" (1989). Sadly, Ainley's performance is not well regarded and he comes across as a silky, Machiavellian, even pantomime villain. Ainley seems to grit his teeth and grin throughout his portrayal, and continually gives a "heh-heh-heh" chuckle as he contemplates his dastardly machinations. This is, of course, partly the fault of the producer and the directors, who dress him in black velvet to emphasise his villainy – subtle, that – and give him some very silly schemes. In "The King's Demons" (1983), the Master attempts to stop the signing of Magna Carta for no very good reason; even the Doctor notes that this is small time villainy by his standards.

The Master's transformation, under John Nathan-Turner, into a stereotyped villain is of a piece with the new style of the series in the 1980s. As the costuming was fixed and simple, so was the characterisation. Nathan-Turner preferred his regulars to wear costumes – even uniforms in Tegan's case – rather than clothes. The Master's character was now an off-the-peg villain: gone was the charming, complex villain faced by Pertwee; in came the pantomime villain disliked by fans, wearing the same black velvet outfit for every appearance bar one. Until Nathan-Turner arrived, Tom Baker had varied his hat and scarf-based outfit from story to story, opting for boots, shoes, waistcoats, cravats and a variety of coats. Under Nathan-

Turner, his costume was fixed into a uniform burgundy (once described by Tom Baker as, "the shitty one") which sported the question marks on the shirt collar (to suggest "Doctor…*Who?*" and to add to the confusion about our hero's name). The question marks were a ghastly addition retained by all subsequent Doctors in the original series and, as the equivalent of Batman's bat logo or Superman's S, unfortunately moved the Doctor into the world of the superhero. Adric, Nyssa and Turlough would all wear virtually the same costumes for every story and air hostess Tegan usually sported the air hostess uniform which she wore when she first climbed aboard the TARDIS in "Logopolis" (1981). By the time she left after three years, it must have been pretty ripe.

The Master's continual inclusion in the series also meant that he, like the Daleks, suffered from the law of diminishing returns. Every scheme of his is thwarted by the Doctor and he ends up looking rather like Sylvester Sneaky/The Hooded Claw from the Hanna-Barbera cartoon *The Perils of Penelope Pitstop* who, however badly his scheme to mash Penelope has gone the previous week, returns every episode with a fiendish new plan which is at once thwarted by the resources of the Ant Hill Mob. The Master has been said to be as nutty as squirrel shit and it is difficult to disagree. He, like the series itself, needed a long rest. When he returned, it was in the Paul McGann TV movie of 1996, played with camp charisma by American actor Eric Roberts. The Master's inclusion in the TV movie was probably determined by rights issues. As he had been created by Barry Letts and Terrance Dicks, he was copyright to the BBC, and could be easily included in any rights package for another production company which wanted to make *Doctor Who*.

The Master's first story, "Terror of the Autons" (1971) coincided with the first serious wave of concern about horror and violence in the programme. One of the Nestenes' weapons was a devil doll, which, when animated by heat, strangled its victims. Barry Letts recalled there were reports of children throwing away their teddy bears in fear of suffering a similar fate. The Doctor and Jo are rescued by two policemen in a patrol car. Suspicious because they won't speak to him, the Doctor pulls away one of the policemen's faces to reveal the Auton beneath. The Autons then proceed to blast away at them in a quarry. Letts received letters from the police force, asking him never again to make policemen frightening for children. He conceded the point, although android policemen appear in "Resurrection of the Daleks" (1984, produced by John Nathan Turner) and shoot the Daleks' enemies with high velocity rifles. Questions were asked in Parliament about the level of violence in what was still considered a children's programme and the newspapers weighed in. A *Daily Telegraph* article, published just after "Terror of the Autons" had aired, protested that the forms taken by the Autons were from a child's domestic sphere and were therefore more frightening than such fantasy creatures as the Daleks and Cybermen. The writer perhaps had a point: suffocation by plastic chair and strangulation by telephone cable are not the usual fare of early evening family viewing. Letts reined in some of the programme's violence after, he thought, going a little too far with the second Auton story, and tried to confine violence to the realms of ray guns and the Doctor's own brand of the martial arts, Venusian aikido. This consisted of Pertwee crying "Haiii!" and flipping a stunt man over his shoulder.

Either the production team took its eye of the ball or relaxed its restrictions when the fuss had died down, as there was some real violence in later Pertwee stories: characters are graphically shot down with arrows in "Death to the Daleks" (1974), for example. The programme came to the attention of Mrs Mary Whitehouse with "Planet of the Spiders", Pertwee's final story in 1974. She criticised the story for playing on children's arachnophobia and suggested the programme should be put on after 6.30 p.m., or that the BBC should commission an analysis of its special effects on the under fives. It might be argued that the quality of the spider effects provided its own dampening of any horror. Although the spiders are very effective in some sequences, there is an awful lot of ropey blue (actually yellow) screen; some of the spiders are virtually static and obviously puppets; some just bob up and down on a visible wire. Indeed, visual effects designer Ian Scoones had made a huge, horror-movie type spider as a prototype for the story, which was vetoed by the production team as too terrifying. I watched this serial aged nine on its first broadcast and, as so often with 1970s *Doctor Who*, was quite aware that the effects weren't terribly good. This at once took the edge off my fear while it in no way interfered with my enjoyment of the story: ropey special effects was something you accepted at the time, put to one side, and then got engrossed in the plot. Anyway, the spiders scared me much less than the materialisation of the false Aggedor in the same season's "The Monster of Peladon"(1974): my twin brother and I delighted in terrifying each other as we climbed up our house's darkened stairs by imitating the noise of the monster's materialisation.

The BBC's research in the early 1970s confirmed that 60% of *Doctor Who*'s audience were adults; although it was perceived as a children's programme, only 40% of the audience actually were children. At the same time, an internal report by the corporation into violence on television revealed that the pre-watershed *Doctor Who* was the most violent of its dramatic fiction series, with an average of four violent incidents per twenty five minute episode. The first Doctor, William Hartnell, claimed around this time that he had left the programme in 1966 because it was no longer made for children and that too much evil had entered into the spirit of the thing. This may have been a case of rationalising after the event; Hartnell had been ill and exhausted after three years in such a demanding role. Jon Pertwee said he was sometimes approached by parents who complained to him that *Doctor Who* was much too frightening for their children. "Well, it's very simple," he replied to them, "You reach out for the on/off switch on your television and turn it to the 'off' position."

Regular repeats of Pertwee adventures were one splendid innovation of his time as the Doctor. The black and white stories had been very seldom repeated, presumably because of the hassle of negotiating repeat fees with the actors' union, Equity. There had in fact been only two repeats in the 1960s: "An Unearthly Child" was reshown before the second episode for the benefit of those who had understandably concentrated on President Kennedy's assassination a week before and "The Evil of the Daleks" (1967) was repeated to fill the gap between the fifth and sixth seasons over the summer break. In Pertwee's time, repeats took the form of (heavily cut) episodes edited together to make a feature film, and fans' hearts leapt when they read the words, "A complete adventure in one programme" in the *Radio Times*. The BBC presumably thought that people wouldn't have the patience to sit through unedited episodes; having seen them once already, would people really want to sit through all those title sequences and cliffhangers again? The same thinking prevailed when *Doctor Who* was first released on VHS in 1984 with the 1975 story "Revenge of the Cybermen", which had its opening titles and cliffhangers lopped off. Such editing wasn't confined to *Doctor Who* video releases: even the first commercial videos of *Fawlty Towers* cut most of the title sequence because it was though viewers wouldn't have the patience to sit through them. Video tape buyers protested that they didn't want their programmes cut, and BBC Enterprises graciously conceded the point; they were happily able to release the programmes on video again, uncut, to a public that was thrilled to pay for them twice over.

Back in the 1970s, however, the repackaging of episodes into feature film repeats was determined by the still-prevailing notion that television was trivia and ephemera; cutting it didn't really matter. The same notion dictated the wholesale burning of old episodes. The stories weren't best served by cutting them: chunks of story disappeared, rendering the plotting as incoherent as some of the Sylvester McCoy episodes. Furthermore, the pacing no longer really worked. *Doctor Who* episodes were designed to build to a climax every twenty two (or so) minutes: it seemed very lame to have our heroes facing certain death one minute and perfectly safe the next. The same objections were raised by some viewers in the United States at the end of the 1970s, whose local public broadcasting stations opted to show episodes as TV movies with the opening and closing titles removed (although not as heavily cut as the BBC in house compilation repeats). Similarly, script editor Eric Saward and other writers said how difficult it was to write forty five minute episodes for Colin Baker's first season, arguing that *Doctor Who* lent itself best to short, twenty five minute, bite-sized instalments.

In spite of all these objections, the repeats were a huge treat for young fans who were desperate to see old stories again. These were the days before Target books made it possible to relive old adventures through the novelisations (indeed, some have argued that one reason people consider Pertwee adventures so good is because the novels are so good: returning to the original programme, some viewers were disappointed); only those with expensive cassette recorders could tape the soundtrack and there was, of course, no home video. "The Sea Devils", "The Green Death" and "Planet of the Spiders" were repeated as TV movies. The BBC started to screen the Peter Cushing Dalek movies on a regular basis, sometimes as replacements for rained-off test cricket; it even showed the compilation of "The Sea Devils" as a cricket substitute. Much to my rage, I missed it. A few of the Tom Baker stories were repeated as edited movies: "The Ark in Space" (1975) was cut together; "Genesis of the Daleks" (1975) was first repeated over the Christmas holidays. "The Sontaran Experiment" (1975) was shown as one programme, but as it was only two episodes long, it didn't need to be cut. In Tom Baker's time as the Doctor, the BBC realised that tastes had changed and viewers would accept unedited repeats. A pattern emerged of a couple of stories being repeated every year over the summer holidays, often with one episode being screened every evening. These were eagerly awaited by fans and the viewing figures held up well for the time of the year.

*

With four seasons under his belt, Pertwee felt that the team around him was breaking up. Katy Manning had announced her intention to leave at the end of the tenth season; Barry Letts and Terrance Dicks also intended to move on to new projects. The death of Roger Delgado had affected Pertwee and the whole cast; with so many others departing, he felt the time was right to move on as well. In his one man show "An Evening with Jon Pertwee", which successfully toured British theatres in the 1990s, Pertwee repeated the story that he had been prepared to stay for the twelfth season but had asked for more money. The BBC declined and Pertwee moved on. Years later, Barry Letts questioned the story's veracity. If Pertwee had wanted to stay and had asked for a rise in his fee, he would have approached Letts who would, in turn, have asked for a bigger budget from Shaun Sutton, the Head of Drama, to cover the star's pay rise. This was the normal procedure in BBC television. Letts said no such approach was made. It is also suggested that Pertwee was actually *offered* a sixth season as the Doctor, but turned it down. He would leave at the end of season eleven.

Season eleven introduced Sarah Jane Smith as the new companion. Elisabeth Sladen, who played her, recalled that Pertwee missed Katy Manning very much during the filming of his final season and became more withdrawn as the season went on; he would sit aside and answer his fan mail instead of chatting with the other actors between scenes. Pertwee was mentally preparing himself to break from the series. When he filmed the regeneration scene with Tom Baker, the two actors barely spoke to one another. It was an understandably difficult time for a man who had starred in the show for five years. Another factor which had perhaps upset the equilibrium in the final season was the fact that Sladen wasn't the first actress who had been tried for Sarah Jane. Some rehearsals and even shooting had begun with another actress who was apparently too buxom for the role (a disadvantage when running down corridors). Elisabeth Sladen was cast and almost immediately bussed down to the location filming for "The Time Warrior" (1974), the first story of the new season. Sladen hadn't been to a rehearsal or read through; these had been completed with the other actress and the show had to stay on schedule.

Some critics have argued that Pertwee became bored with the series in his final season, and his boredom is sometimes reflected in his performance. He certainly admitted to impatience with the scripts, and not just in his final season. Interviewed in the 1970s, he stated that some of the scripts he did were absolutely dreadful, all of them six episodes. He did, however, like Robert Sloman's stories, and hardly altered a line of them; others, he altered a very great deal. Terrance Dicks recalled that Pertwee particularly disliked what *Star Trek* fans call "technobabble" – pseudo-scientific gobbledegook uttered to explain away an unlikely event or to move the plot forward. Pertwee did, however, once tell Dicks that he liked a line saying he was to "reverse the polarity of the neutron flow": easy to remember and it tripped off the tongue. Pertwee used variations of the line in several of his stories and it became something of a catchphrase. At conventions in the 1980s he apparently sang about the Doctor's early days to a tune from Gilbert and Sullivan's comic opera *HMS Pinafore*: "When I was a lad I served a term, As office boy to a Gallifreyan firm, When they shouted "Jump!" I had to go And reverse the polarity of the neutron flow... I reversed that flow so easily, That I vowed I'd do it twice before episode three." Dicks gave Pertwee the line in the twentieth anniversary special "The Five Doctors" (1983), and he smiles as he says it, perhaps relishing its repetition. He said it again in the run of the 1988 stage play *Doctor Who – The Ultimate Adventure*, again by Dicks. When Colin Baker replaced Pertwee as the Doctor later in the show's run, the line was changed as it was considered only suitable for the Third Doctor.

Bored or not, Pertwee was given a run for his money in his final season. He loved gadgetry and often drew the production team's attention to new vehicles: he found the balloon-wheeled, powered tricycles that the Doctor and Jo escape on in "Day of the Daleks" (1972). In fact, the tricycles didn't go very fast, so the Ogrons chasing them had to move *very slowly*. Pertwee had a futuristic car called "the Alien" designed and built for himself. It resembled a small silver hovercraft with wings sweeping towards its tail; the police banned him from driving it in traffic as other drivers, watching it with amazement, took their eyes off the road. As the Whomobile, it appeared in "Invasion of the Dinosaurs" and "Planet of the Spiders", where, in a very unconvincing blue (actually yellow) screen sequence, it is seen to fly. Being Pertwee's own property, the Whomobile vanished from the series when Tom Baker took over and the Fourth Doctor had to make do with Bessie. Part two of "Planet of the Spiders", Pertwee's swan song, is a very long chase between the Doctor and Lupton, who has stolen the blue crystal from Metebelis III that is vital to the plans for universal domination of various arachnid factions. The Doctor pursues Lupton in a one man helicopter, the Whomobile, Bessie and a hovercraft. The sequence was exciting on first viewing but entirely superfluous to the story: its one advantage was that it could be neatly pruned out of the compilation repeat.

"Planet of the Spiders" is a splendid, Buddhist-influenced tale by Barry Letts and Robert Sloman (although only Sloman is credited). It refers back to events in "The Green Death", a year before. A running joke in the series had been the Doctor's wish to take Jo to Metebelis III, the fabulous blue planet of the Actaeon galaxy. He eventually manages this in episode one, and is attacked by giant eagles and tentacle plant life for his pains. He does, however, manage to get hold of one of the blue Metebelis crystals, which he brings back to Earth. These have strange powers: they can clear the mind and amplify its powers; the Doctor uses his to release Mike from his programming by BOSS to murder him. In "Planet of the Spiders", a mentally handicapped worker in the community called Tommy is "cured" by the crystal and goes from reading Ladybird early readers to William Blake in the same evening.

In episode one, Mike Yates and Sarah are investigating strange goings on in a meditation centre in "darkest Mummerset" (Sarah's words). They discover that the guests' meditations have formed a link with the giant spiders in the far future of Metebelis III. One of the guests, Lupton, allows a spider (they are about fifteen inches in diameter) to jump on his back and share his mind. Lupton is a convincing study of a small-minded, embittered, twisted man: once sales manager of his firm, he was broken and dismissed by bullying managers; he now seeks to use the spiders' power to take his revenge on his managers by dominating the whole Earth. The other members of the meditation community are similar unfortunates suffering from stress: one of their number, Barnes, says that he came to the community in search of peace of mind. They are broken enough to be dominated by Lupton and the spiders.

The monastery is led by Cho-Je, a Tibetan monk, and the mysterious abbot K'Anpo Rinpoche, whom no-one ever sees. Cho-Je warns his western disciples against the demons and divinities which they may encounter in the course of their meditations; he later identifies the spiders as such, thus confirming their symbolic function as representations of their human carriers' repressed greed, desire and rage. The Doctor and Sarah eventually meet the Abbot in episode five. The Doctor asks if they have met before and, in one of the Pertwee era's most effective scenes, remembers K'anpo as the old hermit who lived behind his house on Gallifrey. K'anpo is a Time Lord and the Doctor's guru (in a reference to the Eastern religions in which Westerners were becoming increasingly interested at the time of the story's broadcast). He tells the Doctor that he must return the Metebelis crystal to the Great One, a spider the size of a cathedral that thirsts and aches for it to complete her web, giving her power over all of time and space and turning her into God. She taunts the Doctor that he is afraid of her ("You are not accustomed to feeling frightened, are you, Doctor? You are very wise to be afraid of me!") and K'anpo tells him that he must face his worst fear. As the smaller spiders represent the lesser humans' repressed darkness, so the Great One represents the Doctor's greed: he explains this to Sarah as his greed for knowledge, for information. If he hadn't gone to fetch the crystal in "The Green Death", none of these events would have happened. The Doctor accepts that all the story's horrors are basically his own fault: to make amends and to atone, he must give the crystal to the Great One even though the radiation in its cave will destroy him. The Doctor does so; the power from the completed web is too great and destroys the Great One; the Doctor is lost in the time vortex until the TARDIS brings him home, to UNIT headquarters. Before the eyes of the Brigadier and Sarah, he regenerates.

Much of "Planet of the Spiders" is excellent. John Dearth, who had voiced BOSS in "The Green Death", steals the show as the scruffy, villainous Lupton; the actresses who provide the spiders' voices – including Kismet Delgado, Roger's widow – are wonderful in their hysteria and absolute conviction. The story prepares for the new Doctor by using the term "regeneration" for the first time in the series; K'anpo is attacked by the possessed humans, collapses and regenerates into Cho-Je. Cho-Je is, of course, a projection of K'anpo's own self and doesn't really exist: this puzzles the Doctor and indicates K'anpo's highly developed mental powers as a very senior Time Lord. The scenes set on Metebelis III aren't nearly as dreadful as some claim: there is some ropey acting from the human natives but at least we get to see Gareth Hunt in his pre-*New Avengers* days sporting a gringo moustache as Arak, the leader of the two legs. (The spiders dislike being called "spiders" and, in a piece of intelligent verbal coinage, insist on being called "the eight legs"; the word "spider" is forbidden and insulting. Humans are dismissively termed "two legs", thus building on Orwell's slogan in *Animal Farm* : eight legs good, two legs bad.) Robert Sloman recently said he was unhappy about the treatment of Tommy and argued that such a piece of scripting wouldn't be considered now: who are we, he asked, to sit in judgement over the unfortunate? For children watching at the time, however, Tommy was an attractive and sympathetic character whom they immediately liked: my nine year old self was horrified to see him mistreated by Barnes and Lupton, who made him cry. John Kane, who played Tommy, was a veteran of the Royal Shakespeare Company and gives a beautiful and rounded performance. We might object now to the word "cured" to describe the change that has come over him, but it is still touching to see that he is not affected by the rays of energy with which the spiders' servants blast down their victims; nor is Mike Yates. "His compassion protected him," K'anpo explains to Sarah, "just as Tommy's innocence was his shield." This is a powerful metaphor for the qualities which evil can never overcome. Equally poignant is an exchange between Tommy and Sarah: noticing his change, Sarah exclaims, "But you're different! You're just like everybody else!" Glancing at the murderers, sinners and misfits around him, Tommy replies, "I sincerely hope not."

There is also some critical objection to the supposedly Tibetan K'anpo and Cho-Je being played by a white British and a white Australian actor respectively (George Cormack and Kevin Lindsay, who had played Lynx the Sontaran at the beginning of the season). In the highly-regarded Tom Baker story "The Talons of Weng-Chiang" (1977), the leading Chinese character was played by the white Englishman John Bennett, under heavy make-up. Smaller Chinese parts were played by Chinese actors and the serial is considered racist by some. On the other hand, the Chinese characters are partly seen through the eyes of racist white characters in the nineteenth century, who spout the Imperialist platitudes of their time, and are not really allowed to speak for themselves, unless it is in poor English ("Bag gone, Lord!"). It could even be argued that the Chinese tong members are stock characters, rather than stereotypes. Such arguments wouldn't wash with the Australian Broadcasting Authority, which refused to show the serial. Racial politics in the entertainment business was crude in the 1970s. It was not until the end of the decade that directors started to listen seriously, for example, to black actors' objections to Othello being played by a white actor in make-up. The part is never now played by a white actor (except for one production starring Patrick Stewart – Captain Jean Luc Picard in *Star Trek: the Next Generation* – in which Othello was white and all the other characters were black). There are distant echoes of this controversy over the portrayal of other nationalities in the objections to "Dalek" (2005). Some American fans argued that the serial was anti-American because a) Van Statten is the villain and b) Van Statten is American. By this reasoning, we could argue that "The Seeds of Doom" (1976) is anti-British because a) the villain, Harrison Chase, is British and b) he is a baddie. Nevertheless, the revived, post-2005 series is much more inclusive in casting non-Caucasian actors in lead roles and cannot be accused, unlike the original series, of unintentional racism.

7

Fourth Time Lucky

With shooting on 1973's season eleven well underway, it fell to Barry Letts to find a new Doctor. Many actors were considered and invited to meet Letts at the BBC. He usually greeted them with the formula that he wasn't offering them the part, but if it were to be offered to them, would they be interested? Several distinguished actors were under serious consideration. One was Michael Bentine, an actor and comedian who had found fame for his collaboration with *The Goons*, the long-running radio comedy by Spike Milligan featuring Milligan, Peter Sellars and Harry Secombe. Bentine said he was interested but insisted that he would have to have considerable input into rewriting the scripts: this was how he had always worked and he expected to have the same latitude on *Doctor Who*. This wasn't the way *Doctor Who* worked, however, and Letts passed over Bentine.

Another actor who was interviewed was Richard Hearne, who had played the popular children's character Mr Pastry. Letts recalled that Hearne didn't seem to understand what he was being offered: he said that he liked *Doctor Who* but that he didn't think that Mr Pastry was right for the character and they weren't the same at all. Letts moved on to consider Jim Dale, a lead in many of the *Carry On* films, who might have recalled the comic persona of Troughton. Dale was flattered and interested, although the discussions ultimately came to nothing. Graham Crowden was also interviewed: he said he would enjoy it but might want to leave after one year if there was a lovely part going at the National Theatre. One year wasn't enough (although it was for Christopher Eccleston), and Crowden put out himself out of the running. Letts and Dicks thought of Fulton Mackay, who became famous as the disciplinarian prison office Mr Mackay in *Porridge* (BBC 1974-1977). Mackay had played Dr Quinn to perfection in "Doctor Who and the Silurians"; Letts and Dicks considered him a fine actor who, like Troughton and unlike Pertwee, would give a performance that was quite unlike his private self. Again, this discussion came to nothing.

Time was getting on and the new actor would have to be cast soon if he were to rehearse the shows for the new season. Bill Slater, the Head of Serials at the BBC, asked Letts if he had considered an actor called Tom Baker? Baker was a National Theatre player and had been the lead in Slater's BBC production of *The Millionairess* by George Bernard Shaw, which co-starred Maggie Smith. Letts and Dicks interviewed Tom

Baker in their BBC office and were immediately enthusiastic about him playing the Doctor. Letts told Baker that he seemed ideal, but the problem was that he had never seen him act. Tom Baker replied that he had played the villain in the feature film *The Golden Voyage of Sinbad*, then showing in London, and Letts and Dicks could see him in that, if they liked. Producer and script editor took an afternoon off from the office to see the film, loved Baker's performance as the wicked magician, and cast him as the Doctor.

The BBC had let it be known that Jon Pertwee would leave the programme at the end of the season and that the search was on for the new Doctor Who (sic). Baker's casting was announced while "The Monster of Peladon" was airing on television. He appeared in the papers aside Elisabeth Sladen and a Cyberman from "The Invasion" (1968) (regular Pat Gorman in the costume). As a child, I was horrified to see him in my father's *Guardian* newspaper. How could this man be the Doctor? I only had vague memories of Patrick Troughton and, aside from the Peter Cushing films, only knew Jon Pertwee as the Doctor. Certainly, Tom Baker was virtually unknown among the public at the time, yet he became arguably the most successful of the Doctors, playing the role for longer than anyone – seven seasons to Pertwee's five – and dominating viewers' conception of what it meant to be the Doctor for the rest of the original show's run. Colin Baker said people who recognised him as the Doctor kept asking, "Where's your scarf?", which had been Tom Baker's distinguishing item of dress. Just weeks before the series returned in 2005, *The Observer* hoped that Christopher Eccleston would be wearing the "loop the loop" scarf. Baker came into the studio to record the transformation scene for "Planet of the Spiders"; he changed into Jon Pertwee's costume and the regeneration was achieved by a simple cross-fade between the actors.

The regeneration scene completed, and broadcast on 8th June 1974, an alternative fourth Doctor was soon to be on offer at the Adelphi Theatre in London. Christmas 1974 saw the debut of Terrance Dicks's play *Doctor Who and the Daleks in Seven Keys to Doomsday*. Never since the clumsily titled film *Daleks: Invasion Earth 2150 AD* (1966) had there been such a mouthful of a title for a *Doctor Who* spin off, but the play's producers presumably thought that "*Doctor Who* **and** the Daleks" was a bigger pull than *Doctor Who* alone. Indeed, some viewers who had only a glancing acquaintance with the series thought it was called "*Doctor Who and the Daleks*" anyway; various friends in the primary school playground had sometimes tried to convince me that the show's original monsters had always been the Daleks and other creatures had only arrived much,

much later. They were presumably repeating their parents' imperfect memories of the Hartnell era, when, granted, there *were* lots of Dalek episodes, but I knew better and wasn't having any of it.

This was the second commercial *Doctor Who* play after *Curse of the Daleks* by David Whitaker in the early 1960s. *Seven Keys to Doomsday* begins with a projected film sequence of Jon Pertwee collapsing. On stage, the Doctor gets up not in the form of television Doctor Tom Baker (whose first episode had not yet been screened) but as Trevor Martin, an actor who had played a Time Lord in "The War Games" (1969). Two youngsters rush onto the stage from the front row of the audience: these were to be the Doctor's companions for his adventure and one of them, Jenny, was played by Wendy Padbury (Zoe in Troughton's final season). The plot rattles along cheerfully: in an echo of "The Keys of Marinus" (1964) and anticipating the Key to Time season (1978-9), the Doctor must collect seven keys from Karn in order to thwart the Daleks' schemes. He is opposed by the Master of Karn, played by Simon Jones (who was to become the original Arthur Dent in *The Hitchhiker's Guide to the Galaxy*), and crocodile-like humanoids called Clawrantulas.

The play's run was curtailed by fears of an IRA bombing campaign in the capital: they had already bombed pubs in Guildford, only a few miles from London, and in Birmingham. Television advertisements for the play were put out in the ITV London region in an attempt to drum up punters. These consisted of a caption of the poster with a Dalek voice announcing "Doctor Who and the Daleks at the Adelphi Theatre in London" and were about ten seconds long, but they failed to entice a scared public into the west end and *Seven Keys to Doomsday* closed early. A kindly family friend had tickets to take my brother and me to the play but the performance was cancelled. The kindly family friend asked if we would like to see *The Sound of Music* (or some such thing) instead, an offer that we rejected with the utmost scorn. Terrance Dicks re-used some of the plot elements of the play in "The Brain of Morbius" (1976), including the name Karn for the planet, but the show was never revived until it was issued as an audio play in 2008 by the company Big Finish, which had released many original *Doctor Who* dramas. Trevor Martin reprised his role as the Doctor.

Tom Baker's first story, "Robot" (1974-5) was the last to be produced by Barry Letts. Terrance Dicks wrote it as a freelance writer, having handed script editing duties over to Robert Holmes. Dicks had persuaded the BBC that it was always a *Doctor Who* tradition that the outgoing script editor wrote the first story of the new season; the BBC bought the idea, which Dicks had just then made up.

"Robot" was essentially a Pertwee story with a new Doctor: the Brigadier, Benton and Sarah Jane were all present and the Doctor continued to work for UNIT. It was made back-to-back with "Planet of the Spiders" and Elisabeth Sladen had to use her rest days from that serial to go and shoot its location sequences. Dicks wrote the new Doctor as an essentially generic Doctor: he is eccentric, excitable, brilliant and very funny. I remember one of my brothers remarking on the first episode, in the non-politically correct language of the time, "Well, Patrick Troughton was a clown but this new Doctor is a loony." Dicks admitted that he had written the part as very eccentric, but said that future script editors could tone the Doctor down if they wanted to, and anyway, his manic nature could always be put down to the unsettling effects of his latest regeneration.

Like Malcolm Hulke before him, Dicks concentrated as a freelance writer on prose after leaving the show, writing the bulk of the *Doctor Who* novelisations. He adapted his own stories and, if the script writer didn't want to write the book, would make him a reasonable offer: I do the work and you get half the money. Robert Holmes was quite happy for Dicks to write up his stories, saying that he found writing prose fiction about as much fun as digging trenches. By the end of the seventies, Terrance Dicks was writing about nine books a year and had established a shorthand for descriptions. These became affectionately regarded, and occasionally parodied, by fans: the Fourth Doctor was "a tall man in a collection of vaguely bohemian looking garments… a broad brimmed hat jammed onto a mop of curly hair"; the TARDIS's materialisation and dematerialisation noise (originally created by recording and distorting the noise of a key running down the strings of a grand piano) was "a wheezing, groaning sound". Fans laughed at the endless repetition of this image, so Dicks amended it in a much later novel to, "a *defiant* wheezing, groaning sound." The books contributed enormously to children's literacy in the United Kingdom and were in constant demand in school libraries. Some people came to *Doctor Who* through the novelisations rather than the televisions series. Novelist Eion Colfer spent his childhood reading them and only caught the TV series later. It was Hartnell who most clearly matched the Doctor of his imagination and Colfer duly used Hartnell's Doctor in his e-book *A Big Hand for the Doctor* in January 2013. The novelisations were celebrated by Mark Gatiss in a BBC Radio Four documentary in 2008; a correspondent to *The Times Educational Supplement* lamented the lack of novels based on the revived series, arguing that some children needed to have visual images (here, memories of a television programme) to support their reading. The BBC was producing original *Doctor Who* novels from 2005, rather than novelisations, and presumably felt that there was a limit to the number of types of *Doctor Who* books that shops would take. Besides, the new series was endlessly repeated on BBC 3 and freely available on DVD; a major reason for the success of the original novels – which sold over eight million copies across the range – was that they were a record of a programme that was usually only screened once. Nevertheless, the BBC did reprint some of the old Target novelisations, five in 2011 and another five in 2012, with new introductions by *Who* luminaries and notes on the text's puzzling contemporary references to, for example, feet and inches, rather than centimetres.

In "Robot", the Doctor regenerates under the eyes of Sarah and the Brigadier. Dicks felt the dramatic crux of whether the new Doctor is who he says he is had been dealt with before (in "The Power of the Daleks" (1966) and "Spearhead from Space" (1970)) and repeating it would get in the way of telling the story. The new Doctor is provided with a new assistant. This is Lieutenant Surgeon Harry Sullivan, on secondment to UNIT from the Royal Navy, played by the square jawed, good looking Ian Marter. Barry Letts had cast him before the Doctor was cast; it was felt that Harry, a young action hero, could handle the rough stuff if an older actor as the Doctor could not. As Tom Baker was then forty, the Doctor was quite capable of looking after himself in a fight, and this function of Harry's character quickly became redundant. Nevertheless, he was an engaging and entertaining companion, British to the core and liable to call Sarah "old thing" or "old girl", and exclaim "I say!" at the sight of a new wonder. When he disguises himself as a man from the Ministry in order to infiltrate the sinister Think Tank organisation, he sports a bowler hat and looks just like John Steed from *The Avengers*. Sarah confirms his status as a hallmarked English hero by telling him that his undercover work gives him the chance "to be a real James Bond".

Tom Baker liked the script of "Robot" and gives a splendid performance as the Doctor. He is clearly working very hard, in his first few stories, to give a performance; he relaxed more into the role by the end of the season and thereafter apparently played the part effortlessly. Tom Baker admitted that the best way to play a benevolent alien with secrets was to play it as Tom Baker; unlike Troughton, but like Pertwee, he played the Doctor as himself.

In the first episode, the Doctor vanishes into the TARDIS to find a new outfit: he appears, with astonishing rapidity, as a Viking and a Pierrot. The Brigadier objects, reminding him that UNIT is a secret organisation: "Do you think I might attract attention?" asks the Doctor, wide eyed under a huge Viking helm; "It's just possible," the Brigadier replies, stony faced. The Doctor's final outfit is the familiar Bohemian collection of red corduroy jacket, golfing jumper, tie, floppy hat and enormously long scarf, a much more anarchic assembly than Pertwee's smart velvet jackets. The costume was designed by James Acheson (who eventually designed the film *The Last Emperor* (1987)) and inspired by Henri de Toulouse Lautrec's poster for the nightclub star Aristide Bruant: Bruant's heroic, striding pose in the poster is exactly right for the new Doctor. A lady called Begonia Pope was asked to knit the scarf; nobody told her how long it should be and she used all the wool she was given. The finished article was about fourteen feet long and was immediately adopted into the new Doctor's costume and repertoire. By the end of part two of "Robot", he is stretching it between two pillars in an attempt to trip the Robot up, and Tom Baker devised business with the scarf throughout his seven year run. The scarf did for him on location filming for his third story "The Sontaran Experiment" (1975): Baker tripped over it on location in Dartmoor, broke his collar bone and had to be taken to hospital. Without the Doctor, the production team hurriedly decided to carry on filming with Baker's stuntman Terry Walsh playing the Doctor in long shot, Walsh imitating Tom Baker's loping stride. When he returned from hospital, a somewhat immobile Tom Baker shot all the close ups, the scarf concealing his neck brace.

"Robot" is a good, straightforward story designed to introduce the new Doctor. The plans and parts for a new disintegrator gun are stolen; several people are killed in the robberies and one involves a tunnel into a subterranean vault. Benton observes that it has no pit props and whoever was in it wouldn't have been able to breathe; the Doctor replies darkly that whoever was in it wouldn't have needed to breathe. The culprit is experimental Robot K1, designed by the environmentalist Professor Kettlewell; made of living metal, with the capacity to grow, it can think and has been imprinted with the Professor's own principles. Unfortunately, the Robot has become a weapon in the hands of the Scientific Reform Society (SRS), a crackpot organisation led by Miss Hilda Winters that wants to reorganise the world along "scientific" (i.e. totalitarian) lines. Forced to go against Kettlewell's prime directive ("I must serve humanity and never harm it"), it goes mad. The SRS gets hold of the launch codes for the world's nuclear weapons, which the governments of the world handed over to a responsible power. This power would publish them if international tension looked likely to develop into nuclear war; faced with other governments accessing and perhaps using their missiles against their own countries, the nuclear powers would back down. "Naturally enough," states the Brigadier, "the only country that could be trusted with them was Great Britain." "Well naturally," replies the Doctor, "I mean, all the rest were foreigners." The disintegrator gun is built and assembled, the SRS retreats into a nuclear bunker to blackmail the world, and the Brigadier attempts to dispose of the Robot using the disintegrator gun. Unfortunately, the energy released causes the Robot to grow to giant size: the Doctor eventually destroys it with a virus which attacks Kettlewell's living metal.

Terrance Dicks admitted that the story was heavily influenced by the movie *King Kong* (1933). Sarah strikes up a friendship with the Robot, as Fay Wray had become attached to Kong, and Sarah is similarly saved by the beast when the giant Robot goes on the rampage. This borrowing was perhaps inspired by a maxim of Malcolm Hulke's, often quoted by Terrance Dicks: "What *Doctor Who* needs is good, original ideas. They do not, however, have to be your good, original ideas." The new producer, Philip Hinchcliffe, who took over after "Robot", and his script editor Robert Holmes shamelessly raided the movies and stories of popular culture for the three years of their tenure. The SRS is the sort of tin-pot fascist organisation that sprang up in Germany in the 1920s. Its origins can be seen by removing its middle letter, and one of its nerdy members, who tells Sarah her trouser suit would forbidden in the new order, is described as a "Himmler type" in the script.

Sarah, who refused to be patronised by the Doctor in her first season, had been introduced as a response to the feminism which was now coming into mainstream popular consciousness; in the early 1970s, news magazine programmes, like the BBC's *Nationwide*, had invited feminist thinkers to appear so that they could be chortled at for suggesting we should use such outrageous terms as "chairperson" or "house husband". Dicks decided to make "Robot"'s villain a woman in response to the agitation for women to be more visible in society. This was a sympathetic attempt to give a strong female role to a character in a drama, and a meaty part for an actress, but Miss Winters herself comes across as suggesting the stereotyped feminist. She wears glasses, is strident and apparently uninterested in men, shouts, and is aggressive. On the other hand, and following the fascist origins of the SRS, such women had crewed the concentration camps; the horror felt by the

Allies at finding some of the most vicious SS guards were female had quickly killed off the patronising nineteenth century assumption that women were naturally the gentler sex. Miss Winters was, in any case, one of the more successful and believable of *Doctor Who*'s few female villains. A previous villainess had been vetoed. Michael Briant had cast Susan Jameson as the IMC's vicious security chief Morgan in "Colony in Space" (1971), but reports of a female sadist wearing pvc and shooting colonists had caused cluckings of alarm in the top floor of the BBC, who demanded that Morgan's gender was changed. Susan Jameson was paid off and the part went instead to Tony Caunter. In "Robot", the Brigadier pulls a gun on Miss Winters and orders her to cancel the destructor codes; she taunts him by saying, "You won't shoot, Brigadier," which is of course true: the Brigadier could *never* shoot a lady. Sarah, however, has no such qualms, and trains the gun on Miss Winters, who backs down.

"Robot" was directed by Christopher Barry, a veteran *Doctor Who* director. He was perhaps chosen because of his experience in introducing a new Doctor to the public: he had previously directed "The Power of the Daleks" (1966), Troughton's first serial. Mindful of the problem of mixing film and video which had marred so many composite shots in the previous season's "Invasion of the Dinosaurs", Letts and Barry opted to shoot all location sequences on video. Previous stories had always shot location sequences on film, not least because film cameras were portable while video cameras were lumbering monsters. However, the BBC had recently invested in new, lightweight video cameras designed for outside broadcasts: these had been successfully used to shoot an episode of *Z Cars*, the BBC's long-running police drama, and "Robot" was the second BBC production to use them. Rodney Bennett employed them again to shoot "The Sontaran Experiment", which was entirely made on location. With studio and location footage on video, the sequences with the Robot at giant size were combined with a degree of success: the sequences are certainly much more effective than the risible dinosaurs. The Robot strode around a blue screen set (in fact, with yellow used as the keying-in colour), smashing down model telegraph poles and stomping on miniature wooden huts. Viewing the rushes, it was found that the Robot's silver costume reflected the yellow of the keying-in colour; when the location footage was added, his legs kept disappearing and a reshoot was ordered. There are still some see-through legs in the final programme, but the money had run out, as it had for the tank ordered up by the Brigadier to take care of K1. With no time or money, the production team opted to use an Action Man toy tank against blue screen: fans cringed with embarrassment and their enemies chortled with glee, ready to tease them about the dreadful shot when schools resumed after Christmas.

Much of the production's effectiveness comes from James Acheson's wonderful design of the Robot. Dicks had wanted it to be massive and terrifying, yet human and appealing as well. Acheson's design succeeded on all counts, not least because its fan-shaped head grille suggests eyebrows raised in puzzlement at the terrible orders it is given. The Robot was played by Michael Kilgarriff, who had been an Ogron in "Frontier in Space" (1973) and the Cybercontroller in "The Tomb of the Cybermen" (1967) (and, later, in "Attack of the Cybermen" (1985)). His Robot costume was so heavy that he wore a lightweight foil and balsa version for rehearsals. In an interview, he recalled that he couldn't get up when he fell over but lay there like an upturned beetle; he also lacerated his legs from the sharp edges of the aluminium. The Robot costume still exists and was for many years displayed in the window of the Museum of the Moving Image on London's South Bank; Terrance Dicks said he liked to wander over to it when passing, "to have a look at my Robot".

Terrance Dicks and Barry Letts moved on after "Robot", although both were to return. Dicks wrote more stories for the show and Letts directed "The Android Invasion" (1975) before returning as executive producer for Tom Baker's final series, mentoring the inexperienced producer John Nathan-Turner. Back in 1974, Robert Holmes continued as script editor and Philip Hinchcliffe took up the reins of producer. They faced a similar situation to their predecessors in 1970 in that a previous production team had set the shape of the new season, commissioning stories which neither much liked. Bob Baker and Dave Martin had provided another Sontaran tale; the Cybermen were to return after an absence of seven years; John Lucarotti had submitted an unfilmable science fiction story and Terry Nation had turned in the third Dalek story in as many years. Lucarotti had written three historical stories for Hartnell's Doctor: the well regarded "Marco Polo" (1964, the fourth story of the first season), "The Aztecs" (1964) and the curiosity "The Massacre" (1966), concerning the slaughter of Huguenots on St Bartholemew's Eve by Catholics in Paris in 1572. The latter tale hadn't been well regarded by the then production team, who thought its subject matter too obscure for popular television; the then story editor Donald Tosh rewrote the scripts, to Lucarotti's dissatisfaction. What became "The Ark in Space" (1975) was Lucarotti's first science fiction script for *Doctor Who*: it was uneven in pacing and required special effects that were way beyond the series' budget. Robert Holmes completely rewrote the scripts and received the sole on-screen credit for the new story. In doing so, Holmes extended a practice which would last throughout his time as script editor and anticipate the way of working of the revived series' show runners, Russell T Davies and Steven Moffat: the script editor would rework scripts into the new house style, even undertaking root and branch re-workings of stories, and even rewriting scripts from experienced *Doctor Who* writers. It seems likely that Holmes wrote some of "Genesis of the Daleks" (1975); he certainly completely rewrote the twelfth season's final story, "Revenge of the Cybermen" (1975). This was to be made back-to-back with "The Ark in Space", using the same impressive sets of the Ark as a cost-saving measure.

Gerry Davis, who had created the Cybermen with Kit Pedlar, produced his first script for the programme in eight years. As "Return of the Cybermen", he confined the Cybermen to the Ark and included both the Doctor's five hundred year diary (a Troughton hallmark) and the destruction of the Cybermen by something called an X-ray laser. Philip Hinchcliffe immediately took exception to the latter as too childish. He wrote to Davis to explain that the show's audience was now proven to be much more dominated by adults than when Davis had been story-editor; some of them were very conversant with science and wouldn't put up with nonsense like an "X-ray laser". Holmes rewrote the script, introducing the Vogans and their planet of gold. Gerry Davis later said Holmes had done so because the BBC suddenly discovered it had more money than it thought, and that he didn't like what appeared on screen at all.

To be fair to Davis, "Revenge of the Cybermen" is one of the weakest of the early Tom Baker stories. There are only three Cybermen, their costumes slightly redressed versions from "The Invasion"; they want to destroy Voga because it supplied the gold ammunition which did for the Cybermen in the last Cyberwar. This new piece of Cybermen lore is only really sold to us by the absolute conviction with which Tom Baker delivers a line about the Cybermen being defeated by the advent of the "glitter gun". The Cyberleader is vastly overplayed and the Cybermen clump around the planet of gold for three episodes taking pot shots at the Vogans. Kevin Stoney, who played the villain Tobias Vaughn so marvellously in "The Invasion", turned up as Tyrum, leader of the Vogans, but he is wasted as a goodie and invisible under all the high forehead, heavy eyelidded Vogan make up.

The Vogan sequences were shot in Wookie Hole in Somerset, a cave system supposed to be haunted; Elisabeth Sladen was nearly killed when she was swept away by an underground river. She was saved by a stuntman just before she vanished with the water into a cave. Director Michael E. Briant thought the script dull and just an excuse to "bring back a boring monster"; he was wary of directing "The Robots of Death" in 1977, fearing that he would have to make yet more expressionless robot creatures exciting. Even the Doctor seems irritated by the Cybermen:

> You've no home planet, no influence, nothing. You're just a pathetic bunch of tin soldiers skulking around the galaxy in an ancient spaceship.

Hinchcliffe and Holmes intended to direct the programme towards the upper age range of the family audience. In doing so, more overt horror was allowed than had been the case in the Pertwee seasons and Hinchcliffe and Holmes were responsible for the three seasons that are among the most highly regarded of the programme's fifty years. The Fourth Doctor is less of a reassuring, fatherly figure than the Third and voyaging with him is not the comforting experience it had been for his companions. There is no longer the same sense that everything will be all right and they need only run to the Doctor for him to protect them: this new Doctor was apparently younger, more vulnerable, more liable to physical pain than his predecessor. In "Genesis of the Daleks", the Doctor is punched and beaten by Kaled soldiers. He appears quite as hurt as a human being would be, when Pertwee would have cried "Haiii!" and whisked them over his shoulder in no time. The new Doctor is also more alien, given to moods of distant abstraction when he stands, eyes wide and unblinking, gazing into the middle distance while the Morestrans strut around in "Planet of Evil" (1975) or Sarah tries to cheer him up in the first TARDIS scene of "Pyramids of Mars" (1975). (Mark Gatiss picked up on the Doctor's alien nature in his script for the third story of the revived show, "The Unquiet Dead" (2005). Christopher Eccleston's Doctor is at his most alien when he tells Rose that the Gelth's request for human cadavers as vehicles for their disembodied bodies is perfectly reasonable: she can get used to it, or go home.) The Doctor's universe is similarly a more frightening place as Hinchcliffe and Holmes immediately increased the horror content on Letts' departure: Styre the Sontaran tortures humans to death in experiments designed to test their weakness to invasion, which also gratify his sadism; Noah, the commander of the Ark in Space, slowly transforms into an insectoid Wirrn, the hideous new form burning into his flesh. Hinchcliffe also thought the UNIT set up was childish and silly, disliking what he referred to as all these soldiers running around shooting at things. The familiar characters of the Brigadier and Sergeant Benton were phased out after "Terror of the Zygons" (the first story of season thirteen) and Nicholas Courtney didn't return as the Brigadier until "Mawdryn Undead" in 1983. He had been was written into "The Android Invasion" (1975) and "The Seeds of Doom" (1976), but Courtney, seeing that his days as a regular were over, was unavailable and had returned to the theatre. He was replaced by Colonel Faraday (Patrick Newell, who had played Mother in *The Avengers*) and Major Beresford (John Acheson), two generic military types. There was an immediate rise in the number of complaints from viewers that the programme was now much too frightening. Holmes responded by saying that it should no longer be watched by small children. Nevertheless, all but one of the episodes in Tom Baker's first two seasons went out before 6.00 p.m., the watershed before which programmes were deemed suitable for everyone. The BBC belatedly rescheduled Tom Baker's third season after six o'clock, but concerns about its horrific content had by then become too entrenched to save Philip Hinchcliffe (see chapter eight, "Gothic Horror").

Unhappy with the Cybermen, the new production team was similarly unenthusiastic about the presence of a Dalek story in their first season. To the disappointment of younger viewers, both Daleks and Cybermen were unceremoniously dropped from the new two seasons in favour of new monsters. In a significant shift, single villainous figures like Davros, Sutekh, Morbius, Harrison Chase, Heironymous, Eldrad and Magnus Greel came to replace the uniform races of monsters favoured in the Pertwee years. These megalomaniacs and psychopaths are all too recognisable as science fiction representations of vicious twentieth century rulers; as such, they are arguably much more terrifying and plausible than, say, an undifferentiated cohort of Cybermen. They were also popular with actors. Michael Spice, who voiced Morbius and played Magnus Greel in "The Talons of Weng-Chiang" (1977), said that acting was usually about restraining emotions, suggesting moods with small changes in facial expressions and tone: he therefore loved playing Morbius and Greel because he could really let rip. Yet, in spite of Holmes and Hinchcliffe's unhappiness with the Daleks, "Genesis of the Daleks" (1975) is one of the most intelligent, best acted and best written of all the *Doctor Who* stories. It regularly won the "best ever story" award from readers of *Doctor Who* magazine, until it was knocked off its perch in the most recent (2009) one by "The Caves of Androzani" (1984), Peter Davison's swan song; Steven Moffat's "Blink" (2007) was second and "Genesis" came in at number three.

Barry Letts had commissioned Terry Nation to write him a third Dalek story in 1974. When the scripts came in, Letts spoke to Nation, saying, "It's a very good story, Terry, but you've sold it to us four times already." Nation, amused, asked what he meant and Letts detailed the list of plot elements he had used before. It is something of an axiom among fans that Nation's scripts are always the same: in "Planet of the Daleks" (1973), for example, Rebec hides inside a Dalek which the other Daleks blow up just after she has nipped out of it, as Ian had done in "The Daleks" (1964); the deadly Spiridon jungle is much the same as the deadly Kembel jungle in "Mission to the Unknown" (1965), killer plants and all. Letts said to Nation that he had never told us where the Daleks came from and asked him to write their origin story. Enthused, Terry Nation went away and came up with the scripts for "Genesis of the Daleks". Around this time, Terry Nation buttonholed Robert Holmes at a social event for *Who* writers and told him he thought there should be a Dalek story every year. Holmes, who hated the Daleks, replied, "Do you, Terry?" and wandered off. (Holmes, shadowing Terrance Dicks as script editor in 1974, had named Pertwee's final Dalek story "Death to the Daleks" as an expression of his disdain.) He was somewhat surprised to receive a letter from Nation's agent saying that he had agreed to commission a Dalek story annually from his client.

Presumably rewritten to some degree by Robert Holmes, "Genesis of the Daleks" (1975) is a fine piece of science fiction that debates the ethics of eugenics, genetic engineering and philosophy in the context of a strong adventure story. Forseeing a time when the Daleks will have dominated all other life forms, the Time Lords send the Doctor back to Skaro just before their creation. They give him three options: to avert their creation; to alter their genetic development, so that they evolve into less aggressive creatures, or to destroy them utterly. (Fan historians in 2005 argued that these are the first moves in the Time War which led to the annihilation of the Daleks and the Time Lords by the Doctor.) After a thousand years of war, Skaro is a hideous, barren wasteland peopled by mutations: the warring sides, the Thals and the Kaleds, have retreated to their respective cities under protective domes. The war is a virtual stalemate and resources are almost exhausted: Harry and Sarah observe that one of the dead soldiers wears both animal skins and synthetic fibres, and carries both a single shot rifle and a large ray gun (a prop reused from "Galaxy Four" (1965)). General Ravon, the very young general who interrogates Harry and the Doctor, informs his men that ammunition must be conserved: thus the time travellers will be hanged rather than taken out and shot, as in the past, as a happy piece of economy.

The Thals first appeared in the original Dalek story and returned in "Planet of the Daleks": the Kaleds are new to the series. Black haired when the Thals are blond, they are dominated by an elite scientific group which operates from its own bunker. This Elite is now so powerful it can demand anything it wants, much to the regular army's resentment. Their leader is Davros, a crippled scientist confined to his wheelchair. The Elite's original intention was to produce weapons capable of ending the war; they soon realised this was futile and directed their efforts towards the survival of their race. Davros has experimented on Kaled flesh, treated it with chemicals and finally discovered its ultimate evolutionary form: a shrivelled and malevolent green bundle of tissue. As it cannot survive without artificial intervention, this creature will clearly need a mobile machine as a life support unit. The mutation and the life support machine combine to become the Dalek: an anagram of the origin race, Kaled.

Davros, however, has become obsessed with the development of the Daleks: they are to be creatures made in his own megalomaniacal image, without morals and without pity, and eventually become his shock troops and bodyguard. Others among the Kaled scientists are alarmed: Ronson helps the Doctor and Harry escape, charging them to report Davros's experiments to the few members of the Kaled government who still have the power to stop him. Councillor Mogran orders an investigation, which Davros welcomes with great interest, agreeing to stop work on the Dalek project. He immediately betrays the Kaleds to the Thals, giving them the necessary chemical formula to allow their rocket to destroy the Kaled city; he has Ronson exterminated as the traitor responsible. The Doctor is recaptured and forced to tell Davros the reason for every Dalek defeat in the future: they will be programmed with this knowledge and there will be no defeats. Davros explains that the Doctor will tell him because "You are afflicted with a conscience": if he does not co-operate, and in a scene which exemplifies the fearless approach to violence of the new production team, Harry and Sarah will be tortured to death in front of him.

In a quiet conversation after this session, Davros plays the kindly host and offers to talk to the Doctor "as men of science". Davros argues that the Daleks are not a power of evil, but of good: when all other life forms are suppressed, then there will be peace. Nation here emphasises that Davros is evil because he believes, as did the Nazis on whom he is modelled, that the end justifies the means: the Doctor is a hero, and is good, because he never believes that, and is filled with outrage at the treatment of human or other intelligent beings as means, not ends: as less than themselves in any scheme, however well intentioned. In "Robot", the Doctor tells Professor Kettlewell that he cannot stop the nations polluting the world by threatening them with a nuclear war. In a much-praised sequence, the Doctor asks Davros if he would allow the use of a virus which would destroy all other forms of life. Davros is fascinated and says he would indeed allow it: such power would set him up above the gods, "and through the Daleks I shall have that power!" The Doctor thus proves him to be a megalomaniac and a madman, and no philanthropist. Later in the story, he agonises over the ethics of means and ends. With no option left but genocide, he questions his right to destroy the Daleks: some things might be better with them, future worlds will stop warring against each other and combine together, just because of their fear of the Daleks. If he commits genocide, wiping out an intelligent race, he is no better than the Daleks. He asks Sarah if someone who knew the future pointed out to her a child who would grow up to be a ruthless dictator who would destroy millions of lives, could she then kill that child? Sarah dismisses the argument: matters are far simpler for her, the Daleks are the most evil creatures ever invented and they must be destroyed. The Doctor is saved from making the decision by the apparent success of a coup against Davros.

Both of these sequences show Tom Baker at the height of his powers as the Doctor, absolutely convincing in his anguish and in his careful argument about the virus that traps Davros into revealing his true nature as a megalomaniac. It has been pointed out that it would be hard to see Pertwee playing the same scenes with such intensity and success.

Other characters in the story debate the ethics of science. Gharman applauds the intention to allow his race to survive in the new travel machine, but insists that the creature must have a conscience, a judgment of right and wrong, "all the qualities that we consider essential in ourselves"; it must do good things and evil ones, "but it cannot be allowed to become a heartless machine". He and the other scientists who oppose Davros are exterminated for their pains, but then, inevitably, the Daleks discover their true nature and start operating independently of their creator. The remaining Elite, still loyal to Davros, are to be exterminated. Davros pleads for their lives, urging the

Dalek leader to have pity: "Pi-ty?" it grates. "I have no understanding of the word. It is not registered in my vocabulary banks." The last Kaled alive in the bunker, Davros implores the Daleks to obey him as he is their creator; but they are the creatures he has made them, and the Dalek leader states that they are the superior beings; Davros, an inferior, must be exterminated. Finally realising the horror he has created, Davros speeds his chair towards the bunker's self-destruct switch, but is gunned down before he can activate it. The Doctor belatedly blows up the Dalek creatures' incubator room but says he has only delayed them for a short time – perhaps a thousand years.

The success of "Genesis of the Daleks" is down to a number of factors other than its excellent script, not least the design and lighting. The bunker is convincingly realised as functional, metallic corridors; the lighting designer intelligently lit the artists, rather than the set, so there are menacing shadows everywhere. Davros's mask is a wonderfully convincing sculpture by John Friedlander, who also created the Ogrons and Draconians; it was based on the Mekon from the *Dan Dare* comic strips of *The Eagle*, enjoyed by the young Philip Hinchcliffe. The Daleks are also well realised. Mindful of the problems experienced by taking them to quarry locations in the previous two Dalek stories, director David Maloney confines them to the studio. Painted a gun metal grey, they are convincing weapons of war and the paint job and low lighting successfully hides the flaws in what were now ageing props. (They are practically falling apart by the time of their reappearance in 1979's "Destiny of the Daleks".) The original script called for the Daleks to be different from the Daleks we now know, simpler, less finished. This accounts for the Doctor's line in episode two, "A Dalek...very primitive, but undeniably a Dalek" when the Mark III travel machine is first exhibited to the Elite by Davros. Given that it looks the same as ever, the line is slightly puzzling to viewers. Presumably the budget wouldn't run to refurbishing the Dalek props. Some fans objected to the rewriting of Dalek history: the original Dalek story back in 1964 had called the Daleks' ancestors the Dals, not the Kaleds, and some of the Dalek annuals and comic strips (considered by some fans as canonical) had posited a different history of the Daleks as created by a scientist called Yarvelling. Back in 1975, however, and with memories of the original Dalek story dimmed to extinction by its single screening, no-one cared about such things (and perhaps they shouldn't now).

Michael Wisher's performance as Davros is superb and he dominates every scene; he is by turns ranting, demented, wheedling, reasonable and soothing. His Davros is a perfect match for Tom Baker's towering performance as the Doctor. Wisher was a *Doctor Who* regular, having appeared as Wakefield in "The Ambassadors of Death" (1970); Rex Farrell in "Terror of the Autons" (1971) and Kalik in "Carnival of Monsters" (1973). He provided Dalek voices for "Death to the Daleks" (1974) and went on to play Magrik in "Revenge of the Cybermen" and Morelli in "Planet of Evil" (1976), both of them minor roles. Wisher reasoned that Davros's effectiveness would be primarily determined by his voice as his face and eyes would be hidden beneath the mask. He therefore elected to rehearse the part with a paper bag over his head, which gave Tom Baker hysterics. Baker similarly went into hysterics when he saw Frederick Jaeger's anti-man-beast make up for "Planet of Evil" (1975), which rendered him as an ape-like Mr Hyde.

The Nazi origins of the Daleks were emphasised by the production. The Kaleds wear SS-style uniforms and give each other Nazi salutes. Davros's henchman Nyder (another wonderful performance by Peter Miles) wears Himmler-like wire framed glasses and, for the first studio session, an Iron Cross, which he was asked to remove for subsequent recordings. These elements follow the clear lead of the scripts, with its reference to the Bunker as the leader's last refuge and the expulsion of the mutations – Mutos – into the wasteland with Nyder's explanation, "We must keep the Kaled race pure. Imperfects are rejected." Nation had originally intended Davros to be in an ordinary wheelchair, but David Maloney elected to make it look like the lower half of a Dalek. This made explicit the link between Davros and his creations, and the Doctor's point that Davros is trying to perpetuate himself in the Daleks; it also led to a mistake common among viewers who watched the show *very* casually, that Davros was what a Dalek looked like when you took its top off.

Nation's decision to have Davros attempt to destroy his creations was absolutely right as a dramatic decision. It also fitted completely into the philosophical logic of the story: an aggressive creature programmed to survive and to consider itself superior to all other beings would destroy those it considered inferior. Having said this, it seems a contradiction that Nation immediately blurred the boundaries by insisting that we were not to see Davros actually be exterminated on screen, in case he, or a future production team, should want to bring him back. Here, Nation explained that he was trying to learn from his errors in the first Dalek story: at the end, the Daleks were so thoroughly and utterly destroyed that he had to scratch his head to work out how he could resurrect them for "The Dalek Invasion of Earth" (1964). The solution was to set the second story before the events of the first. This wasn't entirely satisfactory as the Daleks who invaded Earth were much more advanced than the Daleks of the original story, supposedly set in the future, who couldn't even leave their city and apparently had no space travel.

That Davros was resurrected, and appeared another four times in the original series, was to contradict his determination to destroy his creations and therefore dramatic nonsense. When he returns in "Destiny of the Daleks" (1979), all his qualms have been forgotten and he is keen to lead the Daleks again. He is also a much less interesting character and his resurrection is not helped by David Gooderson's lacklustre performance. To add insult to injury, the budget in inflation-wracked 1979 couldn't stretch to a new mask. Michael Wisher's original mask was returned to the BBC after being displayed at the long running *Doctor Who* exhibitions at Longleat House in Wiltshire and on Blackpool's Golden Mile. It didn't fit Gooderson, visibly wobbles on screen, and apparently didn't meld with the new actor's mouth: what looks like melted chocolate appears to be applied to his face to hide the join.

Davros returned again in "Resurrection of the Daleks" (1984) to menace Peter Davison's Doctor. In his ninety year imprisonment on board an Earth ship he has learnt all about regeneration and was now played by Terry Molloy, best known as milkman Mike Tucker in the BBC Radio 4 soap opera *The Archers*. Michael Wisher had been signed up to reprise Davros for this story, but production dates were shifted when it was moved from the twentieth to the twenty first season because of industrial action. Molloy was apparently cast because of his abilities to imitate the original: his Davros sounds quite like Wisher's but is more of a ranting lunatic, which might be explained as character development. Molloy is certainly better than David Gooderson. The BBC had even found enough money to make him a new mask. Much bigger than the original, as Molloy was a much bigger actor physically than the slight Michael Wisher, the mask is yellow tinged and impressed Russell T Davies as zombie-like and very frightening. Molloy gives a fine performance in the Colin Baker story "Revelation of the Daleks" (1985), in which Davros, now apparently a decapitated head in a transparent tank, calls himself The Great Healer and heads a death care facility called Tranquil Repose. Here, the rich can deposit their loved ones at the moment of death, to be kept in suspended animation until a cure can be found for the diseases that killed them. Davros then cheerfully harvests the corpses to create a new breed of Daleks, before he is carted off by a race of Skarosian Daleks to stand trial for his crimes. He finally appears inside the Emperor Dalek in Sylvester McCoy's "Remembrance of the Daleks" (1988) at the head of the Imperial Daleks, thus revealing a capacity to escape from certain death that rivals the Master's.

Russell T Davies resurrected Davros in "The Stolen Earth" / "Journey's End" (2008), paying more attention than previous writers to Davros's character and origins in "Genesis of the Daleks". Perhaps because he had tried to destroy them in his first story, Davros's relationship with the Daleks is now ambivalent and uneasy. They appear to have accepted him, perhaps because they acknowledge his past achievements: he did try to help them win the war against the robot Movellans in "Destiny of the Daleks", after all. Certainly, there is no more talk of putting him on trial or pitched battles between his Daleks and the "official" Daleks. However, Davros is confined to a vault on the giant spaceship The Crucible, where he is attended by only a few Daleks as servants and his role is merely to advise. The Tenth Doctor asks him what exactly his relationship is with the Daleks: Davros replies, uneasily, "We have...an arrangement." The Doctor taunts him by putting his finger on its exact nature: he is the Daleks' "pet".

Julian Bleach plays Davros in this story and his nuanced performance, clearly modelled on Wisher's original, is hugely effective. He is quietly menacing and acidly intelligent, noting that the Doctor prides himself as the man who abhors violence and never carries a gun because he takes ordinary people and turns them into weapons: a fair comment on the bomb-wielding Jack Harkness and gun-toting Rose and Jackie Tyler. The Doctor is silenced by the argument. Davros recognises Sarah Jane, now among the Tenth Doctor's companions, as having been there at the beginning on Skaro. Bleach saves his energy for occasional demented outbursts which out-Wisher Wisher: he screams at the Dalek Supreme to "Detonate the reality bomb!" which will destroy everything in every Universe that is not Dalek. Davros is left in the burning Crucible as the Doctor's human clone (don't ask) destroys all the Daleks on board; Davros ignores the Doctor's offer of rescue and shrieks, "I name you forever, the Destroyer of Worlds!" The ship collapses around him and he is apparently helpless; no doubt he has escaped to return another day. As the Master says at the end of the novelisation of "Frontier in Space", "Oh well. There's always tomorrow."

8

Gothic Horror

There had been some trepidation at the BBC about Tom Baker's debut as the Doctor: would the public accept a new actor after five years of Jon Pertwee? The early viewing figures for episode one of "Robot" were promising but, according to Terrance Dicks, some thought they might be accounted for by people wondering what the new man would be like. But the viewing figures stayed strong: ten million for "Robot", eleven million for "The Ark in Space" and never falling much below nine million for the rest of the season (even for the lacklustre "Revenge of the Cybermen"). Tom Baker was a success, but his first season was cut short at a mere twenty episodes: the shortest season in the programme's history so far. This was owing to a decision to change the running slot for *Doctor Who* from midwinter (January or December) running through to June, to a September start with the season running through the winter and into spring. The BBC felt *Doctor Who* would beef up its autumn season in the ratings war with ITV, which was to begin scheduling glossy American shows – such as Gerry Anderson's *Space: 1999* - against it. Today, the BBC and ITV might come to a gentlemen's agreement not to show the same types of programmes against each other – thus, a truce was arranged not to screen the BBC's *Strictly Come Dancing* against ITV's *The X Factor* – but in the 1970s, it was war. Before the days of home video, science fiction fans who wanted to watch both programmes had to choose between *Space: 1999* – quickly followed by *Buck Rogers in the Twenty Fifth Century* – or *Doctor Who*. Actually, this wasn't too much of a dilemma of choice as the former was dull and the latter was rubbish, but we didn't know this as the time. There is no doubt that both new shows ate into the BBC viewing figures.

Nevertheless, the autumn to spring run was popular amongst viewers and prompted newspaper articles to warm the cockles of your heart about the pleasures of taking your children to see the football match, arriving home on a dark and cold evening to be refreshed by hot tea and crumpets, and settling down together as a family to watch *Doctor Who*. Steven Moffat justified his shifting of Matt Smith's third season (2012) to an autumn start by arguing that the programme worked better against dark winter evenings than sunny summer days. This appeal to the experience of watching the Tom Baker stories was slightly undermined by the first batch of Smith's third season episodes concluding in late

September 2012, in glorious summer sunshine.

The change of scheduling meant that the cast and crew worked continuously on *Doctor Who* from season twelve to season thirteen: there was no summer holiday after shooting wrapped on "Genesis of the Daleks", the final season twelve story to be made. A six episode version of "Terror of the Zygons" had been planned to end season twelve, but it was held over to start season thirteen and cut down to four episodes by Robert Holmes, who rewrote it extensively.

Season thirteen, like season eight for the previous production team, was the first season under the exclusive control of Philip Hinchcliffe and Robert Holmes. Their vision of *Doctor Who* ran riot for the next two years, with even more of an emphasis on horror than season twelve. Both producer and script editor raided the back catalogue of literature and films that they enjoyed, writing shameless pastiches to rework them into the *Doctor Who* world. Cosy old monsters and enemies were dropped in favour of new and terrifying ones. The only adversary to return was the Master in "The Deadly Assassin", and he had been given a Hinchcliffe/Holmes horror make-over in his new guise as a decaying corpse.

After a slow start of seven and a half million for "Terror of the Zygons", viewing figures for 1976 and 1977 went through the roof, averaging ten million per episode and peaking at nearly twelve million for "The Android Invasion" (why?) and "The Deadly Assassin" before reaching almost thirteen million for "The Robots of Death". The series was at a peak of popularity that it hadn't achieved since Hartnell's days, loved by the public and the fans. The three years of Hinchcliffe and Holmes' tenure are regarded as among the best episodes ever made. I remember general disappointment among my comprehensive school friends at the new episodes produced by Graham Williams and still starring Tom Baker; they were generally held to be not as good as the Hinchcliffe stories and the general feeling at morning break was that the series was past its best.

Yet in spite of its popularity, the show again attracted unwelcome attention in the form of renewed criticism of its violent and horrific content. Eventually, these unseated Hinchcliffe as producer and took *Doctor Who* in yet another new direction.

There is much less political and social commentary in the Tom Baker stories than there had been in Pertwee's time, not least because the trio of Dicks-Letts-Hulke had moved on; aside from isolated stories like "The Sun Makers" (1977), the show now avoided such political engagement. Tom Baker's first three seasons were instead rollicking science fiction/horror adventures, but always with the strong moral driving force of good against evil, and the moral message that good can triumph against apparently overwhelming odds if it asserts itself. In "Pyramids of Mars" (1975), the Doctor is captured by Sutekh, an Osiran imprisoned beneath a pyramid in Egypt and powerless to move. Sutekh and the Osirans were hailed as gods by the ancient Egyptians and Sutekh is still possessed of awesome powers. He is also a moral relativist: the Doctor tells him fearlessly that he is evil, and he replies, "Evil? Your evil is my good. I am Sutekh the Destroyer. Where I tread I leave nothing but dust and darkness. I find that good." The Doctor curses him as a "twisted abhorrence" and is blasted into agony for his pains: before Sutekh he is a "grovelling insect" whom Sutekh might "keep…alive for centuries wracked by the most excruciating pain … an amusing diversion". Yet the Doctor heroically defies him, pitting his puny goodness against Sutekh's mighty evil. Eventually, of course, Sutekh is destroyed.

The dialogue of "Pyramids of Mars" is delicious in its richness and melodrama, both hallmarks of Robert Holmes, who is rightly regarded as one of the programme's most talented writers. Holmes delights in language and his scripts, and scripts rewritten by him as script editor, are jammed with wonderful and quotable lines. Like Dickens, he delights in giving each character an individual idiom. In "The Talons of Weng Chiang" (1977), Leela and the Doctor journey back to London in the 1880s; a toothless old crone, who has stepped straight out of the pages of Dickens' *Our Mutual Friend*, spies a corpse floating in the Thames. "It's a floater, ain't it guv?" she gabbles to the policeman hooking out the body with a boathook. When they see the corpse is mutilated (by a giant rat), the crone is subdued: "Oh my eye! You wouldn't want that served with onions. Never seen anyfing like it in all me puff." Arrested with a Chinese tong member, Leela demands of the police desk sergeant, "Put our prisoner to the torture!" "Well, if that don't take the biscuit," the sergeant chuckles. "This ain't the Dark Ages, you know, miss."

"Pyramids of Mars" is also notable for including a thoughtful and influential scene on the paradoxes of time travel. If Sutekh is freed, he will destroy the world. Sarah protests that they know the world didn't end in 1911: "Do we?" asks the Doctor, and takes her and Lawrence Scarman, a contemporary gentleman, forward to 1980, Sarah's time, in the TARDIS. They look out on a landscape of hell, roaring winds whirling around desolate rocks and shattered buildings. This is how Sutekh would leave Earth, the Doctor explains: a dying planet circling a dead sun. "Fascinating," Lawrence Scarman interjects. "Do you mean the future can be chosen, Doctor?" "Not chosen. Shaped. It takes a being of Sutekh's almost limitless power to destroy the future." The trip forward in time silences the objections of Sarah and the viewers, who might have been wondering what all the fuss is about. Sarah realises that they have to go back to 1911. This was one of the first scenes since "Day of the Daleks" (1972) to suggest the existence of what became named as alternative time lines. Russell T Davies was so impressed by it that he suggested repeating the scene in Christopher Eccleston's season in 2005 (in fact, it doesn't appear).

"Pyramids of Mars" is, of course, a pastiche of horror films with mummies and Egyptologists awakening ancient curses with their meddling. The original script was written by Lewis Griefer, who had written for Patrick McGoohan's cult series *The Prisoner* (1967-8), but who couldn't adapt to the requirements of *Doctor Who*. Robert Holmes said Griefer's script largely took place in the British museum and the mummies were given as much prominence as the Doctor. He wrote to Griefer, explaining that for the show's audience, Egyptology meant ancient curses and mummies lumbering out of the fog. Griefer was eventually paid off and the story was completely written by Holmes, but it went out under the pseudonym of Stephen Harris. The horror was given a science fiction makeover and the mummies were lumbering robots, servants of Sutekh seeking to free him from his ancient bonds.

Most of the other stories of seasons thirteen and fourteen were literary and film pastiches. "Planet of Evil" (1975) was inspired by *Doctor Jekyll and Mr Hyde*. A Morestran expedition led by Professor Sorenson lands on Zeta Minor at the edge of the known universe. The planet is on the boundaries between the universes of matter and anti-matter and Sorenson raids its ore, rich in the power needed to refuel the dying Moretran sun. This is a glance at the perennial energy crisis of the 1970s but, unlike the Pertwee stories, the reference to the real world is quickly buried under the horror and adventure. The anti-matter creature of Zeta Minor silently registers its displeasure at its planet's despoliation by killing off the Morestrans, sucking all life from their bodies and leaving them as withered, skeletal husks. The influence of *Dr Jekyll and Mr Hyde* is seen in an imaginative extrapolation of the transformation of the planet by day and night: by daytime, it is relatively harmless; at night, the anti-matter creature stalks its prey. Sorenson is infected by the anti-matter and becomes anti-man, who shambles around the Morestran ship and murders its crew: his make up is directly influenced by Hollywood's Mr Hydes in numerous horror films.

As a child, I found "Planet of Evil" the most frightening thing I had ever seen. I had seriously to consider not watching the summer repeat or reading the novelisation: my first exposure to it had led me to sleep with the light on for a fortnight.

Having raided Stevenson, the production team turned their attention to the other Hollywood staple and earliest of Gothic novels, Mary Shelley's *Frankenstein*. This became "The Brain of Morbius" (1976), a splendid tale which turned the dial of horror and violence up full. On the storm lashed planet of Karn, the obsessed scientist Dr Mehendri Solon (Philip Madoc at his best) lurks in his castle, guarded by his deformed servant Condo, and protecting the terrible secret he keeps hidden in his crypt. He has preserved the brain of the renegade Time Lord Morbius, executed by the Time Lords for his crimes and run to ground on Karn, where he had promised his followers the elixir of eternal life, venerated by the Sisterhood of the Flame. Solon has made a body for Morbius's brain, sewing together bits of corpses from the crews of spaceships which regularly crash on Karn. He needs only a head, and the head of the Doctor would do so well (another Time Lord, he chuckles to Morbius: "The crowning irony"). The Doctor is unwilling to lend his head to the project, so Solon opts for an artificial brain case – looking like a goldfish bowl – to contain the brain, and Morbius lives again. The story concludes with the Doctor and Morbius locked in a contest of mind-bending: Time Lord wrestling in which one opponent thinks the other back through his life to his beginnings. "It's usually a game but it can end in death," the Doctor tells Sarah. Morbius loses, becomes a ravening animal and is herded off a cliff by the Sisterhood of the Flame: as he goes over, stuntman Stuart Fell, playing the Morbius monster, catches the camera with his brain case and there is a visible shake on screen.

"The Brain of Morbius" is rightly highly regarded but had a troubled production history. Hinchcliffe asked Terrance Dicks to provide a story about a robot and in the original, it is the robot which preserves Morbius's brain. Having delivered his draft, Dicks went on holiday and couldn't be contacted when Hinchcliffe decided he'd gone off the robot idea. In Dicks's absence, Robert Holmes rewrote the script and introduced Solon. He was very apologetic about the changes when Dicks returned, but the latter objected to the new script. There are certainly some plot holes, which Dicks remedied in his novelisation: why doesn't Solon use Condo's head or Sarah's for the Morbius creature? (The novel explains both are too small, which doesn't quite fit Condo's hulking appearance.) Why does Solon need to build a body at all, when he could just use Condo's?

Dicks also protested against the mind bending match. The Doctor and Morbius are each connected to a headset at the end of a tubular metal lash up topped by a screen. As he begins to lose, the Doctor's previous incarnations appear on this screen – photos of Pertwee, Troughton and Hartnell – and Morbius shrieks, "Your puny mind is powerless against the strength of Morbius! Back, back to your beginnings!" and yet more faces appear. These, is seems, are the Doctor's previous selves: in fact, they are photographs of the production team, including Hinchcliffe, Holmes and regular director Douglas Camfield. The scene is a continuity howler as it goes against the established idea that the Hartnell Doctor was the first. In his novelisation, Dicks writes that there was a confused flurry of faces on the screen and the BBC later suggested the pre-Hartnell faces were Morbius's, which doesn't fit the dialogue. Dicks told Holmes he wanted his name taken off the script. What name should go on it? Holmes asked. "I don't care," Dicks said, "just put it out under some bland pseudonym." He was amused when he saw the listing in the *Radio Times* a few weeks later: the story credited to one Robin Bland.

Other stories followed the lines of pastiche. *The Android Invasion* (1975) was a doppelganger story and Terry Nation's first script without the Daleks since *The Keys of Marinus* in 1964: was it commissioned to placate Nation and his agent, who had said Robert Holmes had promised a Dalek story ever year? Perhaps not: the production team were just using an established writer. Much as they wanted to encourage new writers for the show, both the Hinchcliffe and, later, the Williams production teams found that new writers often didn't understand what they were supposed to produce; their scripts had to be heavily rewritten or abandoned, so commissioning established writers saved time, work and money.

"The Seeds of Doom" (1976) relied heavily on *The Day of the Triffids* for its central premise, plant life dominating animal life; "The Deadly Assassin" was inspired by the film *The Manchurian Candidate*; "The Robots of Death" was a science fiction version of such Agatha Christie tales as *Ten Little Indians* and "The Talons of Weng Chiang" (1977) was a heady, eclectic mix of borrowing. Corpses in the river came from Dickens's *Our Mutual Friend*; Magnus Greel lurking under the music hall came from *The Phantom of the Opera* (which Holmes was again to mine as a source for "The Caves of Androzani" (1984)); the Doctor investigating the crimes which baffle Scotland Yard is pure Sherlock Holmes, and, to reinforce the point, Tom Baker substitutes a deerstalker and cape for his usual hat and scarf; there are murderous Chinese gangs; a murderous ventriloquist's dummy (actually the Peking Homonculous, a cyborg with a pig's cerebral cortex, which has a murderous hatred of humanity); giant rats in the sewers, girls disappearing off the streets to have their life forces fed into Weng Chiang…

"The Talons of Weng Chiang", like "Genesis of the Daleks", is another frequent winner of the Best Ever Story poll in *Doctor Who Magazine*. It is a wonderful pot pourri of imagery and borrowing, bound together with a strong story, excellent acting and splendid dialogue and characterisation. The Doctor is assisted by Henry Gordon Jago, a colourful owner and manager of the music hall, modelled perhaps on Vincent Crummles from Dickens's *Nicholas Nickleby* (Christopher Benjamin, who played Jago, went on to play Crummles in the RSC's nine hour epic production of *Nicholas Nickleby*: on the DVD commentary, he notes the similarities of the characters). Holmes gives him some wonderful lines. When the Doctor suspects Jago has been recently hypnotised, he hypnotises Jago with a pocket watch. Jago is scornful and protests, "I am a man of determination and character, sir. The Rock of Gibraltar could be more easily… more easily…" as he comes under the influence. Leela and the Doctor also team up with Professor Litefoot, "England's premiere pathologist," according to Jago. Litefoot (Trevor Baxter) is impressed with the Doctor's diagnosis in the autopsy of the murdered cab driver – the chisel like teeth marks suggest a giant rat – and invites him and Leela to supper. This cold collation has been laid out by Litefoot's housekeeper, a Mrs Hudson, named after the housekeeper in ITV's popular contemporary series *Upstairs, Downstairs* (which was created by Jean Marsh, Jon Pertwee's first wife and actress of Hartnell companion Sara Kingdom). Leela seizes the joints of beef in her hands and tears the meat off the bone; as a Victorian gentleman, it is part of Litefoot's code never to make a guest feel uncomfortable, so he puts down his knife, fork and plate and uses his hands to eat. Jago and Litefoot eventually team up against Weng Chiang in the final two episodes. Weng Chiang – actually a fifty third century war criminal called Magnus Greel ("The Butcher of Brisbane!") – snarls that they will die slowly, to give entertainment to his wolves. "You filthy bounder," Litefoot observes with dignity. The line is hilarious and absolutely just: to a Victorian gentleman, Greel has trespassed over the bounds of what is acceptable, thus he is indeed a bounder.

"The Talons of Weng Chiang" was originally written by Robert Banks Stewart, who had turned in strong scripts for the previous season's "Terror of the Zygons" and "The Seeds of Doom". Holmes rewrote it extensively and received the sole on-screen credit. He originally toyed with including the Master as the phantom beneath the theatre, crippled by his failed regeneration and using the life force of abducted young women in an attempt to renew himself. Holmes replaced the Master with Magnus Greel, a war criminal whose Zygma experiments in time travel led mankind up a technological cul-de-sac. Greel arrived in his time cabinet in nineteenth century China, where he was hailed as the god Weng Chiang by Li H'sen Chang (John Bennett), who gives him shelter and protection. The time cabinet is claimed as booty by British soldiers, who take it to England, where it ends up in the home of Professor Litefoot. Greel and Chang follow the time cabinet to London and search for it desperately. Greel's experiments in time travel have made him ill to the point of death; only recovering the time cabinet will heal him. He holes up beneath Jago's theatre, guarded by rats he has enlarged to the size of lions. The Doctor protests that activating the Zygma beam of the time cabinet will destroy London, but Greel goes ahead anyway, only to be killed by the Peking Homonculous who has grown bored and is indulging its hatred of mankind in a killing spree. The production is only let down by the now notorious giant rat, a cuddly and shapeless costume which bumbles down the sewer sets to seize Leela by the leg. Louise Jameson screams valiantly but the sequence is embarrassing. The rat's head and teeth aren't too bad, though.

The increased level of horror and violence under Hinchcliffe once more drew the programme to the attention of Mrs Mary Whitehouse. This lady's somewhat unimaginative interpretation of the Christian faith called her to campaign against violence and something called "dirtiness" in television and radio programmes. In the late 1960s, she gathered fellow minded citizens together to protest about the malign influence of television on our youth, positing a connection between what one saw on television and what one enacted in one's own life. Nigel Kneale's prescient satire on what would now be called reality television, *The Year of the Sex Olympics* (1968), was termed one of the dirtiest plays Mrs Whitehouse had ever seen; other dramas were attacked for their brutal portrayal of violence.

Sir Hugh Greene, Director General of the BBC from 1960-1969, cheerfully admitted that he viewed Mrs Whitehouse as a "persona non-grata and persona non-exista" and ignored her. However, perhaps as a consequence of popular fears of an increasingly violent society – the Troubles in Northern Ireland had claimed many lives – Mrs

Whitehouse's views were finding increased favour among the public in the mid-seventies. Letters to the *Radio Times* complained that children would be able to see little difference between the opening sequence of "Genesis of the Daleks" and events in the Falls Road area of Belfast. These sequences included soldiers in gas masks being gunned down in slow motion; the Doctor, Sarah and Harry wrenching respirators from corpses to avoid suffocation and worse in a gas attack on the Kaled trenches. One other middle aged and middle class woman of similar imagination and faith was the new Leader of the Opposition and the Conservative Party, a Mrs Margaret Thatcher, who expressed sympathy for Mrs Whitehouse's views. In this new political climate, the BBC started to pay some attention to the NVLA.

Tom Baker's second season was criticised by Mrs Whitehouse for its depictions of strangulation by "obscene vegetable matter" (the Krynoid in "The Seeds of Doom") and "by claw" in "The Brain of Morbius", when the Morbius monster strangles one of the Sisterhood of Khan (my ten year old self was unconvinced by this sequence on first broadcast as I noticed that the claw didn't move when it was around the woman's neck). *Doctor Who* was lumped together by Mrs Whitehouse with such adult fare as *I, Claudius* and deemed similarly harmful to the nation's health. Hinchcliffe and script editor Robert Holmes continued full steam ahead on this sea of sin for Baker's third season but hit trouble in the third story, "The Deadly Assassin" (November, 1976). At the end of episode three, in a filthy river blazing with ignited marsh gas, the Doctor and Chancellor Goth (the Master's agent) battle in the dreamscape of the Matrix, apparently intent on beating each other to death. In a sequence famous among fans as a turning point in *Doctor Who*'s history, Goth holds the Doctor's head under the water and splutters, "Finished, Doctor! You're finished." The end theme crashes in over a three second close-up of Tom Baker's face underwater.

Hinchcliffe was not a cavalier producer and took his responsibilities seriously. He had already edited out a shot from the previous season's "The Seeds of Doom", of a character slowly mutating into a Krynoid, as being too disturbing for children. Viewing the ending of episode three of "The Deadly Assassin", Hinchcliffe decided to let the "drowning" shot go through. He argued that the audience knew that it wasn't really the Doctor underwater: the whole episode has established, and reinforced through cutaway shots, that the Doctor himself was actually lying on a coach in the Time Lords' archive room: only his mind was in the Matrix, so he couldn't actually be drowned. The episode was transmitted uncut and Mrs Whitehouse pounced. Interviewed in the

1990s, she said she "[could] see until this day, the final shot of Doctor Who drowning". Fans would perhaps be more upset by her calling the Doctor by the title of the programme, but the BBC took the complaint seriously: this marked a turning point in its attitude to Mrs Whitehouse, whom the BBC had previously regarded as a nuisance and ignored. The BBC agreed that the ending as transmitted had been a mistake and cut the final sequence from the repeat of the story in the summer of 1976. It was only restored to the VHS and DVD release from an American, uncut, copy: the consequent fall-out in picture quality on both is very obvious.

This was the beginning of the end for Hinchcliffe. He and Holmes were planning a fourth season for Tom Baker and had started work on a new breed of monsters who they promised would be more terrifying than the Daleks or Cybermen, both of whom Hinchcliffe disliked as old hat. As production of the final stories of the 1976-7 season got underway, Hinchcliffe found a young man called Graham Williams trailing him at planning meetings. This was his first inkling that Williams was to be the new producer and that he, Hinchcliffe, was to move on; in fact, to develop a new post-watershed police series called *Target*, created by Graham Williams, starring 1970s heart throb Patrick Mower. Here, Hinchcliffe would continue to do damage to the nation's psyche with a series full of unbridled violence and sexual content. In effect, he and Williams had exchanged jobs.

Graham Williams took over *Doctor Who* with a brief from the Head of Series and Serials to reduce the violence and to make it more suitable as family-friendly viewing. The obvious thing to replace the violence with was humour, something very much in tune with Tom Baker's inclinations for the show. Williams was also concerned about the "improbability" of the Doctor arriving on a planet in peril at the start of every story owing to a malfunctioning TARDIS: perhaps an odd thing to worry about, given that it had served the programme well for fourteen years. He proposed an umbrella theme for the new season. The Doctor was to be given the task of assembling the six segments of the Key to Time: an awesomely powerful MacGuffin which would restore the balance (of what, exactly, was never made clear) of the Universe. One segment would be found in each story and the quest was to be directed by the White Guardian: an awesomely powerful being opposed by the equally awesomely powerful and equally opposite Black Guardian. These demi-gods partly owed their creation to Williams's feeling that the Time Lords had lost their god-like status in the series. Certainly, "The Deadly Assassin" had portrayed them as a squabbling, decadent and politically corrupt race: rather like the human beings whose form they resembled.

Production time was pressing, however, and Williams was unable to get the Key to Time arc up and running for the fifteenth season: it was held over to the following year (1978-9). Williams' first season was an uneasy hotch-potch of tone, quality and style, overshadowed by the departure of Robert Holmes as script editor after three and a half years, and of Louise Jameson as Leela. *Who* veteran Terrance Dicks had penned the first tale, a Gothic piece luridly entitled "The Vampire Mutations". This almost immediately ran into trouble as it clashed with the BBC's consanguineous production of *Dracula*, with Frank Finlay and Louis Jourdan: perhaps unsurprisingly, the producers of that serious television movie were not keen to have their project "undermined" by a *Doctor Who* story that could be seen as a spoof. "The Vampire Mutations" was pulled from the fifteenth season (it would eventually resurface as the eighteenth season story "State of Decay") and Terrance Dicks hurriedly wrote a four part replacement, "The Horror of Fang Rock". Set on a nineteenth century lighthouse, the story belongs to the pseudo-historical vein of *Who* in which the historical setting is enlivened by the inclusion of an alien and science fiction elements. (The purely historical stories had been abandoned by producer Innes Lloyd after "The Highlanders" in 1966, deemed insufficiently exciting compared with the programme's science fiction yarns.) Robert Holmes instructed Dicks to research the historical background of lighthouses thoroughly, perhaps as a revenge for a similar request Dicks had made of him when Holmes wrote the 1974 medieval tale "The Time Warrior". "The Horror of Fang Rock" has much to recommend it: strongly drawn, well-acted characters, excellent lighting, a building menace (and a menaced building) as the lighthouse's inhabitants are murdered one by one by the marauding Rutan. On the debit side, the Rutan resembles a luminous football and the story is too slow to act as an effective season opener. Episode one ends with the dullest cliff-hanger in years as a hideously unconvincing balsa-wood model yacht crashes into the island. The story, uniquely in the programme's history, was shot in Pebble Mill at Birmingham. Paddy Russell, the director, praised the innovation and dedication of the technical team but the lack of resources away from London is all too obvious on screen. "Horror of Fang Rock" also suffers from its juxtaposition with the final story of the previous season, the much loved "Talons of Weng-Chiang", also set in Victorian times.

From Fang Rock, the TARDIS careered wildly back into the world of space opera for the second story, "The Invisible Enemy". Space opera was always difficult on *Doctor Who*'s limited budget, as demonstrated by 1973's "Frontier in Space", whose Earth ship was piloted by actors sitting on office chairs, propped up on pallets. "The Invisible Enemy" boasted some impressive and ambitious model work from *Thunderbirds* veteran Ian Scoones, but the plot – a space virus attempts to become the dominant species in the galaxy – veered about as crazily as the space shuttle that crashes into the asteroid hospital in episode three. Long term script writers Bob Baker and Dave Martin borrowed heavily from *Fantastic Voyage* (1966) for scenes where miniaturised clones of the Doctor and Leela clamber around in the Doctor's brain, hunting for the nucleus of the virus. "What was that?" Leela asks as a light zaps by them. "Just a passing thought," replies the Doctor. The nucleus itself is eventually manifested as a giant prawn on castors which has to be pushed around by its minions; Tom Baker quipped that "a large deep fat fryer would have put paid to its schemes".

Entertaining mess and witty lines aside, "The Invisible Enemy" was notable for introducing K9. This computer, in the form of a robot dog, was equally loved and derided by fans and is still a feature of the programme thirty five years after his/its introduction. Scoones, who eventually handled only the miniatures in the story's special effects, did some initial designs of K9 as an alarming robotic Doberman; like the Daleks, Scoones envisaged him as big enough to contain an actor who would provide the movement. Tony Harding, the story's other visual effects designer, came up with K9's cute and familiar look and it was his design which found favour with the production team.

K9 effectively filled the tonal gap created by the removal of horror from *Doctor Who*. Robert Holmes quickly spotted its potential and told Baker and Martin, "Well, I think it's a knockout, this dog." He sought – and gained – approval to use K9 in future stories. Hedging his bets, Williams nevertheless had two endings shot for "The Invisible Enemy": one where K9 remains with Professor Marius and one where he goes with the Doctor.

In fact, K9's inclusion in the regular line up caused enormous problems. Scoones' original idea of having him/it controlled by an actor in a prop might have been better technically than the radio controlled K9 used in the studio. Harding lamented that K9's frequency was the same as the cameras', which often scrambled his radio control and sent him crashing into the scenery. The dog's motor was so noisy that he almost obliterated dialogue (something solved by the introduction of a new prop K9 Mark II in the next season opener, "The Ribos Operation"). Like the Daleks, K9 had only been designed for one story, which created difficulties for future appearances: the Daleks had to be heavily modified for their second appearance in "The Dalek Invasion of Earth" (1964), given bigger bumpers with larger rubber wheels to cope with London paving and save them from (in designer Raymond Cusick's words) "rattling along like biscuit tins" on their original castors. K9 found it similarly hard to cope on location: he had to run on wooden boards rather obviously laid down on grass in "The Stones of Blood" (1978) and refused to work altogether on Brighton beach in "The Leisure Hive" (1980), in spite of an expensive refit. The bathetic beach solution was to pull along a hollow K9 prop on fishing line. A more radical solution to the K9 problems frequently employed by despairing writers was to leave him out of a story altogether. K9 was too big to get through the door of the TARDIS: there was always an obvious cutaway shot when he disembarked until new producer John Nathan Turner had the bright idea of opening both doors on the new TARDIS prop introduced in "The Leisure Hive". Terry Nation refused to allow K9 to encounter the Daleks in 1979's "Destiny of the Daleks" for fear that he would upstage them and the Daleks weren't alone in the fear of being upstaged. Tom Baker thought K9 "insufferable" and allegedly booted him around the set; he quickly tired of the inevitable two shot to fit dog and Doctor into frame and was only reconciled to the character by his friendship with K9's voice artiste, John Leeson, who, like Baker, was a devotee of *The Times* crossword. There is a story of Baker, in costume, apparently solving the clues with K9 in breaks between filming. In fact, Leeson was offering his contributions via a fold back speaker from the other side of the studio, but the spectacle equally bemused and amused onlookers.

Older fans, ever-sensitive to taunts that *Doctor Who* was a children's programme, lamented K9's introduction into the series as a lurch into childishness and it is hard to see Hinchcliffe sanctioning his inclusion. Children, on the other hand, loved him. Like the Daleks, he was easy to draw, had a character that could be immediately grasped and a voice that could be imitated. (Interestingly, when the series was revised in 2005, Russell T Davies insisted that the aliens could be drawn easily by children.) Like the Daleks again, the BBC made vast sums from merchandise – a Talking K9 appeared almost immediately, with a smaller plastic figure joining Denys Fisher's *Doctor Who* toy range – and the designer, Tony Harding, like Dalek designer Raymond Cusick before him, got not a penny. As a BBC employee, he received a salary instead of royalties: the royalties from K9 were divided between the BBC and the writers, Bob Baker and Dave Martin.

The third story of the fifteenth season, "Image of the Fendahl", is a splendid throwback to the horror of Hinchliffe's time as producer. It was the last story for writer Chris Boucher, who had written both "The Face of Evil" and "The Robots of Death" the previous year: the latter regularly featured in the top ten "best" stories polls in "Doctor Who Magazine". Boucher went on to script edit Nation's new science fiction series *Blake's Seven*, notable for having an even smaller budget than *Doctor Who*: Matt Irvine recalled that the special effects budget was fifty pounds per episode. Once John Nathan-Turner arrived as *Doctor Who's* producer in 1980, Robert Holmes found his services as a scriptwriter were no longer required: Nathan-Turner was keen to encourage new talent and to use his own writers. Chris Boucher repaid the favour Holmes had done him by commissioning three *Doctor Who* stories: he commissioned Holmes to write for *Blake's Seven*.

Before the fifteenth season fell apart completely, Robert Holmes wrote one of the series' best loved stories, "The Sun Makers" (1977). Set on Pluto in the far future, Holmes presented a humanity cowed by an oppressive regime run by the Collector, a Usurian who keeps his work units docile by working them to death and taxing the life out of them. "The Sun Makers" had its roots in Holmes's annoyance with the then Labour government's high taxation policies, and the story's biting satire, and splendid design based on Fritz Lang's 1927 film *Metropolis*, delighted viewers. The Collector sported bushy eyebrows as a reference to Chancellor of the Exchequer Denis Healey (who also had them) and his pin striped robe alluded to Middle Eastern oil potentates, then frequently blamed for high oil prices that were driving the country into recession. There was some criticism from right-wing viewers of the Doctor behaving like Fidel Castro and starting a revolution among the work units (a splendidly rousing speech delivered by Baker at the height of his powers: "Remind them that they're human beings, and human beings always have to fight for their freedom!") but this criticism could be offset by the equally beastly treatment of James Callaghan's Labour government by the story. "The Sun Makers" was notable too for the Usurian's use of a gas pumped into the city to keep the populace docile and frightened at all times. This was lifted by Holmes from a story pitched to the production team by a new writer bursting with innovative science fiction ideas, one Douglas Adams.

As the season continued, it became clearer and clearer that the money was running out. *Doctor Who*, like the United Kingdom, was becoming a victim of high inflation. Some of the scenes in "The Sun Makers" appear to be performed against magnolia-painted flats or black drapes:

Williams later lamented the need to find story reasons to perform scenes against those black studio drapes as an economising measure. "Underworld" (1978), the fifth story of the season, starts strongly on an impressively designed spaceship around which a whole planet begins to form. However, having spent all the budget on episode one, the production team found they had nothing left to finance three episodes set in a cave system. Location filming, or building studio sets, were non-starters. They eventually opted for shooting the episodes against blue screens, keying in model caves using chromakey. The results are questionable to say the least: either dreadful or, if one feels like being kind, an interesting case of the first virtual set in science fiction. "Underworld" also suffered from including, as the Doctor said, "another machine with megalomania" (after the previous season's Xoanon in "The Face of Evil"), poor acting (often a problem in the series' original run 1963-1979) and aliens wearing what appear to be waste paper baskets on their heads with chocolate buttons for eyes and nose.

If "Underworld" was full of problems, the season finale, "The Invasion of Time" (1978), was a work of desperation. Pennant Roberts had submitted a script set on Gallifrey which featured the planet's other, previously unheard-of, inhabitants, a race of intelligent cat people. The story ("The Killer Cats of Geng Singh") called for an arena filled with thousands of the things. Although some designs were completed, including an impressive cat person, Williams cancelled the story when it became clear it was far beyond the programme's means. He had recently been disheartened by the release of *Star Wars* in 1977; returning to the production office after seeing the film, he lamented that there was no way they could match its production values and special effects. (In-house effects designer Mat Irvine recalled that he had been asked if the BBC Visual Effects Department could do effects "like *Star Wars*" and he had replied, "Sure, if you give us the money.") Williams and Anthony Read, the new script editor, wrote "The Invasion of Time" quickly, keeping the Gallifrey setting and following Robert Holmes's advice that a six parter should be written as a four parter followed by a linked two parter: a structure Holmes had used with great success in "The Talons of Weng Chiang".

"The Invasion of Time" is a mess with little to recommend it. It requires the viewers to have seen, and to have remembered, the Gallifrey story "The Deadly Assassin" from the previous season: a tall order in the days before domestic u-matic video recorders were available to anyone save the very rich. (U-matic was the home video system which preceded VHS and Betamax and u-matic video recorders had just started to appear in British schools.) As a twelve year old, I remember being confused and upset by the portrayal of an apparently evil Doctor who sides with the Vardans (tinkly aliens made, it seemed, of tin foil) and is only revealed to be good in later episodes, by which time some of the viewers had given up. Gallifrey is invaded and the Vardans manifest themselves as singularly unimpressive short humanoids dressed as East German traffic policemen. They bark orders and are promptly banished by the Doctor, only to be replaced by the Sontarans in part four's cliff hanger: the story's single effective moment. The Sontarans then run around Gallifrey (or "rampaging", as the *Radio Times* had it); the Doctor and his friends take refuge in the TARDIS's many rooms, but there was no money for sets – again – so the scenes were shot in the brick corridors of a disused lunatic asylum (a metaphor for the story's tone?). Leela is hurriedly written out, staying on Gallifrey with a wet Time Lord called Andred at whom she has never previously looked but with whom she is now apparently in love, K9 is left on Gallifrey only to be replaced by K9 mark II … and mercifully the season came to an end.

Season fifteen's problems perhaps contributed to a decline in viewing figures. Although they rarely dipped much below eight million and peaked at ten and a half million for "The Invasion of Time", this was some way off the eleven million who watched "The Hand of Fear" (1976) and "The Face of Evil" (1977), let alone the twelve million who watched "The Deadly Assassin" (1976) and the whopping twelve and a half million who tuned in to "The Robots of Death" (1977). The figures seem huge by today's standards, where producers, in a multi-channel age, would bath in champagne if their shows garnered an audience of eight million (something regularly achieved by the re-tooled, post-2005 *Doctor Who*), but there were only three channels in 1977 and *Doctor Who*, although by no means a worrying failure, appeared to be in decline.

Determined to get a grip on the series, producer Graham Williams finally managed to launch his Key to Time arc the following season. Under Anthony Read's stewardship as script editor, the sixteenth season's stories were better written and better made than season fifteen's. Ratings held up, but didn't greatly improve. Tom Baker was proving harder to control and his "antics" – Williams' word – often left the producer exhausted. Philip Hinchcliffe had said managing Baker was like riding a huge and powerful horse, but one that was pointing in roughly the right direction. Under Graham Williams, the horse appeared to have thrown off its rider and galloped off.

Another development was the acceptance of a story by a new writer. Nothing very new in that, except that this writer was simultaneously at work on *The Hitch Hiker's Guide to the Galaxy* for Radio 4, and his name was Douglas Adams.

9

The Key to Time and the Talking Cabbage

There were some good stories in the Key to Time season, which ran from September 1978 to February 1979. It was the series' fifteenth season, which saw it notch up its five hundredth episode and one hundredth story, "The Stones of Blood" (1978). Producer Graham Williams had asked Elisabeth Sladen to return as Sarah Jane Smith, but she turned him down: asked about this offer at an American convention, she said she had thought, "How lovely – but no". Much as she had enjoyed *Doctor Who*, Sladen had found there was only so much you could do with the part of a companion and playing second fiddle to two Doctors had sometimes had limited charms. John Nathan-Turner later asked Louise Jameson to return as Leela, perhaps for another story set on Gallifrey, but she also declined.

Williams thus had to devise another companion character. He came up with Romanadvoratrelunder, a young, female Time Lord assigned to the Doctor by the White Guardian to help him in the search for the Key to Time. She is only one hundred and forty years old and had graduated from the Academy with a brilliant degree (far better than the Doctor's): script editor Anthony Read said that, like most brilliant young graduates, she thought she knew everything but lacked experience. Travelling with the Doctor would teach her what the Universe outside Gallifrey was really like. By the end of episode one of "The Ribos Operation", the first story, Romanadvoratrelunder is trapped under a descending stone door and screaming as an awakening Shrivenzale, a local crocodile-like monster, advances on her. "I never imagined…!" she exclaims after escaping. "Are there many creatures like that in other worlds?" "Millions! Millions!" the Doctor snaps back. The Doctor's role in teaching Romanadvoratrelunder recalled Philip Hinchcliffe's initial idea for Leela as an Eliza Doolittle character to the Doctor's Professor Higgins (from Bernard Shaw's 1914 play *Pygmalion* and its sanitised, sentimentalised musical version *My Fair Lady* (1956)): Leela, an alien savage descended from the crew of a crashed Earth ship, would be introduced to civilised behaviour by encountering other humans. The premise appears in "The Talons of Weng Chiang", when the Doctor takes her to see her nineteenth century ancestors, and in numerous stories like "Image of the Fendahl" where he tries to teach her that violence isn't the answer. Leela wants to attack a security guard and his guard dog at Fetch Priory:

Leela:	There is a guard. I shall kill him.
Doctor:	No!
Leela:	Why not?
Doctor:	You'll frighten the dog.

Relations between the Doctor and Romanadvoratrelunder are initially frosty and the Doctor resents being given an assistant: perhaps a reflection of Tom Baker's insistence that he could manage without one and could carry the show on his own. The Doctor tells Romanadvoratrelunder that her name is far too long, and by the time he had called, "Look out, Romanad – ", something awful would have happened to her.

Doctor:	I'll call you Romana.
Romana:	I don't like Romana.
Doctor:	It's either Romana or Fred.
Romana:	All right, call me Fred.
Doctor:	Good. Come on, Romana.

Graham Williams was somewhat more dismissive of Romana's character genesis than Anthony Read, saying that now they had done the primitive savage it was time to do the ice maiden, and this was going from one stereotype to another. We might compare the comments of script editor Eric Saward, who lamented that the character outline for Tom Baker's final companion Tegan was "an Australian", and for Peter Davison's final companion Peri, "an American": both nationalities were chosen to boost the appeal of the series further in these respective countries, where it was doing well.

Mary Tamm was cast as Romana and her first costume – making her look like illustrations of the White Witch in *The Lion, the Witch and the Wardrobe* – emphasised her ice maiden character: white furs, suitable to the icy world of Ribos. Mary Tamm was best known for her role as Sigi in the 1974 film *The Odessa File*, based on the novel by Frederick Forsyth, and was hesitant about taking on the role in *Doctor Who*. This hesitancy might explain her somewhat uncertain performance in some episodes. Romana's introduction wasn't helped by poor management of the press releases, which said she was a "new time lady companion" for the Doctor. "Time Lady" apparently meant female Time Lord (Lord/Lady – see?) but this wasn't a term the show had ever used before and was ambiguous for many, not least my twelve year old self. I assumed that "time lady" just meant "lady who travelled in time", and since almost all of the Doctor's female companions had done that, I couldn't understand why being a "time lady" made Romana special. As a character, Romana suffered from the same problem as Dr Liz Shaw, Jon Pertwee's first companion: she was simply too clever and there was no need for the Doctor to explain things to her. Douglas Adams tried to get round the problem in "The Pirate Planet" by having her and the Doctor explain things together to the simple natives – much to the Doctor's irritation, who thought that explanations were his job – but the writers soon fell back on the expedient of the Doctor telling her things which, as a Time Lord, she should already know. John Nathan-Turner thought Romana didn't work and wondered why she and the Doctor didn't just wink at each other and say, "It's solution number 93". She was written out in Tom Baker's final season.

With Romana came K9 mark II, apparently made by the Doctor after the original had been left on Gallifrey. In the real world, a technological innovation was the domestic video recorder, now becoming more widely available now that VHS had replaced the cumbersome, expensive and unreliable u-matic system. VHS recorders had begun to appear in British homes in 1977 and some fans had taped the fifteenth season off air. The machines were still hideously expensive, as were the tapes, but renting expensive electrical equipment was a more common option in the 1970s and 1980s than it is now, and came with the advantage of free servicing and upgrades when the models were superseded. My brother and I bought our first VHS video recorder – a Ferguson Videostar, no less – in time to tape the repeat season "The Five Faces of *Doctor Who*" in September 1981. It cost £400 (perhaps £800 in today's money) and a three hour tape was £10: hugely expensive for sixth form students like us on a tight budget when we also had to buy beer. You could fit seven episodes on a tape; there was only standard play, not long play and the Ferguson Videostar was mechanical: you had to jam down its mighty play and record buttons together (like a contemporary cassette player) to make it record and there was no remote control. How I kicked myself when the Ferguson Electronic Videostar came out a few months later, with a remote control and long play, doubling the number of episodes you could get on a tape! At least we didn't get a Betamax, the rival system to VHS which died a death in the mid-1980s. Nevertheless, with video, fans could watch the show as many times as they wanted and not reply on summer repeats to see it again. We could notice, for example, that "The Power of Kroll" (1978) used the same shot of the native Swampies running towards the camera twice in different episodes, and that the Mute who menaces the Doctor on the space station, outside the

TARDIS, in "The Armageddon Factor" (1978) kicks up the set's carpet as he comes into shot. We didn't know it at the time, but home video would revolutionise the way we watched television and greatly influence the way television was made. Fans would be able to sneer when John Nathan-Turner denied that the programme had been better in the past when speaking on air about "The Trial of a Time Lord" (1986): we had the tapes and could see that he was wrong. Some critics could even justify incoherent story telling on Sylvester McCoy's stories by saying that they made perfect sense if you watched them fifteen times (note: they still didn't).

The sixteenth season begins strongly with Robert Holmes's "The Ribos Operation" (1978), featuring Iain Cuthbertson as con-man Garron who is trying to sell Ribos to the fanatical warlord, the Graff Vynda-K (Paul Seed, who later directed the BBC's *House of Cards* trilogy with Ian Richardson as silky Conservative Prime Minister and murderer, Francis Urquhart). The Doctor is given the task of finding the six segments of the Key to Time (sometimes referred to on screen as the Key *of* Time as the scriptwriters or actors slip up) by the White Guardian (Cyril Luckham), a civilised cove in a 1920s linen suit, chatting about the end of order in the Universe as he sips a green brandy. The Doctor is reluctant to go on a quest and asks what will happen to him if he refuses. "Nothing," says the White Guardian, pleasantly. "Nothing? You mean, nothing will happen to me?" the Doctor asks hopefully. "Nothing at all," the White Guardian repeats. And then quietly adds: "Ever."

The first segment recovered, the Doctor and Romana travel to Calufrax to find the second in "The Pirate Planet". Their first attempt at landing is aborted: something appears to be trying to materialise in the same space as the TARDIS. With Romana at the helm, showing off, their second attempt is successful. Checking the readings, the Doctor congratulates her on arriving at precisely the right point in space and precisely the right point in time. But on the wrong planet. "This planet," states the Doctor gravely, "wasn't here when I tried to land."

The Time Lords have arrived on Zanak: a hollow, space jumping planet built by the Captain (Bruce Purchase) under the direction of Queen Xanxia. Zanak materialises around other planets, sucks out its minerals and wealth and leaves it, and its inhabitants, for dead.

This was Douglas Adams' first commissioned story for *Doctor Who*. Adams had previously submitted some story ideas to Graham Williams for the fifteeenth season. He suggested a story about an aggressive planet where the people had been pacified by the Time Lords, who built an enormous statue that sucked all the aggression out of them; unfortunately, the Time Lord engineer who maintained the statue gets stuck inside it and absorbs all the aggression. Adams explained in an interview that the story was very complicated, even in its story break-down form, and that after he had read it to Graham Williams, Williams slid down in his chair and muttered that he now knew how Stanley Kubrick felt. The pacifying element was purloined by Robert Holmes for "The Sun Makers" as the Usurians' means of keeping the human workforce quiet and docile. Adams was invited to pitch for the series again and came up with "The Pirate Planet". He was simultaneously commissioned to write six episodes of a science fiction comedy for BBC Radio 4. This was *The Hitch Hiker's Guide to the Galaxy*, which would make him famous and would eclipse his work on *Doctor Who*. Adams, however, had always loved *Doctor Who* and explained often that it, and *Dan Dare* in the *Eagle* comic, were huge influences on *Hitch Hiker's*. He was a graduate in English Literature from the University of Cambridge and interested in real science (he introduced his friend Richard Dawkins to Lalla Ward, who would become Dawkins' wife): both science and literature, and a spell writing for the Monty Python team, were hugely influential on his work for *Doctor Who*.

"The Pirate Planet" is a fine story with wonderfully inventive ideas, but suffers in its last episode from a huge information dump of technobabble to explain how the Doctor releases Calufrax from the jaws of Zanak. This explanation apparently makes scientific sense to science graduates, but was way beyond most viewers at the time. The story also suffers from some dreadful acting by two supporting artists: as is common with so much of *Doctor Who* in the 1970s, actors in minor roles can sometimes be embarrassingly bad. One of the show's directors accounted for this by saying that directors sometimes owed someone a favour, or an agent a favour, and felt obliged to use "actors" in certain roles. It might also be argued that some actors have no idea how to approach science fiction: considering it nonsense, they therefore under- or over-act, or make no attempt to apply their training (assuming they have had any) in creating a character, or character background, for their part. Better actors realise that the way to play science fiction, like anything else, is with total conviction: however preposterous the situation, it must be played for real. In Shakespeare, this sells to an audience the idea that girls can dress up as boys and nobody notice; in *Doctor Who*, it sells to viewers the idea that you are an embittered cyborg space pirate engineer who has invented a space-jumping planet. Adams himself was unhappy with some of the acting in "The Pirate Planet".

He approved of, and injected, much humour into *Doctor Who* but deplored what he saw as a tendency for some actors to see a joke and think it gave them licence to give their character a silly voice, or a funny walk, or to camp it up in general. This view is slightly at variance with Adams' account of writing "The Pirate Planet". He said he left a note in the script's margin saying, "It needs something silly in it, so how about a robot parrot?" He returned to the note, thought, "God, don't be stupid," and then thought, "Why not?" Adams also thought the robot parrot – the Polyphase Avatron – would be a specially designed enemy for K9 to fight, and the two square up in part three, the parrot apparently defaecating electronic globs onto K9 as he blasts it with his nose laser. At the fight's conclusion, K9 presents the destroyed Polyphase Avatron to the Doctor in the manner of a gun dog presenting its master with its game. Adams said the parrot originally had lines like "Pieces of silicate!" and "Pretty Polyphase Avatron!" but he thought them so awful that he cut them. Dick Mills, who designed the wonderful sound effects for the show for many years, said he thought the parrot was a good idea but the problem was it didn't look much like a parrot on screen. It couldn't be painted parrot colours of green, yellow or blue because these were the colours used for colour separation overlay or chromakey (now generally called "green screen"), so it had to be painted brown and therefore wasn't obviously recognisable as a parrot to all the viewers.

One actress who gave her all to the story was the uncredited elderly lady who played Queen Xanxia, held immobile in the last moments of her life by the Time Dams powered by Zanak's plundering of other planets' energy (a typically inventive Adams science fiction idea). If Graham Williams would agree to increase her fee, this lady would offer to remove her teeth to look more decrepit. This was thought to be a splendid idea and the actress complied.

The season's third story, "The Stones of Blood" (1978) was hailed by fans at the time as a classic and won the season poll in the *Doctor Who* Appreciation Society's magazine, *TARDIS*. It is actually quite a forgettable affair, with a cult worshipping an ancient goddess that appears to have stepped out of "The Daemons" (1973). An almost identical cult appears in the lamentable spin-off *K9 and Company* three years later (1981). The eponymous stones of blood monsters are giant lumps of rock on castors that are pushed into shot by stage hands. The fourth story, "The Androids of Tara" (1978), is a wonderful Ruritanian romp and a return to the sort of pastiche favoured by Philip Hinchcliffe and Robert Holmes. It is virtually a re-telling of Anthony Hope's novel

The Prisoner of Zenda (1894) with Peter Jeffery as a splendid villain, Count Grendel (we can tell he is the villain because he has the same name as the monster in the Anglo-Saxon poem *Beowulf*). Grendel attempts to seize the Taran throne by various daft schemes involving android copies of the Princess Strella, engaged to marry the rightful heir, Prince Reynart. Romana is the spitting image of Strella and is blackmailed into assisting Grendel; Grendel kidnaps the Prince to prevent the coronation but the Doctor, working for Reynart's party, provides an android copy of the Prince to be crowned in his stead. The story ends with a splendid swordfight between Grendel and the Doctor on the castle ramparts: Grendel dives into the moat with the parting line, "Next time I shall not be so lenient!", setting himself up for a return match which sadly never materialised.

One interesting notion in "The Androids of Tara" is that the engineers and technicians are the peasants: Reynart and his court have no idea how a horse works, let alone an android, and the Doctor is treated with some disdain for his technical skills. This is presumably a satirical point about the useless, pampered aristocracy who are maintained by the toils of the peasants or workers: an idea in science fiction that goes back to H. G. Wells' *The Time Machine* (1895) where the workers evolve into the Morlocks who devour the skill-less and useless descendants of the aristocracy, the Eloi. (*The Time Machine* appears to have heavily influenced the plot of the first Dalek story back in 1963, with the Daleks as the Morlocks and the Eloi as the Thals; the imagery of the television and film version, *Dr Who and the Daleks*, borrows heavily from the 1960 film of Wells' novel.) "The Androids of Tara" also contains some sexual references which are highly unusual in the original series (although a prostitute quietly appears in episode three of "The Talons of Weng Chiang" as one of Li H'sen Chang's abducted victims). Grendel's android engineer, a woman called Madame Lamia, appears to have been his mistress: he tells Romana that she is attached to him "for certain favours I once showed her" and she hates Romana for having attracted Grendel's attention. Grendel also threatens Lamia that their past relationship will not preclude her punishment if she makes a mistake: "I shall have you flogged, and don't imagine that I won't."

Robert Holmes provided the script for the penultimate story "The Power of Kroll". It is one of the more disappointing of the stories he wrote for *Doctor Who* and was his last until "The Caves of Androzani" in 1984. Holmes was perhaps constrained by the brief from Anthony Read to include "the biggest monster ever seen in *Doctor Who*". This wasn't a great idea on the series' budget and Holmes wasn't keen: having said this, the story has many good points and intelligent ideas. A methane refinery on the third moon of Delta Magna is sending the gas back to the main planet as an energy supply, energy crises being a perennial theme in 1970s *Doctor Who*. The planet's original inhabitants, termed "Swampies" by the racist humans, have been moved to reservations on the third moon in a manner analogous to the Native Americans in the nineteenth century. They are now in the way again and Thawn, the ruthless human leader, wants to wipe them out as his company establishes more refineries. The source of the methane is in fact Kroll, a giant squid hideously mutated and enlarged by the fifth segment of the Key to Time: once the Doctor has extracted the segment, the power source is removed, Kroll disintegrates into lots of little baby squids, and the humans have to find a new modus vivendi with the Swampies.

The story was shot in Norfolk. The boggy terrain was completely unsuitable for K9, who didn't appear. John Leeson, who provided K9's voice, played refinery member Dugeen instead. The actors playing the Swampies are green and their make-up had to be waterproof. This proved difficult to remove and the actors had to repair to a local RAF base and scrub themselves down with Swarfega, a heavy duty cleaner used by engineers to remove oil from the skin. Tony Harding, the story's visual effects designer, explained that the refinery model was about two feet across: on screen, it looks even smaller and Harding was very disappointed with the shots transmitted. Kroll was a much more effective model, four feet across, and operated as a puppet. The live action scenes shot in Norfolk were to be combined with the footage from the model studio of Kroll waving his tentacles around: visual effects decided on a soft edged wipe to achieve the combined shot. Unfortunately, Harding explained, the cameraman on location was very young and had been given the wrong information about how to achieve a soft edged wipe. On screen, the division between the two pictures is marked by a dirty great flickering black line which appears to cut off the marsh's reeds half way up. There was no possibility of returning to Norfolk to reshoot, and Harding was desperately disappointed with the imperfect shots transmitted.

The season's final story is "The Armageddon Factor" by *Doctor Who* stalwarts Bob Baker and Dave Martin. They had to conclude the Doctor's quest for the Key to Time: Williams had set it up but hadn't determined on a clear ending, although it was also claimed that the Doctor, having assembled the Key, would always have said, "Well, there it is – I'm going to chuck it away now." Baker and Martin opted for the bi-partite structure of a six part serial favoured by Robert Holmes (write it as a four parter followed by a two parter). The first three episodes are set on the planet Atrios, which is locked in a nuclear war with Zeos, its neighbour, and losing heavily. *Doctor Who* was clearly drawing on the threat of nuclear war again, something it would return to with much less subtlety in the execrable "Warriors of the Deep" (1984). The possibility of a nuclear war and the accelerated arms race with the Soviet Union deeply alarmed sections of the British public at the time, as did the election of Ronald Reagan as President of the United States in 1980. Reagan's advisers had seriously considered the possibility of a pre-emptive nuclear strike against the USSR. Membership of the Campaign for Nuclear Disarmament soared, as did hostility to the movement, dubbed "Communist, Neutralist Defeatists" by such mushrooming opposition groups as Women for Defence, led by the Conservative MP Lady Olga Maitland (itself dubbed Mummies for Missiles by the actress Emma Thompson). The Atrians are led by the Marshall, played by John Woodvine at his Churchillian best. In a clear echo of right wing alarm about the enemy within (as CND was perceived by some at the time), he accuses pacifists Surgeon Merak and Princess Astra of colluding with the enemy Zeons to bring about a swift end to the war.

The Marshall is under the influence of the Shadow, the Black Guardian's agent. While the Doctor has scoured the Universe for the first five segments, the Shadow has sensibly located the sixth segment and waited patiently for the Doctor to bring him the other five. He traps the Doctor in his lair, the planet of evil (actually a space station), where Doctor wanders about for several episodes. The Shadow's lair was originally conceived as a fun fair or ghost train, with strange noises and sudden giggles heard from dark corners. Dick Mills revealed this was dropped when people began asking why there should be people giggling in dark corners: altogether too suggestive for the time slot. The Doctor meets Drax, a Time Lord with a cockney accent in the Shadow's employ, who addresses the Doctor as Theta Sigma. This upset people at the time as the non-classically educated among us assumed "Theta Sigma" was the Doctor's name, now finally revealed on television. One fan reviewer transcribed it as "Feet Asigma". Theta and Sigma are of course two Greek letters, but comprehensive school educated boys like me didn't know this, or recognise that it was unlikely the Doctor was named after two Greek letters. The BBC let it be known that Theta Sigma was the code by which the Doctor had been known at the Time

Lord academy, and Terrance Dicks explained it as such in his novelisation of the story. There were shades here of the retrospective continuity applied to the multiple faces of the Doctor in "The Brain of Morbius" and the BBC's subsequent explanation (see chapter eight). Again, the point wasn't made clear on screen and viewers scratched their heads.

Another minor continuity mistake is the Doctor's line "I've never seen him do that before" as K9 revolves on the spot before communicating with Mentalis, the Shadow's war computer. Dick Mills noted that K9 *had* done it before in "The Pirate Planet", because he had provided the whirling sound effect for it. The point was made during the recording but time was pressing and the mistake went through.

In a clever piece of scripting, the sixth segment is revealed to be Princess Astra (Lalla Ward). She calmly accepts her destiny and is transformed into a component. Romana is appalled, as is the Doctor, who nevertheless insists they have to return the Key to the White Guardian. The Doctor is himself affected by the Key and Tom Baker has a speech of ranting megalomania in which he insists that he could become a god: the scene is played and scripted for laughs and we see the influence of Douglas Adams again, who had just taken over from Read as script editor. Presumably the Doctor's experience of the Key's effect on himself is one reason for his decision to dismantle it, as it is too powerful for any one being to possess, but the point again isn't made clear on screen. The Black Guardian arrives and poses as the White Guardian to persuade the Doctor to hand the Key over. As he now looks and sounds like Valentine Dyall and not Cyril Luckham, the Doctor should have spotted the substitution. He does so when he asks the Guardian about Astra's fate: the Black Guardian says it's regrettable that Astra has died but with the future of the Universe at stake one can't be too careful. Knowing that the White Guardian would never have such a callous disregard for human life, the Doctor activates the TARDIS's defences (we know this because the Black Guardian has the line, "Doctor! You have fully activated all the TARDIS's defences!"), dematerialises and scatters the Key again in time and space. This restores Princess Astra to her human form and to her drippy lover, Surgeon Merak.

The story's ending is hugely unsatisfactory and as full of holes as the original premise for the Key to Time. It is never clear what the Key is supposed to do: "restore the balance", yes, but of, or between, what? The Doctor says at the end of "The Armageddon Factor" that there should always be a struggle between good and evil: this is one reason why he hesitates about destroying the Daleks for ever in "Genesis of the Daleks". If the balance were restored between good and evil, would there then be no conflict, or would the sides just be evenly matched? Certainly if conflict would end then so would the series, but this is never made clear. "The Ribos Operation" suggests the Key is needed to balance much vaguer cosmic "forces" in the Universe, without which the Universe will fall apart. Is this some reference to the threat of entropy in "Logopolis" (1981), through which the Universe is disintegrating and is only held together by the block transfer computations of the Logopolitans? Dispersing the Key might thus mean the Universe is still under threat of collapse. As the Doctor has failed his mission for the White Guardian as well, won't he be looking for revenge as well as the Black Guardian? Yet when the Fifth Doctor encounters both again in "Enlightenment" (1984), the White Guardian seems to have forgotten all about his threat of eternal nothingness as a punishment for the Doctor's lack of co-operation, and is as civil and avuncular as ever. Both Guardians are ludicrously costumed in this Peter Davison story, the Black Guardian wearing a vulture's head as a hat, and the White Guardian a dove: perhaps their choice of headgear indicates a weakening of their mental powers, which would explain the White Guardian's forgetfulness of his threat of eternal punishment for the Doctor.

With filming on the season nearly completed, Graham Williams thought that the umbrella theme had been a success but couldn't be repeated easily. It had, he thought, imposed too many constraints on the writers. Next season would see the Doctor resume his random travels in time and space and "The Armageddon Factor" ends with the Doctor fitting a new device to the TARDIS console. This is a randomiser, which, he explains, operates on the "very, very complex scientific principle of pot luck". "Now no-one knows where we're going," sighs Romana, "Not the Black Guardian. Not even us." "No," says the Doctor, and smiles hugely as the season ends.

The chaos generated by the randomiser was mirrored by more chaos in the show's production. Mary Tamm was adamant that she would do one season only and not renew her contract. Graham Williams kept trying to persuade her to do one more year – "Mary will come back next year, won't you Mary?" he's said to have kept saying – but she kept saying no. By the time Williams realised that she really wouldn't return, the final scenes of "The Armageddon Factor" had wrapped and Mary Tamm hadn't been written out. Tamm suggested to Lalla Ward, who had played Princess Astra, that she should put herself up for the role of the companion. Lalla, who had enjoyed a regular part as Lottie in *The Duchess of Duke Street* (BBC, 1976-77), was interested. She had found favour with the production team for her sensitive performance as Astra. Someone realised that, as Romana was a Time Lord, she could regenerate and Lalla Ward could play her, rather than another character.

The problem was that a regeneration scene hadn't been shot and Mary Tamm would not have agreed to return to shoot one. The Doctor's regeneration had always been carefully planned and built up to in the course of a story. How then could Romana regenerate at the beginning of the new season? The new script editor, Douglas Adams, solved the problem with his application of his customary humour, or, if you would rather, flippancy. In the opening scene of season seventeen's first story, "Destiny of the Daleks" (1979), Romana is seen trying on bodies as an Earth woman would try on clothes: one midget form, dressed in Zilda's garb from "The Robots of Death" (1977), says, "I quite like this one, but it's a bit short." "Well, lengthen it then, go on," the Doctor replies. Fans hated the scene for its flippant tone and the frivolity with which it dealt with the serious concept of regeneration: a Time Lord has twelve regenerations but Romana apparently wastes more than half of them trying on different forms. Viewers are also asked to swallow that Time Lords can wear copies of bodies and the Doctor tells Romana that she can't wear Princess Astra's body: "Why not?" says Romana, "I thought it looked very nice on the Princess." To be fair to Adams, he was making the best of a bad job and trying to write an impossible scene. However, this was a huge and indigestible change in tone from the previous season which, though often funny, had largely kept Tom Baker's performance, and the humour, under control and subordinate to the drama. Now it seemed that the series had become *The Hitch Hiker's Guide to the Galaxy*. Romana's rapid changes of form recalled the Hagunenons, the super evolving species from the original radio series, who would evolve a longer arm instantaneously if they needed to reach a cup of coffee from the other side of the room. In fact, this sequence was written by John Lloyd rather than Adams, who was busy with *Doctor Who*, but perhaps Adams recalled it anyway when faced with the problem of Romana's changing face.

Graham Williams had offered Adams the post of script editor partly because he felt that the combination of Adams's inventiveness and humour, and Tom Baker's sense of humour, would lead to an explosion of creativity. In fact, it radically changed the programme, inflecting it towards humour and auto-referentiality (where the fiction reminds its audience that it is a fiction) in a way that influenced it permanently. It has been argued that Russell T Davies was influenced by Adams' sense of the absurd in his treatment of the revived series after 2005. In 1979, some fans rejoiced at the fresh inventiveness of the show; others lamented its lack of seriousness and "undergraduate" humour, and fandom was split down the middle. Adams allowed Romana and the Doctor to speculate about flying down from the top of the Eiffel Tower rather than taking the lift in "City of Death" (1979). This has been seen as a charming and amusing moment, or as irritating beyond words because it treats Time Lords as Superman-types with super powers, when it has never been established in the show that they are like this. Douglas Adams would not let continuity stand in the way of a joke, however good or bad it was. As script editor, he pitched several story ideas to Williams that the latter rejected. One was to pitch the Doctor against a race called the Krikkitmen: Adams postulated that every planet had variations on a game called cricket, and the English game was related to the sinister variety played by the evil Krikkitmen. This was a variation on a *Hitch Hiker's* idea that every planet had a drink called gin and tonic or its homophonic equivalent. Williams said the Krikkitmen were too silly and Adams replied that this seemed a strange thing to say about a series which centred on an alien clad in a hat and scarf who travelled the Universe in a police box with a robot dog. He tried to turn the script into a film, *Doctor Who and the Krikkitmen*, but nothing came of it. Never one to discard old story ideas, Adams re-used the material in his third *Hitch Hiker's* novel. He similarly recycled Professor Chronotis from the abandoned story *Shada* (1979) into his novel *Dirk Gently's Holistic Detective Agency*. Adams also submitted a story in which the Doctor retires from saving the Universe, arguing he has done enough, before being drawn back into his heroic role by a new threat. Williams toyed with the idea and then turned it down, but it perhaps formed the basis for the Eleventh Doctor's retirement in "The Snowmen" (2012). Distraught at the loss of his companions Rory and Amy, the Doctor goes into seclusion in Victorian England and ignores repeated attempts by Silurian Madame Vastra, her maid Jenny and Sontaran manservant Strax to re-engage him with combating evil. Adams's enduring influence on the series can perhaps be seen in the triumvirate of bizarre characters in the 2012 Christmas special, "The Snowmen". The Doctor (Matt Smith) of course has his interest reawakened by the enigmatic Clara (Jenna-Louise Coleman) and the animated snowmen, manifestations of the Great Intelligence…

The seventeenth season also hit problems with the rampant inflation of the late 1970s. Former producer Philip Hinchcliffe submitted a story called "The Valley of the Lost", centering on a plane crash in a South American jungle. Adams turned it down on the grounds of cost, explaining in a letter to Hinchcliffe that they now made *Doctor Who* on about one third less of the money that had been available to the former producer. In a margin of the proposed script, Adams wrote, "*Close Encounters* of the extremely expensive kind...?" The production values of the seventeenth season were poor in comparison with the sixteenth, let alone the Hinchcliffe/Holmes serials. The Daleks looked reasonably good on location for "Destiny of the Daleks", but were bashed about considerably when they returned to the studio, allegedly after being hired out to *Blue Peter* and to private users. For a small fee at the time, you could hire a Dalek from the BBC for, say, a parish fete: Dick Mills lamented the need to provide a tape for hired Dalek voices. My brother Simon and I tried out a BBC Dalek in 1979 in its "Destiny" livery. It had been hired by a local picture framer who wanted to use it as a model for two Daleks he intended to build (and I think never did) for his youth club.

In the studio, the Daleks were decrepit: their paint was chipped, their wheels squeaked (apparently the budget didn't run to a can of oil) and one had a diamond panel banged onto its base section to hide its damage. The props were also so old that each was slightly different from the others, with different coloured dome lights and rings around the same and so on. This meant that it was therefore very obvious which Dalek prop was doubling as another Dalek once it had been exterminated.

There appeared to be almost no money at all for the final two stories, "Nightmare of Eden" and "Horns of Nimon". Some of the former's spacecraft scenes were shot against black drapes and the passenger extras were clad in head-to-toe cagoules, complete with hoods, and dark glasses: no doubt to save money on costumes. The Skonnon parliament in "The Horns of Nimon" contained about five members sitting on black rostra, doubtless indicating how far Skonnon democracy had declined under the despotism of Soldeed (Graham Crowden). It seemed that much of the money was spent on "Creature from the Pit", the first story to be shot, which had included expensive jungle sets and filming at Ealing Studios. "City of Death" was partly filmed in Paris, but apparently the location filming was no more expensive than shooting in this country, thanks to the canny budgeting of the production unit manager, one John Nathan-Turner, who became producer for the eighteenth season. The team kept costs down by shooting on the hoof: they set up the camera without permission to shoot the Doctor, Duggan and Romana in Paris and hurriedly decamped when the local gendarmerie started to take an interest. "Shada" would presumably have been an expensive finale but was abandoned because of industrial action at the BBC, with only one of its three studio sequences, plus its location filming, completed. John Nathan-Turner attempted to remount it in the following year but was unable to make it work. It was eventually released as a commercial VHS in 1992, with Tom Baker providing linking narration (in character as the Doctor) for unfilmed sequences. Big Finish remade it as an audio with Paul McGann as the Doctor and Lalla Ward reprising her role as Romana. It was available to stream on the BBC website, with limited animated visuals, and was eventually published as a novel by Gareth Roberts in 2012.

The seventeenth season was thus a chaotic one with a hotch-potch of stories of even more varying quality and tone than season fifteen. John Leeson had left as the voice of K9 and his replacement, David Brierley, had none of the original's charms. Adams attempted to explain K9's change of voice as an attack of laryngitis in "Destiny of the Daleks", but this explanation, which could be described as lazy or hilarious scripting, depending on your taste, was undermined by the Doctor asking, "How can a machine get laryngitis? I mean, what do you need it for?" No answer was forthcoming. John Nathan-Turner persuaded John Leeson to return as K9 for Tom Baker's final season and Leeson has provided K9's voice ever since for *Doctor Who*, *The Sarah Jane Adventures* and Bob Baker's lamentable Australian children's series *K9* (2009-10).

Adding to the general sense of confusion was Tom Baker. He had now played the Doctor for five years and was embarking on his sixth, longer than any previous incumbent in the role. Tom Baker felt that he knew the part and understood the series better than anyone else. Asked to stay on for another season, Baker wrote a long letter to the Head of Series and Serials saying that he would only stay on if he had more control over the scripts. He suggested that his new companion should be a fat girl who couldn't keep up, or a talking cabbage who would sit on the Doctor's shoulder and offer opinions. Strangely, neither of these suggestions were taken up, although he did have more and more control over the scripts – which he and Lalla Ward would apparently rewrite in rehearsals – and over what appeared on screen. He appeared to enjoy Adams's sense of humour and ad-libbed constantly. There is one sequence in "Nightmare of Eden" when the Doctor is attacked by the Mandrels; Baker, off screen, ad-libs, "Oh my arms! My legs! My everything! OOO!" He then staggers towards the camera in a ragged coat, looking like a cartoon character who has experienced a terrible disaster: say, Tom from *Tom and Jerry* after a bomb has gone off. Other Baker interpolations followed. In "The Horns of Nimon", he gives K9 the kiss of life and draws attention to the woefully unfrightening Nimon costumes by asking, "Tell me, Nimon, are you terribly fierce?" Lalla Ward, perhaps trying to compensate, plays the whole story completely straight. Graham Crowden, apparently infected by all the hilarity, laughs his head off during his death scene; he was, it seems, unaware that this was a take, not a rehearsal. Graham Williams recalled that "we would be tearing our hair out in the gallery while Tom was going through his antics" on the studio floor. He and Baker clashed to the extent that they had a meeting with Shaun Sutton, the Head of Drama and another senior BBC executive, Graham McDonald. Knowing the problems with Tom Baker not taking the material seriously enough – they had sent Williams notes expressing reservations about the level of humour in the new scripts – McDonald nevertheless told Williams that Tom Baker's Doctor delivered up to thirteen million viewers a week, and that, if a choice had to be made between them, Williams would go and Baker would stay. The pair agreed they could work together. In his autobiography, Baker rather decently expresses regret at his behaviour to Williams and realises that his suggestions exhausted his producer.

In spite of all the mayhem off screen, the viewing figures for season seventeen were exceptionally good. "Destiny of the Daleks" gained thirteen and a half million viewers, and "City of Death" fourteen and a half million: the programme's highest ever audience. As Letts and Dicks had found when they opened the ninth season with "Day of the Daleks" (1972) – nine and a half million viewers and the season's biggest ratings winner – Daleks were a great hook for casual viewers in the opening episode. The exceptional figures for "Destiny" and "City" were partly explained by the lack of competition, as ITV was again blacked out by industrial action. This plagued all television production in the 1970s as show business unions, like others, ignored the pleas of the then Labour government and the Trades Union Congress to keep wage demands low and reasonable. In some cases, unions selfishly and recklessly did neither, demanding preposterous settlements and raising their own nemesis in the form of Mrs Thatcher's Conservative government, whose legislation castrated the union movement. The industrial craziness hit the BBC in a yearly dispute about which union was responsible for the clock on *Play School* (the BBC's main programme for under-fives). For *Doctor Who*, union silliness manifested itself as an endless dispute about who should operate and maintain the time rotor which rose and fell on the TARDIS console. Philip Hinchcliffe got so fed up with this that he wrote the time rotor out in the fourteenth season, which introduced a new, Jules Verne type control room whose console was based on a davenport and had no time rotor. Graham Williams, anxious to restore the show's science fiction look, reintroduced the gleaming white control room in "The Invisible Enemy" (1977), time rotor and all: based on the Hartnell set, it was basically used until the original series folded in 1989.

As is the case with most of the seasons, viewing figures drained away in the course of the season, falling to eight and three quarter million for "The Horns of Nimon" (1979-80). The decline was attributable in part to ITV broadcasting again. It might also be argued that the final Nimon story was so dreadful that it put viewers off *Doctor Who* for much of the next season. "The Leisure Hive" (1980) barely managed to scrape together five million viewers, and the eighteenth season averaged about six million, peaking at just over seven million for the excellent "Warriors' Gate" (1981). Although hailed as a Saturday evening institution, people weren't watching *Doctor Who* much. The decline led new producer John Nathan-Turner to push for a change of scheduling and Peter Davison's three seasons as the Doctor transmitted twice weekly on weeknights. There was an immediate improvement in ratings: Davison's first story garnered nearly ten million viewers and the rest of his season averaged over nine million. Davison himself expressed some regret at the change in timeslot but acknowledged Nathan-Turner's reasoning for it.

There are some good stories in season seventeen. "City of Death" (1979) is often hailed as a classic and is packed with inventive science fiction ideas. Douglas Adams and Graham Williams, working under the in-house pen name of "David Agnew", which had been used as a credit for "The Invasion of Time" (1977), rewrote a script from David Fisher about art theft. This had featured a detective in the Bulldog Drummond mode who became the bumbling Duggan, engagingly played by Tom Chadbon. At the dawn of time, a Jagaroth spaceship explodes on take-off on prehistoric Earth, scattering its single survivor across different periods in Earth's history. Each of the separate selves tries to push forward mankind's development so that its twentieth century self, Count Scarlioni (Julian Glover) in Paris, will have sufficient technology to build a time machine, return to the past and stop his original self from launching the ship. The time experiments are financed by art thefts, including the theft of the Mona Lisa. The story is witty, well-acted and entertaining but arguably spoilt by Tom Baker's performance, now almost wholly inflected towards comedy and undermining the dramatic moments.

"Nightmare of Eden" (1979), Bob Baker's solo writing venture for the series, is also a good story. Coming out of hyperspace, the cruise liner *Empress* and the cargo ship *Hecate* half materialise around each other. The *Empress*'s mayday is answered by the Doctor and Romana. In a nice touch of realism, the Doctor poses as an insurance agent trying to sort out the rival claims for damages from each of the captains. Also on board the *Empress* is zoologist Tryst, whose continual event transmuter has allowed him to store sectors of the planets he has visited on data crystal. He is financing his experiments with drug running: the monstrous Mandrels, reduced to ashes, form the basis of the drug vraxoin. The Doctor is appalled at the presence of vraxoin on the ship: he reinforces the story's anti-drug message repeatedly by reiterating the evil of drug running, which destroys whole planets while the merchants make fortunes. The original script called the drug "zip" but Lalla Ward was concerned that this sounded too attractive a name for children, so it was changed. At the story's end, Tryst appeals to the Doctor to understand, as a fellow scientist, that he never wanted to be a drug runner but had to finance his research. The Doctor, who never acknowledges that the end justifies the means (at least, until his Sylvester McCoy incarnation: a disgraceful distortion of the series' morality), disgustedly tells him to go away.

Good as these stories are, there are moments to make the viewer wince. Both feature a scientist with a cod Germanic accent: Kerensky in "City of Death" and Tryst in "Nightmare of Eden". Williams really should haff spotted zis und put a schtop to it. Colin Mapson was the visual effects designer on "Eden" and lamented Williams's decision to save money by shooting his beautiful and elaborate models on videotape. On the model stage, with high speed film cameras, effective filming of spaceships was possible; in the television studio, with lumbering electronic video cameras the size of a piano, it wasn't. Williams expressed himself very pleased with the time and the money saved: Mapson hated it. Colin Mapson also criticised the design of the Mandrels, which hugely resembled the larger muppets from *The Muppet Show*, then running on ITV, and provoked hysterics across the land when one lunges out at the Doctor and Captain Rigg at the end of episode one. As was common in *Doctor Who* for the period, the spaceship sets were over-lit, which exposed the cheapness of their construction. The public address system is very clearly a drain cover screwed into a flat. The story also collapsed behind the scenes. Alan Bromley, who had directed "The Time Warrior" (1973-4), walked out half way through following disputes with the cast and Graham Williams had to handle the final studio session.

The less said about "The Creature from the Pit" and "The Horns of Nimon", the better. Christopher Barry returned to direct the former and found a very different Tom Baker from the actor he had worked with in "Robot" and "The Brain of Morbius". He objected to Baker reworking scenes and would wait till he had finished improvising before trying to shoot the scene as he, Barry, wanted it. Much of the season's money appears to have been spent on an impressive jungle set at Ealing studios and the eponymous creature is a Kroll-sized disaster. Special effects designer Matt Irvine and his team created Erato – for that is the creature's name – from weather balloons and it bundled greenly along the studio floor with a huge penile probe extended when it wanted to communicate with people. There was a pause when it was unveiled in the studio, broken by one of the cameramen saying, "Who's a big boy, then?", followed by general hilarity. Christopher Barry was furious and modifications were made to the creature for the second studio session, where it looked less obscene. Barry, Williams and Irvine were involved in an internal BBC inquiry to discover who had sanctioned such a disaster. As usual, it was trying to deliver an ambitious effect with a lack of time, communication and money. A similar disaster occurred five years later with the Myrka, the Silurians' dinosaur pet in "Warriors of the Deep" (1984). Released to destroy the humans on the sea base, the Myrka was operated by the two pantomime horse actors from *Rentaghost* and was about as realistic. It wasn't ready for the studio session and was still wet with paint; its verisimilitude wasn't assisted by guest star Ingrid Pitt, who decided to launch into a karate kick against it and presumably got her feet covered in paint. The Myrka was in good company in this story. Working against the clock, the director screamed at the Sea Devils who had just fallen over and died – their costumes buckling at the back in the process, revealing the actor underneath – to get up and die again. "Creature from the Pit" concerns the planet Chloris, rich in vegetation but lacking metal, visited by the Tythonian ambassador – the Creature – from a planet rich in metal but lacking vegetation. He hopes a swap can be arranged but is thrown into the pit by the wicked Lady Adrasta, who has a monopoly on the metal and doesn't want the price to fall. Erato is freed and kills her. There is a silly sub plot with some bandits whose leader sounds and looks like Fagin from various films of *Oliver Twist*: he even calls his henchmen, "my boys".

"The Horns of Nimon", the season's final story, is extraordinary. Anthony Read's script is actually pretty good and in the pastiche tradition of Hinchliffe and Holmes, via "Underworld" (1978): the latter was a version of Jason and the Argonauts, "Nimon" is a version of the Minotaur legend, signposted by the virtual Nimon/minotaur anagram in case we can't work this out for ourselves. The Nimon are a plague of galactic locusts who land on a planet, promise its inhabitants great wealth, then strip it of all its riches and energy before moving on. This is called "The Great Journey of Life". One Nimon has promised Soldeed (Graham Crowden) such riches and technology but endlessly defers it while it accepts tribute from Aneth (i.e. Athens), defeated by Skonnos (Knossos) in war. The tribute takes the form of highly ineffectual young men and women whom the Nimon slaughters for no good reason. One was played by Janet Ellis, who went on to become a presenter on *Blue Peter* and looks and sounds like one in this story. The Nimon has high opinions of itself and lives in the Power Complex (geddit?). Romana and the Doctor defeat him and Soldeed and the season lurched to a premature end: the next story, "Shada", was abandoned because of industrial action.

"The Horns of Nimon" is perhaps the worst story of the 1970s. Tom Baker sends the whole thing up and sucks any dramatic tension out of every scene. In episode one, the Doctor is dismantling the TARDIS console to make it work more effectively: when he tests it, it emits a stock comedy sound effect of whoops and boings first used in *The Goons* and familiar from shows like *The Goodies*. This is an effective metaphor for what Tom Baker and Douglas Adams were doing to *Doctor Who* at this point: taking it to pieces and reassembling it as puerile comedy. This wouldn't be so bad if it were funny but it isn't and comedy can never be excused or acceptable if it isn't funny. Graham Crowden catches the general mood of hilarity and grotesquely overacts as Soldeed. Only Lalla Ward tries to keep things on an even keel by playing it straight and she is fighting a losing battle. The money has clearly run out by this point, too. The Nimon are played by dancers in black body stockings, clad in wispy golden loincloth and clumping around in the sort of platform shoes favoured by glam rockers of the period. Their heads appear to be bull masks sculpted in plastic and are so unconvincing that original viewers thought they must be helmets to hide the real, hideous alien within. This was indeed the plan but there wasn't enough money to make real, hideous aliens, so the production team hoped the ridiculous helmets would suffice. They didn't. The co-pilot shot by the Nimon splits his costume and reveals his red underpants.

As a penultimate story before a six part epic, "The Horns of Nimon" might have been quietly forgotten as an embarrassment. As the final story of the season, it is a disaster and left many fans depressed and miserable about the show's prospects. It seems odd to think of now, when Tom Baker remains one of the most popular Doctors and is so loved, that many fans wanted him to go by the start of season seventeen, hating the way he sent the show up and fearful that the public wouldn't accept a new actor as the Doctor. Douglas Adams departed for other *Hitch Hiker's* related projects at the end of season seventeen and Graham Williams left the BBC altogether to run a hotel. BBC executives had continued to be concerned about Tom Baker not taking the show seriously for some years; Graeme McDonald had even asked Williams to fire him, which Williams thought completely unnecessary. The new producer was one John Nathan-Turner and his first brief was to keep Tom Baker under control.

10

The first of the modern Doctors

John Nathan-Turner had been production unit manager on both *Doctor Who* and the BBC's long-running vet saga *All Creatures Great and Small* (1978-80; 1988-90), based on the autobiographies of James Herriott. He was thus the keeper of the purse strings and was adept both at bringing in his shows on budget and making that budget go a long way. As such, he was thought to be a safe pair of hands for *Doctor Who*. However, the BBC noted his inexperience as a producer and appointed Barry Letts as executive producer for the eighteenth season. Letts read and commented on all the scripts and mentored Nathan-Turner in the role of a producer.

John Nathan-Turner immediately set about "putting the money on the screen". Season eighteen's production values were far higher than season seventeen's although the budget was more or less the same. Nathan-Turner cut back on expensive location work and alien environments were convincingly realised in the television studio: "The Leisure Hive" had only one location sequence on Brighton beach; "Meglos", "Warriors' Gate" and "The Keeper of Traken" had no location filming at all.

A new title sequence was commissioned from graphic designer Sid Sutton. In place of the familiar time tunnel – which Nathan-Turner thought looked like racing down the tube of a vacuum cleaner – was a star field which forms the Doctor's face. The stars also formed the new logo: the shield, which had been used since Pertwee's last season and for seven years, was replaced by a tubular logo. Both title sequence and logo were disappointing. A shield suggested the Doctor's role as knight errant fighting evil; a tubular logo suggested inventive domestic lighting. The star field put the theme of space travel across convincingly enough but time travel was now absent. Furthermore, the stars weren't particularly well realised: they appeared fully formed in the middle distance, rather than coming into shot gradually, and the star field was far less effective than that used in *Star Trek*'s opening titles which dated back to 1966. That they recalled *Star Trek* at all showed how old hat the new titles were. Nathan-Turner used a new portrait of Tom Baker for the titles, arguing that the original portrait had been used since 1974 and didn't match the actor's ageing. Baker's face would be replaced by Peter Davison's for the following season – which appeared from a venetian blind-like wipe, thus complementing the domestic interior design theme of the logo – and eventually by Colin Baker's, which broke into a huge and ghastly grin. The closing titles ended with a white star exploding onto the screen in a white out. Composer Peter Howell recalled that Sutton had been advised not to use this image, as white outs always showed up the viewers' dirty television screens, but he used it anyway. The new theme was a more boppy, disco version of Ron Grainer's original, which began with the scream that had signalled the cliffhanger of previous years (something copied in the new theme for Christopher Eccleston and David Tennant's Doctors). The scream was repeated for the cliffhanger, but was too high pitched and short to generate excitement as had the deep bass original of previous years. *Doctor Who* had entered the colourful eighties and the new theme was apparently played in British discos at the time to warn the staff that there was a fire. When the show returned in 2005, Russell T Davies's team looked to the original Baker sequence for inspiration, thus perhaps indicating the enduring worth of its star field replacement. The 2005 sequence copied the Tom Baker TARDIS hurtling through the time tunnel and the imagery within the programme itself showed the TARDIS travelling in the same tunnel when in flight (the original series had tended to use a space background for sequences when the TARDIS flew). This re-use of 1970s imagery confirmed the original Baker sequence as representing the time vortex, something that had never been made explicit at the time. Davies and Moffat dispensed with the Doctor's face for all the title sequences until the 2012 Christmas special, "The Snowmen", where Matt Smith's face appears fleetingly against cosmic clouds.

Nathan-Turner was unhappy with the six part serials, correctly feeling that they sagged in the middle and were usually padded with running up and down corridors. He asked for an extra two episodes for Tom Baker's final season (the eighteenth) so that he could make seven four part stories rather than five four part stories and a six parter, the twenty six episode pattern that had been standard for the past five years. Nathan-Turner made the request with some trepidation, thinking that he might be asked to make two episodes fewer instead, but the BBC, in a sign of their confidence in him and their hope the show could be revitalised, agreed. Had they insisted on twenty four episodes we might have been spared the dreadful "Meglos", a tale not of a talking cabbage but a talking cactus, but that's another story. In the course of making season eighteen, Nathan-Turner apparently felt the strain of stretching the budget over twenty eight episodes and requested a twenty six episode run again for season nineteen, Peter Davison's first, concentrating the money saved into the twenty six episodes. Nathan-

Turner avoided a sagging six episode tale in Davison's first season by making six four part stories and one two parter: the historical 1920s tale "Black Orchid" (1981) by Terence Dudley.

Nathan-Turner intended to write out both Romana and K9, thinking both were far too clever and made it too easy for problems to be solved. Unfortunately, the announcement that K9 was to go led *The Sun* newspaper to run a "Save K9" campaign ("Save him! Save K9 from the beastly Beeb!") and Bill Cotton, the outgoing Controller of BBC 1, insisted that K9 should return to television within a year. This either meant including him again in *Doctor Who* or giving him his own show. Thus a pilot episode for a new series, *K9 and Company* (1981), was made. Elisabeth Sladen returned as Sarah Jane Smith with John Leeson as the voice of K9. Elisabeth Sladen was horrified by the technical limitations of the K9 prop and not over-enamoured of the script, which concerned a cult of pagan goddess worshippers led by a greengrocer, played by Bill Fraser. This plot wasn't a good idea as it had been already done in "The Stones of Blood" eighteen months previously and such tales were arguably an ill fit with a science fiction show. Sarah Jane Smith's character had undergone some alterations: she was more acerbic than the Sarah we had last seen in "The Hand of Fear" (1976) and she had learnt to dispatch bad guys with high kicks. Had writer Terence Dudley confused her with Leela? It was nice to see Sarah's Aunt Lavinia make an appearance, played by the fine actress Mary Wimbush (Julia Pargetter in *The Archers* and Aunt Agatha in *Jeeves and Wooster*, both formidable ladies) but hard to see how the pilot could be stretched into a series. Apart from a coven of witches, what other evils could threaten the village of Moreton Harwood? *K9 and Company* remained a single-episode spin-off, but was assimilated back into the parent show and thus regarded as canonical when Sarah reappeared with K9 in the twentieth anniversary special "The Five Doctors" (1983) and in the revived series in "School Reunion" (2006).

New companions were introduced towards the end of the season. The first was Adric, a mathematical boy genius, described in the brief to writers as fifteen, small for his age, wiry and strong. Boy geniuses in science fiction shows are the sort of idea which production teams feel are excellent and viewers dislike intensely. Adric, like Wesley in *Star Trek: the Next Generation* was conceived as a character for younger viewers to identify with but, as Sydney Newman noted when planning the series in 1963, such viewers tend to identify with the next generation up and find characters their own age irritating and patronising. While *Next Generation* fans were hoping that "that brat didn't save the ship again", *Doctor Who* fans squirmed in embarrassment at Adric. Adric might have worked if a good young actor been cast but Matthew Waterhouse's range is somewhat limited. In his first story, "Full Circle", he is upstaged by Richard Willis as his brother Varsh and some critics wondered why the casting was not reversed. Fans breathed a sigh of relief when Adric blew up with the Earth freighter on prehistoric Earth ("Earthshock", 1982). Some even considered he didn't quite merit the end titles rolling in silence over his smashed badge for mathematical excellence – a trick used for Charlie's death in *The Duchess of Duke Street* (season two, 1977) – or Nyssa and Tegan's grief in the following story, "Time Flight".

The second new companion was Nyssa (Sarah Sutton), introduced in "The Keeper of Traken" and retained as a companion at short notice after that story's conclusion. "Logopolis" had to be hastily rewritten to incorporate her; she was brought from Traken by the Watcher, the intermediate projection of the Doctor between his fourth and fifth incarnation. Completing the trio was Tegan (Janet Fielding), an Australian air hostess whose aunt is murdered by the Master in the first episode of "Logopolis". All three new characters were much younger than either version of Romana and presumably introduced to lower the show's demographic in an attempt to appeal to a younger audience. This created problems when a younger Doctor was added to the mix. Peter Davison was only twenty nine when he began playing the part and was strictly forbidden from putting his arm around either Nyssa or Tegan: Tom Baker could, but didn't, because that would have been fatherly, whereas if Davison had done it, that might suggest indulgence willy-nilly in hanky-panky in the TARDIS. He was, however, allowed to put his arm around Adric and, later, Turlough. Nathan-Turner thought that including more companions would allow each to have her or his own sub plot, thus increasing the dramatic possibilities available to the writers and reproducing the multiple plot structures of the Hartnell and Troughton stories.

Arguably the biggest problem facing the new producer was the show's star. Nathan-Turner had firm ideas about how Tom Baker was to play the Doctor and cut back on the control the actor had had on the character in the Graham Williams seasons. Partly in an attempt to "tidy him up" in Nathan-Turner's words, the new producer introduced a new version of the Doctor's costume; the greatcoat, scarf and hat were retained but in a uniform burgundy. Thus Baker's choice over a simpler, more comfortable costume, often stripped of waistcoat, jumper, jacket and tie, was removed. John Nathan-Turner also instructed directors to insist that Baker stuck to the script and limited his ability to re-write, ad-lib and improvise. Baker gives a more subdued and intense performance as the Doctor in his final season; with the humour now under control, this is one of his most effective years as the Doctor. However, the new approach understandably led to friction between the producer and his star. Nathan-Turner apparently felt that the only way to establish proper control over the Doctor was to cast his own actor in the role. Tom Baker was offered another season, on the same conditions of performance as the eighteenth season, but he declined. In his autobiography, Baker explained that one reason for leaving was his unhappiness with the new companion characters (Adric, Nyssa and Tegan). His departure from the series was announced on the BBC *Nine O'Clock News* while "Meglos" was being broadcast and illustrated with a clip from that lacklustre serial. Now married to co-star Lalla Ward, Baker returned to the theatre, playing Oscar Wilde in *Feasting with Panthers* at the Chichester Festival Theatre (which I saw: he was excellent) and Frank in the original production of Willy Russell's *Educating Rita*, a twentieth century version of *Pygmalion* and a perennial favourite for GCSE English Literature. Willy Russell took advantage of Baker's casting to insert an in-joke into the play. Rita, who has decided to drop her Liverpudlian accent in favour of a posh one, alarms Frank into saying that "I am not giving a tutorial to a Dalek." Rita replies "I am not a Dalek" (a version of the oft quoted line "I am a Dalek" which, like "Beam me up, Scotty", was never said). The line was understandably cut in the film with Michael Caine, as he had never played the Doctor and it was presumably felt that American cinema audiences wouldn't have got the reference; although, with the wide dissemination of Tom Baker serials on PBS stations, many of them probably would have done so. When Katy Manning played Rita in a production in Australia, the Dalek line was retained and *Doctor Who* fans in the audience laughed their heads off.

Nathan-Turner asked Christopher H. Bidmead to join the show as the new script editor. Bidmead wasn't keen. He was a scientist and writer who hated recent versions of the show and particularly deplored its reliance on "magic". He might have been thinking of the sequence in "City of Death" where the Doctor and Romana suggest that they fly down from the top of the Eiffel Tower. Nathan-Turner reassured him that the show was to be re-tooled with a harder science fiction edge, and Bidmead came on board. Like Holmes and Adams, he rewrote many of the serials presented to him. David Fisher's "The Leisure Hive" had been written for the previous production team and concerned an alien

Mafia organisation muscling into the entertainment industry: it was full of humour, which Bidmead tamed, to Fisher's disappointment. The aliens were the Foamasi (an anagram of Mafiosi), trying to buy out the Argolin Leisure Hive. This was established by the Argolins as a multi-cultural meeting and learning place where different races can put aside their differences as a move of reconciliation after a hideous war with the Foamasi. In the serial's best lines, the Doctor asks the Argolin leader Mena how long the war lasted. "Twenty minutes," she replies. "As long as that?" the Doctor comments, surprised. Wry smiles all round from viewers thinking of nuclear holocaust with the election of Ronald Reagan and the renaissance of CND. Bidmead rewrote "Full Circle" by an eighteen year old fan, Andrew Smith, who had been submitting stories to the production office for some years. He also tried to rewrite "State of Decay" by *Doctor Who* veteran Terrance Dicks. This had been originally submitted to the production office as the first story of season fifteen, entitled "The Vampire Mutations", and had been vetoed because it clashed with the BBC's new film of *Dracula*. High camp Gothic horror, however, was not easily rewritten as hard science fiction and in the end it was Dicks's version that was made. One wonders if the experienced Dicks might have had something to say about his work being heavily rewritten by a novice production team.

The fifth story was "Warriors' Gate". Steve Gallagher was a prose writer of science fiction and his submitted scripts and story ideas read like a novel. Bidmead agreed to rewrite them as a script, and the result is a superb science fiction serial. Slavers on Captain Rorvik's spaceship The Privateer trade in Tharils, time sensitive aliens who can navigate the time winds for vessels when plugged into its consoles. The slavers and the TARDIS arrive in a limbo between universes. Here, the Tharil empire once stood, the Tharils themselves enslavers of human beings who rose up against them, building the robot Gundan to drive them out. The story is wonderfully witty and beautifully shot. The actors are superimposed onto a pure white void for the scenes in limbo, or onto black and white photographs of Powis Castle for the scenes in the Tharils' empire, both achieved through green screen. Rorvik's crew are a bunch of bored, recalcitrant malcontents, with very funny performances from Kenneth Cope and David Kincaid as engineers and a wonderful Rorvik in Clifford Rose. Rose was famous as the SS Standartenführer Kessler in the BBC's *Secret Army* (1977-1979). Anxious not to make that character a stereotype, Rose developed a private life and a girlfriend for him. He brought the same level of research and seriousness to Rorvik. Interviewed on the DVD release,

Clifford Rose said he found the scripts hard to understand (and they do contain some baffling science fiction concepts) but got a handle on Rorvik by seeing his similarity to Captain Mainwaring in the BBC's long running *Dad's Army*, another character of limited competence and authority who has to motivate a crew of even greater incompetence. Rose's performance as a man struggling to stay in command of his crew and of himself is a delight.

"Warriors' Gate", like "Nightmare of Eden" in the previous season, hit serious problems behind the screens. Paul Joyce, the director, was experienced in theatre and brought an innovative style to the show which grated with BBC routines. He elected to shoot off the set into the lighting gantry, which had been used as a double for machinery in 1973's "Carnival of Monsters": the technicians objected. The set design for the Privateer ship was a two level gantry supported by scaffolding: health and safety said it wouldn't take the weight of artistes or cameras, so Joyce opted to use a hand held camera when shooting on it. He borrowed a spaceship corridor from the BBC television version of *The Hitch Hiker's Guide to the Galaxy*, then shooting at the same time, to increase the sense of space on board the Privateer. Joyce apparently took ages setting up shots and the show became dangerously behind schedule; he was sacked and then apparently brought back when no-one else could figure out how to shoot the rest of the script. Nathan-Turner apologised to his superiors for employing Joyce and accepted full responsibility for his mistakes; he also congratulated Joyce on the finished product. On the DVD extras, Joyce recalled Nathan-Turner saying, "They're great shows, Paul" but admitting that he didn't understand them. This was a worrying presentiment for a new producer and it has often been alleged that Nathan-Turner brought in the show on budget, and it often looked good, but he left the story-telling to others.

Bidmead also reworked Johnny Byrne's script for "The Keeper of Traken", concerning the intrusion of the evil Melkur into the pastoral idyll of Traken. Nathan-Turner wanted to bring back the Master and Bidmead worked him into the script. The Melkur statue became the Master's TARDIS, which is odd since it walks around a lot and we'd never seen a TARDIS do that before, and the Master returns in his withered "Deadly Assassin" state. His regeneration cycle used up, he employs some of the powers acquired as the Keeper of Traken to steal the body of Tremas (an anagram of Master), Nyssa's father, who becomes the new Master. Both Tremas and the Master were played by Anthony Ainley. "The Keeper of Traken" is a fine story and very much better than Johnny Byrne's next effort, the Gallifrey based "Arc of Infinity" (1983), known to some fans as "Arse of Inanity"; the difference in quality suggests that much of the good writing came from Bidmead, not Byrne.

Bidmead wrote the season's final story, "Logopolis", which rather belies his dislike of magic for its inclusion of two extraordinary ideas. In the first, the Master's TARDIS has appeared inside the Doctor's TARDIS console room. This leads to lots of excellent scenes of "recursive occlusion", when the Doctor and Adric walk through the Master's TARDIS – also disguised as a police box – into another TARDIS control room, inside which is another police box, which they enter to find themselves in another TARDIS control room containing another police box, which they enter to find themselves in another TARDIS control room containing another police box, which they enter to find themselves in another TARDIS control room containing another police box ... and so on, to apparent infinity. The Doctor decides the best way to flush the Master out of the TARDIS is to land it under the Thames, open the doors and let the water do its work. He and Adric stay in the console room and viewers notice the obvious flaw: wouldn't he and Adric drown?

The second strangeness concerns the mathematical race of Logopolitans. The Universe has passed the point of its normal heat death according to the third law of thermodynamics – entropy increases. Here, the dialogue fulfils some of the series' original educational function from 1963 in getting some real physics across to its dullard viewers. The Universe is only prevented from collapsing by the block transfer computations of the Logopolitans. This seems to involve them muttering or intoning numbers which mathematically map the universe and therefore keep it from collapse (eh?). "The Daemons", following Isaac Asimov, established that alien science advanced beyond our comprehension would be indistinguishable from magic, but, to the non-scientific viewer, block transfer computation looks awfully like magic. Barry Letts, the executive producer, thought it was a stunningly imaginative concept.

Also in "Logopolis", the Master broadcasts to the entire Universe from the Pharos Project on Earth, a Jodrell Bank-like radio telescope, demanding its complete obedience to his will or its annihilation. Quite what the Master would want with the whole Universe is never explained and former script editor Douglas Adams criticised his reappearance in the series. Adams argued that if you had someone with a black beard and an evil laugh, you didn't need to give him any plausible motivation.

He satirised the Master in the end narration for an episode of *The Hitch Hiker's Guide to the Galaxy,* which wondered whether its heroes would face an exciting threat, "or will it be a monster trying to take over the Universe for no very good reason?"

In looking for a new Doctor, John Nathan-Turner wanted someone as unlike Tom Baker as possible. He also wanted an actor who might be more biddable. In casting both the Fifth and the Sixth Doctors, Nathan-Turner had a clear idea of who he wanted and didn't hold auditions: Peter Davison and Colin Baker were his first choices. When it came to casting the seventh, auditions were held – with Janet Fielding – perhaps an indication of Nathan-Turner's weariness at still being in charge of the show after seven years and no longer having the enthusiasm to choose decisively. Richard Griffiths was apparently considered (later famous as the chef/detective in *Pie in the Sky*) and Ken Campbell was auditioned but the part went to Sylvester McCoy. The producer got on well with him and found a new lease of life for himself in the show's final three years.

Back in 1981, Nathan-Turner phoned Peter Davison and asked him if he would be interested in playing the Doctor. Davison was very surprised to be asked and had never considered himself as the Doctor, thinking he was far too young for the part. He took several days to consider, under strict instructions to tell no-one about the offer, apart from his immediate family. Still undecided after a week, Nathan-Turner took him out to lunch and finally persuaded him. Davison recalled that one reason he accepted was because he thought it was a marvellous opportunity, but also because he couldn't bear the thought of someone else playing the Doctor after he had turned it down. Furthermore, he would be sworn to secrecy about the offer after declining it. Davison was well-known for playing Tristan Farnon in *All Creatures Great and Small,* one of the three leads with Christopher Timothy and Robert Hardy. He wondered how he was to play the Doctor and sought advice from some younger *Doctor Who* fans, one of whom said he should be "like Tristan, but brave". Davison thought this was admirable advice and went through his first season with wide-eyed innocence, recapturing some of the wonder felt by the Doctor as he encounters new and extraordinary worlds and situations. He was still feeling his way into the part when shooting "The Visitation" (1982), which was made second but actually transmitted fourth. Davison recalled that the director, Peter Moffatt, assumed that he knew how to play the Doctor and allowed him to get on with it, affording him the customary respect as the star that had often been given to Tom Baker. Davison actually wanted some direction and asked Moffatt for help in shaping the part, which Moffatt was pleased to give him.

The nineteenth season, then, was shot out of sequence, as the changing length of Davison's hair between stories testifies. "Four to Doomsday" (transmitted second) was followed by "The Visitation" and "Kinda" (transmitted third) before work started on Davison's first story "Castrovalva" by Christopher Bidmead, a sequel to "Logopolis". Nathan-Turner had been forced into shooting the season out of sequence because of problems with the script for the first story, "Project Zeta-Sigma", which had run into several drafts and eventually had to be abandoned. "Castrovalva" was a late replacement and the script wasn't ready for the first shooting session. Nathan-Turner made a virtue out of necessity by arguing that shooting the season out of order helped Davison get into the role. Certainly, his performance in "Castrovalva" is much more assured than in "The Visitation" and "Four to Doomsday", although his performance in "Kinda" (actually written for Tom Baker) is splendid. Some reviewers questioned whether it was quite such a good idea to make "Castrovalva" a sequel to a story that had been broadcast nine months previously, but the problem was smoothed over by a repeat of "Logopolis" in October 1981.

"Logopolis" was the Tom Baker/Peter Davison offering for a series of repeats on BBC 2 in the autumn of 1981 under the umbrella title of "The Five Faces of *Doctor Who*", commissioned by Nathan-Turner to remind viewers that there had been other Doctors before Tom Baker and to prepare them for Peter Davison. These were the first repeats on the BBC to include Doctors other than the present incumbent, and they were well received by the public, grateful fans and the press. *The Guardian* hailed them in its listings guide with the rapturous, "O tempora! O TARDIS!" (a play on Cicero's despairing comment on Roman times under Mark Antony: "O tempora! O mores!" – "Oh the times! Oh the manners!"). Hartnell was represented by the first story "An Unearthly Child", Troughton by "The Krotons", Pertwee by "The Three Doctors" and "Carnival of Monsters". The episodes were stripped across weekday evenings from Monday to Thursday. At the *Doctor Who* Appreciation Society convention in 1981, Frazer Hines despaired of the choice that represented his Doctor – "Oh, not 'The Krotons'!" – and said that he, Troughton and Wendy Padbury had hated it and, while filming it, they had inevitably called the enemies "the croutons".

Nathan-Turner was so pleased with the reception of the repeats that he arranged for three more stories to be shown the following year

(1982) under the title of "*Doctor Who* and the Monsters": "The Curse of Peladon" (Ice Warriors), a hacked four episodes edit of "Genesis of the Daleks" and "Earthshock" from Davison's first season, representing the Cybermen. The success of "The Five Faces of *Doctor Who*" apparently led Nathan-Turner erroneously to believe that, because so many people loved the old episodes, they would want to see elements of the old episodes – characters and enemies – in new stories. This led to the poorly-scripted and poorly received second Davison season, which contained a returning element from the series' past in every story. This twentieth season started *Doctor Who*'s slide from hugely popular family viewing to a cult show arguably made for, and watched by, fans, many of whom ironically didn't like what was being offered them anyway. Viewing figures thus slid from ten million in 1982 to under four million in 1989, when the axe finally fell.

Peter Davison was himself disappointed with the scripts for his second season. He was under contract to make a third season but had to decide if he wanted to stay for a fourth year during his second. He decided to move on, not least because of the quality of the scripts and because he wanted to do other things. Elisabeth Sladen recalled that she and Tom Baker would take time out of rehearsals to peep in at other shows being rehearsed simultaneously. While she and Baker thought they looked awfully dull, and Baker telling her they should go back to saving the Universe, Davison looked longingly at his fellow actors in rehearsals on exciting projects. There was some improvement in script quality in his third year as the Doctor and he did sometimes regret his impending departure, but the die was cast – and so was Colin Baker.

Season nineteen was rescheduled from Saturdays to a bi-weekly slot, retained for all three of Davison's seasons, apparently to test the water for a bi-weekly soap opera which eventually materialised as *EastEnders* in 1985. Episodes were transmitted at about 7.00 p.m. and the later timeslot anticipated and deflected complaints about horror or violence. Both, however, were on the wane in Davison's time – with one or two notable exceptions – and the heat had gone out of Mrs Whitehouse's campaign against *Doctor Who* anyway now that the BBC had assimilated her criticisms in shaping the programme. By this point, the length of an episode was something of an anachronism. Soap operas were the only other dramas in 1982 which had half hour, or twenty five minute, episodes: forty-five minutes, or one hour, slots were preferred. One reason for showing two episodes a week was to satisfy the demands of viewers used to longer running times for their favourite shows. They might not get a single forty-five minute episode of *Doctor Who* until

"Resurrection of the Daleks" in 1984, but they did get fifty-odd minutes' worth if it was shown twice a week. *Blake's Seven* had had considerable success with its forty five minute running time, which was eventually copied for Colin Baker's first season (1985) in another attempt to inject life into the flagging *Who*. In 1986, ITV achieved great success with its two hour long episodes of *Inspector Morse*, which became the standard length for other detective dramas like *Frost, Dalziel and Pascoe* and *Rebus*. Next to these mighty juggernauts, made effectively as a collection of television movies, the last four seasons of the original series, with their twenty five minute episodes, looked ridiculous. Furthermore, they only broadcast once a week and by this time, audiences were demanding more content to be rolled out weekly for its entertainment. Again, *Doctor Who* looked like an old show which couldn't change with the times: this was certainly how Peter Cregeen saw it, which is why he decided it was ripe for the chop in 1989.

Nathan-Turner wasn't entirely happy with the twice weekly timeslot, or the inevitable consequence that the programme now ran for thirteen weeks a year, rather than the twenty six or so with previous Doctors. He tried to get the programme shifted back to an autumn timeslot, not least so that it would be on the air during the twentieth anniversary on 23rd November 1983. The controller of BBC 1, Alan Hart, turned him down. Starting the programme in the autumn would mean that Peter Davison wouldn't be available to shoot *Sink or Swim*, the BBC comedy in which he co-starred with Robert Glenister (Salateen in "The Caves of Androzani") and which ran for Davison's first two years as the Doctor. Hart wasn't prepared to tell comedy to move its production schedules just to accommodate *Doctor Who*. He did, however, agree to Nathan-Turner's plan B, which was for a special drama to be made and broadcast on or around the twentieth anniversary. Extra money was thus found for the ninety minute special, "The Five Doctors" (1983).

There are some very good stories in Davison's first season. There are also signs of the incomprehensible and garbled elements which would baffle the general public and lead to the programme's decline. "Castrovalva" is a good story based on the graphic works of M. C. Escher. Recovering from his regeneration, which he fears is failing, the Doctor seeks a dwelling of simplicity – known as Castrovalva – in which he might rest and heal. There are effective scenes of the Doctor and his companions running around Escher-esque architectural impossibilities: running away from a village square, they only run back to it and so on. One of Castrovalva's senior members is the Portreeve, a gentle soul who helps the Doctor recover. The Portreeve is in fact the Master in disguise: a genuine revelation for some viewers, thanks to Anthony Ainley's subtle and beautiful performance as the Portreeve. The *Radio Times* and end credits kept the surprise by listing the Portreeve's actor as "Neil Toynay", an anagram of "Tony Ainley". Castrovalva isn't real either: it's a block transfer computation conjured up by the Master and vanishes into the ether.

With only two stories under his belt, the new Master was already starting to become samey and irritating. As with his appearance in every story of season eight, his continued reappearance in Davison's and Colin Baker's time suffered from the law of dimishing returns and unfortunately, we don't have Roger Delgado's wonderful performance to enjoy. The Master returns in season nineteen's last story, the incomprehensible drivel of "Time-Flight", in which he disguises himself for no reason at all as a magician called Kaleed; here, the actor is credited as Leon Ny Taiy, another anagram of Tony Ainley. In "The King's Demons" (1984), the Master pops up again in disguise as Sir Giles Estram (another anagram of "Master"), credited as James Stoker (an anagram of "Master's joke"). By this point, some were in agreement with Douglas Adams that a man with a black beard doesn't need any motivation; there certainly doesn't seem to be any for his determination to prevent Magna Carta from being signed in "The King's Demons" (1983) unless it is a love of mischief for mischief's sake, like Shakespeare's Iago in *Othello*: but this isn't made clear in the scripting.

The third story, "Kinda" (1982), is one of the series' finest, beautifully acted, made and scripted as a heady draught of Buddhism, Christianity and a satire on colonialism. Humans have established a scientific observation dome on the paradise planet Deva Loka, inhabited by the mute, peaceful, humanoid Kinda. The military head of the expedition is Sanders, a suitably British colonial name for a colonial administrator played, in a coup of casting, by British war movie veteran Richard Todd. He tells the Doctor the Kinda are ignorant savages, "But they smile a lot. Or at least they used to. Before we took the hostages." Sanders' deputy, Hindle (Simon Rouse) has a complete nervous breakdown and goes mad, threatening the Doctor and Adric with death and the surrounding rain forest with obliteration. The jungle, convincingly realised as a studio set, is an idyllic Eden, and in every Eden there is a snake. This is the Mara, a being from "the dark places of the inside", which possesses Tegan when she falls asleep in the place of the Dreaming. Several scenes are set in Tegan's mind, where she encounters figures from Buddhist teaching (which includes the Mara itself). Eventually, the Mara manifests itself as a giant snake (like Satan in Eden). The Doctor surrounds it with reflective panels from the dome, arguing that evil can never face the sight of itself. The Mara panics at its reflection and is banished back to the dark places of the inside.

The story is an intellectual tour de force. It also works well as exciting drama and the supporting cast are terrific. Nerys Hughes was cast as Todd, in an early example of Nathan-Turner's preference for casting actors principally known for light entertainment in *Doctor Who* (Nerys Hughes was one of the leads in *The Liver Birds* (1969-78)). Ever-concerned that it would provoke ridicule from the uninitiated, fans worried that this tendency undermined the seriousness of the drama, but Nerys Hughes gives a wonderful performance (she wasn't just capable of comedy, after all) and there is some erotic tension between her and the apparently younger Doctor, culminating in the parting will he/won't he kiss her goodbye. Mary Morris, who had excelled as one of Patrick McGoohan's tormenters, Number Two in *The Prisoner*, is superb as the wise seer Panna, who is apparently dispatched by her visions of the Mara. "Kinda" was written for Tom Baker's Doctor and writer Christopher Bailey considered him more suited to the Doctor's role as wise man in the story; he was somewhat concerned that Peter Davison wouldn't exert as much authority, but he needn't have worried. Bailey was less happy with some aspects of the production and disliked the appearance of the Kinda, beautiful Caucasian extras who looked as though they had just stepped out of a Timotei shampoo advertisement. His hopes for his story were somewhat at odds with those of the director, Peter Grimwade, who viewed the script with some impatience, thinking that Bailey wanted to write *Play of the Month* and was trying to shoehorn a religious allegory into the unreceptive vessel of *Doctor Who*. Bailey in turn grew weary of some of the rewrites he was asked to perform, especially those which required him to give more explanations or information. He believed that he was expected to explain absolutely everything, and memorably said that if *Doctor Who* had tackled "Little Red Riding Hood", he would have been obliged to fit a transmogriphication device on the wall of grandmama's cottage to explain why Little Red Riding Hood didn't spot that her grandmama was actually the wolf in disguise.

Some critics have said that the Doctor's statement that evil cannot stand its own reflection is optimistic at best. However, there is a story that Reinhard Heydrich, responsible for the so-called "final solution" and the Nazi extermination camps, caught sight of his own reflection in a full-length mirror and emptied his revolver into it. This incident has been variously interpreted as indicating Heydrich's self-loathing and disgust; it might be an historical example of evil loathing its own reflection.

The Cybermen stomped back onto our screens in "Earthshock" (1982), hijacking an Earth space freighter which they intend to crash into an interplanetary peace conference. This is captained by Briggs, described in the script as a tough and physically imposing woman, and played on screen by light comedy actress Beryl Reid, who was neither of these things. Reid's unfamiliarity with science fiction led her to quip, "We're going to Warp Drive. Is that near the Awkright Road?" during rehearsals. The Cybermen were redesigned but retained the basic features of their last appearance in "Revenge of the Cybermen" (1974). The basis of the costume was now a military pilot's uniform rather than a rubber wet suit and, in keeping with the eighties look, they wore silver sprayed moon boots rather than sprayed wellies. Topping the helmet, and replacing the forehead guns of their "Revenge" counterparts, was a piece of hologram paper that changes colour when it changes direction. Like the bubble wrap used to make the Wirrn grubs in "The Ark in Space", this was very effective when first broadcast but looks a little ridiculous today as such holographic paper is a staple of gift wrap. These new Cybermen lost the teardrop but gained a hang-dog look to their mouths which turn down at the corners; this feature was criticised at the time as being too like the stormtroopers from *Star Wars*. John Nathan-Turner asked for the chin piece to be transparent plastic so that the actor's jaw (inexplicably painted silver) should be visible: a reminder of the Cybermen's organic origins to viewers who might have thought they were robots. This detail was abandoned for subsequent appearances and replaced by a solid silver jaw. As with "Revenge of the Cybermen", the Cybermen were voiced by the actors who played them, rather than by another artist as in the sixties and post-2005 stories. David Banks made his first appearance as a Cyberleader; he was to play Cyberleaders in the following three Cyber stories and argued that there was an element of the Cyberleader which survived into all its replacements. He eventually published a book about the Cybermen which theorised about their origins and nature. Cybercontroller Michael Kilgarriff thought the book showed Banks had become a bit too mystical about the whole thing.

The *Radio Times* offered John Nathan-Turner a cover photograph to mark the Cybermen's return. This would have been the first *Radio Times* cover since Jon Pertwee's day, but Nathan-Turner turned it down, preferring to keep the enemies' identity secret until the surprise at the end of episode one. Hence David Banks was credited as "Leader", rather than Cyberleader, in the magazine's cast listings. "Earthshock" was well received but contained some of the worst lines ever to be inflicted on an actor. The Doctor expresses sarcastic surprise that the Cyberleader can understand a word connected with emotion, as they hurtle towards planet Earth:

> Cyberleader: It is a word like any other. And so is "destruction". Which is what we're going to do. To that planet.

(They are going to "destruction" it?) The Fifth Doctor lets the linguistic abuse pass: the Fourth picked it up when a Cyberleader said their bombs would "fragmentise" Voga, the planet of gold. "Fragmentise? Oh well, I suppose you can't expect good English. From a machine." A BBC technician also appears on screen in one shot, behind one of the space frieghter's stairwells; he can only be spotted if you turn your television brightness up high, which presumably wasn't done on the vision mixer's monitor in the Television Centre gallery, which is presumably why the mistake wasn't noticed.

"Time Flight", the season's final story, vies with "The Horns of Nimon" as one of the worst ever made. It was apparently commissioned because British Airways offered the BBC some filming on their supersonic airliner, Concorde; somehow, a *Doctor Who* story had to be shaped around the aircraft. This particular black spot fell to Peter Grimwade, who proceeded to turn in the weakest of his three weak scripts for Peter Davison's Doctor. Concorde travels back in time to prehistoric Earth, where the Doctor and his companions meet the Plastmatons and the Master, stroll around a bit and then go back to Heathrow. It seems extraordinary that anyone thought it was possible to realise Concorde landing on prehistoric Earth on the show's budget but the rest of the script is up to the standard of this concept. Veteran British film actor Nigel Stock – who had appeared with William Hartnell in the Boulting Brothers' wonderful film of Graham Greene's *Brighton Rock* (1947) – wanders around looking embarrassed and speaks his lines without attempting to give much of a performance. Tegan is left behind at Heathrow, apparently written out, only to reappear again in the first story of season twenty, "Arc of Infinity", where the Doctor finds her in Amsterdam of all places.

Perhaps boosted by the positives of "Earthshock", "Time Flight" managed to gain nine million viewers. Perhaps memories of "Time Flight" caused "Arc of Infinity" to shed almost two million – and three million since "Castrovalva" – from a public which thought that *Doctor Who* was now a bit rubbish. Viewing figures hovered around the seven million mark for the whole of season twenty. Sadly, "Arc of Infinity" (1983) is very poor fare indeed. In the first sign that Nathan-Turner intended to use the series' back catalogue with a vengeance, "Arc" is set again on Gallifrey with Omega (from "The Three Doctors", 1973) attempting to return and control the Matrix. The story required viewers to remember Omega from a story transmitted ten years previously, and Gallifrey from stories broadcast in 1976 and 1977. For viewers who couldn't remember, the story was baffling; for those who could, it seemed ridiculous to bring back Omega when he had been so comprehensively destroyed in "The Three Doctors". "Arc of Infinity" is notable for Colin Baker's appearance as Commander Maxil, commander of the Chancellery Guard. Baker's performance isn't especially memorable but it is recalled because he was soon to be cast as the new Doctor and does, as Baker himself recalled with relish, get to shoot his predecessor in the back. There is also a dreadful alien in the Ergon, a giant chicken, and Peter Davison scowls most dreadfully when Omega assumes the Doctor's form. The story's one good moment is a small child smiling at Omega; Omega smiles back at him, remembering what it was like to have physical form and contact with his fellows. Tegan rejoins Nyssa in the TARDIS and the trio go off to Manussa, to encounter the Mara again in "Snakedance", a story that is virtually a retread of "Kinda" minus the religious references, but which does at least include a young Martin Clunes as the bored and spoilt Lon, heir to the throne. This is the best story in a woeful season. Valentine Dyall returns as The Black Guardian in three stories but now he has a stuffed vulture on his head. Again, viewers are expected to remember who he is after his last appearance in 1978. The Black Guardian recruits Turlough (Mark Strickson), an alien posing as an English public schoolboy, to destroy the Doctor in revenge for the Black Guardian's humiliation in "The Armageddon Factor" (1979). He tells Turlough that "I may not be seen to act in this", but doesn't explain why not. The Black Guardian then pops up in the course of the next few stories to nudge Turlough gently along in his murderous Faustian bargain; Dyall bellows such lines as "In the name of all that is evil! Destroy him!"

Turlough becomes Adric's replacement as a companion and is never entirely trusted by Tegan, although he is fully accepted once the Black Guardian spontaneously combusts in "Enlightenment". John Nathan-Turner worried that Strickson's blond hair would make him look too like Peter Davison in long shot, and Turlough was thus manifested as auburn. In keeping with his preference for the regulars to wear a uniform rather than clothes, the producer decreed that Turlough should always wear his school uniform. This stretched credulity to the limit for younger viewers: they could accept dimensional transcendalism and regeneration, but not the voluntary wearing of school uniform. British secondary school pupils tended to hurl off their uniforms as soon as they got home and, as Turlough presumably only had one uniform when he stepped on board the TARDIS, his presumably was as ripe as Tegan's after repeated wear. Viewers worried about such things and their worry affected their ability to suspend their disbelief. Nathan-Turner, who provided Tegan and Nyssa with a bedroom to highlight the chastity of sleeping arrangements aboard the TARDIS, didn't extend the courtesy – or realism – by allowing them regular changes of clothes.

Turlough joined the series in "Mawdryn Undead", which featured David Collins as the eponymous Mawdryn, an alien stuck in an undead state ("dryn maw" is Welsh for "dead man"). Mawdryn is mistaken for the Doctor after an aborted regeneration by Tegan and Nyssa. In a typical example of Peter Grimwade's crass scripting, they don't consider what tragedy might have caused the Doctor to regenerate: perhaps they thought he had fallen off an exercise bike, the apparent cause for the Sixth Doctor's regeneration in "Time and the Rani". Tegan and Nyssa realise their mistake when Mawdryn recovers his true form and they notice his spaghetti-like brain falling out of his head. Mawdryn and his mutant companions seek death, which can only be provided by the Doctor donating the rest of his regeneration cycle to them: the energy of one regeneration will cause the death of one of them. This is an intriguing addition to Time Lord lore in an otherwise uninteresting and poorly developed script: Mawdryn says that donating his regenerations will mean "the Doctor will cease to be a Time Lord. That is the price of compassion." The implication is that being a lord of time lies in the capacity to cheat death through regeneration, rather than to control time as suggested in "The War Games" (1969). The Doctor is willing to make the sacrifice and presumably to die at the end of his fifth incarnation, but the energy is supplied by two versions of the Brigadier meeting in a temporal paradox: as they touch, the energy created releases Mawdryn and his brothers from life. The Brigadier has been brought back for the story as a Mathematics teacher in Turlough's public school. He has a nervous breakdown as a result of the events of the story on his younger self and, when the Doctor meets him seven years after the death of Mawdryn, has forgotten his time at UNIT. The Doctor reunites him with his younger self to complete the time paradox that frees Mawdryn. It is as disappointing to see the Brigadier tamed as a schoolmaster as well as it is unlikely; this can be explained by the original plan to use Ian Chesterton, one of William Hartnell's first companions, as the teacher, but actor William Russell was unavailable and the Brigadier was substituted instead. The production team themselves seemed unhappy about Lethbridge-Stewart's change of career and, when we next see him in "The Five Doctors" (1983) and "Battlefield" (1989), there are no references to his teaching days; it seems that that timeline has been quietly erased.

Steve Gallagher contributed an intelligent script about space leprosy for "Terminus", named "lazar's disease" after the Middle English word for leprosy. The story is notable for the intelligent designs of the lazars' carers, the Vaneer (based on Anglo-Saxon images of death) and a giant talking dog with light-up eyes, the Garm. Again, the execution let down the script; a problem that had plagued the series as far back as "The Krotons". Space travellers' terror at contracting lazar's disease is spoilt by hysterical overacting from Dominic Guard ("That's it! That's WHAT IT'S ALL ABOUT! WE'RE ALL GOING TO DIIIIIIIIIIIIIE!") and Lisa Goddard wearing a fetching white outfit more suited to *Barbarella*, frizzy hair and a big bubble space helmet. The story attracted complaints from the Leprosy Society for its negative portrayal of leprosy and from the Tannoy company which complained about the word "tannoy" being used for the ship's public address system. The company quite reasonably pointed out that "tannoy" was not a generic term but a copyright brand name, in the same way that Hoover is not a synonym for vacuum cleaner. The BBC apologised to the Tannoy company.

The season ended with the lacklustre two parter "The King's Demons", another pseudo-historical by Terence Dudley who had supplied the well-regarded "Black Orchid" the previous season. The Master appears again in disguise ("Oh my dear Doctor, you have been naïve!") and has substituted a shape-changing android called Kamelion for King John in order to carry out a baffling and pointless scheme to prevent the ratification of Magna Carta. Kamelion was an animated, computer controlled robot made by a firm called C P Cybernetics. John Nathan-Turner was enthusiastic about its possibilities as a companion but it quickly became apparent that its capabilities as a mechanical prop, like K9's before it, were very limited. Peter Davison recalled that Kamelion's dialogue had to be pre-recorded and fed into the robot for its lip movements to synchronise with its speech. This meant recording sessions with Kamelion were frustrating and slow and there was no possibility to vary its performance as Davison et al were not interacting with another actor. Although a remarkable piece of work for the time, Kamelion actually looked so human it might as well have been played by a human actor and some viewers were surprised to learn it was actually a robot. Sadly, the only person who understood how to program him died and he was banished to the realms of the TARDIS corridors. Here, he was largely forgotten for the next season until he was unceremoniously written out in "Planet of Fire" (1984).

"The King's Demons" was to have been followed by a story called "The Return". Of what? Of the Daleks of course, their inclusion being kept as a surprise as the Cybermen's had been in "Earthshock" and as the dinosaurs had been in "Invasion" (part one of "Invasion of the Dinosaurs" (1973), the retitling of which caused much trouble: see chapter six). A strike by BBC electricians put paid to "The Return", which was held over to the following season where it became "Resurrection of the Daleks" (1984).

"Resurrection of the Daleks" typified the problems of this period of the show. Penned by script editor Eric Saward, the plot seemed to be made up as it went along. One minute we were on Earth, with android policeman controlled by a gangster called Lytton (Maurice Colbourne, who had played Coker in the BBC's excellent adaptation of *The Day of the Triffids* (1981) and who would play the lead in the BBC yachting drama *Howard's Way*), then we were on an Earth ship in the far future under attack by the Daleks; then the Daleks have made androids of the Doctor and his companions, intending to use them to assassinate the High Council of the Time Lords; then the Doctor intends to assassinate Davros... such plot as there was consisted of a series of set pieces sustained by a bunch of cardboard characters. Again, the casual viewer was required to remember chunks of continuity from years-old stories: the Daleks' war against the Movellans from "Destiny of the Daleks" five years previously is discussed (the Daleks lost) and we were expected to know – and care about – what is meant by the High Council of the Time Lords. There was yet another flashback sequence of clips from old episodes: as the Daleks drain the Doctor's memory of his past companions, all are seen on screen, except for Leela, whom the production team forgot to include. These clip sequences were a hallmark of Nathan-Turner's in the eighties: in "Logopolis", the fourth Doctor sees images of his old enemies; in "Earthshock", the Cybermen watch clips from old Cybermen stories to remind themselves of the Doctor; in "Mawdryn Undead", the Brigadier sees clips of his UNIT days. The clips were intended to please the fans, which was very sweet of Nathan-Turner, but arguably meant nothing to other viewers; except perhaps to remind them of happier periods in the show's history or to get a parlour game of the "Who's that?" variety started. They certainly slow down the action and were mercifully abandoned by the time Colin Baker became the Doctor.

"Resurrection of the Daleks" also suffers from some very poor acting by co-stars better known for light entertainment, thus, for once, fulfilling the prophecy of fans that some actors were not up to the high drama of the series. Rula Lenska has no character to work with; Rodney Bewes (from *The Likely Lads*) is absolutely without grit as a Dalek agent; Chloe Ashcroft, who often presented *Play School*, is utterly unconvincing as Professor Laird. Michael Wisher was to have reprised his role as Davros from "Genesis of the Daleks" (1975) but the change of shooting dates rendered him unavailable, and Terry Molloy plays Davros instead. He is certainly much better than David Gooderson ("Destiny of the Daleks") but is too much of a ranting lunatic for this author's taste. The Doctor carries a revolver while hunting a Dalek mutant and a blaster when threatening to execute Davros, both anathema to the tradition that the Doctor never carries, or uses, firearms. Some sequences are frankly nasty. The Daleks' allies release a nerve gas that destroys human flesh: one character raises his dissolving hand and asks, "What's happening?" in real distress. *Doctor Who* now seemed to be a show that had lost its way; meandering plots, poor acting and a neglect of the casual viewer would be hallmarks of the show until its cancellation in 1989.

Perhaps mindful of the need to do something to stop the rot, Davison was keen to inject some more humour into the proceedings. He felt that his Doctor was awfully straight-laced. Nathan-Turner, mindful of the horrors of Tom Baker's clowning around, rejected the idea.

There were some good stories in the rest of Davison's run. One is the twentieth anniversary special, "The Five Doctors". This was broadcast two days after the actual anniversary on 25th November 1983 as part of the BBC's annual Children in Need telethon appeal. Some regions ran captions over the action detailing the donation hotline number and the amount raised so far. Canada saw the special two days before the British, on the actual anniversary itself.

Robert Holmes was the first person to be approached to write the special. Saward had wanted him because he had written for the show for fifteen years and knew it backwards. Holmes warned Saward that he wasn't sure he'd be able to make the script work and turned in a treatment called "The Six Doctors", in which the Cybermen have made an android copy of the First Doctor which doesn't look entirely like William Hartnell and thus explains the necessary recasting. Holmes eventually abandoned the script, having succumbed to his own fears that it was impossible to write, and Eric Saward turned to another *Who* veteran, Terrance Dicks. Dicks wrote a story akin to a role-playing game, in which an unseen villain removes the Doctors and their companions from time and space and plonks them down in the Death Zone on Gallifrey: an ancient wilderness where the founders of Time Lord society brought aliens to fight each other for their entertainment. This loose structure allowed the script to adapt to whichever actors might be available, although Saward would soon be tearing his hair out to accommodate additions like Caroline John (Liz Shaw), Richard Franklin (Mike Yates), Frazer Hines (Jamie) and Wendy Padbury (Zoe), asked to appear at the last minute by John Nathan-Turner. In the end, all appear as phantoms generated by Rassilon's Dark Tower in the Death Zone. The Second Doctor only realises that Jamie and Zoe are illusions by recalling that, as the Time Lords had wiped their memories in "The War Games" (1969), they shouldn't be able to recognise him. This is in fact a continuity mistake and an example of Terrance Dicks's axiom that continuity in *Doctor Who* was like the definition of history in *1066 And All That*: What You Can Remember. The Time Lords wiped Jamie and Zoe's memories of all their adventures with the Doctor *except for the first one*: thus they would have been able to recognise Troughton's Doctor. Robert Holmes made a similar continuity blunder in "The Two Doctors" (1985): the Time Lords use the Second Doctor as an agent to do their dirty work, when in fact it had been the Third and Fourth Doctors who had been used thus. Holmes had forgotten.

Nathan-Turner decided to recast the First Doctor before work on the special began. William Hartnell had passed away in 1975. He chose Richard Hurndall, whom he had seen in an episode of *Blake's Seven* and thought closely resembled Hartnell. Hartnell himself is represented in a clip from the last episode of "The Dalek Invasion of Earth" and Hurndall turns in a good performance, copying a few of Hartnell's mannerisms but otherwise making the part his own.

The problem of the First Doctor was dealt with; the problem of the Fourth Doctor soon arose. Tom Baker had agreed to be in the special and a substantial role had been written for him, but he was having second thoughts. He had only left the show two years previously and appeared to feel it was too soon to return: he also wondered if he would think "Who are all these people?" pretending to be the Doctor. Baker withdrew and Terrance Dicks was left with an almost identical situation to the one he had faced ten years earlier with "The Three Doctors", when a substantial role for Hartnell's Doctor had had to be abandoned. Heather Hartnell, William Hartnell's wife, had telephoned the production office to say that Bill couldn't possibly do all the running around that was required in the script. Dicks cheerfully employed the same solution on "The Five Doctors" that he had employed on "The Three Doctors": the attempt to lift the Doctor from his time stream had been unsuccessful. The First Doctor had been stuck in a travel capsule in a time eddy (in 1973) and the Fourth Doctor was stuck in limbo in the new story. John-Nathan Turner got Baker's permission to use some clips from the abandoned "Shada" (1979) to represent his Doctor, and the actor agreed. Mindful of the friction between Pertwee and Troughton in filming "The Three Doctors", Dicks structured the new script to keep the Doctors apart until the final scenes.

"The Five Doctors" is a vastly enjoyable, nostalgic romp and a reminder of how the programme should be made and scripted. It features a Dalek, the Cybermen and the Master as the main enemies, with cameo appearances from a Yeti and a new enemy, the Raston robot. Susan, the Brigadier, Sarah Jane and K9 return as companions as do some Time Lords from "Arc of Infinity", although Colin Baker was replaced as Captain of the Chancellery Guard so that viewers wouldn't be confused when he appeared as the Sixth Doctor at the end of the following season.

Season twenty-one began two months later, with a sad return to dreadful form in the appalling "Warriors of the Deep" (1984), a Sea Devil and Silurian tale scripted by Johnny Byrne. The season contained two excellent stories in "Frontios" and "The Caves of Androzani". "Frontios" is a fine piece of science fiction by former script editor Christopher H. Bidmead, in which a human colony in the far future is under attack from meteors from the sky – which apparently destroy the TARDIS – and burrowings from underground, which claim colonists' lives. Those responsible are the Tractators, mindless burrowing creatures controlled by the Gravis – a Tractator that has developed extreme intelligence and psycho-kinetic powers – whose control over the other Tractators recalls the Animus's control over the mindless Zarbi in "The Web Planet" (1965). Bidmead was inspired to create the Tractators by a plague of woodlice that kept infesting his flat and the design does recall a woodlouse. Director Ron Jones cast dancers to realise the Tractator movement, but the costumes were unfortunately far too rigid to do much more than shuffle along.

Davison's final story is the superb "The Caves of Androzani", by Robert Holmes, a tour de force of excellent writing, directing, acting and design that recalled the heights of the Holmes/Hinchcliffe/Tom Baker years and won the most recent "Best *Doctor Who* story" poll in *Doctor Who* Magazine. Holmes re-used some elements which worked well in his previous stories, but "Androzani" is none the worse for that. On the planet Androzani minor (shades of the third moon of Delta Magna in "The Power of Kroll", 1979), the scalded and embittered Sharaz Jek lurks in the planet's cave systems (shades of Greel's lair below the theatre in "The Talons of Weng-Chiang", 1977), holding Androzani major to ransom by keeping sole hold of its supply of spectrox. This precious element slows the ageing process and grants a human being twice his normal life span. "Would you think I was eighty?" the President asks the villainous industrialist Morgus. "Fifty, at most," that worthy replies. Jek has let it be known that the people of Androzani major can have all the spectrox they like, if they give him the head of Morgus in return. He and Morgus were once in partnership but Morgus destroyed his life by leaving him to be scalded near to death in a mud burst in one of the Androzani caves; Jek's thirst for revenge has become an obsession and driven him to the point of madness. Jek is one of the planet's foremost android engineers and is protected by android troops of his own making, armed by the gun runner Stotz, whom Jek supplies with spectrox in return for weapons. Stotz is himself in Morgus's pay, who receives Jek's spectrox through him and thus has a monopoly on the limited supplies available on Androzani major. Morgus is simultaneously financing the President's armed campaign against Jek, but the Praesidium's troops are bogged down against superior forces. Jek has also kidnapped their General Chellak's deputy Salateen (Robert Glenister) and replaced him with an android duplicate: he thus has a perfect spy in his enemy's camp.

Into this murky world of political intrigue, double-crossing, cave systems and soldiers, come the Doctor and Peri. They are first suspected of being gun runners and are then captured, or rescued, by Sharez Jek, who falls violently in love with Peri and allows the Doctor to be taken back to Androzani major by Stotz. Investigating the tunnel systems, both time travellers stumble into a nest of raw spectrox and quickly fall victim to spectrox toxaemia, for which the only cure is the milk of the giant queen bat that lives in the cave system's lower levels. The gun runners, aided by Morgus in person when his treachery is discovered and his business empire collapses (he has murdered the President), over-run Jek's lair and are beaten back by Jek and his androids. Jek murders Morgus and dies of his wounds. The Doctor conserves enough oxygen in his respiratory bypass system (last seen in "Pyramids of Mars", 1976) to enter the airless levels of the queen bat, but there is only enough milk for Peri. He collapses on the floor of the TARDIS and regenerates.

There is much to delight the viewer in "The Caves of Androzani", a story full of guts and high drama. Holmes, believing that there were reserves of untapped heroism in the Fifth Doctor, gives Davison some moments of real gusto and physical violence. When Sarez Jek drools over Peri, the Doctor stands up and eyeballs him silently, forcing Jek to divert his attention from his companion; the Doctor defies Stotz in turning the ship back to Androzani minor and runs for his life through the sand dunes as the gun runners machine-gun him; he uses his fists on Salateen when he needs to escape. As Morgus, John Normington gives a performance of Jacobean coldness and villainy, turning to deliver his soliloquys directly to camera in the best traditions of BBC Shakespeare. In fact, this was the result of Normington's misunderstanding of Graeme Harper's direction, but Harper liked it and kept it in. Christopher Gable excels in the Phantom of the Opera melodrama of Sharez Jek, making him both pathetic and genuinely frightening. He turns from ranting to being quietly terrifying on a heartbeat, as in this exchange with the exhausted Peri:

Jek: And it is Morgus who has done this to me! Morgus destroyed my life. Do you think I'm mad?
Peri: (lying) No.
Jek: I *am* mad.

Never has Peri been in greater peril in the series. Holmes intelligently has her sympathise with her captor and tormentor and Nicola Bryant conveys Peri's physical deterioration as spectrox toxaemia takes hold with great subtlety and conviction. Holmes also re-uses a powerful image from "The Talons of Weng-Chiang" as Jek, like Greel before him, rips off his leather mask to reveal his disfigured face beneath, to the hysterical terror of Morgus and, when she spots him, Peri. Jek gibbers with distress at her fear and hides under the table in a touching and realistic moment: a considerable dramatic achievement in the midst of a battle between humans and androids. Graeme Harper's inventive direction on his first *Doctor Who* story is rightly praised: even small details surprise, as in the holographic viewer in Morgus's office when it would have been so much simpler to use a two dimensional monitor.

Harper was swiftly re-employed to direct "Revelation of the Daleks" in the following season; he would have directed the aborted BBC Enterprises thirtieth anniversary special "The Dark Dimension", but returned to helm several episodes of the revived series from 2005, including the four Cybermen episodes in David Tennant's first season (2006).

Peter Davison collapses on the floor of the TARDIS, asks "Is this death?" and his features reform – after the inevitable nostalgia sequence featuring his past companions – into the sixth Doctor, Colin Baker.

11

Doctor Wholigan?

Colin Baker is a fine actor and could have been one of the great Doctors, but he was let down by poor scripts and various eccentric decisions by the production team. The other Doctors were all fully committed to the programme and cared deeply about it: Colin Baker shared that commitment, but he went further and was, in effect, a fan. He had watched the first episode when he had been studying the law, before he became an actor; he was always generous with his time in giving interviews to fans and wrote some of the comic strips for his Doctor. Baker was delighted to be offered the part. He had been reluctant to play Commander Maxil in "Arc of Infinity" because he thought taking a part in the show meant he would never get a chance to play the Doctor; when Nathan-Turner asked him if he'd like to be the new Doctor, his jaw dropped and he simply said, "Yes please!"

Colin Baker drew on William Hartnell's portrayal of the Doctor in preparing his characterisation. Hartnell, he said, was "the guv'nor", and he wanted to return to his irascibility and alien quality. The sixth Doctor would be inconsolably grieved over the death of a butterfly, Colin said, but might react with indifference to the departure of a companion: "All right. Go then." He wanted to beat Tom Baker's record of seven years in the part and determined to play the Doctor, initially, as somewhat unlikeable: then, as time went on, he would peel back the layers of the character like the layers of an onion, and we would see the real man inside. This perhaps wasn't a good idea as the unlikeable Doctor that Colin portrayed in his first season repelled many viewers: at the end of "The Twin Dilemma" (1984), he turns to Peri, who misses his "sweet" fifth incarnation, and says, "I am the Doctor, whether you like it or not." The trouble was, lots of viewers didn't. Furthermore, by the time we got to the centre of the Doctor's being, he would presumably turn out to be much the same person we had been used to for the past twenty two years. Events, of course, prevented Colin's plans from being realised.

By this point in the series' history, John Nathan-Turner was attracting almost as much publicity as its stars. He enjoyed being photographed with Davison and Colin Baker, always in his trademark Hawaiian shirts. He attended many conventions in America, where he was as feted as the Doctors themselves, and introduced Colin Baker as the new Doctor to American fans before the British, much to the latter's disgruntlement.

British convention organisers in the 1980s were finding it difficult to attract any of the programme's stars to their events; they couldn't match the fees of their American counterparts, and actors understandably thought an event in Los Angeles might be more fun than one in Milton Keynes. There was consequently a certain amount of resentment felt towards American fans and the production team. The inclusion of the American companion Peri was seen as pandering to American fans, which is perhaps unfair (and a bit racist) as almost all the previous companions except Tegan had been unmistakeably British, whether or not they hailed from the planet Earth, and Nicola Bryant gave an excellent performance anyway.

Pat Godfrey, the costume designer on "The Twin Dilemma" (1984), asked John Nathan-Turner what sort of clothes he would like the new Doctor to wear. Nathan-Turner asked for something "totally tasteless and clashing", like his own Hawaiian shirts. Apparently several designs were sent back as not being outrageous enough, but the eventual hideous look of the Technicolor dreamcoat, striped waistcoat and spotted cravat was settled on. The coat still had the cut of the Edwardian outfits favoured by previous Doctors but the ensemble was manifestly a costume, and criticised by some as drawing attention to the Doctor (although most characters, ridiculously, didn't comment on it) when he should be able to slip in and out of events when he wants to. Even Peri says, "You're not serious," when he tries it on. The costume was presumably supposed to be very funny but looked like a parody of previous Doctors' outfits and recalled Verity Lambert's criticism of the later show, that it sent itself up and wasn't taken seriously by its production team. Colin Baker himself wanted to wear black, to emphasise the mystery of the Doctor's character, but was told this wasn't possible as the Master wore black: it was presumably too difficult to adapt the Master's costume accordingly, such was the rigid thinking of the time. Colin said the best thing about his costume was that, as he was inside it, he didn't have to look at it. Philip Segal, the executive producer of the Paul McGann TV movie (1996), said one of the worst faults of the original series had been its costume design in its final years. A telling comment was made by the costume designers on J. Michael Staczynski's excellent *Babylon 5* (1994-9), who shopped for interesting garments in Hollywood stores: they wanted their human characters to wear clothes, not costumes. (*Babylon 5*, while it ran, was a worthy comfort for the lack of *Doctor Who* and comes highly recommended. Straczynski himself admired and liked *Doctor Who*, which, like *Blake's Seven*, was one inspiration for his five year arc story. Watching *Blake's*

Seven, he was amazed that, unlike *Star Trek*, here was a crew of people who *didn't like each other*: this he carried into the rivalries and feuds between *Babylon 5*'s leading characters. He also tried to get Tom Baker aboard as a guest star.)

It appears that Colin Baker was encouraged to play up his performance in his first story, "The Twin Dilemma". If other Doctors had suffered from post-regeneration trauma, which had made them somewhat erratic, the Sixth Doctor's regeneration made him positively psychotic. He sneers and snarls at Peri throughout, calls her evil and tries to strangle her. Nathan-Turner elected to change the established pattern of a new Doctor starting a new season by appending "The Twin Dilemma" to the end of Davison's final season. This was intended to establish Colin as the new Doctor before the summer break between seasons but proved disastrous as "The Twin Dilemma" is one of the worst stories ever made, although Nathan-Turner apparently thought it was brilliant. While its immediate predecessor came first in the Best Story poll, "The Twin Dilemma" came bottom out of over two hundred stories. The juxtaposition of excellent and execrable highlighted the schizophrenic quality the show was beginning to demonstrate. Watching "The Twin Dilemma" was like watching a different programme; perhaps a particularly bad episode of the children's drama *Captain Zep – Space Detective*. The Doctor goes mad, lands on a planet to cure himself to find it ruled by Mestor, a giant slug, who intends to explode a star to scatter his eggs all over the Universe. The costumes for the human characters – shiny black nylon uniforms – would have been thought cliched in the 1960s; the acting is often appalling, especially from Helen Blatch as Fabian, and the dialogue is excruciating. Blatch gets to utter immortal lines like "May my bones rot" for giving an uncongenial order; the Doctor says ludicrously over-melodramatic lines like "The very core of my being is on fire with guilt and rage!" Denis Chinnery, who had played Gharman beautifully in "Genesis of the Daleks", is that sit-com figure, the father who is out of his depth, trying to cope with boy genius twins called, you've guessed it, Romulus and Remus. The poor lads – identical twins - who were cast as these characters have identical speech impediments and say "w" for "r", but no-one thought to change the characters' names, so they were cruelly exposed to ridicule by viewers when they introduce themselves: a wholly unnecessary indignity for actors in their first television engagement. Distinguished actor Maurice Denham played retired Time Lord Azmael, an old friend of the Doctor, but even an actor as excellent as he – who would make a reading of the phone book interesting – couldn't save the story from being anything other than risible rubbish. The season ended with fans in dismay.

It would be nice to say there was an improvement in Colin Baker's first full season. There were some good stories amidst the dross, but the first story – "Attack of the Cybermen" (1985) – appeared to continue the downward trend of "The Twin Dilemma". Season twenty two was moved back to Saturday evenings, where *Doctor Who* stayed as long as Colin Baker played the lead. For the first time in its history, the series was made as forty five minutes episodes: the standard episode length for the post-2005 revival. The previous season's "Resurrection of the Daleks" (1984) had been re-edited as two forty five minute episodes to avoid programming clashes with the winter Olympics. This was thought to have worked well and a necessity became a virtue as all of Colin Baker's first season was scripted and shot as forty-five minute episodes. This decision may also have been influenced by the successful length of the recently-defunct *Blake's Seven*, whose fifty minute episodes helped that show to be accepted as more adult fare. Were longer *Doctor Who* episodes staking a claim for the programme to be taken more seriously by the viewing public? Certainly, both the Saturday screenings and the innovative episode length were intended to boost the ratings, but the timeslot – around 5.20 p.m. – didn't help. It was, as *The Guardian* pointed out, too early for families to catch after the Saturday afternoon trip to a local football match; it was also before the six o'clock watershed, which neutered its attempt to move into *Blake's Seven's* viewing demographic (*Blake's Seven* had always been transmitted after 7.00 p.m.). Furthermore, the timeslot was far too early for the amount of horror and violence contained in the season, both heavily criticised by the fans. In spite of all the effort, season twenty two failed to garner more viewers. It averaged about seven million, the same as Peter Davison's last two seasons; much better than Tom Baker's final season but respectable rather than spectacular. The ratings nevertheless gave the lie to Michael Grade's claim that the show was unpopular when his cancellation announcement was made during the broadcast of "The Two Doctors" (1985).

Season twenty two's first story, "Attack of the Cybermen" was another dreadful script which, like "Resurrection of the Daleks", appeared to make things up as it went along. It lurched from set-piece to set-piece, subjecting cardboard characters to all manner of indignities. It has been pointed out that the Cybermen lose their menace as emotionless, dehumanised versions of ourselves if the human characters are equally dehumanised because of bad writing. "Attack of the

Cybermen" was written by one Paula Moore, actually a pseudonym for a friend of Eric Saward and Saward himself, working from ideas fed to the production team by unofficial series consultant, Ian Levine. Levine was the fan record producer who had saved many of the black and white episodes from being wiped. He suggested a sequel to "The Tenth Planet" (1966) and "The Tomb of the Cybermen" (1967); all very well, but these serials were long forgotten by the general public and even by the fans. "The Tomb of the Cybermen" was still one of the stories that was lost (it was returned to the BBC from Hong Kong in 1992) and neither was available on the BBC's fledgling home video collection of *Doctor Who*, so there was no possibility of re-watching them to try and make sense of the new story.

"Attack of the Cybermen" is apparently aimed at pleasing the fans with numerous continuity references. Fans, who wanted good, new, original ideas, weren't impressed at yet another raid on the programme's back catalogue. The Doctor lands in I. M. Foreman's junkyard, last seen in the first story "An Unearthly Child" (1963). This might have been exciting if it was tied in with the plot, but it wasn't, and so comes across as a gimmick. The production team also spells "Foreman"'s name wrongly, which only serves to irritate the handful of viewers who actually get the reference. There are Cybermen lurking in the sewers (as in "Invasion", 1968) and Lytton is back from "Resurrection of the Daleks" (1985), as scowly as ever. The Doctor distrusts him as he seems to be working for the Cybermen, this time with a bunch of London villains led by that fine actor Brian Glover, who apparently enjoyed the part enormously. Lytton, however, is inexplicably revealed to be a goodie who was working to undermine the Cybermen all along, and the Doctor regrets misjudging him. So far, so baffling. The Cybermen want to crash Haley's comet (then about to appear in our skies again) into Earth, and so prevent the events of "The Tenth Planet", a story a mere nineteen years old, which we are expected to remember; all this is offered to the viewer with minimal explanation so we can't follow the plot (such as it is). The action then switches to the Cybermen's tombs on Telos (taken from "The Tomb of the Cybermen" again), now redesigned to look like an Iceland or frozen food store: those chest freezers are just the right size to take a Cyberman! The Cybercontroller – from "Tomb" – returns, again played by Michael Kilgarriff in a fan-pleasing piece of casting; not a good idea as Kilgarriff had put on weight and had a cyberbeerbelly. There are various scenes where the Cybermen convert some shouty humans into Cybermen (see most previous Cybermen stories) and then the Doctor defeats them, shooting the Cybercontroller with his own cyber-weapon. One of the story's few effective points is the Cryons, the other inhabitants of Telos, female humanoids who recall the Sensorites in design (see "The Sensorites", 1964) with interesting and beautifully choreographed hand movements which I nicked for the witches in a student production of "Macbeth" in 1985. Although production values are high and the story looks great, the script is drivel and should never have been made.

There were, however, three good stories in the season, or two good and one reasonable. The issue of "video nasties" was causing public concern at the time. These were an apparently uncontrolled feature of the wide availability of home video recorders and commercially available video tapes: extremely pornographic and/or violent videos with titles like *Driller Killer* copied illegally and circulating the video rental shops without certificates. Such was the concern of Mrs Thatcher's second government that a law was passed requiring videos to be classified in the same way as films. The press agonised over what sort of people would want to watch these sorts of horrors and the issue was addressed in playwright Philip Martin's story "Vengeance on Varos", the second of season twenty two. This was an intelligent satire on the media and capitalism that recalls similarly politically engaged stories like "The Green Death" (1973) and "The Sun Makers" (1977). The economy of the planet Varos is drained by its obligations to the reptilian Mentors and their ambassador, Sil (Nabil Shaban). Its main exports are Ztyon 7, a mineral needed to power space and time craft (the TARDIS runs out of Zyton 7, which necessitates the Doctor's visit), and extremely violent videos made to keep a bloodthirsty population dormant and content while living in poverty. These are manufactured in the Punishment Dome by the sadistic Quillam and include burning by lasers, hanging, immersion in acid bath and being eaten alive by cannibalistic, atavistic savages dressed in nappies. The Doctor and Peri are caught up in the Dome and subjected to all manner of horrors as they try to escape. Watching at home are Arak and Etta, a middle aged, apparently working class couple whose function, Philip Martin explained, is the same as a Chorus in a Greek tragedy: they comment on the action beamed from the punishment dome and punch in their appreciation ratings in their interactive control unit. Interactive television was then only in its infancy and largely confined to phone-in chat shows like the Saturday morning BBC children's show *Multi-Coloured Swap Shop* and its successor, *Saturday Superstore*, on which Tom Baker, Peter Davison and Colin Baker had appeared at various times to be quizzed on *Doctor Who* by children at home. Punching in your appreciation of a programme while watching it, or even voting in elections, was the stuff of *Tomorrow's World* in 1985, but Philip Martin's prescient anticipation of such technology is brilliantly handled and worthy of Nigel Kneale himself. In one sequence, Varos's Governor (Martin Jarvis) subjects himself to the will of the people, whose punch-in electronic votes of approval or disapproval will result in his re-election or live torture on television under green disintegrator beams. If the ratings are bad enough, the beams will eliminate him and ensure the election of his successor. Viewers mused on the excellence of this idea and wondered if it could be applied to some of our own politicians. "Vengeance on Varos" is an excellent treatment of human thoughtlessness and cruelty. The Doctor saves the day by telling the Governor the true market price of Zyton 7: this splendid piece of market economics means that Varosians can stop making video nasties and being exploited by Sil, who is so enraged that his translator unit self-destructs.

Martin Jarvis gives a wonderful, silky performance at the Governor, who tries to protect Peri from torture but whose conscience has been worn away by his exposure to such a corrosive political system. Jarvis, who had played a Menoptra in "The Web Planet" (1965) and Butler in "Invasion of the Dinosaurs" (1973), was pleased to return to *Doctor Who* not least because of his friendship with Colin Baker, who had played Laertes to Jarvis's Hamlet in the theatre. Nabil Shaban is also excellent as Sil. Shaban, an actor with osteogenesis imperfecta (also known as brittle bones disease), had submitted a story idea to the production office with himself cast as the Doctor. He explained in an interview that the idea was the Time Lords, who were really out to get the Doctor this time, forced him into a disabled body for his next regeneration. Nathan-Turner wrote to Shaban explaining that he couldn't play the Doctor but auditioned him for the role of Sil, a role which he clearly relished. Shaban developed a revolting, rattling laugh for Sil by lapping his tongue vigorously against his lips while gurgling. He tried this out in the read-through; there was a stunned silence, then vigorous applause from the other actors. The laugh, Shaban explained, was Sil's catchphrase equivalent of the Daleks' "Exterminate", and would, he hope, "get the kids back behind the sofa where they belong."

The trouble with "Vengeance on Varos" is, that in attempting to show that torture and horror are vile, it shows vile torture and horror and was much criticised at the time. Quillam is a monstrous bully with greasy black hair, a leather costume and a horribly scalded face; the cannibals are frankly very disturbing, nappies notwithstanding, and a sequence where the Doctor and Jondar (Jason Connery, Sean's son) are hanged – we see them fall through the trap door – is real violence of the type not shown in the programme before. That the Doctor and Jondar are immediately shown to be unharmed is presumably an excuse for the sequence's inclusion, but mock hangings are hardly the stuff of family viewing. Peri is transmogriphied into a bird for Sil's slavering pleasure in a sequence that could only be described as kinky. Worst of all for some viewers is that the Doctor is no longer the reassuring figure of moral outrage we could hide behind: Pertwee's Doctor might have mocked the terrors and Tom Baker's Doctor might have raged at their perpetrators, but the unsympathetic harshness of Colin Baker's Doctor means that the story lacks a reassuring moral centre. Two guards sent to dispose of him in the Punishment Dome are dispatched to their deaths in baths of acid: instead of showing horror or sympathy, the Doctor quips "You'll forgive me if I don't join you," in a psychopathic aside worthy of James Bond. This lack of care and general unkindness on the part of the Sixth Doctor led some to label him Doctor Wholigan. The production team radically toned down his nastiness for the twenty third season, when it eventually appeared, and Colin Baker's Doctor is a much more conventionally likeable figure in his second season.

The uneven tone and quality of the first two stories combined with other extraordinary moments to suggest a production team that had taken its eye off the ball and a series that had lost its way. There was unnecessary and nasty violence in "Attack of the Cybermen" when two Cybermen crush each of Lytton's hands until they bleed copiously. A character is murdered with cyanide powder in "The Two Doctors". Some of the story ideas were just plain odd. Nathan-Turner let it be known that he was going to change the TARDIS's exterior form as no-one knew what a police box was any more. This was a publicity stunt which resulted in mothers writing in asking him to change his mind as their children were in tears. Nathan-Turner had no intention of making such a change permanent, but the chameleon circuit works for a bit in the first story and we have lots of fun, apparently, when the TARDIS appears as a pipe organ (with no door: how does the Doctor get in and out?) and a pair of silver doors in the Cybermen's control centre. It becomes a police box again at the end of the story but only when the gimmick has been milked to maximum viewer irritation. In "The Mark of the Rani", a character is transformed into a tree (a ludicrous costume straight out of a pantomime) by the Rani's land mine. Peri is about to step on one but the tree, apparently still sentient, reaches out a protective branch and grabs her. The Borad in "Timelash" was once mistaken for the Loch Ness Monster, which doesn't seem very likely as he's only about six feet tall and *Doctor Who* had already explained that the Loch Ness Monster was the Zygons' Skarasen cyborg ("Terror of the Zygons", 1975). Some of the ideas are simply poor or cheesy: the tiresome Herbert, whom the Doctor encounters in "Timelash", is H. G. Wells, who gets his story ideas from his trip in the TARDIS (a very unoriginal conceit). The inhabitants of Karfel in the same story have a painting of the Doctor so they know who he is. However, the painting is an American fan's portrait of Jon Pertwee included by Nathan-Turner as a favour; no-one comments on the fact that the Doctor doesn't look like this any more but they are still able to recognise him from the portrait of an apparently entirely different person. "Timelash" also graces the TARDIS with seatbelts attached to the console, which the Doctor and Peri stand upright in, lean back against, and run around as they hit turbulence. Robert Louis Stephenson's workshop in "The Mark of the Rani" has the completed Rocket in the background, just in case we don't know who he is. We have two refugee actors from *Blake's Seven* in the twenty second season. Jacqueline Pearce, who played chief villain Servalan in that series, is very effective as Chessene, the villain in "The Two Doctors". Paul Darrow, who had played Avon, is dreadful as Tekker, the villain in "Timelash"; he admitted he played it as Richard III, complete with limp, and hammed it up ludicrously because he was allowed to. Asked what he thought of the story, Darrow said it was "rubbish". "Timelash" is as bad a story as "The Twin Dilemma". A villain called the Borad sends his enemies down the Timelash, a tube literally decorated with Christmas tinsel – the money had run out – which dumps them elsewhere in time. There is a sock puppet Bandril ambassador with a silly voice and Peri is tied up – again – and menaced by a giant diplodocus-like creature while she screams and screams. And screams. And screams. "Timelash"'s plot development and characterisation makes "Attack of the Cybermen" look like a masterpiece.

And yet, among the dross, and in spite of all their problems, there are good stories in "Vengeance on Varos", "The Two Doctors" and "Revelation of the Daleks". These, however, are not the sure footed, well-written fare of seasons past but succumb to the general silliness or uncertainty of tone of the rest of the season.

Patrick Troughton enjoyed his time in "The Five Doctors" so much that he asked to return again as the Doctor. Nathan-Turner obliged two years later with "The Two Doctors" and turned to Robert Holmes to write it. It is effectively a six parter – three parts in the new format – and Holmes was brought back on board because of his experience in writing six part stories. He was asked to include the Sontarans, which Holmes didn't really want to do as he thought bringing back old monsters was boring (his sentiments in his years as script editor), but went along with because he hadn't liked the way his creations had been handled in "The Invasion of Time" (1977). Nathan-Turner also hoped to shoot on location in New Orleans, again to please American viewers, and Holmes had to scratch his head to work both New Orleans and the Sontarans into a story. He reasoned that New Orleans was known for its jazz, which might not work well with the Sontarans, but also for its food, which led to the creation of the new aliens, the Androgums, an anagram of "gourmand". Holmes enjoyed anagrams; the name for the Drashigs from his "Carnival of Monsters" (1973) is an anagram of "dishrag". Unfortunately, the American deal fell through and Nathan-Turner elected to shift the action to Seville in Spain instead. Holmes said he had no idea what the connection between gourmands and Spain was, but the script was shot there anyway.

Patrick Troughton is clearly enjoying playing the Second Doctor again, this time accompanied by Jamie, who had been scripted into "The Three Doctors" (1973) but replaced by Sergeant Benton when ITV refused to release Frazer Hines from shooting on the long-running soap *Emmerdale Farm* (later just *Emmerdale*). The pre-"Five Doctors" TARDIS console reappears for the Troughton TARDIS and the opening moments of the story are transmitted in black and white as a reminder of Troughton's original sixties episodes. There is a wonderful turn by John Stratton as Shockeye, the Androgum's chief butcher and cook, who will eat anything, including rat ("The flesh is rank. Perhaps with a sauce…") and intends to butcher and serve Peri for lunch ("What a fine, fleshy beast!"). John Stratton was best known at the time for playing Mr Bott, or "Botty", in ITV's children's serial *Just William* (1976-7), based on the books by Richmal Crompton. Mr Bott's daughter was the lisping and spoilt Violet Elizabeth, played by one Bonnie Langford who was, it must be said, absolutely superb in the role.

"The Two Doctors" suffers the fate of many six parters (or three parters in the new format) as the final episode is essentially a chase around Seville. The Second Doctor has been transmuted into an Androgum; while he and Shockeye hit the restaurants, the Sixth Doctor hunts them down before the Androgum DNA can hit his system. He eyes a cat and licks his lips, so he finds his younger self just in time. "The Two Doctors" is quite fun but suffers from being the second multi-Doctor story in two years. As with the Master, if the idea is over-used it suffers from the law of diminishing returns. This is perhaps one reason why the revised series proper hasn't attempted a multi-Doctor story yet, although Peter Davison paired up with David Tennant for a witty mini-episode, "Time Crash" (2007), written by Steven Moffat for the BBC's annual Children in Need appeal (and David Tennant is in the fiftieth anniversary special).

There are some good moments in "The Mark of the Rani". John Nathan-Turner wanted to include a renegade female Time Lord, like the Master, as an adversary and antithesis of the Doctor. The producer wasn't sure what she should be called, although he stipulated that it couldn't be "The Mistress". The title Rani was eventually chosen. The word is Hindi and means a Queen or a Rajah's wife. The word was never explained on screen for those few viewers who didn't know it, but Kate O'Mara's imperious performance fits the title well. This was Pip and Jane Baker's first script for the series and was far better than their later contributions. The Rani, unlike the Master, is an amoral psychopath rather than an evil genius. A brilliant Gallifreyan chemist, she has as much interest in human beings as in laboratory animals and doesn't care whether they live or die as a result of her experiments. This indifference and lack of empathy, recalling the Nazi doctors who experimented on prisoners in concentration camps, is hideously plausible. It is, therefore, something of a mistake to pair her with the Master in the story, who is completely upstaged by Kate O'Mara and comes across as a bumbling and incompetent egotist, as she herself tells him. We also get to see the Rani's TARDIS, a jolly design with a gyroscope instead of a time rotor; the story ends with the Rani and the Master in its console room, powerless to move as her ship hurtles out of control and an embryo tyrannosaurus rex, collected by the Rani on one of her last visits to Earth, starts to grow to adult size… Kate O'Mara's Rani so impressed some American television executives that they offered her a starring role in the glitzy series *Dynasty*, the rival soap to *Dallas*.

The series' final story is Eric Saward's "Revelation of the Daleks". This takes Evelyn Waugh's novel *The Loved One* as its source, a satire on the American "death care" industry which features a lonely undertaker, Mr Joby, as its down-at-heel hero. In "Revelation of the Daleks", Mr Joby becomes Mr Jobel (Clive Swift), the toupeed head of the funeral facility Tranquil Repose. Here, the rich can deposit their dead loved ones in suspended animation, ready to be awakened when a cure is found for the disease that killed them. Tranquil Repose is in fact run by Davros, who is using the corpses to make a new race of Daleks (the "Revelation" of the title) or turning them into foodstuffs to be shipped to other planets, in another reference to cannibalism of questionable taste. Broadcasting to the dead is the DJ, played by comedian Alexei Sayle, who had once submitted an article to Marxism Today entitled "Why I should be the next Doctor Who: the case for a Marxist in the TARDIS". The DJ rejigs his equipment into a weapon and manages to destroy two Daleks with a pure beam of concentrated rock and roll before he is exterminated. Again, the story is well made and, under Graeme Harper's direction, looks great but, in common with many of Eric Saward's scripts, is oddly structured. The Doctor and Peri spend most of episode one trying to get to Tranquil Repose and don't actually engage with the other characters until episode two. In another bit of fan pleasing reference, we have a transparent Dalek, imagined by David Whitaker in his novelisation of the first Dalek story but never realised on screen, and a flying Dalek. The latter was a commercially available kit made by Sevans Models. As it was seen for only a few seconds, the flying Dalek didn't have sufficient impact to stamp out, once and for all, the hilarious jokes about Daleks being unable to conquer the Universe because they can't climb stairs.

With the Dalek story, the uneven, good looking, extraordinary season came to a close. But not before a new threat stirred. On the higher floors of Television Centre,

in an office inaccessible to lesser beings,

a mind immeasurably different from our own,

an intellect cold and cool and unsympathetic,

regarded the programme with hostile eyes;

and slowly,

and surely,

drew its plans against it.

12

Escape into Danger

And so it came to pass that Michael Grade, the Controller of BBC 1, looked upon Colin Baker's first season as the Doctor and liked not what he saw. Grade had come over to the BBC from ITV, Britain's commercial television company, and immediately applied the principles of commercial television to a public service network funded by the licence fee. Grade ruffled feathers at the corporation by a perceived "dumbing down" of the BBC's output: colourful game shows, of the type produced by ITV, were in, and series which didn't garner enough viewing figures were out. Critics wondered why, if competition was so important a motivational and commercial force in Mrs Thatcher's Britain, Michael Grade thought he could compete with ITV by making the BBC's output essentially the same, but Grade ploughed on regardless. He axed the BBC's adaptation of John Christopher's science fiction novels, *The Tripods* (1984-5), after only two of its proposed three series (one for each of the novels), thus leaving the story unfinished. This was the sort of commercial decision only too familiar for American viewers of American networks but it was new in Britain: some were surprised and dismayed by Grade's decision to put viewing figures above artistic considerations. Such was the comparative innocence of the times in the 1980s.

Michael Grade has also been criticised for getting rid of shows that he personally disliked. He was no fan of *Doctor Who* and, in a later interview, remembered how appalled he had been at watching scenes of "shop window dummies calmly mowing down shoppers" (a reference to "Spearhead from Space" (1970)). Although the twenty second season of the programme had many problems, it did produce some good stories; the viewing figures, perhaps helped by the move to Saturday nights and forty five minute episodes, held up reasonably well. But this was not enough to save the show from Grade's pitiless attention. The production team were told half way through the season's run that there was to be no twenty third season.

What happened next is far from clear. We don't know whether the programme was put on hold or cancelled outright, although the latter seems more likely. The immediate effect on *Doctor Who* was to depress the cast and crew thoroughly. Scripts had already been commissioned and partly written for the twenty third season: they were axed (although the audio company Big Finish did eventually release them, in adapted form, as CD plays). The final scene of "Revelation of the Daleks" (1985) has the Doctor wonder where to take Peri next: he triumphantly utters the line, "I know! I'll take you to Blackpool!" This was to have been a lead in to the first story of the new season, "The Nightmare Fair" by former producer Graham Williams, in which Michael Gough would have reprised his role as the first Doctor's enemy The Celestial Toymaker, now operating from Blackpool's pleasure domes. Knowing that this would never be made or broadcast, the production team cut the last word of Baker's line. His speech now ran, "I know! I'll take you to – ": the picture froze before the last word. Freeze frames had been used before to excellent dramatic effect in the programme (for example, Sarah falling off a gantry at the end of episode two of "Genesis of the Daleks"(1976)), but it was somewhat bathetic – and baffling – to use one to cover the Doctor's announcement of his next destination.

Ian Levine was working with producer John Nathan-Turner as a script consultant when Grade's decision was announced. He recalls that Nathan-Turner briefed him to give the inside story of the cancellation to *The Sun* newspaper. With a circulation of four million copies a day and perhaps twice as many readers, this was Britain's best-selling tabloid. Levine was told to use the alias Snowball, which signalled to *The Sun* that his call was genuine and from the BBC; Nathan-Turner, standing in the same room, fed Levine the line about the cancellation that he wanted to be made public. *The Sun* which, for all its faults, had been often supportive of *Doctor Who*, splashed the story across its front page with "*Dr Who* [sic] Is Axed In A BBC Plot". Much was made of the corporation's alleged motivation to cut costs in a recession, as a preparation for its new breakfast television service.

Other newspapers quickly picked up the story: *The Guardian*'s leading article murmured that, while the programme had endlessly recycled plots and was *not* a national institution (*The Guardian* said so, so it must have been true), it did not make sense to axe a programme that was popular simply on cost cutting grounds. The *Daily Mirror* sent journalists to pursue Michael Grade and caught up with him on a skiing holiday. By this time, the story had changed. Grade opined that everyone was making a lot of fuss and that the fans were hysterical; he announced that the programme had not been cancelled (which was news to the production team), but was merely being rested. The idea was mooted that a long break would give an exhausted production team time to rethink their approach to the show. *Doctor Who* fans smelt a whole sewer full of giant rats and were not convinced.

The series went into an eighteen month hiatus. Colin Baker, who cared deeply about the programme, was bitterly disappointed. There was a brief respite from the gloom when BBC Radio Four commissioned six ten minute episodes from Eric Saward (an experienced radio writer) to be part of their new magazine show for children, *Pirate Radio Four*. The story, "Slipback", was inflected towards comedy and showed the influence of *The Hitch Hiker's Guide to the Galaxy* on *Doctor Who* yet again in, for example, its ditsy computer with a split personality. Valentine Dyall gave a strong performance as the melancholy spaceship captain and the story ambitiously focused (yet again for the series) on the creation of the universe and its possible prevention. Derivative though it was, "Slipback" was also light hearted and rather jolly. One of the technical staff who worked on it pointed out that it didn't fully exploit the creative possibilities of radio where, unlike television, there were no budgetary and technical limitations on what could be featured. He suggested that the monster should have fourteen penises, but this idea was surprisingly not picked up by the production staff.

There were stories that Michael Grade, who had tried to kill off *Doctor Who*, was cross that Radio Four had resurrected the show. Nearly twenty years later, fans' collective stomachs lurched when they learned that Grade was to be the new chairman of the BBC, just after BBC 1 had announced it was re-launching the series with Christopher Eccleston. Was the prize of a new series to be snatched away, after they had waited so faithfully and so long? To calm such fears, Grade let it be known that he had no intention of interfering in the revival; after the first series had screened, he even congratulated everyone concerned and said how much he and his young son had enjoyed it. For some, this was as improbable as seeing the Master repent of his evil ways and becoming an Anglican clergyman.

After a holiday, the production team had to decide what to do about the twenty third season. Rumours hit the *Doctor Who* Appreciation Society that the number of episodes was going to be cut. The BBC denied it and pointed out that the new season would have fourteen episodes, one more than the previous season's thirteen. What they neglected to mention was that the new season's episodes were returning to the twenty five minute length that had been standard for the programme: fourteen episodes of twenty five minutes each was significantly less screen time than thirteen forty five minute episodes, and fans sank into a black gloom.

Michael Grade was consulted about what he wanted the new season to be like: the production team was anxious to find out and, if possible, propitiate him if the programme was to avoid his attention in the future. Colin Baker recalled that Grade had opined, "Yes, more humour, less violence." This was exactly the same brief given to Graham Williams after the supposed excesses of season sixteen had drawn down the wrath of Mary Whitehouse. Reluctantly, Saward and Nathan-Turner went back to the drawing board. The scripts which had been already commissioned for the season were axed and a new umbrella theme emerged. As with season sixteen's Key to Time season, the twenty third season would comprise several – in fact, four, because of the reduced episode count – stories united by a common theme. The Doctor was to be put on trial by his own people for interference in the affairs of other races. This sounded promising to some fans, who recalled it was exactly the same premise as the final two acclaimed episodes of "The War Games" (1969), Patrick Troughton's last story. So obvious was the repetition (perhaps *The Guardian* had a point about the series recycling its plots) that Lynda Bellingham's Time Lord Inquisitor notes in the first episode: "The Doctor has been tried for these offences before."

Saward and Nathan-Turner used the trial theme as a cheeky metaphor for the way the show itself was on trial. The season's structure was borrowed from Charles Dickens's *A Christmas Carol*: in the same way that that tale had three ghosts of past, present and yet to come, so the fourteen episode "The Trial of a Time Lord" would feature three stories taking place in the Doctor's past, present and future.

"The Trial of a Time Lord" is, sadly, generally perceived as a failure and even worse than the season which had preceded it. Eighteen months had not given the team the energy or motivation to rethink the series and it suffered from unprecedented upheaval behind the scenes. Nathan-Turner wanted to move on from the show, having produced it for six years (including the hiatus): a year longer than any previous producer. However, BBC management made it clear to him that *Doctor Who* would be the only show he would work on as producer: if he left the programme, he would leave the BBC. It also appears to have been suggested that, if Nathan-Turner left, the show itself would be axed; such was the low esteem in which it was held at the corporation. When the show reached its twenty fifth anniversary two years later in 1988, seventh Doctor Sylvester McCoy said that the BBC didn't care about *Doctor Who* and had no interest in its place in broadcasting history.

Eric Saward was tired, having acted as script editor for four seasons of production. When he mentioned this to Robert Holmes, who was returning to write for the new season, Holmes told him, "You're mad. I did three years and that was enough." The strain of endlessly commissioning, polishing and occasionally rewriting whole scripts had worn Saward down.

"The Trial of a Time Lord" started unambitiously and pleasantly enough with a four part story by Robert Holmes. Some eyebrows were raised by the first shot – the TARDIS is dragged aboard a Time Lord spaceship by a tractor beam – as it was news to the fans that the Time Lords had spaceships at all: they always assumed that the Time Lords' great power had led them to transcend such simple mechanical devices when the universe was less than half its present size. The effects shot itself was superb for the time, but used up much of the season's effects budget: something made obvious by the number of times the shot was repeated in the season. There was yet another new arrangement of the theme tune, apparently written and recorded in five days: it was as twinkly as the programme's messy title sequence.

Holmes' story (called either "The Mysterious Planet" for convenience or "The Trial of a Time Lord" episodes one to four) concerns a planet called Ravalox which appears to be Earth in the far future, moved to a different location in space and peopled by an iron age tribe led by *Carry On* star Joan Sims. There are some effective scenes set in a ruined Marble Arch tube station and an amusing Holmes double act called Glitz and Dibber, a pair of con-men who recalled "The Ribos Operation"'s Garron and Unstoffe (1978). The Sixth Doctor's relationship with Peri has softened from the previous season and they treat each other like old friends. Colin Baker quite reasonably said that this was entirely believable for two people who had travelled together for so long and, had they continued their abrasive previous relationship, Peri would have left long ago. Location filming was replaced by video for the final four years left to the original series' run: presumably a cost-cutting decision which didn't help the programme to look less cheap when compared, as some in the BBC sneeringly did, with glossy American science fiction films and series.

Some of the first story's action takes place on Ravalox, the rest on the space station where the adventure is screened as evidence in the Doctor's trial. The Prosecutor is called the Valeyard and played with relish by Michael Jayston; he knows the Doctor well but the Doctor has no memory of him or of how he himself came to be in court.

This was all well and poor but the ratings were disastrous: "Attack of the Cybermen", which had opened season twenty two in 1984, garnered over seven million viewers: "The Mysterious Planet" managed just over four million. The decline demonstrated how far the programme had declined in the affections of the public and its transformation from a family show loved by millions to a cult show popularly held in derision. The viewing figures were never to rise above five and a half million until the end of the original series' run in 1989. Some argued that it was inevitable that people wouldn't watch as long as the production values were so poor and the stories so incoherent: yet the production team battled valiantly on against a BBC that had little time for the series.

The second story (sometimes called "Mindwarp") saw the return of the amphibian Mentors and Sil from "Vengeance on Varos"(1985). At this point, the season falls apart. The Doctor is again acting strangely and appears to be evil (a la "The Invasion of Time" (1978)): the Doctor protests to the court that the evidence has been tampered with and that this wasn't how it happened. He appears to betray Peri to the Mentors and sides with a sadistic scientist called Crozier (a wonderfully cool performance from Patrick Ryecart). Colin Baker recalled that he went from writer Philip Martin to script editor Eric Saward asking whether the Doctor was really evil, just pretending to be evil, or whether the evidence had been tampered with. Martin said he had no idea and suggested Baker consult Saward; Saward said he had no idea and suggested Baker consult Martin. The resulting incoherence on screen made for unhappy viewing and perhaps contributed to the show's declining fortunes in popular affection (although the viewing figures did pick up again, averaging some five million for the rest of the season).

It was at this point in production that the first rumours circulated that the BBC was to relinquish production of *Doctor Who* to an independent television company. The policy of commissioning programmes from independents was the BBC's response to a Conservative government hostile to public service broadcasting and the BBC in particular. Denis Thatcher, the Prime Minister's husband, had once said, "Of course, the BBC is full of Marxists". To head off any attempt to privatise the BBC, it attempted to prove its free market credentials by commissioning programmes from the private sector. The Government was appeased for the time being. Rumours reached the production team that *Doctor Who* was considered ripe for the independent treatment: the team's sense of insecurity deepened overnight. Brian Blessed was playing King Yrcanos in "Mindwarp" and recalled that he had been named as a possible future Doctor in an independently produced show. On set, he reassured a troubled Colin Baker that this was not true. The sword of Damocles, in the form of cancellation or independent production, hung over the show until the end of its run in 1989.

The final straw that triggered Saward's resignation was a dispute about the final story of season twenty three. Set in the Matrix (and retreading – yet again after "The Invasion of Time" – the events of "The Deadly Assassin" (1976)), the Doctor was to have battled the Valeyard in a dreamscape. Saward had the two of them fight to the death and fall into the vortex at the end of episode fourteen, a dramatic climax and an inconclusive ending which reflected the uncertain fate of the programme as a whole: would the Doctor, or *Doctor Who*, return? Nathan-Turner rejected the storyline as too negative. Saward, upset at the death of Robert Holmes (who had written episode thirteen), resigned, saying he had had enough, and refused to allow Nathan-Turner to use his script. He then gave a blistering interview to the science fiction magazine *Starburst*, attacking Nathan-Turner as uninterested in the stories of the show and only caring about budget and merchandising. (It is a frequently cited criticism of Nathan-Turner's ten years on the series that the stories are only as good as the current script editor.) The cast, including Colin Baker, comforted and supported an extremely wounded Nathan-Turner, who now had to find a replacement script for the final episode.

He turned to the writers of the third instalment of "The Trial of a Time Lord", husband and wife writing team Pip and Jane Baker. Arriving at his office, they were somewhat surprised to find a solicitor in attendance. Nathan-Turner explained that the solicitor was present to witness that the producer did not even breathe a word of plot detail about Saward's cancelled final episode. Pip and Jane Baker had to come up with a replacement on their own.

The season's final two stories unwound unevenly on screen. Pip and Jane Baker's story, called either "The Terror of the Vervoids" or parts eight to eleven of "The Trial of A Time Lord", was an Agatha

Christie-type yarn set aboard the spaceliner Hyperion, in which the passengers and crew are being murdered by intelligent plant creatures, the Vervoids. The story was reasonably engaging but suffered from the gleaming white lighting so beloved of eighties *Who* for spaceship interiors, which reveals only too clearly the limitations of the set: the Hyperion, for example, looks like an upmarket health club. The Vervoids' design was effective but some viewers drew attention to their penile faces; the crew's guns are called phasers, which presumably infringed a *Star Trek* trade mark. *The Avengers* star Honor Blackman played Professor Lasky, injecting some much needed gravitas into the proceedings, but that was not arguably enough to counter-balance the casting of the new companion. Bonnie Langford made her first appearance as Mel.

Ian Levene had apparently been appalled her casting and rang up Nathan-Turner in the hope that it was so ridiculous it couldn't be true. But he knew that it was. Bonnie Langford was best known to British viewers for her wonderful performance as a child actress as Violet Elizabeth Bott in ITV's *Just William* (1976-7). A talented singer and dancer, she was appearing in a revival of *Peter Pan* on stage during the eighteen month hiatus. Nathan-Turner arranged for publicity photos of her and Colin Baker – she in her Peter Pan costume, he in full *Doctor Who* rig: Baker was grinning madly, Langford smiling sweetly, and the pictures were duly printed in the newspapers. Fans' faces across the country got longer and longer.

"Terror of the Vervoids" is set in the Doctor's future and he has no memory of its events, including how he comes to be travelling with Mel, whose character brief was "a computer programmer from Pease Pottage". This was almost as feeble as the brief for Peri, which ran, said Saward, to two words: "An American". Mel was a generic companion character and was never given an introduction to the Doctor. Saying goodbye to her at the end of the following season, Sylvester McCoy's Doctor notes, "I haven't even met you yet." Bonnie Langford threw herself into the part and gave an enthusiastic performance, but it was too theatrical for the small screen and confirmed fans' views that Nathan-Turner was interested in generating publicity rather than telling good stories. Casting actors primarily known for light entertainment in a serious drama show like *Who* was scandalous: this view grew out of a remark by Nathan-Turner that *Doctor Who* was like *The Morecombe and Wise Show*. He later said he meant the remark in the sense that everyone wanted to be in it (something that certainly appeared to be true of the post – 2005 revamped series), but fans took it as meaning that he saw the show itself as light entertainment. They looked on in disapproval as subsequent seasons saw roles for Ken Dodd, Hale and Pace and even Sylvester McCoy, then best known as the Prof, an eccentric figure who raced around at high speed in the BBC's magazine show for deaf and partially-hearing children *Vision On*. (Was the name of this character the inspiration for the seventh Doctor's companion Ace continually calling him "Professor"?)

Seeing no alternative, the Doctor eliminates the Vervoids and the Valeyard attempts to keep the lurching plotline going by arraigning the Doctor for genocide. It seems extremely strange that a defendant standing trial for one charge could, in the same trial, be suddenly made to answer another charge but presumably the Time Lords' legal system was like the season's plotting: they made it up as they went along. The final two episodes reveal that the Valeyard is an evil future incarnation of the Doctor, somewhere between his twelfth and thirteenth regenerations (though this idea is not explored beyond a throwaway line); the Master comes to the Doctor's rescue because he would rather face the Doctor he knows than a rival in an evil and resourceful Doctor. The Doctor saves the day somehow or other and goes off in the TARDIS with Mel, who intends to put him on a strict exercise regime. Colin Baker's final words as the Doctor are the bathetic, "Carrot juice, carrot juice, carrot juice." The Valeyard escapes, grins evilly into the camera, and the season lurched to a halt. Viewers all over the United Kingdom scratched their heads.

13

All at Sixes and Sevens

Production wrapped on the twenty third season and Nathan-Turner still didn't know if there was to be a twenty fourth. Colin Baker's contract lapsed. Michael Grade has asked Sidney Newman, *Doctor Who*'s creator, to come up with some ideas for revamping the series; Newman made some suggestions but they came to nothing.

Eventually, Colin Baker got a phone call from Nathan-Turner. "I've got some good news and some bad news." "Go on," said Baker. "The show is coming back but they want a new Doctor." Grade had taken the simple step of replacing the lead as a panacea for the show's woes. Very unhappy that he was to leave a part he loved, Colin Baker went to see Jonathan Powell, the Controller of BBC 1. Powell, an experienced television producer of such excellent series as *The Barchester Chronicles*, was no fan of *Doctor Who*. He had reviewed all the scripts for "The Trial of a Time Lord" and commented on them harshly: didn't like this, didn't like that, thought that was too silly. Experienced writers like Robert Holmes were unused to such treatment; fans were later aghast when Powell commented that Holmes's name linked to a film version of the series was far from a guarantee of good quality. Colin Baker recalled that Powell was charming, said he was quite happy with the actor's performance as the Doctor, but was adamant that it was time for a change. Baker asked if he could do one more season so that he could continue to play a part he loved in a series to which he was committed; then he could leave with some dignity. He was offered one more story. Shooting "Time and the Rani" would have made it difficult for him to find other work; he had to make a living, so he opted out of the series. After one complete season, a radio series, eighteen months off, and a curtailed season of fourteen episodes, the era of the Sixth Doctor came to an uneremonious end. *The Sun* published an account of the acrimonious parting and claimed Colin Baker blamed Michael Grade for his removal.

It was again made clear to Nathan-Turner that, if he wanted to remain working in the BBC, he had to stay with *Doctor Who*. Bonnie Langford was to reprise her role as Mel in the twenty fourth season but a new script editor and Doctor were needed. Scottish actor Sylvester McCoy (born Percy James Patrick Kent-Smith in 1943) put himself forward through his agent, auditioned with Janet Fielding and was quickly cast. Ken Campbell was also under consideration. McCoy was best known for his performances in *Vision On* but was an accomplished stage actor, then working in a production of *Antony and Cleopatra* with Timothy Dalton; McCoy recalled that he was cast as the Doctor at about the same time that Dalton, in the same show, learnt he was to be the new James Bond.

Fourteen more episodes were commissioned. The ratings had been poor for season twenty three and, after returning to Saturdays for all of Colin Baker's run, the programme was again shifted to a midweek slot. It was eventually scheduled against ITV's *Coronation Street*, then the mightiest ratings winner of all, a catastrophic mistake which guaranteed low viewing figures. (Or was it a mistake? Some fans suspected a conspiracy to wipe out the programme once and for all.)

A replacement for Eric Saward was found in Andrew Cartmel, a young television writer relatively new to the industry who had a background in computer journalism. He amused Nathan-Turner at his interview with his statement that he would like to use *Doctor Who* to bring down the Conservative government; Nathan-Turner quietly suggested that the most they could hope for was to make stories which showed good defeating evil. Critics later noted the similarity in looks and vocal range of the dictator Helen A, played by Sheila Hancock in "The Happiness Patrol" (1988), and Mrs Thatcher, but the story's satire of a society in which happiness is compulsory hardly qualified it as leftist criticism of a Conservative government.

Cartmel inherited scripts written for Colin Baker's Doctor, which were quickly adapted to McCoy. Pip and Jane Baker had contributed the first story, "Time and the Rani", execrated by fans and described by Russell T Davies, the 2005 show runner, as "a low point". With Colin Baker unavailable, Cartmel and the Bakers were faced with the problem of how to regenerate the Doctor. Under attack from the Rani, the TARDIS is buffeted about in time and space: while the Third Doctor faced his fear and died from radiation poisoning in the cave of the Great One, and the Fifth Doctor sacrificed his life to save Peri from spectrox toxaemia, the Sixth Doctor apparently regenerates after falling off his exercise bike. It was the silliest regeneration since Romana's in 1979's "Destiny of the Daleks". Sylvester McCoy wore Baker's costume and a blond wig: something very obvious when the regeneration effect begins on a shot of a face that is clearly McCoy's and not Baker's.

Previous producers and script editors had had traditional career backgrounds in writing and a university education: Terrance Dicks once said, "I don't think about it very much any more, but I have a degree in English". Cartmell's preferred inspiration was comics and he suggested writers read *Halo Jones* from *2000 AD*, a wandering chap given to gnomic utterances. The comic strip style arguably influenced the new title sequence, which took advantage of advances in computer generated imagery to show a galaxy forming, the TARDIS flying overhead in a bubble (why a bubble?), and McCoy winking at the camera. There was a new logo: the word "Who" tumbled out towards the centre of the screen and the word "Doctor" swished open above it in a handwriting font: merchandisers disliked it as it could only be reproduced against a black background. Oliver Elmes, who created the title sequence, said his inspiration was his thought that *Doctor Who* was like a comic strip. Questioned about why the Doctor gave a cheesy wink, Elmes replied that he thought he had always winked in the title sequence. He never had: so much for careful research. There was a new, more serious arrangement of the theme music to replace the twinkling fairy tricks of the previous year's version.

It might be argued that not much of Cartmell's influence could be seen in "Time and the Rani" (1987), which had the recognisable Pip and Jane Baker signatures: lots of colour and memorable images, including Bonnie Langford in a bubble trap that careered around a quarry and threatened to explode, thus bringing Mel's life to an early close (it didn't), and a plot that raced along and made little sense. There was the Rani trying to create a giant brain from geniuses of the universe including Einstein (who rather wistfully tries to understand the TARDIS; the Doctor gently tells him, "I'll explain it all later"), some very effective three-eyed bat creatures called Tetraps, and Kate O'Mara giving a wonderful, and very funny, impersonation of Bonnie Langford as she tries to inveigle her way into the confused new Doctor's confidence. Not much made sense but it was colourful hokum.

More troubling was McCoy's uncertain performance as the Doctor. He races around, plays the spoons, gurns, tries on his predecessors' costumes and eventually settles down a little in episode four. Perhaps confused by the mess, only 4.7 million people tuned in; newspaper television critics gave scathing reviews.

Needing new scripts quickly, Cartmell commissioned "Paradise Towers" from a writer called Steven Wyatt, who had sent in some material on spec. The new script editor then turned to his friends from the BBC script writers' course, Malcolm Kohll and Ian Briggs, who each contributed a story. These included some interesting ideas, excellent images and designs, but showed no notion whatsoever of how to tell a story with a beginning, middle and end that viewers could actually understand. "Paradise Towers" is a dystopian story set in high rise tower blocks inhabited variously by rival girl gangs, cannibalistic grandmothers, and Richard Briers as the Chief Caretaker. Briers put on a silly voice, a Hitler moustache, a cabaret costume and proceeded to send the part up. Sylvester McCoy tones down the Doctor considerably and there is a good scene where he persuades his caretaker guards that their instructions are unreasonable and he should be released. "Delta and the Bannermen", Kohll's third story, features comedian Ken Dodd, who was then linked in the public mind with McCoy as a light entertainer: not perhaps a good idea when McCoy was trying to establish his serious credentials as the Doctor. It is a tale of Chimeron queen Delta who travels back to the 1950s to a Butlins-style holiday camp, pursued by Don Henderson and his Bannermen; Stubby Kaye turns up as a CIA agent, the plot bumbles along incomprehensibly, and I switched the television off in disgust for the first time ever during a broadcast of *Doctor Who*.

The final story, "Dragonfire", featured a villain called Kane, a space station called Ice World, and some excellent design. The dragon creature itself resembled the alien from the *Alien* film series and Kane melts at the end as he exposes himself to the sun. The McCoy era saw fans of the show, and members of the *Doctor Who* Appreciation Society, actually work on it: a trend that became the norm with the post-2005 incarnation of the series. Susan Moore, herself a fan model maker, created the effect of Kane's face melting. She was briefed that she wasn't to use any red in the effect; cast and crew stayed to watch the head being slowly melted by blowtorches and the speeded-up shot is one of the best effects in the programme to date.

"Dragonfire" also featured an unusually incoherent script: guards have impenetrable conversations as they pursue the Doctor and, in an extraordinary sequence at the end of episode two, Sylvester McCoy climbs over a railing to hang over a cliff by his umbrella for no reason at all. This was apparently an auto-referential joke about a cliff hanger ending (geddit?), and there is a handy ledge for the Doctor to fall onto at the start of part three, but viewers, used to entertaining and comprehensible fare from the show, were baffled. Cartmell's era was littered with in-jokes: guards in "The Happiness Patrol" quote from the academic tome *"Doctor Who: The Unfolding Text"* (1983), which is most amusing for the ten people who get the joke, but leaves the other five million viewers alienated and scratching their heads. I was studying for my PGCE in Oxford at the time and remember my undergraduate friends saying, *"Doctor Who* is just so weird now", and refusing to watch it.

Bonnie Langford leaves at the end of "Dragonfire", to be replaced by Sophie Aldred's Ace. Ace is a companion much loved by fans of the McCoy era and Aldred herself was dedicated to the show. In scripting typical of the Cartmel era, Ace, whose real name is Dorothy (a reference to *The Wizard of Oz*), arrives at Ice World in a time storm (whatever that is; it is never explained, but is apparently another plot device borrowed from *A Wizard of Oz*). She is a streetwise teenager given to setting off explosives with Nitro-9: how a British comprehensive school student could have access to such things, or to have acquired such knowledge, is never explained in the comic strip shorthand storytelling favoured by Cartmel, but it does mean Ace can produce some pretty bangs and flashes. As a streetwise teenager, Ace should have colourful language, but the timeslot and censorship obviously prevented this, so she is given to calling people "scumbug", "toerag" and so on. She also calls the Doctor "Professor" for no very good reason (unless it is a reference to Sylvester McCoy's role as the Prof in *Vision On*), but reverts to "Doctor" in moments of stress (why?).

Season twenty four came to a close with ratings that were no better than "The Trial of a Time Lord": the shift to a midweek slot had not done the trick. The show was renewed for a new season; Nathan-Turner made one of his periodical attempts to quit but said he was persuaded not to do so by Sylvester McCoy.

Having cut his teeth, Cartmel now started to take firmer control over the series. He attempted to reintroduce mystery to the Doctor's character: perhaps a tall order, given that viewers knew he was a Time Lord from the planet Gallifrey, had two hearts, could regenerate twelve times, was blessed with a respiratory bypass system, was a member of the Prydonian chapter, had scraped through his degree at the second attempt, and in fact had twenty four years of history of the character on which to draw. Cartmel proposed rewriting the established continuity of the programme in what would now be called retrospective-continuity, or ret-con, and devised what has come to be called the Cartmel master plan. The Doctor, he decreed, was not just a mere Time Lord, but a survivor of Rassilon's dark time on

Gallifrey; he was one of the founders of Time Lord society with Omega and Rassilon, and a stellar engineer on the first TARDISes. The Doctor was to become a much more amoral figure, one for whom the ends justify the means, who would put the lives of his companions in danger if necessary because he would know the ultimate outcome of events. Again, the influence of comics is clear in the dark and mysterious (and not entirely comprehensible) tone and direction Cartmel chose for the series.

Nathan-Turner was ambivalent about Cartmel's ideas and, on screen, they amount to little more than irritating hints. In "Remembrance of the Daleks", the first story of season twenty five, the Doctor tells Ace about the Hand of Omega, "and didn't we have trouble with the prototype." "We?" asks Ace. "They," the Doctor smiles. Some scenes which revealed more of the Doctor's dark history were shot and then edited out of the broadcast version (though they survive as extras on the DVDs). Again in "Remembrance of the Daleks", Davros rants that he will sweep away Gallifrey and its impotent collection of Time Lords: the Doctor, in a cut line, tells Davros that he is so much more than an ordinary Time Lord; in the final story, "Survival", 1989, the Master asks the Doctor, "Who are you?" as they battle to the death on the Cheetah people's dying world: the Doctor gives an evasive answer but again the sequence was cut. Ben Aaronovitch includes some intriguing flashbacks to the Old Time on Gallifrey in his novelisation of "Remembrance of the Daleks": here, the Doctor is called "The Other" and works alongside Rassilon and Omega on the eponymous Hand.

Again, the narrative of the series is incomprehensible to the viewers, who could make little of Ace's comment "No-one knows who the Doctor is" (I thought we knew, non fans perhaps murmured) and "Doctor, who are you?" at the end of "Silver Nemesis" (the Doctor puts his finger to his lips). Perhaps the script writing was influenced by the tendency of the new American series *Star Trek: the Next Generation*, which spent much time exploring its own continuity (also called, going up its own arse) in the forms of Klingon and human culture when the original series had told exciting space adventure stories. Perhaps Cartmel's approach left viewers irritated and baffled. Although the viewing figures picked up slightly for season twenty five, they collapsed completely for the final season: "Battlefield" (1989) did not even get four million viewers and only the final story, "Survival", got anything approaching five million after a five minutes to midnight publicity blitz by the BBC, which had finally awoken to the fact it had spent a considerable amount of money on a programme that no-one much was watching.

The Cartmel "Time's Champion" version of the Doctor was picked up by Virgin's "New Adventures" series of novels which began after the television series ended. Promoted by their editors as a direct continuation of the television series, the authors enthusiastically took the opportunity to explore the Doctor's origins: but this was for a series of books that sold thousands of copies, rather than for a television series that had to appeal to millions if it was to survive. In book form, the new version of the Doctor flourished; on television, it baffled and confused. When the series was resurrected in 2005, Russell T Davies and his team quietly ignored the Cartmel masterplan as they had ignored the Paul McGann TV movie's revelation that the Doctor was half human, and returned to the original series' notion that the Doctor was a wandering Time Lord.

Things looked up for the season twenty five opener, "Remembrance of the Daleks" (1988), a comprehensively told and well executed story. Set in London in 1963 at Coal Hill School and I. M. Foreman's junk yard, both revisited from Doctor Who's first episode "An Unearthly Child", the story features a conflict between rival gangs of Daleks for the Hand of Omega, a stellar manipulation device brought by the Doctor from Gallifrey before the events of that first story. Ben Aaronovitch's script treats its theme of racism with intelligence: the Imperial and renegade Daleks "hate each other's chromosomes" as "impure in their blobbiness", as Ace puts it. Some of the human characters share the racism: the builder Ratcliffe is attracted to the rebel Daleks as he was imprisoned as a Nazi sympathiser in the war, and Ace leaves her bed and breakfast in disgust when she finds her landlady has put a sign saying "No Coloureds" in the window. The Emperor Dalek is revealed to be Davros: Ben Aaronovitch noted that this was a late addition and was the idea of one of the special effects men (presumably Mike Tucker) who said, wouldn't it be great if the Emperor Dalek's head swung open to reveal Davros inside?

"Remembrance of the Daleks" regularly wins a top ten position in "Doctor Who Magazine" story polls, and deservedly so. However, the following stories of season twenty five arguably reverted back into incoherent story telling. Verity Lambert, the series' original producer, criticised the McCoy seasons as sending up the show and showing actors who seemed to be terribly pleased with themselves but not playing scenes for reality, without which any science fiction programme, dependent as it is on a suspension of disbelief, must fall apart. She was perhaps thinking of scenes in which the Doctor threatens to melt the candy made Kandyman in "The Happiness Patrol", a character whose design irresistibly recalled Bertie Bassett, then used to promote the sweets liquorice allsorts. Bassett Foods plc complained to the BBC about copyright infringement but were placated by an assurance that there was no connection between the characters (although viewers instantly made one, to the detriment of the show) and that the Kandyman would not appear in the series again.

In 1983, the BBC had celebrated *Doctor Who*'s twentieth anniversary by commissioning a 90 minute special, "The Five Doctors", shown as near as possible to the anniversary date itself (23rd November, 1983) and featuring all the surviving Doctors. In 1988, the BBC celebrated *Doctor Who*'s twenty fifth anniversary by doing nothing at all, although Noel Edmonds did put a "Happy Birthday *Doctor Who*" card on the set of that week's *Telly Addicts*. An untried writer called Kevin Clarke wrote a Cybermen story called "Nemesis": this was quickly amended to "Silver Nemesis" when it became clear that the story would be broadcast on the silver, twenty fifth, anniversary. Interviewed on an American television documentary, "The Making of *Doctor Who*" – which was subsequently released on VHS with a revised cut of the story – Clarke said he had been thinking about anniversary elements and thought that, because it was the silver anniversary, the Cybermen should be in it because they were silver. "Silver Nemesis" was reviled by fans at the time of broadcast as utterly incoherent nonsense. Its plot was virtually the same as "Remembrance of the Daleks", two stories previously: viewers were asked to believe again that William Hartnell's Doctor had escaped from Gallifrey with two Armageddon-inducing weapons, the Hand of Omega and, in "Silver Nemesis", a living statue of a metal called veridium. The statue is pursued by Nazis (compare the fascists in "Remembrance"), Cybermen (taking the place of the Daleks) and a sorceress from the seventeenth century called Lady Peinforte. Once again, the shorthand narrative explanation of comic strips is used to explain (or not explain) how Lady Peinforte came to be in our time: it is apparently by magic. Asimov had famously written that extremely advanced technology would look indistinguishable from magic (a maxim employed to good effect in

1972's "The Daemons" and an explanation which would just about excuse Ace's time storm in "Dragonfire"), but, in "Silver Nemesis", magic looked indistinguishable from magic. Magic sits ill with the science fiction elements of *Doctor Who* and only made the narrative – which also featured the Queen, corgis, Windsor Castle, Haley's comet and Gallifreyan legend – even more garbled. The Cybermen also suffered from a chrome accessoried redesign; their vulnerability to gold – a criticised plot feature of 1975's "Revenge of the Cybermen" – here became absurd as they are dispatched by Ace with gold coins fired from her catapult.

The final story of the season, when coupled with the name of the programme in television listings magazines, was witty entitled "*Doctor Who*: The Greatest Show in the Galaxy". This concerned a psychic circus run by the Gods of Ragnarok, a race of beings who force performers to entertain them or die. It featured T. P. McKenna as the Captain and Jessica Martin as Mags, his werewolf (in a science fiction programme?) companion. As with Vorg and Shirna in 1973's "Carnival of Monsters", these were mirror images of the Doctor and Jo/Ace, promoting much enjoyment for viewers who spotted the links. Allegedly, Nathan-Turner included a character called Whizz Kid as a parody of the fanboys who had been a thorn in his side for suggesting that *Doctor Who* wasn't very good any more. Played by Gian Sammarco, an actor who had recently played Adrian Mole on ITV (casting which sardonically emphasised the production office's view of *Doctor Who* fans), Whizz Kid is an irritating geek who states that he hasn't seen the early versions of the Psychic Circus, but everyone knows they are much better than its present incarnation. Like "Shada" in 1978, "The Greatest Show in the Galaxy" was hit by industrial action at the BBC and production was only salvaged when it was elected to record the circus scenes in a tent in the BBC car park. Sylvester McCoy recalls his back and behind were singed by a huge explosion detonated by over-enthusiastic special effects men at the climax of the story.

The show was renewed for one more season and many fans began to be more optimistic about its quality. Even DWB ("*Doctor Who* Bulletin"), a widely circulated fanzine that was blistering in its unremitting criticism of Nathan-Turner's output, remarked that people seemed more cheerful about the programme and things were looking up. The Brigadier returned in 1989's season opener, "Battlefield", a sword and sorcery tale by Ben Aaronovitch which he had pitched to the production office before "Remembrance of the

Daleks". Again, magic sits uneasily with science fiction as the Doctor is recognised, by knights from another dimension, as the sorcerer Merlin, and Morgaine (Jean Marsh) cures a character's blindness with magic and tries to start a nuclear war before she is led off – inexplicably, given her great powers – to prison. There was a near disaster in the studio when Sophie Aldred (Ace) was trapped in a glass tank filling with water. McCoy saw that the glass was bulging and yelled for Aldred to be pulled clear, which she was, just before the glass broke and water flooded the studio floor.

Marc Platt's second story, "Ghost Light", was the last story of the original series to be made. Acting again as Time's Champion in keeping his motivation secret, the Doctor returns Ace to a haunted house which had terrified her as a child. Here, Josiah Samuel Smith (Ian Hogg) lives with his Neanderthal butler: it is never explained why he has a Neanderthal butler, but the casual viewer was just expected to accept it. He attracts the attention of the Reverend Mr Matthews (John Nettleton), who questions Smith's interest in the blasphemous theory of evolution and ends up, in a memorable image typical of this period in the show's history, as a monkey clutching a banana in a glass case. An alien called Light is cataloguing life on Earth but destroying that which he catalogues. The story is intriguing, but very complicated. Apologists for Sylvester McCoy's era argue that his stories often have to be watched several times on video (then widely available) for them to yield up their secrets: this is all very well for fans, but too much to expect of the general public, who, expecting comprehensible entertainment, couldn't be bothered to watch a programme repeatedly. The viewing figures hovered around a disastrous four million.

There were two more stories to go. One is the well regarded "The Curse of Fenric", set in a secret base in the Second World War and featuring enigma machines, vampires from the future, Viking runes and an enemy of the Doctor from the dawn of time with whom he had played chess (in a reference to the film *The Seventh Seal*). Again, some critics found the story rushed and confusing, partly owing to the episodes over-running drastically. Cartmel had instructed his writers to write as much as they wanted and not to worry too much about the twenty five minute running time: thus episodes were pruned down in the cutting room, plot and explanations (such as they were) were lost and confusion reigned. Cut footage was restored to "The Curse of Fenric" for its VHS release: critics of the story opined that it was still confusing, only longer. There is a ridiculous moment when Ace asks Kathleen (her grandmother) about the father of her baby (Audrey, Ace's mother). Ace assumes the father is Kathleen's "partner" and is embarrassed when Kathleen slaps her down by telling her she has a husband. This is political correctness unrealistically intruding into the characterisation; it is highly unlikely that Ace, even with the education she has had, wouldn't know that having children out of wedlock was socially unacceptable in the Second World War, but such inattention to characterisation was typical of this period of *Doctor Who*.

The show's final story was written by another newcomer, Rona Munro, who became an accomplished playwright. It featured a comprehensible and intelligent script and allowed Sophie Aldred to shine in a story which centred around Ace. In contemporary Perivale, Ace's friends are disappearing to the planet of the cheetah people, who snatch humans from our world to hunt them in theirs. The cheetah people were well conceived and designed: there is a memorable and effective sequence in part one when Ace cowers inside a child's climbing frame as a cheetah person on horseback stalks around its circumference. The cheetah people's planet, effectively realised as a quarry but enhanced by new video technology as a convincing alien world, exerts an influence on the humans, who become more like the cheetah people themselves and eventually transform into them. Episode two ends with Ace's eyes changing colour, effectively indicating her infection by the planet. (As a footnote, some viewers were still watching in black and white in 1989: not noticing the transformation in eye colour, they missed the significance of the cliff hanger.) The Master lurks on the cheetah people's planet as well, fighting off his own transformation as a cheetah person: in his finest performance as the character, Anthony Ainley battles the Doctor at the end of the planet's life. The Doctor, also transforming, rejects his animal nature and refuses to kill the Master, howling "If we live like animals, we die like animals!" as he is hurled back to Earth, to Ace and to the TARDIS.

A final, late publicity push by the BBC saw "Survival" gain the highest ratings of the season, but only to five million viewers. At home, Sophie Aldred got a phone call from Sylvester McCoy. "Are you sitting down?" he asked. "You'd better sit down. The show's been cancelled." There was to be no new season. A monologue was recorded for the Doctor and played over the last minutes of "Survival" as the Doctor and Ace walked back to the TARDIS: in a piece of Carmel, Tolkeinesque, whimsy, the Doctor reminded Ace that there were planets to visit where cities were made of smoke and people made of song. "Come on Ace," he enthused, "we've got work to do."

The Doctor did not return to television for seven years.

14

The Wilderness Years and The TV Movie

Andrew Cartmel had made plans for the new season. Ace was to have left and, as a subtle contrast to a working class companion, was to be replaced by an upper class companion who was also a safe cracker (interestingly, a premise used for the character played by Michele Ryan in the 2010 special "Planet of the Dead"). There was to have been an atmospheric introductory scene in which the new companion entered a dark building, found the safe, opened it in triumph to reveal the Doctor inside, saying, "What kept you?" Sylvester McCoy would have left at the end of the season.

Instead, the production office closed its doors and Nathan-Turner finally left the BBC. Andrew Cartmel returned eventually to journalism. The word "cancellation", as in 1985, was never actually used by the BBC, but it was fairly clear to fans that this was what had happened. Concerned viewers wrote to the BBC listings magazine *Radio Times*: one wrote that people should realise that "Survival" was the last ever episode of "Doctor Who". Not so, replied Peter Cregeen, the new controller of BBC 1, in the *Radio Times* letter pages: there might be a longer wait than usual before a new series, but options were being explored to resurrect the Doctor at some point, when the series would be new and fresh rather than featuring "a battle-weary Time Lord languishing in the backwaters of audience popularity".

In fact, the wait between full seasons was fifteen years.

DWB confirmed in a late 1989 edition that there would be "No New *Doctor Who* in 1990". Officially, the BBC was looking at independent bids for making the series. Cregeen eventually explained, in the extras to the DVD release of "Survival", that he had come to the BBC to find several old series still in production and haemorrhaging viewers. One was Peter Davison's former vehicle *All Creatures Great and Small*: another was *Doctor Who*. Cregeen considered recomissioning them, but decided that their time had passed. Perhaps wary of exasperating fans and creating a storm of adverse press reaction as with the 1985 cancellation, the BBC avoided saying that the programme had in fact been cancelled and kept telling anyone who enquired that it would probably, eventually, be made by an independent company.

It seems that the BBC effectively forgot about *Doctor Who* for a few years and, with a sigh of relief, turned its attention to other projects. There were some approaches from independent producers to revamp the series. Gerry Davis, the co-creator of the Cybermen and script editor of the Hartnell era, put together a proposal to the BBC; so did Terry Nation, the creator of the Daleks. Neither got anywhere. Derick Sherwin, Troughton's last producer, proposed a new series featuring UNIT but excluding the Doctor: again, nothing came of it.

With the BBC refusing to make the show, the corporation's commercial arm, BBC Enterprises, began to look at options for a straight-to-video thirtieth anniversary special. *Doctor Who* had been kept alive by a very successful series of VHS releases in the 1990s: the newly found "Tomb of the Cybermen" had been rushed into release in 1992 and shot to the top video spot in the retail chain W. H. Smith. *Doctor Who* was a merchandising cash cow, and BBC Enterprises was grateful. They wanted to "give something back to the fans" and considered a documentary, then a drama. Tom Baker expressed an interest in playing the Doctor again and was swiftly signed up to the project. Fan Adrian Rigelsford wrote a script for a story called, variously, "The Dark Dimension" or "Lost in the Dark Dimension". This featured all the surviving Doctors but centred on Tom Baker's and Sylvester McCoy's. It also featured a character called Summerfield (presumably Bernice Summerfield, a companion from the Virgin novels) and the Doctor's funeral: his body is pushed out to sea on a Viking long boat and then set on fire. (This striking image was coincidentally used by Steven Moffat in the opening scenes of "The Impossible Astronaut" in 2011.) The premise was that the Fourth Doctor had not regenerated at the end of "Logopolis" (1981) and had to reunite himself with his seventh incarnation if he was to remain whole. On the way, he meets his other selves, Daleks, Yeti, Cybermen and a villain who was to have been played by Brian Blessed.

Graeme Harper, who had directed "The Caves of Androzani" (1984) and "Revelation of the Daleks" (1985), was appointed as the special's director; Tony Harding, who had designed K9, was the visual effects designer and started work on revamping the special weapons Dalek from 1988's "Remembrance of the Daleks". Designs were completed, locations chosen, studios booked, the cameras were ready to roll and several hundred thousand pounds were spent on preparing the project.

However, Colin Baker, Peter Davison and Jon Pertwee were far from happy that their Doctors were only to appear as cameos. They also noted the naivety of BBC Enterprises, which was a merchandising, rather than a production, company, in writing directly to them about their involvement in the special rather than contacting them through their agents. It seemed unlikely they would agree to the script as it stood. Meanwhile, BBC 1 got wind of the production and expressed an interest in screening it; they also offered to put up much of the budget. Other parts of the BBC protested at Enterprises making programmes, which was not its role, and "The Dark Dimension" started to flounder on rights issues and BBC internal politics. It was eventually vetoed by Philip Segal, who was unhappy about a BBC produced *Who* clashing with his version of the show (which eventually became the 1996 TV movie), and the BBC closed the project down. There were some attempts by Enterprises to remount it: Tom Baker was still under contract and the film could be made as a straight-to-video release with only one Doctor, but by then it had run into the sand. Fans who had read eagerly of the production learnt glumly, and with a sense of inevitability, that it was not going to happen after all: "Disinterest [sic] Kills The Dark Dimension", stated *DWB*.

The disappointment of fans was not appeased by the BBC's replacement special, two short segments in 3D for its annual *Children in Need* telethon called "Dimensions in Time". This did feature all the surviving Doctors and as many companions as could be found, including the Brigadier, Leela, Victoria and Romana II, in an incomprehensible skit shot on the *EastEnders* lot. Kate O'Mara returned as the Rani with as many monsters as could be found and the cast did their best with a preposterous and appalling script. There were two versions of episode two, in which one of two characters from *EastEnders* helped the Doctor: viewers were invited to phone Noel Edmonds and vote on which version they wished to see. Only one version was shown and nobody much cared to see the other one. The escapade confirmed for some that the series was held in contempt by at least some sections in the BBC.

The BBC's thinking in the early 1990s is somewhat opaque and documentary evidence is not readily available, but it seems that it was interested in two approaches to revamp the programme. A company called Lumiere Pictures (later Green Light) wanted to produce at least one feature film. Scripts were written by Johnny Byrne, who wrote "The Keeper of Traken" (1980) and "Arc of Infinity" (1983), and featured, at various times, K9, an alien companion called Pog, Amelia Earhart, Shakespeare, the Master and a replacement renegade Time Lord called the Mandrake. Negotiations continued into 1995; some design sketches were completed; the company released a publicity leaflet for the film, now called "Last of the Time Lords", with the strapline: "Doctor Who: the man: the myth: the motion picture." It seems that the negotiations culminated in a three film deal to start shooting in 1996 with Piers Brosnan (soon to be cast as James Bond) as the Doctor. The deal collapsed when the BBC opted to go with the Universal/Fox TV movie with Paul McGann, and Green Light took them to court for breach of contract. They got nowhere.

The other approach that the BBC was considering was a new television series, co-produced by an American network, and linked with Steven Spielberg. This decision was a culmination of the decades old sense that *Doctor Who* couldn't compete with the production values of American science fiction series: the budget for two episodes of *Star Trek: the Next Generation* was about the same as a fourteen episode season of *Who*. Furthermore, the BBC had been impressed by the popularity of *Doctor Who* in the States. A four season package of Tom Baker episodes had been sold through Time Life television to American PBS companies in 1978; the show had become a massive cult programme, although it never penetrated mainstream American viewing as, unlike *The Avengers*, it had never secured a slot in an American network. An American co-production for a US network, the BBC mused, could take advantage of the show's stateside publicity and attract the sort of budget that Nathan-Turner et al could only dream of.

In fact, Spielberg was only involved on the peripheries of the negotiations, although he was aware of *Doctor Who* and liked it. In 2009, he accepted Steven Moffat's resignation as chief scriptwriter on the Tintin movies when Moffat was offered the post as show runner on *Who*: Spielberg gave Moffat his blessing and told him that the world would be a poorer place without *Doctor Who*. The driving force behind the American negotiations was Philip Segal, an executive producer on such science fiction shows as *Seaquest DSV*. Segal had grown up in the United Kingdom and had happy memories of sitting on his grandfather's knee to watch William Hartnell as the Doctor. He produced a series bible for the new show, purportedly written by Cardinal Borusa (who had featured in the four Tom Baker/Peter Davison Gallifrey stories) as the Doctor's mentor. Segal touted it around American television companies saying, "Isn't this fantastic?" He later wryly recalled that the reply was, "To you, maybe; to us it's just gobbledegook."

Segal moved employers several times in the 1990s and took his *Doctor Who* proposal with him. In the UK, meanwhile, a champion for the programme was found in the shape of Alan Yentob. As controller of BBC 2 in the early 1990s, Yentob had endeared himself to fans by agreeing to a repeat season of classic stories including "The Time Meddler" (1965), newly returned to the archives, and "Genesis of the

Daleks" (1975); now, as controller of BBC 1, he sanctioned more repeats and a documentary in 1993, "Thirty Years in the TARDIS". Interviewed at its conclusion, Yentob was asked if it was true that he was in discussion with Steven Spielberg about *Doctor Who*. Quoting from the popular political drama *House of Cards*, then running on BBC1, Yentob replied: "You might think that. I couldn't possibly comment." He then relaxed and said "You know what the American networks are like, so there are no promises." For the first time in four years, the BBC was making something like positive noises about the show's return. In private, Yentob was trying to hammer out a deal with Segal. Several networks had turned the project down as a television series; Segal took it to News International's new network, Fox TV, which declined to commission a series but agreed to a one-off television movie. This, it seemed, could act as a back door pilot to a series. Universal Television was to make the film for Fox with support from BBC Enterprises: thus three companies had had to be fully satisfied before the project could go ahead and it was something of a miracle that it ever got off the ground.

Once the film had been given the green-light, things moved very quickly. Before *Doctor Who* fans were fully aware that there was indeed to be a television movie, they learnt that it had already begun shooting in Canada and Paul McGann was playing the Doctor. The BBC was pleased with the choice: McGann was an accomplished actor who had given an acclaimed performance in the BBC's First World War series, *The Monocled Mutineer.* Segal had the choice of two possible scripts. One, which he preferred and wondered later if he should have made, effectively pressed the reset button on the series and took the Doctor back to Gallifrey, where his brother, the Master, was in charge and his father, the great explorer Ulysees, was lost in time. Pursuing his father is the Doctor's motivation for leaving Gallifrey, and the story featured both Davros and the Daleks (redesigned and looking like Cybermen). Dramatic blockbuster though it would have been, this was a far more radical reimagining of the series than the 1960s Peter Cushing movies had ever been and would, perhaps, have been too much for British viewers to accept.

In the end, Segal opted for a script by the British writer Matthew Jacobs, who was briefed to introduce the series to an American audience which might be unfamiliar with it, while simultaneously including "kisses to the past" for a British audience who knew it backwards. As well as squaring this circle, Jacobs was briefed to tell a simple story. The Master was chosen as the main villain, as with several scripts for the Green Light/Lumiere movie: this may have been because copyright for the Master was owned by the BBC and could easily be included in the film's rights package. Other monsters, such as the Daleks (who have a cameo in the TV movie), were owned by their creators or by their creators jointly with the BBC, thus creating tiresome rights issues for anyone who wanted to use them again. (Green Light had apparently thought that the Master was not available in their rights package; they replaced him in some draft scripts with a similar character called the Mandrake.)

Strangely for a movie that was supposed to introduce the programme to a new audience, Segal and Jacobs elected to include Sylvester McCoy as "the Old Doctor" and make the film a regeneration story. The BBC weren't happy with the inclusion of a Doctor from a period of the show that had not found favour with the corporation and asked for Tom Baker instead. Segal, who had more of a sense of the programme's continuity than the corporation, insisted on McCoy and the BBC eventually concurred.

The film was shot in Canada to take advantage of various tax deals, and Vancouver doubled for San Francisco. The BBC faxed over designs for the police box exterior of the TARDIS and Segal enthused that "our carpenters have done a wonderful job" when the prop was finished. Daphne Ashbrook, an actress who had appeared in *Star Trek: Deep Space Nine,* was cast as Grace, the female companion, a doctor working in the emergency room when the Seventh Doctor is brought in, dying from gunshot wounds. Yee Jee Tso played Chang Lee, a young Asian gangster companion, and Eric Roberts, brother of Julia, was cast as the Master. Roberts was much better known in the States than in the UK and Fox's promotional material for the film featured his Master much more prominently than McGann's Doctor. "Two time travellers arrive in San Francisco on December 31st 1999: only one will leave alive", growled the movie poster. The British poster featured the cheery strapline: "Time Waits For No Man… Except One". Roberts knew McGann, having trained with him at RADA, and the two actors apparently enjoyed each other's company on the shoot.

The film's budget was set at five million pounds: enough for five seasons of McCoy *Doctor Who.* A voice over from Paul McGann introduces the story. The Master has been put on trial by the Daleks on Skaro and exterminated. The Seventh Doctor has been charged by the Daleks to take Master's ashes away from their planet. Unfortunately, the Master's remains are only dormant; a timing malfunction forces the TARDIS to land in San Francisco on December 30th, 1999. The Doctor leaves the TARDIS, only to be shot down by a hail of bullets intended for Chang Lee. The Master's casket has by this time broken open and his essence, a transparent goo, leaks from the TARDIS's keyhole. Ambulanceman Bruce (Eric Roberts) takes Chang Lee and the Doctor to the hospital. Grace tries to operate but is unfamiliar with the Doctor's alien physique and the Seventh Doctor dies on the operating table. He regenerates in the morgue, terrifying the mortuary assistant as he rises from his slab, and steals some fancy dress clothes from hospital lockers in a sequence inspired by an identical scene in "Spearhead from Space" (1970), Jon Pertwee's first story. (Steven Moffat repeated the scene again in "The Eleventh Hour" (2010) with Matt Smith's newly regenerated Doctor.) Meanwhile, the Master's essence has taken over Bruce, who dies, rises as the Master, kills Bruce's wife and declares that he must have the Doctor's body: Bruce's is already decaying.

The rest of the story is essentially a chase around Vancouver/San Francisco, with the Master and Chang Lee haring after the Doctor and Grace. Both are captured, the Doctor is strung up in a device that resembles Christ's cross and crown of thorns (the film uses Resurrection imagery throughout in its treatment of regeneration) and the Master prepares to take over the Doctor's body. He kills both Chang Lee and Grace; the Doctor is freed and throws the Master into the Eye of Harmony, the energy source at the heart of the TARDIS. (This contradicted "The Deadly Assassin", which established that the Eye of Harmony is situated on Gallifrey and all TARDISes draw their power from it.) In an incomprehensible twist, the TARDIS then decides it likes Chang Lee and Grace so much that it rolls back time and brings them back to life. This "get out of jail free" card had been outlawed by 1970s script editor Douglas Adams, who forbade writers from letting the Doctor return to a point in time to prevent the cataclysmic events of the story from happening in the first place. Adams wisely saw what Jacobs and Segal missed, that this plot line could be used to save the day in every single adventure. The Doctor drops his new companions back to Earth and asks Grace to come with him: "You come with me!" she replies, and they part. The TARDIS spins off into the vortex and *Doctor Who* was again absent from British television screens; this time, for nine years.

Well-acted and well made, the TV movie had much going for it and gained nine million viewers on this side of the Atlantic: proof that there was still an audience and affection for the programme. Perhaps the BBC had been wise to rest *Doctor Who* if it could be so welcomed when it returned? There were some problems. Segal and Jacobs came to the conclusion that, as the Doctor kept returning to Earth and loved the planet so much, he must be half human (like *Star Trek*'s Mr Spock); in a shorthand for American viewers, the chameleon circuit was renamed a cloaking device (another reference to *Star Trek*) and the evolution of a Time Lord, in which Paul McGann suggests he, like the Master, can transform into another species at the end of his renegeration cycle, was derided by fans. Some fans were unhappy that the previously asexual Doctor kissed his female companion in a definitely non-avuncular manner: this was too radical a departure from the paternalistic figure they had grown up with and gay fans, who made up a large percentage of the programme's followers, felt understandably excluded by this identification of the Doctor as exclusively heterosexual.

Critical opinion was similarly divided and some argued that, in attempting to appeal to both American and British viewers, it had pleased neither. *The Guardian*'s television critic wrote that the film had been stuck mid Atlantic like the isle of Rockall and was "about as interesting"; *The Independent* said that the best word to sum up the film was "derivative" and cited its similarities to the *Terminator* films, not least in Eric Roberts's leather coat and dark glasses. Another *Independent* writer lavished praise upon the attractive figure of Paul McGann ("Doctor FWhooaaarrrr") and said that the BBC would be mad not to commission a series. Asked what he thought of the movie at its premiere screening, Terrance Dicks said it was "incoherent crap" and then wondered if he should have been a little more frank; Barry Letts said the execution of the story was "bad, bad, bad"; Waris Hussein, who had directed the first story "An Unearthly Child" in 1963, said that the movie showed the Americans didn't understand *Doctor Who*.

In the States, the TV movie was scheduled against the final episode of ratings champion *Roseanne* and did very badly. Many felt that there was far too much new information for new American viewers to take in – the first five minutes ask viewers to absorb the concepts of the Time Lords, the TARDIS, regeneration, the Daleks – and it was felt a mistake to have two actors playing the leading role. In 2005, Russell T Davies avoided this problem: he did not script a regeneration scene for Paul McGann and "Rose" only features Christopher Eccleston as the Doctor. Davies stated it would be far too confusing for new viewers to have McGann shot by a laser bolt in the first five minutes, only to be replaced by Eccleston: viewer loyalty should be immediately attached to one hero, not two.

Fox declined to make another movie or to commission a series from this "back door" pilot. It became apparent to fans very soon after the TV movie was shown in May 1996 that there was to be no more *Who*.

Segal was disappointed. Before the rights to the series reverted to the BBC, Yentob wrote to Segal to tell him that the rights to the Dalek movies *Dr Who and the Daleks* and *Daleks: Invasion Earth 2150 A.D.* had come up and that Segal was welcome to remake them. Segal was less than enthusiastic, noting that these movies were themselves adaptations of existing television stories ("The Daleks", 1963 and "The Dalek Invasion of Earth", 1964) and that he was being asked if he would like to make a remake of a remake. He declined.

By the end of 1996, it looked as though the BBC had taken its best shot at bringing back *Doctor Who* and had failed. It seemed very unlikely that the programme would return. Fans consoled themselves with the BBC's series of novels based on the Eighth Doctor: following the TV movie, the BBC had taken back the rights to the novels from Virgin. Terrance Dicks wrote the first novel, "The Eight Doctors", as a direct continuation of the TV movie (Paul McGann's Doctor finally finishes reading *The Time Machine*, which he had been reading in the film, and goes back in time to meet his other selves). The independent company Big Finish was releasing audio CDs of new *Doctor Who* stories featuring Peter Davison, Colin Baker and Sylvester McCoy, and "*Doctor Who* Magazine" continued to be published every month: but it looked as though the Doctor's career on television was over.

But there was a surprise in 2003…

15

Resurrection: New *Who*, 2005

Seven million people listen to BBC Radio Four's *Today* news programme, broadcast six days a week from six to nine in the morning. In November 2003, many listeners dropped their spoons into their cornflakes in astonishment at the announcement, at the end of the six thirty a.m. news summary, "And *Doctor Who* is coming back." There was a short feature explaining that a new series had been commissioned, that Russell T Davies was to be the producer, that the Doctor hadn't yet been cast and that nothing would appear on our screens until 2005. Clayton Hickman, the editor of "*Doctor Who* Magazine", was interviewed on *Today* and said that he and his team had been dancing on their desks.

Several planets moved into a favourable conjunction to create a change of heart at the BBC. Many of the corporation's executives, who now had the power to commission programmes, had watched and enjoyed *Doctor Who* as children; the programme's detractors, like Peter Cregeen and Jonathan Powell, had long since moved on. Lorraine Heggessey had been appointed as controller of BBC 1 in 2000 and had made some positive comments about wanting to bring back the show, perhaps with a female Doctor played by someone like Judy Dench. The fans had heard it all before and grunted non-commitally. The BBC was anxious, in 2003, to beef up its Saturday evening schedule against competition from ITV: it considered which programmes had been popular in the past. One had been *Doctor Who*. Why not do something like *Doctor Who*? In fact, why not just do *Doctor Who*? Proposals for a feature film had grumbled on through the early 2000s, going back and forth and not really going anywhere, and Lorraine Heggessey eventually said, "Enough!" She and Mal Young, the BBC Controller of Continuing Drama Series, agreed that plans for a movie had had their chance; in a later interview, Young said that *Doctor Who* wasn't a movie, it was a television show, and that was how it should return.

The choice of Russell T Davies to produce the new series was, Mal Young said, a "no brainer". Davies had written several very successful series and plays for commercial television, including Channel Four's *Queer as Folk*, which had prompted questions in Parliament about its supposed obscenity and had featured a gay *Doctor Who* fan who watched the programme because it made him happy (something with which fans, called on to justify their appreciation of a "children's programme" by scoffers, could applaud as a simple and good reason to enjoy it). Davies had long been a *Who* fan and had written the novel *Damaged Goods* for the Virgin New Adventures range. Working for Granada Television in the 1990s, Davies had suggested the company should bid for *Doctor Who*, only to be slapped down by a boss who said, "Why should we make that rubbish?" The time was still not right. In 2000, Davies was courted by the BBC to write for them. He held out for *Doctor Who* and submitted a proposal for revising the series: the proposal was headed, "Doctor Who 2000". The BBC passed on the idea, but Davies remained optimistic, assuring "*Doctor Who* Magazine" of his confidence that the series would come back one day.

Knowing that Davies was a fan and a brilliant writer, Heggessey and Young wooed him to join the BBC and produce the new series. Like most fans, Davies was somewhat sceptical at first: he said that he wrote programmes that were going to be made, and was not interested in writing a *Doctor Who* story that would end up as one episode on BBC 3 or as a webcast on the official *Who* website. Such had been the case for Paul Cornell's 2003 webcast, "Scream of the Shalka", featuring Richard E. Grant as the Doctor (claimed by the BBC at the time as the official Ninth Doctor), Derek Jacobi as the Master and one David Tennant as the Caretaker. The BBC reassured Davies: there would be a full series on television, initially planned at seven episodes, and it really would happen.

Davies climbed on board. In execution and storyline, the new series was much influenced by American series like *Buffy the Vampire Slayer* and *The X Files*, not least in its production management. Davies was to be the showrunner of *Doctor Who* in much the same way that Joss Whedon was the showrunner on *Buffy*: unlike previous producers and script editors, Davies effectively combined the two roles as showrunner. He would write the bulk of the scripts and have control over the others: he would outline their stories to other writers and be responsible for rewriting the scripts as necessary to meet the new house style. Davies also persuaded the BBC to commit to thirteen, rather than seven episodes, correctly arguing that it would be much easier to sell a package of thirteen episodes to overseas stations and, not least, to the United States. Once again, the BBC had its eye on selling *Doctor Who* to an American network: a prize that had eluded the series in its original twenty six year run.

Press speculation now turned to casting the new Doctor. Many fans wanted Paul McGann, who had instantly made the role his own in the TV movie and had not, they felt, been given a fair crack of the whip. McGann himself did not rule it out. Unsurprisingly, Davies wanted to cast his own Doctor, perhaps with the intention of making a clean break with the past. Christopher Eccleston had played the Son of God in Davies's television movie *The Second Coming* (2003). Interested in news reports that Davies was to be writing again for "children's television" (Eccleston's description), Eccleston went out for his daily run and decided to put his name forward. He emailed Davies and asked if he could be auditioned as the Doctor. Davies said, "Of course I'll audition you". Other actors were seen but Eccleston's extraordinarily intense performance was acclaimed by Davies and executive producers Mal Young and Julie Gardner, and Eccleston was cast.

The casting was greeted with some surprise by the press: Eccleston had a reputation as an intense actor who chose his roles carefully, often opting for gritty realism in drama. He had been one of the leads, with Daniel Craig, in the 1996 mini series *Our Friends in the North* (another instance of Bonds and Doctors working on the same production) and cited *Doctor Who*, with its thirteen episodes filmed over nine months, as a similar "challenge". *The Guardian* broke the story with the headline, "Shakespeare actor Eccleston reincarnated as Doctor Who" – a reference to Eccleston's recent performance as Hamlet in 2003. In emphasising that the new *Who* was to take the show seriously and eschew the pantomime inflection of the McCoy years, Eccleston's casting was a bold and wise move. It was also an example of Davies's understandable liking for working with actors he already knew: David Tennant, the Tenth Doctor, played the lead in Davies's 2005 BBC 3 series, *Casanova* (an experience which Tennant described as "an extended audition for *Doctor Who*").

The press returned to the theme, common in lazy writing about the series, that its special effects were poor and its sets wobbled (a charge which always made fans cross; they pointed out that any 1970s BBC drama had wobbly sets, as witnessed by episodes of *Fawlty Towers* and *The Fall and Rise of Reginald Perrin*, but no-one was listening). Davies joked that he was six foot four and would lean against the sets to ensure they wouldn't wobble. Quoted in *The Guardian*'s feature on Eccleston, a "BBC source involved in the production" said the production values would be high and they were making the show with serious money: modern audiences wouldn't accept the cheap and cheerful production values of the original series. How much money was not entirely clear and the BBC didn't release details of the budget: it wasn't, it seemed, as much as a million pounds per episode (*Star Trek: the Next Generation* had a budget of one million dollars per episode in the 1990s) but was at the higher end of the BBC budget for drama. Certainly, it was more than the budget allocated to the programme in its original run, when producers had been expected to produce science fiction on a cop show budget.

As for the special effects, advances in CGI (computer generated imagery) were such that excellent, movie standard effects could be created relatively cheaply. The ghost of "laughable" special effects (another charge lazy writers levelled against the original series) was laid to rest. Several effects companies – staffed, perhaps understandably, by *Doctor Who* fans – scrambled over themselves to bid for the CGI contracts; some were willing to undercut their usual fees because, as one employer said, "this was *Doctor Who!*" The contract was eventually awarded to The Mill, a London based effects company which had provided CGI for the Oscar winning film *Gladiator* (2000). In its pitch, the Mill produced an animated version of the octopoid Nestene consciousness that had adorned the cover of the Target book *Doctor Who and the Terror of the Autons* in 1975 (the Nestene on television had appeared as a fluttering lighting effect that looked like rubber gloved hands waggling under a spotlight). This creature was eventually seen as the Bane in the first episode of the spin-off series *The Sarah Jane Adventures* in 2007.

BBC politics of 2005 were radically different from those of 1989, when the show had last been in regular production. Then, all episodes of *Doctor Who* (bar "Horror of Fang Rock" (1977)) had been made in London: initially at Lime Grove studios (much to Verity Lambert's disgust) and eventually in the new BBC Television Centre. Under pressure to justify its licence fee from consecutive Conservative and now Labour governments, the BBC had started to move its programme making away from London. *Doctor Who* was to be made by BBC Wales in Cardiff. New producer Phil Collinson enthused about the excellence of Wales as ripe in locations within easy reach of the studio: there were stately homes (seen in "The Girl in the Fireplace", 2006), Victorian streets ("The Unquiet Dead", 2005), rugged hills and valleys (doubling as the Highlands of Scotland in "Tooth and Claw", 2006) and Cardiff's Temple of Peace (doubling as a space station, a Berlin restaurant, the Silurian parliament, and an art gallery in *The Sarah Jane Adventures*). There was to be a London shoot for the first episode, "Rose", as the Ninth Doctor and his new companion race across Westminster Bridge, flanked by double decker buses: Davies was keen to establish the series' British credentials and wanted its imagery to be as British as the yellow school bus was American in stateside science fiction shows. The BBC's policy of moving out of London continued into the late 2000s as many productions moved up to Manchester and BBC Television Centre itself was sold off in 2012.

Having dealt with wobbly sets, special effects and the casting of the Doctor, the press wanted next to know if the Daleks would be in the new series? In 2003, the audio company Big Finish had produced an audio story called "Jubilee" by the playwright Rob Shearman, a friend of Sir Alan Ayckbourn. The story concerned a single Dalek that is imprisoned and tortured and begins to question its existence. Davies commissioned Shearman to rewrite the piece for *Doctor Who*: it eventually became the fifth episode, "Dalek". Mal Young suggested that the Daleks should feature in the first episode: Davies successfully argued that they should be held back until half way through the season, which would allow the series effectively to relaunch itself. In fact, "Dalek" was broadcast at the time of the 2005 general election: the *Radio Times* cover reprised an iconic image from 1964's "The Dalek Invasion of Earth", now featuring the redesigned Daleks gliding over Westminster Bridge under the headline, "Vote Dalek!"

It was during the writing of "Dalek" that the series hit its first serious trouble. Terry Nation's agent, Tim Hancock, was allegedly unhappy about the treatment of the Daleks in the script and withdrew his permission for their use. *The Times* of 5th August 2004 reported that talks between the BBC and Nation's estate had broken down over issues of editorial control and that the BBC hadn't consulted them carefully about their plans for the Daleks. BBC Wales carried an interview with Davies in 2004 outside "Henrik"'s department store in Cardiff, where shooting was underway for the shop scenes of "Rose". The presenter asked enthusiastically about the new series and commented, "But no Daleks?" "Well, never say never," Davies replied.

In fact, Shearman had been asked to rewrite his episode without the Dalek and to replace it with the Sphere: this was the Toclafane, which Davies had been saving for a future season. Shearman called his redraft "Absence of the Daleks". Eventually, Hancock and the BBC came to an agreement and "Dalek" went into production.

Of the fans who had welcomed the casting of Eccleston, some were less happy when they heard that the new companion, Rose Tyler, was to be played by Billie Piper. Piper had been a pop star in her late teens and had had a number one hit with "Because We Want To": fans feared celebrity casting and thought it would be Bonnie Langford all over again. They were reassured by Billie Piper's performance as Alison in the BBC's *Canterbury Tales* in 2004, and accepted that she could actually act.

The treatment of the companion was another change from the original series. American series like *Buffy the Vampire Slayer* had surrounded the lead character with family and friends, or friends-as-family. Perhaps following this lead, Davies gave Rose a boyfriend, Mickey, and a mother, Jackie, to ground the companion's character on Earth and to make real to the audience the consequences of travelling with the Doctor. It was argued that viewers would no longer accept that human beings could drop homes, families and jobs to take off in the TARDIS or that their lives afterwards could be unaffected by their experiences. To be fair, the original series had sometimes touched on these matters: in the last episode of "The Hand of Fear" (1976), Sarah's final scene has her longing for her lost life on Earth:

I want a bath, I want my hair washed, I just want to feel human again.

"Zeus plug!" calls the Doctor, repairing the TARDIS console and, as usual, not listening.

Rose's family was a backbone to the plotting and themes of the 2005 season. She has to choose between her "stupid boyfriend" (the Doctor's words) and travelling with the Doctor; Mickey, utterly distraught after his experiences of being captured by the Autons and duplicated by the Nestenes, can only hold onto her like a toddler and beg her not to go into the TARDIS. In "Aliens of London", episode four of the new series and the first to be filmed, the Doctor returns Rose to Earth twelve months after they left. He had imagined it to be twelve hours but the TARDIS is as unreliable as ever. In this time, Rose has become a missing person and the Doctor is horrified to find posters asking "Have you seen Rose Tyler?" stuck around the estate. Mickey has been questioned as a murder suspect and Jackie smacks the Doctor hard when he returns Rose to her; so does Martha's mother, Francine, in the 2008 season ("It's always the women!" the Doctor grumbles).

Realism was considered essential in making an otherwise fantastical series acceptable to a modern television audience. In a radical departure from the Sylvester McCoy series, human beings were actually written as recognisable human beings. Insisting on realism, and further insisting that all the first season's stories should be set on or near Earth, Davies was returning to the successful template established in "An Unearthly Child" (1963), itself influenced by literary science fiction. Such writers as John Wyndham had made science fiction mainstream by adding only one or two fantastic elements to an otherwise realistic world: thus the

London of *The Day of the Triffids* is very much the contemporary London of the 1950s, although, granted, there is the addition of carnivorous, semi-sentient, walking plants. Indeed, David Whitaker, *Doctor Who*'s first story editor, greatly admired Wyndham's work and invited him to write for the series. Nothing came of it, but the series produced its own version of the triffid in the 1976 serial "The Seeds of Doom".

If realism was to be a keynote, Davies had to address the other perennial issue repeatedly asked by the series' original viewers: was there hanky-panky in the TARDIS? Most viewers had at least wondered about the Doctor's predilection for attractive young women: science fiction and *Star Trek* writer Harlan Ellison opined that the relationship was never satisfactorily explained for those like him with a nasty, suspicious turn of mind. Tom Baker had once said it was all about "Shagging. Yes, shagging." Davies addressed the matter by having Rose gradually fall in love with the Doctor over the course of the series; he becomes a substitute for Mickey but the relationship is never consummated. A policeman in "Aliens of London" (2005) asks if travelling together for a year meant that theirs was a sexual relationship: both Rose and the Doctor are incredulous and reply, "No" in unison. Nevertheless, the Doctor appears jealous of Rose's affection for Mickey and refers to him as "your stupid boyfriend" or "Rickey". Steven Moffat developed the theme further in his first two scripts for the series, the wonderful "The Empty Child"/"The Doctor Dances" (new *Who* had returned to the early Hartnell practice of giving each episode individual titles: Davies argued that if a story carried the label "part two", those who had missed part one wouldn't watch it). Here, the Doctor is jealous of Rose's infatuation for the handsome Jack Harkness. Dancing is used as a euphemism and symbol for sex in episode two when the Doctor tells Rose that, in nine hundred years, she might imagine he has at some point danced. The Doctor's sexuality had never really been explored in the original series, although some in the 1980s production team were apparently uneasy about the suggestion that Susan really was the Doctor's granddaughter as it would mean he had had sex; surely, they tremblingly suggested, "grandfather" was her name of endearment for him? Steven Moffat settled the matter by arguing that the Doctor was sexual but chaste: something he undermined in his second story "The Girl in the Fireplace", in which David Tennant's Doctor triumphantly declares, "I've just snogged Madame de Pompadour!" and seems content to settling down to a life with her when he is separated from the TARDIS. Eccleston finally gets to kiss Rose in his final episode, but only to draw the time vortex out of her which, in turn, triggers his regeneration.

Having established sexuality in the TARDIS, Rose declares her love for the Doctor in "Doomsday" (2006); he is about to say that he loves her, but the link that allows him to communicate with her across universes is broken. A tear courses down the Doctor's cheek in the TARDIS but this tender moment is broken by the materialisation of Catherine Tate as Donna who demands to know what the hell is going on. Rose is eventually rewarded with a half human regeneration of the Doctor in "Journey's End" (2008) and they settle down to a lovely life together in a parallel universe.

Following the two season story of mutual love, Davies opted for a theme of unrequited love for the third season. Martha is in love with the Doctor but he won't even look at her; finally accepting that he won't love her, she leaves at the end of the season. Some fans were by now tired of the companion mooning around after their hero and wondered if it was the production team who were most in love with the Doctor; some longed for the days when the Doctor and his companion loved each other – arguably the case with the Third Doctor and Jo, or the Fourth Doctor and Sarah – but the show accepted it rather than dwelt on it and got on with telling the adventure story. Perhaps realising this seam had been sufficiently mined, Davies opted to make Donna emphatically uninterested in the Doctor in season four. When the Doctor says he needs "a mate" to travel with, Donna is aghast: "You're not mating with me, sunshine!" There are repeated and very funny sequences in which characters assume that the two are together and the Doctor and Donna deny it in unison. Donna tells Martha that the Doctor is so skinny, if you "hug him, you get a paper cut" ("The Sontaran Strategem" (2008)).

Some wag suggested in the *SFX* letter pages that the Doctor was now as veteran a snogger as James T. Kirk and you couldn't imagine Hartnell behaving like that: Moffat said that he wasn't trying to make the Doctor like Kirk at all but the sexual Tenth Doctor is the Doctor we have. When he became showrunner in 2010, Moffat didn't give Amy a romantic interest in the Eleventh Doctor. She does, at one point, try to get him into bed: Karen Gillan, who played Amy, said this was justified as Amy is an ordinary young woman with ordinary sexual desires; a correspondent to the *Radio Times* disagreed and said Amy was behaving like a tuppenny tart. Otherwise, Amy and the Doctor's relationship is one of a more profound, chaste love. This does not placate Amy's fiancé, Rory, who understandably perceives the Doctor as a rival in the 2010 season. Moffat's decision to move away from the Doctor as a romantic figure was perhaps inspired by his wish to stamp his own mark on the series, not least, by pushing the reset button so that many events in the Davies years never happened. Amy does not recognise the Daleks, for example. Ending the romance might also have been a response to the casting of the gangling Matt Smith as the Doctor, who moves, according to Moffat, like a drunken giraffe and is arguably less conventionally attractive than the dashing David Tennant. The Eleventh Doctor is uncomfortable with sexual matters and is embarrassed to think that Amy and Rory conceived River Song on board the TARDIS. It seemed that Moffat was returning to the original series' Doctors in shearing him of his sexuality.

Davies continued to bring the new series into the twenty first century by reflecting contemporary attitudes to race and sexuality. Casting regardless of colour was common: Mickey is black and Martha was acclaimed by the press as the first black companion (presumably they hadn't noticed Mickey). This was quite a departure from the original series which had treated race sensitively but had a predominantly white cast for much of its run. Bob Baker and Dave Martin had been surprised when a West Indian actor was cast as Cotton in "The Mutants" (1972), a story which satirised apartheid South Africa in its depiction of separate development for the native Mutts and the colonising Overlords. The Mutts are mistreated and kept in poverty while the Overlords live like kings. In the DVD extras, the writer and social commentator Bidisha applauded the story's attempt to tackle racism but was amused by the contrasting depiction of the Doctor: as a Chap, he was a fellow you could trust.

Again reflecting changes in contemporary attitudes, Davies introduced gay characters into the show: another contrast to the original series which, perceived by many as a children's programme even to the end of its run, barely touched on characters' sexuality and, if it did, suggested they were heterosexual. In "The Curse of Fenric" (1988), for example, the Doctor is surprised when Ace tells him she's "not a little girl any more" and proposes to use her sexuality to distract a guard. Davies' correct insistence on including gay characters was a perfectly logical extension of the Doctor's, and the programme's, championing of individual freedom against oppression and prejudice. At a press launch for the 2005 series, a journalist from the gutter tabloid *The Daily Star* asked if the new series would be camper than the original. Davies replied that he thought the journalist was being very rude, that he was only asking that question because he knew he was gay, and then told him to f*ck off. The Doctor's sexuality, such as it was, was identified as heterosexual (in keeping with Paul McGann's revelatory kissing of Grace in the 1996 TV movie), and the main companion was traditionally attractive, female and heterosexual, but Davies did introduce an "omnisexual" companion in Captain Jack Harkness. Jack is from the fifty third century and Davies reasoned that, by that point, people's sexual orientation would no longer be of interest. Jack is in fact omnisexual; in his spin-off series *Torchwood* he criticises twenty first century human characters for their narrow distinctions in sexual matters and pursues vigorous liaisons with male and females. In a very touching scene in "The Parting of the Ways" (2005), Jack kisses Rose and then the Doctor in exactly the same way to say goodbye before he goes to face his death by the Daleks.

Times had changed. In the early 1990s, fans of *Star Trek: the Next Generation* had petitioned Gene Roddenberry to include a gay couple on the bridge of the Enterprise. Like Davies, Roddenberry reasoned that humanity would have transcended arguments over sexual orientation in the future: unlike Davies, he used this as a reason not to include homosexual characters. This was a cop out: Roddenberry had ignored the southern Bible belt's objection to a black character on the bridge in the person of Lieutenant Uhura, but he would not champion a gay one.

16

Season Twenty Seven or Season One, 2005

"Rose" debuted on BBC 1 at 7.00 p.m. on 26th March 2005. The new series was shot in widescreen on video, and then "filmised" to give it a look indistinguishable from film. It was an immediate critical and popular success: 10.8 million people tuned in. There was a technical problem when sound from Graham Norton's new show *Strictly Dance Fever* bled over the sequence where Rose explores the department store's cellars and the Autons come slowly to life behind her, although some viewers assumed this was part of the soundtrack. Finding that the episode under-ran, the production team decided to feature a "Next Time" trailer for "The End of the World". This featured Cassandra, a creature Davies had conceived when watching the Oscar ceremony's parade of women who had had so many facelifts that they could barely speak. Cassandra has had several hundred slimming operations and is now a stretched piece of skin bolted to a metal frame. *The Guardian*'s television critic, new to *Doctor Who*, was enthusiastic and wrote, "I'm damned if I'm going to miss that."

Nearly eleven million viewers was an outstanding achievement in the fragmented age of multi-channel television and the BBC was delighted. It was perhaps inevitable that the second episode dropped two million viewers: after all, people had tuned in to see what the new Doctor, and the new series, was like, and a pattern of falling off in viewers for episode two had been common in the 1970s. Some fickle commentators, including Richard Ingrams in *The Observer*, crowed. Davies had said that he absolutely hoped the new series would work and that a second would be commissioned on the basis of strong viewing figures: a system which, he said, he absolutely supported. He also said that, privately, there was a little voice in his head which whispered "four million", and he had prepared a defence to say that public service broadcasting didn't necessarily have to mean high viewing figures, that the BBC's duty was to serve the public, and so on. It was the BBC's status as a public service broadcaster which had ensured the longevity of the original run: the BBC stuck with the series through troughs of poor viewing figures – at least, before Michael Grade arrived – in, for example, Tom Baker's final season, because it believed in serving a significant section of the public. Contrast Paramount's treatment of the *Star Trek* franchise, the world's second longest running science fiction brand, where various incarnations of the series were axed when their viewing figures dipped. It is highly unlikely that *Doctor Who* would have lasted even to the end of the 1960s if it had been made by commercial television.

Davies and the production team were delighted; the fans were thrilled; the BBC confirmed that there would be a second series before "The End of the World" was broadcast. It was at this press conference that the show came off the rails for the first time since the wrangling over the rights to the Daleks. The BBC bungled a question about whether Eccleston would be returning for the second series. In fact, fans had had their suspicions since his appearance on a special *Doctor Who* themed edition of the BBC's quiz show *Mastermind*. John Humphrys, the show's host, asked if he could call Eccleston "Doctor Who" and the actor replied, "You can for now"; he had said "I can't answer that" when asked if he would return for a second series on BBC News. Eccleston had been offered a second season during the filming of the season's final story "Bad Wolf"/"The Parting of the Ways", but had said he wanted to leave. Nick Briggs, who supplied the Dalek voices, prepared to make the Daleks say, "Christopher Eccleston has filmed his last scene on *Doctor Who*. He will now be exterminated!" on the actor's last day on set, but forgot to perform the joke in the pressures of the studio day.

Thus, when the new series was only two episodes old, the audience learnt that the new Doctor would be gone before they had a chance to get used to him. The press ran some silly stories about crisis in the new series, coupling the reduction in viewing figures with the news of Eccleston's departure; fans reacted grumpily and blamed him for harming the prospects of the fledgling series. The BBC quickly steadied the boat and announced that David Tennant would be the new Doctor in series two and in a Christmas special for 2005. Again, some fans had picked up the intimations of Tennant's casting, noting that he had provided the voice-over for the documentary "The Story of *Doctor Who*", screened on BBC 1 before "Rose" was broadcast.

It isn't entirely clear why Christopher Eccleston left after only one season, but it seems to be that he saw the part, and the intensive shoot, as a similar challenge to *Our Friends in the North* or a one year run of a stage play. He later suggested that he had been unhappy with how some of the crew had been treated on the set. There were the inevitable rumours that he had feared being typecast. Fans complained to the papers; the director Joe Ahearne wrote to *The Guardian* in the actor's defence, ironically asking how Eccleston dared leave a programme after one year of giving such a committed performance to return to other work, and working on the show with such courtesy and patience.

Eccleston's performance as the Doctor was certainly radically different from his predecessors'. His was a darker Doctor even than Sylvester McCoy's, bearing the burden of survival guilt as the last of the Time Lords and spitting with rage at the Dalek in Van Statton's cell. Some of the humour didn't always sit easily with his portrayal and some cast members – like Camille Coduri – while praising Eccleston's performance, hinted that David Tennant would much more in keeping with the public's traditional conception of the Doctor.

It is, however, clear that securing such a respected actor as Christopher Eccleston was a major reason for the audience to take the new series seriously, even if he wasn't necessarily everyone's idea of what the Doctor should be. Some likened him to Tony Blair as the new leader of the Labour Party: not everyone's idea of what a Labour leader should be, but a serious and necessary break with the past who at least got the party elected. Eccleston had helped to get the new series made and renewed for a second season. Some fans couldn't forgive him for not being a fan of the show, unlike David Tennant, for declining requests for interviews about his time as the Doctor and for saying, when asked if he would return, "No. Never bathe in the same river twice." Others correctly argued that the show owed him enormous thanks.

Davies had changed much of the back story for the Doctor. He argued that viewers knew too much about him and there were too many proper nouns: he was a Time Lord, a member of the Prydonian Chapter, a renegade... It was time to sweep away the complications and return, in many ways, to the simplicity of the character as originally played by William Hartnell. The Doctor would again be a solitary wanderer in time and space. The Time Lords were no more. As the season unfolded, we learnt they had been destroyed in the Time War against the Daleks: the Doctor had destroyed both races to bring it to an end. These were all unseen events which presumably took place in the gap between the TV movie and "Rose" and had, we imagined, caused the Eighth Doctor to regenerate. The Ninth Doctor seems to be a new regeneration ("Not too bad. Look at the ears!") and post regeneration trauma – established in "Robot" (1974-5), Tom Baker's first story – might combine with survivor guilt to produce his erratic behaviour. "Not made of plastic are you?" he asks Rose, tapping her on the forehead. "No. Bone head. Bye then." Davies had determined back in his Granada Television days that the Doctor's costume should be modern: in 1996, he had asked a senior colleague what he had thought of the TV movie. "Too much fancy dress", was the reply, and Davies agreed. The Ninth Doctor was therefore scripted as wearing jeans, a sweater and a leather jacket. The Edwardian or eccentric outfits of his predecessors were no more and with them, much to the fans' relief, the silly question mark motif which had featured on all the Nathan-Turner Doctors' costumes. Reading Davies's outline for the season, Lorraine Heggessey worried that the end of the Time Lords would mean no return for the Master. She needn't have worried: Davies had worked out how he could be resurrected and the Master returned for the last three episodes of season three.

Mark Gatiss, the writer of the third episode "The Unquiet Dead", said that the revived series was much more like *Doctor Who* than *Doctor Who* had been at the end of its original run. This was true: garbled story telling was gone, the Doctor was no longer half human, the Cartmel master plan was ignored. Part of the explanation for the clarity of story telling lay in the experienced Davies' overall control of the series as chief showrunner: all the scripts were polished by him to fit in with the house style and the season's overall arc. Seventies script editor Terrance Dicks laughed when he was asked if he would like to write for the new series: "What, and do eight drafts?" Shearman's "Dalek" (2005) had reached eight.

As the programme returned, so did much of its cultural legacy – and even baggage. In its initial research for the relaunch, the BBC had found that adults thought it an old show and children thought of it as their parents' show, making them unlikely to watch it. Pre broadcast, specially shot trailers, pitched *Doctor Who* as a new series, sometimes from Rose's point of view: "I've got a choice. Stay at home with my mum, my boyfriend, my job, or chuck it all in for danger, and monsters, and life or death…" she said, standing next to a silent Doctor and giving viewers their first glance at the new TARDIS interior set. Eccleston recorded a special trailer which featured him racing away down a corridor from an approaching fireball and directly inviting the viewers to join him on his travels. The Eccleston trailer laid fans' fears about special effects to rest, featuring the splendid footage of the Slitheen's spaceship slicing through Big Ben and crashing into the Thames. Rather sweetly, it also recalled Peter Cushing's gentle trailer for the 1965 movie *Dr Who and the Daleks*: "Come with us into that strange new world. I cannot guarantee your safety, but I can promise you unimagined thrills."

The BBC's pre-broadcast research proved erroneous. Parents who had enjoyed the series as children watched it with their children. The concept of families watching a programme together on a Saturday night returned: *Doctor Who* was one of the few programmes which appealed to all ages. The BBC had assumed that family viewing was dead: to their surprise and pleasure, *Doctor Who* brought it back and the corporation celebrated its clean sweep in the Saturday night ratings. *Doctor Who* was a hit and so was *Strictly Dance Fever*. The latter evolved into the top rated show *Strictly Come Dancing* in 2006, *Doctor Who* was renewed and the BBC commissioned *Robin Hood* and later *Merlin* as family-friendly replacements for when the programme was off the air. All were strong ratings winners for Saturday nights. The perennial taunt that fans had endured for the programme's original run – that *Doctor Who* is a children's programme – was silenced by the new series' inflection as family viewing. Adults appreciated the subtext of some witty dialogue; children (and adults) enjoyed the monsters, which Davies, preparing the series, had insisted should always be simple enough for children to draw. As an example of subtext: the Prime Minister in "World War Three" announces that the Slitheen's mother ship contains "massive weapons of destruction – capable of being launched in forty five seconds". This was a reference to the US Republican and British Labour governments' claim that Saddam Hussein's troops could launch weapons of mass destruction in forty five seconds, used as a justification for the Iraq war. In "World War Three", The Doctor wonders if the people will believe a lie. "Why not? They did last time," says Rose.

Is *Doctor Who* for children, for adults, or for everyone? In 2012, Steven Moffat said that if you enjoy the programme, it's for you. Perhaps it is part of the British sensibility to be dismissive of science fiction. Like satire, it has never been seen as a respectable genre in the minds of sophisticates or of some sections of the general public, and dismissing *Doctor Who* as a children's programme, even in its more sophisticated incarnations, is a way of keeping an unrespectable genre in its place. Perhaps the British sensibility is inclined to cynicism, irony, a refusal to take things seriously and a fear of being too enthusiastic: by contrast, the American audiences of *Star Trek* in the 1960s never saw it as a children's programme, in spite of some of the merchandising (I had a rather splendid Captain Kirk's Space Communicator set, based on the old children's toy of two yoghurt pots linked by a string: this was two blue plastic globs, which looked nothing like the series' communicators, linked by a string).

Another part of *Doctor Who*'s heritage was its capacity to disturb and terrify children, at least according to the newspapers. Fans gleefully rejoiced at reports that "The Unquiet Dead" had prompted dozens of concerned parents to complain to the BBC because it was too frightening. *The Times* reported viewers' concern about a sequence in the pre-credits teaser in which a dead grandmother's hand shoots out of a coffin and strangles her grandson. I was watching this with my small daughter, not yet three, who burst out laughing. Gatiss skilfully doused down the terror in any case with undertaker Mr Sneed's comic attempts to jam the coffin down on the old lady ("Gwyneth! Get down here! We've got another one!") and any horror is of the *Carry On Screaming* variety ("The stiffs are getting lively again!"). The BBC rather fumbled its response to the concerned parents, perhaps because it had been a long time since it had handled such complaints about *Doctor Who*. It said at first that the programme shouldn't be watched by under-eights and then said it should. Fans recalled David Coleman fronting the BBC viewers' response programme *Points of View* in 1967: parents had written in to complain about "horrific" sequences in "The Tomb of the Cybermen" and Coleman cheerily introduced the item by presciently asking, "Is *Doctor Who* too frightening for children? Or should that be, is *Doctor Who* too frightening for adults?"

Matters came to a head with the release of season one/twenty seven on DVD. The British Board of Film Classification took exception to scenes in which the Doctor "tortures" a Dalek ("Dalek" (2005)). However cross one might be with a Dalek, the BBFC opined, torturing it is no way to behave; children's identification with the Doctor might lead them to imitate him; the DVD must not be supplied to anyone under the age of twelve. In a display of how quickly the new *Doctor Who* had become part of mainstream British culture, *The Times* took up all of its third page to run the story. In its leading article of 16th May 2005, "Let's not be beastly to Daleks" (a reference to Noel Coward's satirical post war song, "Don't let's be beastly to the Hun"), *The Times* quite rightly ridiculed the BBFC's decision and wondered if a creature intent on exterminating all mankind might not deserve a taste of its own medicine. Championing the series as as a piece of serious children's fiction on a par with Harry Potter and Roald Dahl, *The Times* concluded that the message of *Doctor Who* was that sometimes violence was necessary to defeat evil, and good could only triumph if it asserted itself. This had always been the theme of the original series: that it was clearly the theme of the revival was reassuring and proof that the theme was as vital now as it had ever been.

17

Christmas Time – Sycorax and Wine

What should we call Christopher Eccleston's season? "The Christopher Eccleston months", some wag suggested. BBC documentation and DVD releases treated the revived *Doctor Who* as an entirely new series and went with "series one". American writer Harlan Ellison, who had penned introductions to the American versions of the novelisations (in which the Fourth Doctor eats jelly beans, not babies, and the Brigadier's mustache is neat) and had praised *Doctor Who* above *Star Wars* and *Star Trek* (for which he had written "City on the Edge of Forever"), growled that it was the twenty seventh goddam season, so it should be called the twenty seventh goddam season. Steven Moffat complicated things further when BBC documentation referred to Matt Smith's first series as "series one". He explained to pedantic fans that no-one talked about season eight, they talked about Pertwee's second season, which was why he'd opted for the new naming: we could then talk about Matt Smith's second season and so on. The DVD range stuck with "series five", however.

It appears that David Tennant had been cast as the Doctor before Christopher Eccleston's season had even aired. Tennant had played the lead in Russell T Davies's *Casanova* on BBC4. Davies asked him if he would like to play the Doctor almost at the same time; Tennant was incredulous and laughed heartily. He was a fan of the programme and, as a child, had queued to get Tom Baker's autograph when the actor had visited Scotland. Tennant had been inspired to become an actor because of his love of the show and had a successful career in television and theatre, not least with the Royal Shakespeare Company. Davies said he understood Tennant's reaction as it was too much to take in; he left him to think it over. Like Peter Davison before him, Tennant partly took the part because he couldn't bear the idea of someone else doing it when he'd been offered it. He also eventually came to terms with the idea that it was fine for a fan to play the Doctor.

Russell T Davies suggested to Tennant that he should change his native Paisley accent; Tennant said this was fine, as he spent half his life speaking with an English accent anyway. Davies was anxious to avoid what he called "a tour of the regions" after Eccleston's northern accent, which had caused some controversy among some unimaginative people who reasoned that a Time Lord was a lord and should therefore have an educated southern English, or Received Pronunciation, accent. Davies wrote the issue of the accent into "Rose", when our eponymous heroine asks him, "If you're an alien, how come you sound like you're from the north?" "Lots of planets have a north," the Doctor huffs. In "World War Three", Harriet Jones (MP for Flydale North) makes the same comment when told the Doctor is alien and Rose, showing how she has accepted the Doctor and his accent, repeats his earlier explanation: "Lots of planets have a north". The Tenth Doctor adopts a mild East London accent, which cut dialogue from "The Christmas Invasion" (2005) indicated was imprinted on him by his contact with Rose. Matt Smith speaks in the Received Pronunciation accent we are used to from most of the original series' Doctors.

Tennant's debut was in the 2005 Christmas special, another first for the revived show. Commissioning an hour-long special was an early mark of confidence from the BBC in the new series. Fans hoped for, and got, a Christmas Day slot, and the Christmas special has been a fixture of the new series for the past eight years. There had been one Christmas episode in 1965 entitled "The Feast of Steven" after the companion played by Peter Purves. This was the seventh instalment of the twelve episode epic "The Daleks' Master Plan" but, as it contained neither Daleks nor much of the surrounding plot line, is effectively a separate story. It is basically a good-natured romp in which the TARDIS lands in a 1920s Hollywood studio, where the crew are chased by Keystone Cop-a-likes, and the Doctor is investigated by 1960s police in Liverpool. Director Douglas Camfield had hoped to persuade the actors of the popular Liverpool-based police series *Z-Cars* to play the policemen, but they refused. The Doctor produces champagne for Steven and Sara, who was to be aged to death in episode twelve, and Hartnell then wishes the viewers at home a very happy Christmas. Donald Tosh, the story editor, was apparently furious, saying Bill deserved to be shot as the line wasn't in the script but was just something he'd thought up. Another version of the story is that the line was actually scripted but this breaking of the fourth wall, the riff on *Z Cars* and the pause in the science fiction Dalek adventure, all failed to find favour with the public: audience research suggested they hated the episode. "The Feast of Steven" has inevitably been wiped, so it's hard to assess how good – or bad – it is.

The first Christmas special of the new series, "The Christmas Invasion", was well received by ten million viewers. Davies was enthusiastic about Christmas specials, saying that he loved seeing familiar characters surrounded by tinsel, presents and Christmas cheer; he intended to bring this all to *Doctor Who* and the seven subsequent

Christmas specials to date have all been set at Christmas time. Davies said he had thought of the title – "The Christmas Invasion" – even before he started writing.

In the same way that Sarah Jane bridged the transition between the Third and Fourth Doctors, and so helped viewers accept Tom Baker after five years of Jon Pertwee, so Rose stayed on into a second season to help viewers accept David Tennant: a crucial decision as the programme had only been on the air for three months and a new Doctor was being introduced far too early into the series' run. "The Christmas Invasion" (2005) focuses its first half on the familiar characters of Rose, Jackie and Mickie. The Doctor is in a troubled sleep or coma and looked after by Jackie and Rose, who put him to bed in the pyjamas he wears for the rest of the story. Rose tells her mother about his two hearts; Jackie asks, "He hasn't got two of anything else, has he?" When it looks as though the regeneration is failing, the Doctor is restored to health by the scent of the tea dripping from Jackie's thermos. Rose had greeted her mother's insistence on bringing tea on board the TARDIS by sarcastically saying, "The answer to everything": a good piece of dramatic irony, because of course, it is.

It's a brave decision to keep Tennant in the background for so much of the story, with the result that, when he does appear on the Sycorax ship, his entrance is all the more dramatic, and Rose's – and the viewers' – sense that all is going to end well, is heightened.

As with so much of the original series, "The Christmas Invasion" takes ordinary objects and makes them strange or sinister. Rose and Mickey are wary of a band of masked Santa Claus (Clauses?) playing Christmas carols on their brass instruments in a very Salvation Army fashion. The Santas duly turn their tubas towards the pair and fire them as flame throwers. Jackie's Christmas tree starts to spin and advance towards her, its separate sections apparently razor sharp: whereas the Santas are sinister, the Christmas tree is great fun and entirely in tone with a Christmas special. Both Santas and tree reappear in the following special, "The Runaway Bride" (2006), with some surprises: the Santa abducting Donna (Catherine Tate) is seen to be a robot under the Father Christmas mask, and the tree at her wedding reception launches its baubles to burst as small grenades among Donna's wedding guests.

Davies kept the plot of "The Christmas Invasion" simple, reasoning that people didn't want to be taxed after Christmas dinner and too much booze. The Sycorax are scavengers who want to abduct humans. Davies named them after Caliban's mother in Shakespeare's play *The Tempest*. He remembered studying *Antony and Cleopatra* at school and being pleased with Cleopatra's line, "Give me to drink Mandragora" as it reminded him of the 1976 Tom Baker story "The Masque of Mandragora". He wanted to prepare a surprise for school based *Doctor Who* fans reading *The Tempest*. The other Christmas present buried in the script is the names of the two children suffering from the Sycorax's massed hypnotism, blood control; they were named after Davies' niece and nephew and he said this was a Christmas present to them.

Having recovered, the newly regenerated Doctor asks Rose if he is ginger; he hasn't yet seen his reflection. Told he has brown hair, he is bitterly disappointed and says how much he wanted to be ginger. Is this a reference to Billie Piper's former husband, DJ Chris Evans, a famous ginger celebrity with whom she remained close friends? The Eleventh Doctor (Matt Smith) similarly pulls down a lock of hair for inspection and murmurs, "Still not ginger". This line provoked complaints from some viewers as being anti-ginger, and one correspondent asked why didn't the BBC realise this ridicule of ginger haired people would only reinforce the teasing experienced by some ginger children at school? The BBC sent a soothing reply saying no offence had been intended. The complainants obviously hadn't remembered "The Christmas Invasion" or noted that Donna was a redhead (and so was Amy, but she hadn't appeared yet), and that it was absurd to accuse the programme of redheadphobia.

Davies makes intelligent use of the Christmas dinner, a staple of all Christmas drama specials, to show the differences between the Tenth Doctor and the Ninth. Invited by Rose and Jackie to supper, the Ninth Doctor tells her "I don't do that" and waxes lyrical about visiting some fantastic galactic phenomena instead. The Tenth Doctor is clearly more sociable than the Ninth, and has moved away from his survivor guilt to interacting comfortably among humans. He also doesn't appear to be quite so anti-social and rude. Eccleston, like Colin Baker, had been somewhat unapproachable and spiky; Tennant was warm, funny, reassuring and – according to his legions of female fans – extremely handsome and sexy.

The episode ends with another traditional Christmas special image – snowfall, although this has the alarming cause of being the fallout from the destroyed Sycorax ship. Similarly alarming, and not the usual staple of Christmas drama, are the UNIT personnel reduced to smoking piles of bones by the Sycorax leader's whip ("Oi," says the new Doctor, "You could have someone's eye out with that.") The Doctor loses his hand in a broadsword fight with the Sycorax leader, only to grow a new one from his residual regeneration energy. "Witchcraft," breathes the

Sycorax leader, aghast. "Time Lord," the Doctor corrects. His severed hand falls down to London below, where it is eventually picked up by Jack Harkness and preserved on his desk in the spin-off series *Torchwood*. Jack eventually reunites it with the Doctor, who siphons off more regeneration energy into it in "The Stolen Earth"/ "Journey's End" (2008); it eventually grows into a human clone of the Doctor, which comes in handy for defeating the Daleks. In "The Christmas Invasion", the Doctor saves the day with a satsuma – always, he remarks, left over at the end of Christmas – which he bungs at a control button: the Sycorax ship's edges retract and the Sycorax leader falls to his death. The "next time" trailer was a montage of clips from the new season and a cause of great excitement for viewers. We got our first look at the cat people and the redesigned Cybermen. Cheers abounded through the land when the last clip at the end of "The Runaway Bride" was of the black Dalek Sec, proving that the Daleks would indeed be back in series three. Or twenty nine.

The 2006 Christmas special was "The Runaway Bride". It opened with the sudden materialisation of Donna in the TARDIS reprised from the last moments of "Doomsday" (2006) which temporarily startled the Doctor out of grieving for Rose. Having Catherine Tate as Donna was a serious piece of star guest casting arguably only topped by securing Kylie Minogue as Astrid for the 2007 Christmas special. Catherine Tate had her own series on BBC2 and was famous for her characters and catchphrases; Davies thought it possible she wouldn't want to be in *Doctor Who*, but she was enthusiastic. At the press launch for "The Runaway Bride", Catherine Tate was asked if she would like to return as a regular companion – she elects to return to her family at the end of the special – and she said, "I'd love to, but no-one has asked me." Davies did ask her when Martha left and Tate joined the cast for the fourth (or thirtieth) season. She slightly toned her performance down for her regular role, thus silencing some critics who'd found her too raucous in "The Runaway Bride". Donna, it seems, has regretted her decision not to go with the Doctor and has been looking for him ever since. She eventually runs into him while they separately investigate Adipose Industries in "Partners in Crime" (2008) and slightly alarms him by revealing her cases in her car, including a hatbox, fully packed for climbing aboard the TARDIS. Catherine Tate's performance as Donna was acclaimed by viewers and she was welcomed and celebrated as a woman, rather than a girl, aboard the TARDIS. Tate joked that being buxom made the endless running scenes a bit uncomfortable and it was all right for David Tennant because he didn't have breasts. Being busty had apparently been seen as a problem with the first actress to be cast as Sarah Jane Smith, who had been paid off after a few rehearsals, although this might have been attributable to Jon Pertwee's failure to gel with her.

Again, Davies opted for a simple plot for the second Christmas special. The Racnoss, a giant spider-humanoid creature, is attempting to awaken its young, imprisoned at the Earth's core since the dawn of time. Neil Gorton, whose firm made most of the physically realised monsters for the new series, assumed that the Racnoss would be CGI and was surprised when the production team instead elected for a prop, into which an actress could be fitted. The Racnoss prop was so huge that it couldn't be assembled in the workshop and had to be put together for the first time on location. Sarah Parish played her, standing in the front section of the fifteen-foot-diameter spider; she understandably found filming somewhat uncomfortable and cut the inside of her lip on her prosthetic teeth. Although the Racnoss prop was brilliantly designed and could lurch up and down, it couldn't walk or scuttle, which disappointingly – or mercifully – robbed it of some of the alarm of a real spider. The Racnoss's children climb towards her out of the pipe that leads to the Earth's core. We never see them as the budget wouldn't run to that, but the Doctor drains the Thames into the pipe, thus flushing them down the plughole, and the Racnoss herself is killed. Donna is alarmed at the Doctor's callousness in dispatching so many, and the Racnoss's shrieks of distress are genuinely affecting. Later, Donna tells the Doctor that he mustn't travel on his own: "You need someone to stop you." This sets up an intelligent theme of the revived series, that the Doctor needs the company of human beings to civilise him and to remind him of his conscience. The human cloned Doctor has had no such contact with human beings and little conscience; the Tenth Doctor tells Rose that he is effectively like the Ninth Doctor we met in "Rose" (2005), traumatised and almost amoral after the terrifying slaughter of the Time War. It is the cloned Doctor who kills all the Daleks in "Journey's End" (2008). This is very convenient as then our peace-loving Time Lord Doctor doesn't have to, thus proving Davros's point that he never has to carry a weapon because others do his slaughter for him.

In "The Angels Take Manhattan" (2012), Matt Smith's Doctor asks River Song to travel with him after the loss of Amy and Rory, knowing that he shouldn't be on his own. River, presumably hyperbolically, says that one psychopath per TARDIS is enough. The Eleventh Doctor responds by withdrawing into a depression or sulk in Victorian England, refusing to become involved in saving the world until he encounters Clara (Jenna-Louise Coleman) and The Snowmen ("The Snowmen", 2012).

Kylie Minogue was the guest star in "Voyage of the Damned", the 2007 Christmas special. Perhaps remembering the tendency for ITV and the BBC to show blockbuster movies over Christmas when he was a child – with James Bond films and *Towering Inferno* particular seasonal favourites – Russell T Davies opted to merge the disaster movie with *Doctor Who*. The result is a version of *The Poseidon Adventure*, with the Titanic now a space liner controlled by a creep called Max Capricorn, who swivels Davros-like in his wheelchair and intends to crash the liner into Earth to bankrupt the travel company that has betrayed him. Securing the services of Kylie Minogue is another coup for the show; as an international star, Davies hoped that people around the world who had never heard of *Doctor Who*, but who loved Kylie, would tune in, and it seems that this is indeed what happened. Thirteen million viewers watched at home, making this the highest rated episode of the revived series to date (January 2013). Kylie played Astrid, a waitress aboard the Titanic who wants to see the Universe and is set up as the replacement companion for Martha. She dies disposing of Max Capricorn, which is a good thing as Kylie was presumably busy and couldn't make the filming dates for the thirtieth season. Fans quickly noticed that "Astrid" is an anagram of "TARDIS" and speculated that Kylie would play the TARDIS in human form: they had to wait until Neil Gaiman's wonderful "The Doctor's Wife" (2011) for that to happen.

"Voyage of the Damned" is visually exciting but pretty thin on plot. There are some good ideas. Series regular Jimmy Vee plays a cyborg called Bannakaffalatta; Davies draws some parallels between the emergence of homosexual equality in the twentieth century and rights for cyborgs in this story. The Titanic's guests are served by robot angels called the (Heavenly) Host, which some Christian viewers might find slightly profane, but the revived series under Davies often got in some jolly digs at Christianity. Davies had pretended to be cross with Steven Moffat for including angels in his script for "Blink" in the previous season, since Davies wanted to use them in "Voyage of the Damned", but it is the Weeping Angels that are remembered from the two sets of angels in 2007. There were some complaints from relatives of the victims of the real Titanic disaster, presumably stirred up by the press, who said it was wrong to create entertainment out of a terrible tragedy. The BBC pointed out that the Titanic in the story was a spaceship and not the original. Clive Swift played Mr Popper, a tour guide to Earth who is woefully ill-informed about his subject; he was interviewed about the show by "Doctor *Who* Magazine" and was very rude about the series and television viewers in general; the magazine printed most of the interview in full. The Doctor manages to stop the Titanic from crashing into Buckingham Palace and the Queen appears for the first time since "Silver Nemesis" (1988); she waves and thanks the Doctor for saving the day.

Bernard Cribbins had a cameo role as a newspaper seller, originally called Stan, in "Voyage of the Damned". He reappeared as Donna's grandfather Wilf in the 2008 season and in Tennant's final two episodes. Wilf's role in the season was originally taken by Howard Attfield, Donna's father Geoff in "The Runaway Bride". Howard Attfield managed to shoot a few scenes with Catherine Tate – included as extras on the series four DVD box set – but sadly passed away from cancer. As Bernard Cribbins' newspaper seller had never been named on screen, the production team was able to rename him as Wilf and insert him into Donna's household as her grandfather. Bernard Cribbins's witty and realistic performance, and Davies's scripting, made Wilf one of the most popular characters of the Tennant years.

Great fun and froth though the specials were, Davies made brilliant use of them in his acclaimed story "Turn Left" (2008). This was a "Doctor lite" episode focusing on Donna; the production schedule required two episodes to be made at once for the Tennant seasons and in 2008, the Doctor hardly appears in "Turn Left" and Donna hardly appears in "Midnight". "Turn Left" begins with an alien returning Donna to the time immediately before she met the Doctor. Instead of turning her car right and taking a job where she will eventually encounter him, she turns left, gets another job and never meets him. The events of the revived series unravel. Donna was never with the Doctor when he destroyed the Racnoss, so he is killed before he can escape the deluge and the inferno. As there is no Doctor aboard the Titanic spaceship, it crashes into Buckingham Palace in a nuclear explosion which kills millions and pollutes the whole of southern England. France and other countries close their borders and refuse to accept any more refugees; Donna and her family are sent to hugely overcrowded digs in Leeds. In the poverty and unemployment, resentments build and an Italian family living with Donna are taken away to "resettlement camps". Wilf, Donna's grandfather (Bernard Cribbins), is near tears: "That's what they called them last time". Establishing concentration camps in England is worlds away from the cheery Christmas specials and shows how wildly the tone of the series can vary: the crazy plunge from glee to horror and darkness is worthy of the manic depressive swings in the novels of Dickens.

The 2008 Christmas special was "The Next Doctor", arguably the least successful of the eight. It was effectively two stories. In the first, the Cybermen stomp around Victorian London and wire a lady called Mercy (Dervla Kirwan) into the Cyberking, a giant robotic cybership along the lines of the AT-ATs, the walking ships in *Star Wars*. In the second, much more successful, part of the story, David Morrissey played Jackson, a man who believes he is the Doctor after being imprinted with Cybermen data technology. The Tenth Doctor is fooled for a while, believing Jackson to be a future regeneration suffering from post-regenerative trauma. Jackson eventually recalls his real identity and the Doctor deals with the Cybermen.

It was at this point in the revived series that some felt Davies was both losing his way and his ability to distinguish between a good idea and a terrible one. "The Next Doctor" played on the press and public's obsession with the casting of the leading man in the series. David Tennant noted that, as soon as he arrived, journalists were asking him how long he would be staying; once he had left, they asked him when he would be coming back (presumably for a multiple Doctor story). The press and fans' unease about a new Doctor was presumably a manifestation of the insecurity felt at Eccleston's departure after only one year; perhaps it went back to the TV movie, when Paul McGann had only lasted for only one story. David Tennant had now been in the part for three years and was taking a break in 2009 to play Hamlet at the Royal Shakespeare Company. Instead of a regular series, there would be five specials in 2009-10. There was much speculation about a change of Doctor and "The Next Doctor" teased us that David Morrissey would be the eleventh. Asked if this was true on breakfast television, Morrissey gave an evasive reply. By the end of the episode, we knew that Tennant would be back.

The special also highlighted the production team's, and Russell T Davies's, love of spectacular visuals which, by this point of the series, weren't always accompanied by explanations in the script. Christopher Bailey, the writer of "Kinda" (1982) had indicated that you didn't have to explain *everything* when he complained that, if Little Red Riding Hood were *Doctor Who*, there would need to be a transmogriphication device in grandmama's house to explain why our heroine doesn't recognise the wolf in grandmama's clothing. On the other hand, you had to explain some things, a little. We have some pretty visuals of Victorian orphans in a Cyberman workshop (or workhouse) straight out of *Oliver!* The

Cyberking stomping over London closely resembles the giant gingerbread man menacing the castle in *Shrek 2*. Steven Moffat wisely pressed the reset button when he became showrunner in 2010, wiping out many events from Davies's time including – thank goodness – the Cyberking.

David Tennant had appeared in the BBC's *Who Do You think You Are?* in 2008, a series which invites celebrities to investigate their family tree. At one point, Tennant held up a skull, which prompted Royal Shakespeare Company director Gregory Doran to think he would be a great Hamlet. Tennant would play the Dane for a long run in 2009. The first fans got to know about this was when the RSC released advanced publicity for its new season. Fans immediately knew something was up. If Tennant was in *Hamlet*, he couldn't also do *Doctor Who*. With echoes of its fumbling over the announcement that Eccleston was leaving, the BBC belatedly explained that, as Tennant was otherwise engaged, there wouldn't be a full season of *Doctor Who* in 2009 but some lovely specials instead to keep us all happy. It felt a bit like the 1985 cancellation/hiatus to fans who were old in the tooth. Some asked why, if Tennant was otherwise engaged, didn't they just recast the Doctor? Rumours filtered through that the production team needed a rest to rethink the show. This was one of the reasons given by the BBC when the show was cancelled, then rested, in 1985, and fans were unhappy. The fact the rest and rethinking story was just a rumour was confirmed when we learnt that a new production team, headed by Steven Moffat as showrunner, would take over for 2010. In late 2009, David Tennant announced he was leaving the series live on television from the interval of a performance as Hamlet at the Royal Shakespeare Theatre in Stratford upon Avon; the live announcement had been intended to ensure that the news didn't leak. Again, some wondered why Tennant hadn't left and a new production team hadn't taken over a year earlier, giving us a full series in 2009. The letters pages of genre magazines brimmed with unhappiness. Someone wrote in *SFX* that a two year gap between seasons could be worse; we had once had to wait fifteen years…

The specials of 2009 were variable in quality. The Easter special "Planet of the Dead" (2009), the first to be shot in high definition, was dreadful. Some of the ideas worked well. The Tritovores were a well-designed species of humanoid fly, looking, perhaps unsurprisingly, like the mutant human-fly hybrid in both film versions of *The Fly*. They trade with other planets, offering to take away its waste (on which they feed) in return for technology. Arriving on the planet San Helios, the

Tritovores find a desert. This is all that is left of the planet's ecosystem, destroyed by ravening stingray-like aliens who create wormholes, devour a planet, and move on to the next. Their next target is to be Earth. So far, so good. This story is framed by a nonsensical introduction to the one-off companion Lady Christina de Souza, played by Michelle Ryan, formerly of *EastEnders* and the cancelled revival of *The Bionic Woman*. She is a master cat burglar pulling off the heist of the century in a sequence that baffles and irritates and comes straight out of a *Pink Panther* film. The whole concept is another example of the later Davies era going for pretty visuals, regardless of plot, sense or consideration of whether the sequence fitted into the programme as a whole. The Doctor and Christina are transported to San Helios on a double decker bus, where they hook up with the Tritovores. The bus itself was transported to the United Arab Emirates – the great looking location for San Helios – by sea and the upper deck was smashed to bits on the voyage. Davies hurriedly wrote the damage into the script: this, he said, is what happens to a bus when you pass it through a wormhole. The bus returns to Earth, now augmented with Tritovore technology, and can fly. Lady Christina de Souza evades the police by flying off in it in a sequence that appears to have been borrowed from a *Harry Potter* film.

The autumn special, "The Waters of Mars" was a return to form. On the first manned Mars base, the water is turning hostile; if you touch it, you turn into a ravening, mutated beast (shades of "Planet of Evil", 1975). Water being water, it can get in almost anywhere, as anyone who has had a leaking shower can testify. Lindsay Duncan guests as another strong, mature woman: the companion character for this episode, Captain Adelaide Brooke. The Doctor knows that he has entered a fixed point in time, which cannot be changed. Brooke destroyed the base, killing herself and everyone on board, to prevent the infection from spreading. By this point, the Doctor has been travelling alone for so long that he has become wayward again. Announcing that he is "the Time Lord victorious", he argues that, as the last of the Time Lords, he can make time bend to his will. He rescues Adelaide and brings her home but she shoots herself, thus making time resume its accustomed course and graphically showing the Doctor that he is not all-powerful.

The final David Tennant special was the two part story "The End of Time", broadcast on Christmas Day 2009 and New Year's Day 2010. Russell T Davies asked Steven Moffat, his successor, if he could use the Daleks; Moffat replied that he would like them in the new season (in "Victory of the Daleks", 2010) and Davies opted for the Master instead. A single Dalek appears at the bedroom window of the young Adelaide

Brooke in "The Waters of Mars". Instead of exterminating her, it flies off, thus indicating the Daleks' knowledge of Brooke's importance to history and the time line. "The End of Time" was the first, and to date the only, story of the new series to be specifically billed as a two parter: as we saw, Davies had previously eschewed the practice by arguing that someone who had missed part one wouldn't bother to watch part two. Presumably the viewer's knowledge that this was Tennant's last story, plus the favourable scheduling, encouraged Davies to think that the labelling would work as a one-off. Again, "The End of Time" is a curious tale, the excellent juxtaposed with the execrable. John Simm returns as the Master, resurrected as a peroxide blond which was apparently Simm's idea: he later thought it was a bad one. The Master uses the power of stolen alien technology to duplicate himself into every human being, thus changing the human race into the Master race and proving that he has finally gone completely nuts. The Doctor, Wilf and Donna are unaffected. The Time Lords are back, with Timothy Dalton as Rassilon, who helps defeat the Master, and the Tenth Doctor dies absorbing the radiation which would otherwise kill Wilfred Mott. Davies inevitably goes for unexplained visual thrills, as the resurrected Master can now bounce hundreds of feet in the air (why?) and throw fireballs from his hands (why?). Apparently *Doctor Who* was now in the same stable as *Spiderman* as well as the *Pink Panther* and *Harry Potter*. The programme could now attract Hollywood actors like Timothy Dalton and Brian Cox, who voices the Ood leader, which is impressive, but the script doesn't make it clear who Rassilon is or why his return is a big deal. He was, of course, a founder of Time Lord society who discovered the Eye of Harmony as a power source for time travel (see "The Deadly Assassin", 1976), and the Second Doctor suggests in "The Five Doctors" that he wasn't as pure as history painted him. Dalton kills Time Lords who oppose him and barks "On your knees, mankind" as he appears on Earth.

Tennant's Doctor holds off regeneration long enough to say goodbye to his companions, including Sarah Jane and her adopted son Luke from *The Sarah Jane Adventures*; not necessarily a good idea as the spin-off was watched by about a fifth of the audience of the parent show, and some viewers would not have known who Luke was. Rose appears yet again as the Doctor meets her on New Year's Day 2005, just before she runs off with his ninth incarnation. On board the TARDIS at last, the Doctor says, "I don't want to go" – presumably voicing David Tennant's ambivalence about leaving – and he regenerates into Matt Smith who, like Tennant before him, instantly makes the part his own with four lines of monologue. Such is the incredible force of volcanic energy released by the Doctor's regeneration that the TARDIS control room blows up for no reason at all, which is fine as it looks jolly spectacular. After filming Tennant's last line, Russell T Davies and his team left their chairs and left the set; the chairs were then filled by new show runner Steven Moffat and his team, who handled the final post-regeneration minutes of the episode.

The Christmas specials were by this time a fixture of BBC 1's Christmas Day schedules, and Matt Smith duly appeared in three more. Such is the influence of Charles Dickens' *A Christmas Carol* on our conception of Christmas that three of the episodes made full use of Victorian imagery and two were actually set in Victorian England. 2010's special was actually called "A Christmas Carol", with both Steven Moffat and the Doctor acknowledging Dickens's role in its plotting. The tale of Scrooge had been used twice before in the programme: it provided the past, present, future structure of "The Trial of a Time Lord", Colin Baker's second season; Dickens himself, played by Simon Callow, had appeared in "The Unquiet Dead" (2005), performing the story at a public reading in Cardiff, which is rudely interrupted by the phantasmagorical Gelth. In *Doctor Who*'s "A Christmas Carol", the Eleventh Doctor uses the paradoxes of time travel to soften the heart of Kazran Sardick, a miserly Scrooge figure who rules an Earth-like planet that favours Victorian fashion and design. Sardick is played by Michael Gambon in another triumph of casting. Back in 1967, Innes Lloyd had been asked if Laurence Olivier would soon be in the programme after he succeeded in attracting top names to appear: in 2010, we had Michael Gambon and in 2012, Ian McKellen. The story's only disappointment is its monster, a somewhat uninspiring giant shark.

Having borrowed thoroughly from Dickens, Moffat borrowed from C. S. Lewis for the 2011 special, "The Doctor, the Widow and the Wardrobe", whose title obviously references C. S. Lewis's novel *The Lion, the Witch and the Wardrobe* (1950). The pastiche on Narnia is inspired and cleverly used in the story. It might also be a reference to Lewis's novel's influence on the genesis of the series, with parallels between the wardrobe and the police box as doors into another world. Lewis, who died in 1963, never saw *Doctor Who* but might well have liked it: he enjoyed H.G.Wells' science fiction, wrote three science fiction novels of his own (and they're excellent) and was no literary snob. He had seen the original *King Kong* movie with his brother Warnie and had enjoyed it enormously. In the special, Moffat used the novel's imagery of the wardrobe and the snow clad forest; the castle containing the immobile wooden king and queen recalls the White Witch's castle in the novel and the petrified forms of her enemies, including giants, which litter the courtyard. Madge Arwell and her three children arrive at a vast and deserted country house to escape the bombing, just as the Pevensie children do in the novel. There is an eccentric and wise figure in the house: Professor Kirk in the novel, who has been to Narnia himself, and the Doctor in the special. The Doctor is spending time on his own after dropping off Amy and Rory from their regular travels in the TARDIS.

Moffat also drew on the imagery of the recent film version of *The Lion, the Witch and the Wardrobe* (2005), which opens with German bombers swarming towards London to deliver the Blitz. In the special, these become a single Lancaster bomber piloted by Alexander Armstrong as Reg Arwell, whom the Doctor reunites with his wife, thus un-widowing her. The wife, Madge Arwell, is played by Claire Skinner, immediately identifiable as Sue from the BBC comedy *Outnumbered*, which also rolled out its Christmas specials from year to year.

The final Christmas special to date is "The Snowmen" (2012). Previous specials had taken the Christmas icons of Santa Claus and Christmas trees and made them sinister; Moffat reaches for the Christmas card staple of snowmen, gives them piranha teeth and has them devour humans in Victorian England. Also present are a wonderful cast of characters first seen in "A Good Man Goes to War" (2011): the Silurian Madame Vastra, now established as a private detective; her maid and lover Jenny and their Sontaran butler Strax, who gets some of the best lines in the programme ("Do not attempt to escape or you will be obliterated. May I take your coat?"). The villainous Dr Simeon was played by Richard E. Grant, who had starred with Eighth Doctor Paul McGann in *Withnail and I* (1987). Grant had twice played the Doctor in BBC spin offs "The Curse of Fatal Death" (by Steven Moffat (1999)) and "The Scream of the Shalka" (2003), a webcast that had briefly seen him hailed by the BBC as the Ninth Doctor before Christopher Eccleston was cast. Dr Simeon is apparently in charge of the Snowmen, but answers to a giant globe which issues him with his instructions. The globe's design recalls the snow globe ornaments which you turn upside down to cause a snowstorm: another witty use of snow and Christmas imagery. The Doctor, dressed and hailed as Sherlock Holmes, breaks into Dr Simeon's lair: this is a reference to Moffat's other BBC series *Sherlock*, in which Sherlock (Benedict Cumberbatch) makes brilliant deductions from fragments of evidence. The Doctor, by contrast, makes wildly inaccurate deductions from similar fragments.

The episode's conclusion reveals there is more to the title than a pleasing reference to the Christmas villains of the piece. The voice in the globe is that of the Great Intelligence, the disembodied entity that controls the Yeti in the much loved and lost Patrick Troughton stories "The Abominable Snowmen" (1967) and "The Web of Fear" (1967). The 2012 special's title refers back to the title of the first Great Intelligence story and the plot of "The Snowmen" implies that the Great Intelligence gets the idea of using the Yeti from the snowmen favoured by Dr Simeon. This return of an old adversary is beautifully and intelligently handled, in complete contrast to, say, the return of Omega in "Arc of Infinity" (see chapter ten); in "The Snowmen", it doesn't matter to casual viewers if they don't know who the Great Intelligence is, as knowledge of the entity isn't necessary to follow or enjoy the story. For the fan, the reference is exciting and pleasing, as was the news, issued late in December, that the Great Intelligence was to be voiced by Ian McKellen. For an English graduate and English literature teacher like me, the credit "Voice of the Great Intelligence – Ian McKellen" was one of the best Christmas presents of the year (I also liked the socks thank you). McKellen's beautiful voice is entirely suited to the Great Intelligence's malevolence and recalls Terrance Dicks's descriptions from the novelisations, one of the few ways we still have of accessing and enjoying these old stories. In the treatment of time paradoxes that is one of his contributions to *Doctor Who*, Moffat revealed that this is the Doctor's third encounter with the Great Intelligence but its first encounter with him. To top it all, the Doctor, now one thousand years old (the newly regenerated Ninth Doctor had been nine hundred, so the Doctor has aged one hundred years in the eight years of the revived series), can't remember the Great Intelligence: "Doesn't ring a bell", he says. This line is a really tricky reference to a plot detail in "The Abominable Snowmen": in an untelevised adventure, the Doctor was given the holy ghanta (a small bell) of the Tibetan Det-Sen monastery for safe keeping. In "The Abominable Snowmen", he returns it, only to encounter the Yeti and the Great Intelligence. "Doesn't ring a bell" is a reference to the ghanta. Again, Moffat skilfully gives the über-fan a treat without alienating other viewers. This is surely the way to write *Doctor Who*, true to Moffat's guiding principles as a showrunner: he has said that he has to ignore the fans and write for the other ten million viewers. It is when the programme is directed at the fans, with the tail wagging the dog – as it was for much of John Nathan-Turner's time as producer - that it loses its way.

18

Building on the Myth

Preparing auditions for the Eleventh Doctor, Steven Moffat intended to cast an older actor than Tennant. This was perhaps as an attempt to return to the Doctor as more of an authority figure, as William Hartnell or Jon Pertwee had been. Moffat's intention contrasted with Russell T Davies's view that an older actor could no longer play the Doctor because the hectic schedules and lengthy shoots would simply exhaust him. There is a poignant extra on the series one (series twenty seven) DVD when Christopher Eccleston, looking exhausted and fed up on the TARDIS set, turns to the camera and says, "It's three o'clock in the morning!" Moffat's intention was almost immediately overturned when he saw Matt Smith as about the second actor to audition; when Smith started his piece, Moffat thought, "That's him!" Smith, with his gangling body language and wonderfully eccentric reading of the character, immediately captured the essence of the Doctor. The auditions continued, but Moffat felt they had found their man.

The announcement of the Eleventh Doctor was made in a special edition of the behind-the-scenes companion series *Doctor Who Confidential*. This usually ran on BBC3 immediately after the broadcast of a new *Doctor Who* episode on BBC 1, but the announcement was considered big enough news to run on the flagship channel. Matt Smith, like Tom Baker, was a virtual unknown, and was introduced by Moffat as the youngest actor to have played the Doctor: he was twenty seven; Peter Davison had been two years older when he had been cast. Although not a household name, Smith had starred in *The Ruby in the Smoke* with ex-companion Billie Piper and had played Danny in the 2007 series *Party Animals*. He was also an experienced theatre actor, having performed in Alan Bennett's acclaimed satire *The History Boys* at the National Theatre, which also starred James Corden, soon to guest in *Doctor Who* as Craig in "The Lodger" (2010) and "Closing Time" (2011). Smith was a talented football player and had wanted to turn professional, but a back injury led him to pursue his alternative career as an actor. If the Fifth Doctor was a fine cricketer ("First class bowler and a demon bat", according to Lord Cranleigh in "Black Orchid" (1982)), the Eleventh was a wonderful footballer, demolishing the opposing pub team in "The Lodger", much to Craig's increasing glumness, and performing impressive "keepie uppies" in "The Power of Three" (2012).

Matt Smith's Doctor is joined by Amy (Karen Gillan) in his first story, "The Eleventh Hour". Pre-broadcast photos had shown Amy in a policewoman's uniform with a rather short miniskirt, which led some to grumble about sexism. Moffat wittily reveals that Amy is a kissogram and this is one of her outfits: "It's a laugh," she shrugs. The Doctor first encounters Amy as a young girl, played by Karen Gillan's cousin Caitlin Blackwood. Karen hadn't met Caitlin before they introduced themselves on the set. The Doctor's first scenes with the young Amelia are charming and hilarious; he is starving after his regeneration and demands food ("You're Scottish. Fry something."), eventually settling on fish fingers and custard. The fish fingers were actually coconut cakes and the scene is referenced in later episodes. Amy, knowing that the Doctor will die in the future in "The Impossible Astronaut" (2011), tells his earlier self that she can't reveal the future and he will have to trust her. When she swears on "fish fingers and custard", the Doctor trusts her: "My life in your hands, Amelia Pond." Rory, Amy and the Doctor eat fish fingers and custard together in "The Power of Three" (2012).

Amy's fiancé Rory (Arthur Darvill) is another recurring character and becomes a full companion in Matt Smith's second season. In the first, he appears when the TARDIS returns Amy and the Doctor to Earth. In contrast to Rose and Martha, Amy is not wildly and romantically in love with the Doctor; rather, Moffat makes her relationship with him more like Jo's and Sarah's. She does love him but does not see him as a romantic partner. The Eleventh Doctor is much more uncomfortable about sexual relations that his predecessor, spluttering when kissed by River Song and squirming when Amy tries, on one single occasion, to seduce him. This is a return to the more asexual Doctor, and the more chaste friendship with his companion, of the original series: they love each other, but the Doctor's love isn't sexual. Moffat, however, creates dramatic play from the suggestion that Amy and the Doctor are romantically involved, not least because we are encouraged on occasions to see their relationship through Rory's eyes, who is understandably jealous of Amy's relationship with another man. It's even hinted that the Doctor is the father of Amy's baby, although of course it is Rory. Amy gets increasingly impatient with Rory's failure to believe that she is in love with him, and not with the Doctor. The events of "Journey's End" (2008) suggest that Time Lords and humans might not be biologically compatible anyway, at least as far as breeding is concerned. The Doctor tells Donna, suffering because she has a Time Lord's intellect in her head, that there are no Time Lord-human hybrids "because there can't be."

Moffat has much fun with Rory's character, and sometimes at Rory's expense. He seems to die as many times as Kenny in *South Park*. He turns to dust in the dreamworld of "Amy's Choice" (2011); is consumed by the time rift in "Cold Blood" (2010); returns as a Roman Centurion who is also an Auton in "The Pandorica Opens"/ "The Big Bang" (2010); guards Amy in the Pandorica for two thousand years while still an Auton; returns to human form in "The Big Bang"; is aged near death in "The Doctor's Wife" (2011); ages to death in "The Angels Take Manhattan" (2012) and is finally zapped back in time with Amy by a Weeping Angel in that story, to live out his life with Amy and to die in twentieth century New York. Rory also takes on the mystical persona of the Centurion from time to time, and the persona seems to be enough to cow a fleet of Cybermen into revealing where Amy is imprisoned in "A Good Man Goes to War".

Following the established practice of Russell T Davies' time as showrunner, Rory is given a family and a job. His father Brian, wonderfully played by Mark Williams, appears in "Dinosaurs on a Spaceship" (2012) and "The Power of Three" (2012). Even more of a dignified geek than Rory, it's easy to believe Brian and Rory are father and son. Amy's mother and father appear and disappear according to which timeline we are in, but they attend her wedding to Rory in "The Big Bang" (2010).

One of Steven Moffat's most loved characters is River Song, first played by Alex Kingston in the David Tennant story "Silence in the Library" (2008). Professor Song is an archaeologist whose first words to the Doctor are, "Hello sweetie". She clearly knows him well but the Doctor has no memory of her. River's timeline and the Doctor's run in different directions. The first time he meets her is the last time she meets him and River laments that, every time she meets the Doctor, he knows her less well; there will come a terrible day when he doesn't know who she is. This is the case in her first story: River dies in "The Forest of the Dead" (2008) and the Doctor grants her a form of immortality as part of the computer matrix that sustains the library. In a moment of crisis in the story, River urgently needs the Doctor's trust and proves that she knows him by whispering something in his ear. From the Doctor's shock and silence we know that it's his name, which he never reveals to anyone. Donna asks if River Song is his wife, and the Doctor gives a non-committal reply.

River was intended as a one-off character. Davies and Moffat were delighted to get Alex Kingston to play her. Alex Kingston had been acclaimed in the United Kingdom for her performance as the lead in

Andrew Davies's adaptation of Defoe's *Moll Flanders* (1996); she then moved to the States and played Dr Elizabeth Corday in *ER*. Bringing River Song back depended on Alex Kingston's availability, but she was delighted to return as the character in ten episodes with Matt Smith's Doctor. River Song's story gives Moffat a chance to indulge his delight in time paradox stories which we first saw in "Blink" (2007).

In "The Time of Angels"/ "Flesh and Stone" (2010), River is simply "Dr" Song and is thrilled to learn that she will one day be a Professor. She is accompanied (and guarded) by military clerics, who have allowed her freedom from her prison, where she is held for killing a good man. Which good man? "Spoilers", she smiles, using her catchphrase. Perhaps drawing on the first six seasons on the show for inspiration, which had seen the answer to the question "Doctor who?" endlessly deferred, Moffat continually asks, and doesn't answer, the question, who is River Song? We speculate that she is the Doctor's wife. Is she a Time Lord? Is she his mother? How can she be his mother if the mysterious woman played by Claire Bloom in "The End of Time" (2009-10) was his mother? "A Good Man Goes to War" answers the question for us. Amy and Rory's baby is named Melody Pond. Lorna Bucket, a human soldier from the Gamma forests, gives Amy a piece of cloth on which is her baby's name embroidered in gold. This is the tradition among her people. However, and in fulfilment of the cryptic prediction "The only water in the forest is the river", made by Idris in "The Doctor's Wife" (2011), there is no word for "pond" among her people. The TARDIS telepathic circuits eventually translate the embroidery from "Melody Pond" to "River Song", thus proving that River is Rory's and Amy's daughter. We thus have the fun of an apparently older person being the daughter of two apparently younger people; an image familiar from the apparently younger Doctor being much older than many of his friends and companions.

Amy and Rory are in the process of divorce in "Asylum of the Daleks" (2012), not least because Amy can't give Rory children as a result of her incarceration and forced childbirth on Demon's Run (see "A Good Man Goes to War"). They save their marriage in "Asylum". In a scene scripted but not filmed for the season seven (season thirty three) DVD release, Chris Chibnell reveals that Amy and Rory had another child, a son, in New York after they were sent back in time by a Weeping Angel.

River was conceived on Amy and Rory's wedding night in the TARDIS; having absorbed the energy of the time vortex, she is part Time Lord and able to regenerate. River's story is an example of the fiendishly complicated plotting favoured by Moffat, who answered criticisms of its difficulty by saying that you had to pay attention to *Doctor Who* and couldn't watch it while having a conversation or texting or whatever. Moffat's plotting can be followed by the viewer who is paying attention and it is a delight to follow; unlike the incoherent plots of some of the Sylvester McCoy stories, these detailed plots make sense. River as a child was brought up by Madame Kovarian as a weapon to kill the Doctor. As a child, she inhabits the space suit in "The Impossible Astronaut", is injured when Amy shoots her to prevent the astronaut from killing the Doctor, and regenerates in an alley into Mels. This regeneration isn't the first to show that the process can change skin colour; one of Romana's trial bodies in "Destiny of the Daleks" (1979) is also black. As Mels, River attends Rory and Amy's school ("Let's Kill Hitler", 2011), goes back to Berlin in 1939 and regenerates into Alex Kingston. Looking a little older than she did in "Silence in the Library", River says that she may take the age down a bit; thus is continuity satisfied. River shoots the Doctor, who is dying, and then overcomes her programming by saving him with her remaining regeneration energies. She is thus no longer able to regenerate and is no longer part-Time Lord: this was to have been the Doctor's fate in "Mawdryn Undead" (1983), where donating his renegeration energy to the mutants to free them from life would rob him of his power to regenerate, and he would cease to be a Time Lord. The Doctor partly returns the favour to River by healing her broken wrist with some of his regeneration energy in "The Angels take Manhattan" (2012). The idea that regeneration energy can be accessed at will is new and a bit too much like magic for some viewers' tastes. Regeneration in the rest of the series always results from some massive trauma and River herself is furious at the Doctor for "wasting" his regeneration energy. She storms that he has embarrassed her, and storms off.

After Berlin, River trains to become a Doctor of Archaeology and is recruited again by Madame Kovarian and the Silents. She is returned to the space suit which we saw rising from the lake to shoot the Doctor in "The Impossible Astonaut"; an event that is a fixed point in time and cannot be changed. It then appears that the Doctor she shoots is not the Doctor but a shape-changing machine containing miniaturised humans and the Doctor himself, the Teselecta. It is this machine, taking the Doctor's form, that River marries in "The Wedding of River Song" (2011), rather than the Doctor himself, which makes the question of whether she actually is the Doctor's wife or not a moot point. (Neil Gaiman and Steven Moffat play with the question further by entitling a

2012 episode "The Doctor's Wife", who is eventually revealed to be the TARDIS in human form. "Did you wish really hard?" asks Amy.)

The Doctor's "death" at the hands of the impossible astronaut allows him to drop out of history. He is, he says, becoming too big, hailed as a legend and saviour by almost everyone he meets. The Doctor's quest for anonymity is boosted by his wiping all data on himself from the Daleks' collective hive database. (That there is such a thing as a hive intelligence for the Daleks is perhaps borrowed from the Borg in *Star Trek: the Next Generation*, but *Star Trek* fans must be silent as *The Next Generation* based the Borg on the Cybermen so *Doctor Who* was only doing a little minor pilfering in comparison to *Star Trek*'s dirty great theft.) River has been freed from her incarceration in the Stormcage facility for the murder of the Doctor. Apparently he has wiped himself from all databases in the universe, so she cannot be imprisoned for the murder of someone who doesn't exist.

The revived series resurrected several characters from the original show. Sarah Jane Smith, of course, returns in "School Reunion" (2006), back in her role as investigative journalist. Sarah was now scripted according to the new approach of the revived series. She mourns the loss of the Doctor and asks if she did something wrong, as he just dumped her on Earth. "You were getting on with your life," the Doctor smiles. "You were my life," she replies. In a pleasing addition for fans, she reveals that the Doctor didn't leave her at her home in South Croydon in "The Hand of Fear" (1976), but in Aberdeen. "That's near Croydon, isn't it?" the Doctor offers hesitantly. Sarah comes to terms with her new Earth-bound role in the course of the battle against the Krillitanes and, in a parallel to Elisabeth Sladen's refusal to rejoin the show in the late 1970s, turns down the offer of travelling again with the Doctor (Mickey goes instead). Elisabeth Sladen only agreed to return as Sarah if the character was treated with respect and not just seen in a fleeting cameo. She was evidently delighted with "School Reunion" and returned – occasionally with K9 – in her own-spin off series *The Sarah Jane Adventures* on the children's channel CBBC. The Tenth and Eleventh Doctors guested; so did Katy Manning as Jo Jones (née Grant) and Nicholas Courtney as the Brigadier.

Davies planned for Courtney to return to *The Sarah Jane Adventures* for a second story, but Courtney wasn't well enough to appear. He died in 2011 and his death is marked twice in the *Doctor Who* story "The Wedding of River Song" (2011). In a sequence which shows how much Courtney and the Brigadier were loved by viewers and the production team, the Doctor phones the Brigadier's nursing home only to be told that his old friend has passed away. The Brigadier had always kept two glasses of scotch by his table to the end, in case his old friend the Doctor happened to drop by. The Doctor, shaken and saddened, is shocked into accepting that he must face his own death by the impossible astronaut.

All of Madame Kovarian's team in "The Wedding of River Song" apparently wear eyepatches; in fact, sophisticated devices called eye drives wired into the brain which allow the wearers to remember, and interact with the Silents. The Silents cannot be remembered after they have been encountered: an evolutionary advantage which makes them as dangerous as the Weeping Angels and has allowed them to live alongside mankind for hundreds of thousands of years without being detected. The eyedrives are inspired by a favourite story of Nicholas Courtney's which he trotted out for interviews and conventions. Asked what funny things had happened during filming of the show, Courtney recalled that he had played the Brigade Leader, the Brigadier's fascist counterpart in a parallel universe, in "Inferno" (1970). He had had to swivel round in his chair to reveal the Brigade Leader was without moustache but with a scar on his cheek and an eyepatch. Jon Pertwee and Caroline John decided to make him laugh during a take; when Courtney swung round, he was confronted by the Doctor and Elizabeth Shaw wearing eyepatches. Courtney carried on "as cool as a cucumber" and it was Pertwee and Caroline John who burst out laughing. (Apparently director Douglas Camfield was not pleased at the prank, which wasted studio time and money.) Courtney had told the story so many times that most fans knew it by heart. At one convention, he entered the hall to find the fan audience facing him were all wearing eyepatches, which he thought a good joke. The eyedrives in "The Wedding of River Song" are an affectionate reference to the story and a remembrance of Nicholas Courtney.

Both the Cybermen and the Daleks returned in the new series. The Cybermen originally appear in a parallel universe story, "Rise of the Cybermen"/ "The Age of Steel" (2006). This is effectively a version of "Genesis of the Daleks" (1975), but with Cybermen; Roger Lloyd Pack plays the Davros-like creator of the Cybermen, John Lumic. Like Davros, he is crippled and confined to a wheelchair; like Davros, he has a fanatical desire to perpetuate himself in his creations. The new Cybermen are fashioned by Cybus Industries (Lumic's company) and thus have a large C on their chest units: the Cybus industry logo. Davies apparently decided to source his new race of Cybermen from a parallel universe to sidestep the complicated, and contradictory, history of the

Cybermen established in the original series: necessary if their genesis was to be told. Some fans were unhappy that these were not "real" Cybermen, although Davies was careful to have the Doctor note that "there are Cybermen in our Universe". These don't appear until Matt Smith's era, when a lone, partially dismembered Cyberman attacks Amy in the Pandorica vault ("The Pandorica Opens" (2010)). In a continuity error, this Cyberman still has the C Cybus industries logo on its chest. Perhaps it had fallen through from the parallel universe. Cybermen from our universe, with the C plate replaced by a blank circle, lurk beneath the department store in "Closing Time" (2011) and attempt to turn Craig (James Corden) into their Cybercontroller. The Cybermats, last seen in "Revenge of the Cybermen" (1975), make an effective re-appearance. They now sport vicious teeth and are clearly a cyborg based on an animal, tying them in effectively with the Cybermen (cyborgs based on humans) and solving the mystery of their nature which had been bugging fans for years. Steven Moffat asked the props department if the Cybermen could be seen as battered and broken for "Closing Time". The props department told him that, after six years of being worn, blown up and bashed about generally, the costumes looked like that anyway. Partly as a response to the need for new props, Moffat took advantage of the Cybermen's battered condition to have them redesigned for their reappearance in Neil Gaiman's story in 2013.

The Daleks were also redesigned in Mark Gatiss's 2010 story "Victory of the Daleks". The hybrid Daleks created by Davros reactivate the Dalek progenitor, a device which reforms and duplicates Daleks composed of pure Dalek DNA. The bronze Daleks seen up to this point in the revived series are various bastardised mixes of tissue sourced from humans or Davros himself: as Ace said in "Remembrance of the Daleks" (1988), they are "impure in their blobbiness". As racial fanatics, the bronze Daleks accept their impurity and are happy to be exterminated by the Dalek paradigm, a new race of Daleks. There is a story that this partly came about because the toy company Character Options asked the production team if it had plans to introduce new types of Daleks which it could sell as models. The production team responded enthusiastically by creating five types, or colours at least, of new Dalek. Mark Gatiss, like most fans of his generation, had considerable affection for the Peter Cushing Dalek movies of the 1960s and suggested that the new generation of Daleks in "Victory..." should be like them. In the script, they are described as "big buggers". There are five types: the red Drone (shades of the Borg again): the white Supreme Dalek (Supreme Daleks had previously been black so this is radical stuff); the blue scientist; the yellow strategist and an orange Eternal Dalek. Gatiss named the first four in the script but told Moffat he had no idea what to call the fifth. Moffat suggested "eternal". Neither knew what it meant but both agreed it sounded great.

The new Daleks were designed by Peter McInstry, who had also designed the red Dalek supreme for "The Stolen Earth"/ "Journey's End" (2008). They were not popular with fans, who disliked the disruption of the Dalek silhouette which had been maintained into the revived series. It also seemed odd that, while the bronze Daleks seen from "Dalek" (2005) onwards had included much more intricate surface detail than their classic series counterparts, the Dalek paradigm had much less: and this in the first Dalek story to be filmed in high definition. These Daleks had four, not three, discs in the neck section; swapped the vertical slats of the shoulder section for the horizontal bands last seen in "The Dalek Invasion of Earth" (1964) and replaced the eight hemisphere back panel for a blank panel containing a spine. It was apparently planned that this panel would conceal extra weapons which could be whizzed around the shoulder section to give the Dalek more firepower, but this was never seen on screen. The bright colours of the paradigm encouraged some fans unkindly to dub the new Daleks "Teletubbies".

(The radical redesign of the new Daleks was a case of gilding the lily. The iconic Raymond Cusick originals had often been tweaked, but never before caricatured (or trashed). Moreover, it can be said that one reason for the originals' success rests with a trick played by the human brain. If you draw two dots next to each other, with a line below them, the brain automatically sees that as a face. Add a third dot below and between the other two, and it stays a face, this time with a nose. This works with the Cusick-style Daleks, too. In reductionist form, the lights recall eyes, the eye-stick suggests a nose, and the neck grill suggests teeth. Thus the original Daleks subliminally have a face; as a result, they suggest character and expression. By replacing the neck grill with something that looks like a laundry basket or rubber gear stick housing, the neck stops suggesting a mouth and teeth, the effect is lost, and the Daleks lose a lot of expression. Besides, they've been eating all the pies.)

The production team eventually acknowledged that the new design was not an unparalleled success and restored the bronze variety to prominence in "Asylum of the Daleks" (2012), although the paradigm Daleks appear in the background.

The original series gave images that endure in popular culture: the

Daleks gliding over Westminster Bridge; the Yeti stomping through the London Underground; the Sea Devils rising from the waves; giant maggots hissing from the coal face of a Welsh mine. The revived series has added equally effective images which, according to my secondary school students, have burned themselves into the consciousness of new viewers: a child with a gas mask for a face asking, "Are you my mummy?"; clockwork robots in eighteenth century costumes, striding towards us as French courtiers scream in terror; statues that move when we don't look at them; Munch's painting *The Scream* come to life in a towering Silent, sucking the life force from a middle aged woman in the White House washroom. Beautifully designed and realised, these are all products of Steven Moffat's imagination. The Weeping Angels were voted the favourite monster by fans in a recent poll, unseating the Daleks for the first time ever. They first appeared in the Doctor-lite story "Blink" in 2007, menacing a pre-fame Carey Mulligan (Sally Sparrow) in an abandoned house called Wester Drumlins (named after a house Moffat used to live in), and more or less came about by accident. Moffat was too busy to write a promised two-episode Dalek tale for the third (twenty ninth) season, so, in propitiation, he offered to do the Doctor-lite one instead for Davies. Davies agreed.

Moffat's script for "Blink" was based on a short story he wrote for Christopher Eccleston's Doctor in the 2005 *Doctor Who* annual called "What I did in my Christmas holidays, by Sally Sparrow". Sally is much younger in the short story and receives a message from the Doctor on an old VHS tape, telling her how to bring the TARDIS, stuck in her time, back to him where he's stranded a few years earlier. The Weeping Angels were inspired by the children's game of grandmother's footsteps, in which a group of children creep up on a single child, the leader, while her or his back is turned. If the child whirls round and spots the others moving, they have to go back to the beginning (the origin of the Weeping Angels sending their victims back in time?). The game ends when one of the creepers touches the leader. The Weeping Angels, visually represented as the sort of angels one might see on a sentimental Victorian tomb, are quantam locked and can only move when they are not being looked at. They are also unbelievably fast and can cover many metres in the time it takes you to blink: hence the episode's title and the tendency of children to hold their eyes open as long as possible when playing the episode in the playground. The Angels can be beautiful and look serene, but their true faces are revealed as feral and vicious when they attack. If they reach you, they send you back in time and feed off the energy of the days you would have lived in your own time line.

Moffat had no idea how to end the story and asked Mark Gatiss to suggest some solutions. In the end, the writers realised that the four scavenging Angels could be placed one on each side of a TARDIS wall; when it dematerialised, they would be looking at each other and so would be quantum-locked and harmless.

Moffat was pleased with his story but said it would never win a season poll. He was right: it came second in the latest Best Story poll of *Doctor Who* Magazine, ceding first position to "The Caves of Androzani" (1984). The episode was so highly thought of that American *Who* fans suggested on BBC America that people new to the programme should watch "Blink" as a first taste of *Doctor Who* because it encapsulated the series' imaginative brilliance and introduced its concepts. After watching it, the new viewers could bombard the fan viewer with questions ("What's with the phone box?" etc.). "Blink" implied that all statues might be Weeping Angels in its final montage of images, thus making statues as terrifying for children as shop window dummies had been by the Autons (my daughter wouldn't go past a shop with tailors' dummies in the window for about five years). "The Angels take Manhattan" (2012) confirmed that any statue could be inhabited by a Weeping Angel. "The Time of Angels"/ "Flesh and Stone" (2010) showed their malevolence and cruelty as they torment Amy into thinking she is turning to stone, telling the Doctor they are doing it "for fun".

Given its fifty year run on television, interrupted by two cancellations, how secure is the Doctor's future? Speaking in 2010, Steven Moffat said it is as secure as any television programme can be. Certainly, it still commands huge audiences for a programme in a multi-channel age: ten million viewers watching "Time Flight" in 1982 couldn't get the programme a place in the top twenty but ten and a half million viewers of "Journey's End" in 2008 propelled it to the number one position for that week. Almost every episode of the revived series has been in the top twenty; most have been in the top ten. The programme's merchandising and overseas sales pay for it many times over. Although the BBC was unable to secure a place for the programme on an American network – a prize that also eluded the original series – it played to substantial audiences on the American Sci-Fi channel and, later, BBC America, ensuring that its exposure in the States has never been higher. The programme is still regarded as a critical success by the press and, although press interest has waned a little since its return in 2005, news of a new companion, and certainly a new Doctor, can make the front pages of British newspapers. That serious Conservative

British broadsheet *The Daily Telegraph*, which loves *Doctor Who*, carried a huge colour photograph of Matt Smith on its front page when his casting was announced. The BBC loves *Doctor Who* and lauds it as a flagship programme, protecting its budget at a time that other programmes have had theirs cut to the bone in difficult economic times. The revived series has already lasted eight years, a real achievement for a television science fiction series: the original *Star Trek* series only notched up three seasons; *Star Trek: The Next Generation* and *Buffy the Vampire Slayer*, both considered great successes, were wound up after seven years apiece. *Doctor Who*'s longevity is, to a large extent, attributable to its being made by a licence fee funded, public service broadcaster that doesn't see ratings or advertising revenue as the only reason to make a series. There is still a lingering romanticism in the belief of some at the BBC that, if people still want to watch *Doctor Who*, even if it's a declining audience, they still want to make it. Whether this romanticism will survive a halving of the viewing figures if the programme goes into a decline remains to be seen.

The Doctor is, as Terrance Dicks said, an old fashioned hero. He is good and he fights evil. This is a morality which will never grow old and has ensured the Doctor's appeal in six decades. As a character, he is as immortal as Robin Hood, Sherlock Holmes, Jeeves or Rumpole of the Bailey. He is less respectable than Sherlock Holmes because, like Rumpole, he was created for television, and some people are sniffy about television as a lesser art form than literature. He is not taken seriously by others, who would think this book about him is ridiculous, because he comes from the unrespectable genre of science fiction. Like satire, science fiction is not a respectable form for people who only like Nice stories. Yet as Jonathan Swift held up a satirising mirror to the human race in the creatures and worlds encountered in *Gulliver's Travels*, so the best *Doctor Who* stories hold up a mirror to the human race. They comment on human goodness, wickedness, compassion and greed with characters and aliens we can recognise in ourselves, our history and the world around us. Gene Roddenberry thought romantically that human beings were perfectible, and that by the time of the starship Enterprise we would have eliminated poverty, racism and all forms of conflict. He obviously hadn't read any history, which shows that human beings at any period are much the same and suggests it's highly unlikely we will evolve into mutually loving and caring androids. Indeed, the lack of conflict makes the Enterprise crew in the Roddenberry-helmed early episodes of *Star Trek: the Next Generation* insufferably dull and smug. *Doctor Who* adopts a less romantic, more British pessimism in its depiction of the human race in all its forms and symbols, showing that there will always be evil but triumphantly insisting on the moral message that good must fight evil and, when it does so in the person of the Doctor and his allies, good will always, eventually, win. This is a theme that can never be obsolete and will ensure the Doctor's survival long after any television series has ended. The stories of the Doctor continued in book, audio and comic form in the hiatus between 1989 and 2005; I think that people will always be returning to him as a source for stories and as a figure of moral inspiration.

Let him always be there.

Appendix

Doctor Who Episode Guide

The following list of episodes is intended to help people new to *Doctor Who* to see where the stories mentioned in this book fit in the history of the series and to suggest which might be particularly worth watching. I have scored them shamelessly according to my own views. I have not scored stories which no longer exist in the archives as I don't believe you can rate a story you haven't seen; listening to a soundtrack while looking at screen grabs is no substitute for watching it. I have made perverse exceptions for "The Reign of Terror", "The Ice Warriors" and "The Invasion". "The Ice Warriors" has four out of its six episodes extant; the others have each had their two missing episodes completed by animation for DVD release.

Star ratings, attached to an equivalent monster, are as follows:

★	Appalling (Duvet Monster on the planet of the Ogrons)
★★	Poor (Kroton)
★★★	Good (Cyberman)
★★★★	Very good (Dalek)
★★★★★	Excellent (Weeping Angel)

William Hartnell as the Doctor

Season One

An Unearthly Child ★★★★★	1963
The Daleks ★★★★	1964
The Edge of Destruction ★★★★	
Marco Polo	
The Keys of Marinus ★★★	
The Aztecs ★★★★	
The Sensorites ★★★	
The Reign of Terror ★★★	

Season Two

Planet of Giants ★★

The Dalek Invasion of Earth ★★★
The Rescue ★★★★   1965
The Romans ★★★
The Web Planet ★★★★
The Crusade
The Space Museum ★
The Chase ★★
The Time Meddler ★★★

Season Three

Galaxy Four
Mission to the Unknown
The Myth Makers
The Daleks' Master Plan   1966
The Massacre of St Bartholemew's Eve
The Ark ★★★★
The Celestial Toymaker
The Gunfighters ★★
The Savages
The War Machines ★★

Season Four

The Smugglers
The Tenth Planet

Patrick Troughton as the Doctor

The Power of the Daleks
The Highlanders   1967
The Underwater Menace
The Moonbase
The Macra Terror
The Faceless Ones
The Evil of the Daleks

Season Five

The Tomb of the Cybermen ★★★★★
The Abominable Snowmen

The Ice Warriors ★★★★

The Enemy of the World

The Web of Fear

The Wheel in Space

1968

Season Six

The Dominators ★★★

The Mind Robber ★★★★

The Invasion ★★★★★

The Krotons ★★

1969

The Seeds of Death ★★★★

The Space Pirates

The War Games ★★★★★

Jon Pertwee as the Doctor

Season Seven

Spearhead from Space ★★★★★

1970

Doctor Who and the Silurians ★★★★

The Ambassadors of Death ★★

Inferno ★★★★★

Season Eight

Terror of the Autons ★★★★

1971

The Mind of Evil ★★★★

The Claws of Axos ★★★

Colony in Space ★★★★★

The Daemons ★★★★

Season Nine

Day of the Daleks ★★★★

1972

The Curse of Peladon ★★★★

The Sea Devils ★★★★

The Mutants ★★★

The Time Monster ★★★

Season Ten

The Three Doctors ★★★   1973
Carnival of Monsters ★★★★★
Frontier in Space ★★★★
Planet of the Daleks ★★★
The Green Death ★★★★★

Season Eleven

The Time Warrior ★★★★★   1974
Invasion of the Dinosaurs ★★★★★
Death to the Daleks ★★★
The Monster of Peladon ★★★★
Planet of the Spiders ★★★★★

Tom Baker as the Doctor

Season Twelve

Robot ★★★★★   1975
The Ark in Space ★★★★
The Sontaran Experiment ★★★
Genesis of the Daleks ★★★★★
Revenge of the Cybermen ★★

Season Thirteen

Terror of the Zygons ★★★★
Planet of Evil ★★★★★
Pyramids of Mars ★★★★★
The Android Invasion ★★★
The Brain of Morbius ★★★★★   1976
The Seeds of Doom ★★★★★

Season Fourteen

The Masque of Mandragora ★★★★★
The Hand of Fear ★★★★
The Deadly Assassin ★★★★★
The Face of Evil ★★★★★   1977

The Robots of Death ★★★★★
The Talons of Weng-Chiang ★★★★★

Season Fifteen

Horror of Fang Rock ★★★
The Invisible Enemy ★★
Image of the Fendahl ★★★★★
The Sun Makers ★★★★★
Underworld ★★   1978
The Invasion of Time ★

Season Sixteen

The Ribos Operation ★★★★★
The Pirate Planet ★★★★
The Stones of Blood ★★
The Androids of Tara ★★★★
The Power of Kroll ★★★   1979
The Armageddon Factor ★★★★

Season Seventeen

Destiny of the Daleks ★★
City of Death ★★★★
The Creature from the Pit ★
Nightmare of Eden ★★★★
The Horns of Nimon ★   1980

Season Eighteen

The Leisure Hive ★★★★
Meglos ★
Full Circle ★★★
State of Decay ★★★
Warriors' Gate ★★★★★   1981
The Keeper of Traken ★★★★
Logopolis ★★★

Peter Davison as the Doctor

Season Nineteen

Castrovalva ★★★   1982
Four to Doomsday ★★★
Kinda ★★★★★
The Visitation ★★★
Black Orchid ★★★★
Earthshock ★★★
Time Flight ★

Season Twenty

Arc of Infinity ★   1983
Snakedance ★★★★
Mawdryn Undead ★★★
Terminus ★★★
Enlightenment ★★★
The King's Demons ★★

Twentieth Anniversary Special

The Five Doctors ★★★★

Season Twenty One

Warriors of the Deep ★   1984
The Awakening ★★★
Frontios ★★★
Resurrection of the Daleks ★★★
Planet of Fire ★★
The Caves of Androzani ★★★★★

Colin Baker as the Doctor

The Twin Dilemma ★

Season Twenty Two

Attack of the Cybermen ★   1985

Vengeance on Varos ★ ★ ★ ★
The Mark of the Rani ★ ★ ★
The Two Doctors ★ ★ ★
Timelash ★
Revelation of the Daleks ★ ★ ★ ★

Season Twenty Three

The Trial of a Time Lord episodes 1-4
   (aka "The Mysterious Planet") ★ ★   1986
The Trial of a Time Lord episodes 5-8
   (aka "Mindwarp") ★ ★ ★
The Trial of a Time Lord episodes 9-12
   (aka "Terror of the Vervoids") ★ ★
The Trial of a Time Lord episodes 13-14
   (aka "The Ultimate Foe") ★ ★

Sylvester McCoy as the Doctor

Season Twenty Four

Time and the Rani ★   1987
Paradise Towers ★ ★
Delta and the Bannermen ★
Dragonfire ★

Season Twenty Five

Remembrance of the Daleks ★ ★ ★ ★ ★   1988
The Happiness Patrol ★
Silver Nemesis ★
The Greatest Show in the Galaxy ★

Season Twenty Six

Battlefield ★ ★   1989
Ghost Light ★ ★
The Curse of Fenric ★
Survival ★ ★ ★ ★

Paul McGann as the Doctor

The TV Movie ★★★★   1996

Christopher Eccleston as the Doctor

Season Twenty Seven (season one)

Rose ★★★★   2005
The End of the World ★★★★
The Unquiet Dead ★★★★★
Aliens of London/World War Three ★★★★
Dalek ★★★★★
The Long Game ★★★
Father's Day ★★★★★
The Empty Child/The Doctor Dances ★★★★★
Boom Town ★★★★
Bad Wolf/The Parting of the Ways ★★★★★

David Tennant as the Doctor

The Christmas Invasion ★★★★

Season Twenty Eight (season two)

New Earth ★   2006
Tooth and Claw ★★
School Reunion ★★★★★
The Girl in the Fireplace ★★★★★
Rise of the Cybermen/The Age of Steel ★★★★
The Idiot's Lantern ★★★★
The Impossible Planet/The Satan Pit ★★★
Love and Monsters ★★★
Fear Her ★★★
Army of Ghosts/Doomsday ★★★★

Season Twenty Nine (season three)

The Runaway Bride ★★★★

Smith and Jones ★★★★ 2007
The Shakespeare Code ★★★★
Gridlock ★
Daleks in Manhattan/Evolution of the Daleks ★★★
The Lazarus Experiment ★★★★
42 ★★★
Human Nature/The Family of Blood ★★★★★
Blink ★★★★★
Utopia ★★★★
The Sound of Drums/Last of the Time Lords ★★★

Season Thirty (season four)

Voyage of the Damned ★★★

Partners in Crime ★★★★ 2008
The Fires of Pompeii ★★★★
Planet of the Ood ★★★★
The Sontaran Strategem/The Poison Sky ★★★★
The Doctor's Daughter ★★★
The Unicorn and the Wasp ★
Silence in the Library/Forest of the Dead ★★★★
Midnight ★★★
Turn Left ★★★★★
The Stolen Earth/Journey's End ★★★

Specials

The Next Doctor ★
Planet of the Dead ★ 2009
The Waters of Mars ★★★★
The End of Time ★★★ 2010

Matt Smith as the Doctor

Season Thirty One (season five)

The Eleventh Hour ★★★★
The Beast Below ★★★
Victory of the Daleks ★★★★
The Time of Angels/Flesh and Stone ★★★★★

The Vampires of Venice ★★★★
Amy's Choice ★★★★★
The Hungry Earth/Cold Blood ★★★
Vincent and the Doctor ★★★★★
The Lodger ★★★★
The Pandorica Opens/The Big Bang ★★★★

Season Thirty Two (season six)

A Christmas Carol ★★★★

The Impossible Astronaut/Day of the Moon ★★★★★   2011
The Curse of the Black Spot ★★★★
The Doctor's Wife ★★★★★
The Rebel Flesh/The Almost People ★★
A Good Man Goes to War ★★★★★
Let's Kill Hitler ★★
Night Terrors ★★★★
The Girl Who Waited ★★★
The God Complex ★★★
Closing Time ★★★
The Wedding of River Song ★★★★

The Doctor, the Widow and the Wardrobe ★★★★

Season Thirty Three (season seven)

Asylum of the Daleks ★★★★   2012
Dinosaurs on a Spaceship ★★★
A Town Called Mercy ★★★★
The Power of Three ★★★
The Angels Take Manhattan ★★★★
The Snowmen ★★★★
The Bells of St John ★★★★   2013
The Rings of Akhaten ★★★
Cold War ★★★★
Hide ★★★
Journey to the Centre of the TARDIS ★★★
The Crimson Horror ★★★★
Nightmare in Silver ★★★★
The Name of the Doctor ★★★★★